Strategic Management of Technological Innovation

Strategic Management of Technological Innovation

Fifth Edition

Melissa A. Schilling
New York University

STRATEGIC MANAGEMENT OF TECHNOLOGICAL INNOVATION, FIFTH EDITION

2 3 4 5 6 7 8 9 DOC 21 20 19 18 17 16

ISBN 978-1-259-53906-0

MHID 1-259-53906-7

Senior Vice President, Products & Markets: *Kurt L. Strand*
Vice President, General Manager, Products & Markets: *Michael Ryan*
Vice President, Content Production & Technology Services: *Kimberly Meriwether David*
Managing Director: *Susan Gouijnstook*
Director: *Michael Ablassmeir*
Brand Manager: *Laura Hurst Spell*
Director, Product Development: *Meghan Campbell*
Marketing Manager: *Casey Keske*
Director, Content Production: *Terri Schiesl*
Program Manager: *Faye M. Herrig*
Content Project Manager: *Jeni McAtee, Karen Jozefowicz*
Buyer: *Laura Fuller*
Cover Image: *Andrey Prokhorov/Getty Images*
Compositor: *SPi Global*
Printer: *R. R. Donnelley*

Library of Congress Cataloging-in-Publication Data

Names: Schilling, Melissa A., author.
Title: Strategic management of technological innovation / Melissa A.
    Schilling, New York University.
Description: Fifth edition. | New York, NY : McGraw-Hill Education, [2017]
Identifiers: LCCN 2015043171 | ISBN 9781259539060 (alk. paper)
Subjects: LCSH: Technological innovations—Management. | New products—Management. | Strategic planning.
Classification: LCC HD45 .S3353 2017 | DDC 658.4/012—dc23 LC record available at
http://lccn.loc.gov/2015043171

mheducation.com/highered

About the Author

Melissa A. Schilling, Ph.D.

Melissa Schilling is a professor of management and organizations at New York University's Stern School of Business. Professor Schilling teaches courses in strategic management, corporate strategy and technology, and innovation management. Before joining NYU, she was an Assistant Professor at Boston University (1997–2001), and has also served as a Visiting Professor at INSEAD and the Bren School of Environmental Science & Management at the University of California at Santa Barbara. She has also taught strategy and innovation courses at Siemens Corporation, IBM, the Kauffman Foundation Entrepreneurship Fellows program, Sogang University in Korea, and the Alta Scuola Polytecnica, a joint institution of Politecnico di Milano and Politecnico di Torino.

Professor Schilling's research focuses on technological innovation and knowledge creation. She has studied how technology shocks influence collaboration activity and innovation outcomes, how firms fight technology standards battles, and how firms utilize collaboration, protection, and timing of entry strategies. She also studies how product designs and organizational structures migrate toward or away from modularity. Her most recent work focuses on knowledge creation, including how breadth of knowledge and search influences insight and learning, and how the structure of knowledge networks influences their overall capacity for knowledge creation. Her research in innovation and strategy has appeared in the leading academic journals such as *Academy of Management Journal, Academy of Management Review, Management Science, Organization Science, Strategic Management Journal,* and *Journal of Economics and Management Strategy* and *Research Policy.* She also sits on the editorial review boards of *Academy of Management Journal, Academy of Management Discoveries, Organization Science, Strategy Science,* and *Strategic Organization.* Professor Schilling won an NSF CAREER award in 2003, and Boston University's Broderick Prize for research in 2000.

Preface

Innovation is a beautiful thing. It is a force with both aesthetic and pragmatic appeal: It unleashes our creative spirit, opening our minds to hitherto undreamed of possibilities, while simultaneously accelerating economic growth and providing advances in such crucial human endeavors as medicine, agriculture, and education. For industrial organizations, the primary engines of innovation in the Western world, innovation provides both exceptional opportunities and steep challenges. While innovation is a powerful means of competitive differentiation, enabling firms to penetrate new markets and achieve higher margins, it is also a competitive race that must be run with speed, skill, and precision. It is not enough for a firm to be innovative—to be successful it must innovate better than its competitors.

As scholars and managers have raced to better understand innovation, a wide range of work on the topic has emerged and flourished in disciplines such as strategic management, organization theory, economics, marketing, engineering, and sociology. This work has generated many insights about how innovation affects the competitive dynamics of markets, how firms can strategically manage innovation, and how firms can implement their innovation strategies to maximize their likelihood of success. A great benefit of the dispersion of this literature across such diverse domains of study is that many innovation topics have been examined from different angles. However, this diversity also can pose integration challenges to both instructors and students. This book seeks to integrate this wide body of work into a single coherent strategic framework, attempting to provide coverage that is rigorous, inclusive, and accessible.

Organization of the Book

The subject of innovation management is approached here as a strategic process. The outline of the book is designed to mirror the strategic management process used in most strategy textbooks, progressing from assessing the competitive dynamics of the situation, to strategy formulation, and then to strategy implementation. The first part of the book covers the foundations and implications of the dynamics of innovation, helping managers and future managers better interpret their technological environments and identify meaningful trends. The second part of the book begins the process of crafting the firm's strategic direction and formulating its innovation strategy, including project selection, collaboration strategies, and strategies for protecting the firm's property rights. The third part of the book covers the process of implementing innovation, including the implications of organization structure on innovation, the management of new product development processes, the construction and management of new product development teams, and crafting the firm's deployment strategy. While the book emphasizes practical applications and examples, it also provides systematic coverage of the existing research and footnotes to guide further reading.

Complete Coverage for Both Business and Engineering Students

This book is designed to be a primary text for courses in the strategic management of innovation and new product development. Such courses are frequently taught in both business and engineering programs; thus, this book has been written with the needs of business and engineering students in mind. For example, Chapter Six (Defining the Organization's Strategic Direction) provides basic strategic analysis tools with which business students may already be familiar, but which may be unfamiliar to engineering students. Similarly, some of the material in Chapter Eleven (Managing the New Product Development Process) on computer-aided design or quality function deployment may be review material for information system students or engineering students, while being new to management students. Though the chapters are designed to have an intuitive order to them, they are also designed to be self-standing so instructors can pick and choose from them "buffet style" if they prefer.

New for the Fifth Edition

This fifth edition of the text has been comprehensively revised to ensure that the frameworks and tools are rigorous and comprehensive, the examples are fresh and exciting, and the figures and cases represent the most current information available. Some changes of particular note include:

Six New Short Cases

Tesla Motors. The new opening case for Chapter Three is about Tesla Motors. In 2015, Tesla Motors was a $3.2 billion company on track to set history. It had created two cars that most people agreed were remarkable. Consumer reports had rated Tesla's Model S the best car it had ever reviewed. Though it was not yet posting profits (see Exhibits 1 and 2), sales were growing rapidly and analysts were hopeful that profits would soon follow. It had repaid its government loans ahead of the major auto conglomerates. Most importantly, it looked like it might *survive*. Perhaps even thrive. This was astonishing as there had been no other successful auto manufacturing start up in the United States since the 1920s. However, getting the general public to adopt fully electric vehicles still required surmounting several major hurdles.

A Battle Emerging in Mobile Payments. Chapter Four now opens with a case describing the mobile payment systems that are emerging and competing around the world. In the developing world, mobile payment systems promise to help bring the unbanked and underbanked access to fast and efficient funds transfer and better opportunities for saving. In the developed world, competing mobile payment standards were battling to achieve dominance, and threatening to obviate the role of the major credit card companies—putting billions of dollars of transaction fees at stake.

Reinventing Hotels: citizen M. Chapter Six opens with a case about how Michael Levie, Rattan Chadha, and Robin Chadha set out to create a fundamentally different kind of hotel. Levie and the Chadhas dramatically reduced or eliminated key features typically assumed to be standard at upscale hotels such as large rooms, in-house restaurants, and a reception desk, while increasing the use of technology at the hotel and maintaining a modern and fresh aesthetic. This enabled them to create a stylish hotel that was significantly less expensive than typical upscale hotels. This case pairs very well with the new Research Brief in Chapter Six on *Blue Ocean Strategy.*

The Mahindra Shaan: Gambling on a Radical Innovation. Chapter Seven opens with a case about the decision of Mahindra & Mahindra to make a very unusual tractor. Mahindra & Mahindra had long made traditional tractors and focused on incremental innovation. However, in the late 1990s, Mahindra's management decided to try to find the way to meet the needs of smaller farmers, who could not afford a regular tractor. They ended up creating the Shaan, a tractor/transporter hybrid that could serve for farming, personal transportation, and for transporting goods (a job small farmers performed in the off season to earn additional income). Developing the tractor was a major break with their traditional innovation choices, and this case details how they were able to get this unusual project approved, and nurture it through the new product development process.

Ending HIV? Sangamo Biosciences and Gene Editing. Chapter Eight opens with a case ripped straight from the headlines—the development of ways to alter a living person's genes to address critical ailments. Sangamo Biosciences has developed a way to edit a person's genes with Zinc Finger Nucleases (ZFNs). This innovation has the potential to eliminate monogenic diseases such as hemophilia or Huntington's disease. Even more intriguingly, Sangamo was exploring a way to use ZFNs to cure HIV by giving people a mutation that renders people naturally immune to the disease. In the case, Sangamo must decide how to address this huge—but incredibly risky— opportunity. It already has partnerships with major pharma companies for some of its other projects, but it is unclear whether the pharma companies would want to participate in the HIV project, and whether Sangamo would want to go this route.

Managing Innovation Teams at Disney. Chapter Twelve now opens with a case about how Disney creates and manages the teams that develop animated films. Disney, and Pixar (from whom it acquired several of its current innovation practices) are world renown for their ability to develop magically innovative animated films. This opening case highlights the roles of having a small team size, being collocated, and instilling a culture of brutally honest peer feedback.

Cases, Data, and Examples from Around the World

Careful attention has been paid to ensure that the text is global in its scope. The opening cases feature companies from India, Israel, Japan, The Netherlands, Kenya, and the United States, and many examples from other countries are embedded in the chapters themselves. Wherever possible, statistics used in the text are based on worldwide data.

More Comprehensive Coverage and Focus on Current Innovation Trends

In response to reviewer suggestions, the new edition now provides more extensive discussions of topics such as crowdsourcing and customer co-creation, patenting strategies, patent trolls, Blue-Ocean Strategy, and more. The suggested readings for each chapter have also been updated to identify some of the more recent publications that have gained widespread attention in the topic area of each chapter. Despite these additions, great effort has also been put into ensuring the book remains concise—a feature that has proven popular with both instructors and students.

Supplements

The teaching package for *Strategic Management of Technological Innovation* is available online from the book's Online Learning Center at www.mhhe.com/schilling5e and includes:

- An instructor's manual with suggested class outlines, responses to discussion questions, and more.
- Complete PowerPoint slides with lecture outlines and all major figures from the text. The slides can also be modified by the instructor to customize them to the instructor's needs.
- A testbank with true/false, multiple choice, and short answer/short essay questions.
- A suggested list of cases to pair with chapters from the text.

Acknowledgments

This book arose out of my research and teaching on technological innovation and new product development over the last decade; however, it has been anything but a lone endeavor. I owe much of the original inspiration of the book to Charles Hill, who helped to ignite my initial interest in innovation, guided me in my research agenda, and ultimately encouraged me to write this book. I am also very grateful to colleagues and friends such as Rajshree Agarwal, Juan Alcacer, Rick Alden, William Baumol, Bruno Braga, Gino Cattanni, Tom Davis, Sinziana Dorobantu, Gary Dushnitsky, Douglas Fulop, Raghu Garud, Deepak Hegde, Hla Lifshitz, Tammy Madsen, Rodolfo Martinez, Goncalo Pacheco D'Almeida, Jaspal Singh, Deepak Somaya, Bill Starbuck, and Christopher Tucci for their suggestions, insights, and encouragement. I am grateful to executive brand manager Mike Ablassmeir and marketing manager Casey Keske. I am also thankful to my editors, Laura Hurst Spell and Diana Murphy, who have been so supportive and made this book possible, and to the many reviewers whose suggestions have dramatically improved the book:

Joan Adams
Baruch Business School
(City University of New York)

Shahzad Ansari
Erasmus University

B. Rajaram Baliga
Wake Forest University

Sandy Becker
Rutgers Business School

David Berkowitz
University of Alabama in Huntsville

John Bers
Vanderbilt University

Paul Bierly
James Madison University

Paul Cheney
University of Central Florida

Pete Dailey
Marshall University

Robert DeFillippi
Suffolk University

Deborah Dougherty
Rutgers University

Cathy A. Enz
Cornell University

Robert Finklestein
University of Maryland–University College

Sandra Finklestein
Clarkson University School of Business

Jeffrey L. Furman
Boston University

Cheryl Gaimon
Georgia Institute of Technology

Elie Geisler
Illinois Institute of Technology

Sanjay Goel
University of Minnesota in Duluth

Andrew Hargadon
University of California, Davis

Steven Harper
James Madison University

Donald E. Hatfield
Virginia Polytechnic Institute and State University

Glenn Hoetker
University of Illinois

Sanjay Jain
University of Wisconsin–Madison

Theodore Khoury
Oregon State University

Rajiv Kohli
College of William and Mary

Vince Lutheran
University of North Carolina—Wilmington

Steve Markham
North Carolina State University

Steven C. Michael
University of Illinois

Robert Nash
Vanderbilt University

Anthony Paoni
Northwestern University

Johannes M. Pennings
University of Pennsylvania

Raja Roy
Tulane University

Linda F. Tegarden
Virginia Tech

Oya Tukel
Cleveland State University

Anthony Warren
The Pennsylvania State University

I am also very grateful to the many students of the Technological Innovation and New Product Development courses I have taught at New York University, INSEAD, Boston University, and University of California at Santa Barbara. Not only did these students read, challenge, and help improve many earlier drafts of the work, but they also contributed numerous examples that have made the text far richer than it would have otherwise been. I thank them wholeheartedly for their patience and generosity.

Melissa A. Schilling

Brief Contents

Contents

Chapter 11
Managing the New Product Development Process 235

Chapter 12
Managing New Product Development Teams 265

Introduction

THE IMPORTANCE OF TECHNOLOGICAL INNOVATION

technological innovation
The act of introducing a new device, method, or material for application to commercial or practical objectives.

In many industries **technological innovation** is now the most important driver of competitive success. Firms in a wide range of industries rely on products developed within the past five years for almost one-third (or more) of their sales and profits. For example, at Johnson & Johnson, products developed within the last five years account for over 30 percent of sales, and sales from products developed within the past five years at 3M have hit as high as 45 percent in recent years.

The increasing importance of innovation is due in part to the globalization of markets. Foreign competition has put pressure on firms to continuously innovate in order to produce differentiated products and services. Introducing new products helps firms protect their margins, while investing in process innovation helps firms lower their costs. Advances in information technology also have played a role in speeding the pace of innovation. Computer-aided design and computer-aided manufacturing have made it easier and faster for firms to design and produce new products, while flexible manufacturing technologies have made shorter production runs economical and have reduced the importance of production economies of scale.[1] These technologies help firms develop and produce more product variants that closely meet the needs of narrowly defined customer groups, thus achieving differentiation from competitors. For example, in 2015, Toyota offered 21 different passenger vehicle lines under the Toyota brand (e.g., Camry, Prius, Highlander, and Tundra). Within each of the vehicle lines, Toyota also offered several different models (e.g., Camry L, Camry LE, and Camry SE) with different features and at different price points. In total, Toyota offered 167 car models ranging in price from $14,845 (for the Yaris three-door liftback) to $80,115 (for the Land Cruiser), and seating anywhere from three passengers (e.g., Tacoma Regular Cab truck) to eight passengers (Sienna Minivan). On top of this, Toyota also produced a range of luxury vehicles under its Lexus brand. Similarly, Samsung introduced 52 unique smartphones in 2014 alone. Companies can use broad portfolios of product models to help ensure they can penetrate almost every conceivable market niche. While producing multiple product variations used to be expensive and time-consuming, flexible manufacturing technologies now enable firms to seamlessly transition from producing one product model to the next, adjusting production schedules with real-time information on demand. Firms further reduce production costs by using common components in many of the models.

As firms such as Toyota, Samsung, and others adopt these new technologies and increase their pace of innovation, they raise the bar for competitors, triggering an industrywide shift to shortened development cycles and more rapid new product introductions. The net results are greater market segmentation and rapid product obsolescence.[2] Product life cycles (the time between a product's introduction and its withdrawal from the market or replacement by a next-generation product) have become as short as 4 to 12 months for software, 12 to 24 months for computer hardware and consumer electronics, and 18 to 36 months for large home appliances.[3] This spurs firms to focus increasingly on innovation as a strategic imperative—a firm that does not innovate quickly finds its margins diminishing as its products become obsolete.

THE IMPACT OF TECHNOLOGICAL INNOVATION ON SOCIETY

If the push for innovation has raised the competitive bar for industries, arguably making success just that much more complicated for organizations, its net effect on society is more clearly positive. Innovation enables a wider range of goods and services to be delivered to people worldwide. It has made the production of food and other necessities more efficient, yielded medical treatments that improve health conditions, and enabled people to travel to and communicate with almost every part of the world. To get a real sense of the magnitude of the effect of technological innovation on society, look at Figure 1.1, which shows a timeline of some of the most important technological innovations developed over the last 200 years. Imagine how different life would be without these innovations!

gross domestic product (GDP)
The total annual output of an economy as measured by its final purchase price.

The aggregate impact of technological innovation can be observed by looking at **gross domestic product (GDP)**. The gross domestic product of an economy is its total annual output, measured by final purchase price. Figure 1.2 shows the average GDP per capita (that is, GDP divided by the population) for the world, developed countries, and developing countries from 1969 to 2014. The figures have been converted into U.S. dollars and adjusted for inflation. As shown in the figure, the average world GDP per capita has risen steadily since 1969. In a series of studies of economic growth conducted at the National Bureau of Economic Research, economists showed that the historic rate of economic growth in GDP could not be accounted for entirely by growth in labor and capital inputs. Economist Robert Merton Solow argued that this unaccounted-for residual growth represented technological change: Technological innovation increased the amount of output achievable from a given quantity of labor and capital. This explanation was not immediately accepted; many researchers attempted to explain the residual away in terms of measurement error, inaccurate price deflation, or labor improvement. But in each case the additional variables were unable to eliminate this residual growth component. A consensus gradually emerged that the

FIGURE 1.1
Timeline of Some of The Most Important Technological Innovations In The Last 200 Years

1800 -	1800—Electric battery
-	1804—Steam locomotive
-	1807—Internal combustion engine
-	1809—Telegraph
-	1817—Bicycle
1820 -	1821—Dynamo
-	1824—Braille writing system
-	1828—Hot blast furnace
-	1831—Electric generator
-	1836—Five-shot revolver
1840 -	1841—Bunsen battery (voltaic cell)
-	1842—Sulfuric ether-based anesthesia
-	1846—Hydraulic crane
-	1850—Petroleum refining
-	1856—Aniline dyes
1860 -	1862—Gatling gun
-	1867—Typewriter
-	1876—Telephone
-	1877—Phonograph
-	1878—Incandescent lightbulb
1880 -	1885—Light steel skyscrapers
-	1886—Internal combustion automobile
-	1887—Pneumatic tire
-	1892—Electric stove
-	1895—X-ray machine
1900 -	1902—Air conditioner (electric)
-	1903—Wright biplane
-	1906—Electric vacuum cleaner
-	1910—Electric washing machine
-	1914—Rocket
1920 -	1921—Insulin (extracted)
-	1927—Television
-	1928—Penicillin
-	1936—First programmable computer
-	1939—Atom fission
1940 -	1942—Aqua lung
-	1943—Nuclear reactor
-	1947—Transistor
-	1957—Satellite
-	1958—Integrated circuit
1960 -	1967—Portable handheld calculator
-	1969—ARPANET (precursor to Internet)
-	1971—Microprocessor
-	1973—Mobile (portable cellular) phone
-	1976—Supercomputer
1980 -	1981—Space shuttle (reusable)
-	1987—Disposable contact lenses
-	1989—High-definition television
-	1990—World Wide Web protocol
-	1996—Wireless Internet
2000 -	2003—Map of human genome

externalities
Costs (or benefits) that are borne (or reaped) by individuals other than those responsible for creating them. Thus, if a business emits pollutants in a community, it imposes a negative externality on the community members; if a business builds a park in a community, it creates a positive externality for community members.

residual did in fact capture technological change. Solow received a Nobel Prize for his work in 1981, and the residual became known as the Solow Residual.[4] While GDP has its shortcomings as a measure of standard of living, it does relate very directly to the amount of goods consumers can purchase. Thus, to the extent that goods improve quality of life, we can ascribe some beneficial impact of technological innovation.

Sometimes technological innovation results in negative **externalities**. Production technologies may create pollution that is harmful to the surrounding communities; agricultural and fishing technologies can result in erosion, elimination of natural habitats, and depletion of ocean stocks; medical technologies can result in unanticipated consequences such as antibiotic-resistant strains of bacteria or moral dilemmas regarding the use of genetic modification. However, technology is, in its purest essence, knowledge—knowledge to solve our problems and pursue our goals.[5] Technological innovation is thus the creation of new knowledge that is applied to practical problems. Sometimes this knowledge is applied to problems hastily, without full consideration of the consequences and alternatives, but overall it will probably serve us better to have more knowledge than less.

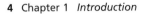

FIGURE 1.2

Gross Domestic Product per Capita, 1969–2014 (in Real 2010 $US Billions)

Source: USDA Economic Research Service, International Macroeconomic Dataset (http://www.ers.usda.gov, accessed August 17, 2015)

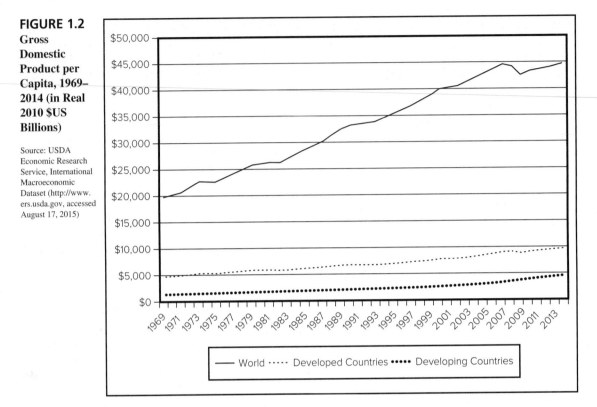

INNOVATION BY INDUSTRY: THE IMPORTANCE OF STRATEGY

As will be shown in Chapter Two, the majority of effort and money invested in technological innovation comes from industrial firms. However, in the frenetic race to innovate, many firms charge headlong into new product development without clear strategies or well-developed processes for choosing and managing projects. Such firms often initiate more projects than they can effectively support, choose projects that are a poor fit with the firm's resources and objectives, and suffer long development cycles and high project failure rates as a consequence (see the accompanying Research Brief for a recent study of the length of new product development cycles). While innovation is popularly depicted as a freewheeling process that is unconstrained by rules and plans, study after study has revealed that successful innovators have clearly defined innovation strategies and management processes.[6]

The Innovation Funnel

Most innovative ideas do not become successful new products. Many studies suggest that only one out of several thousand ideas results in a successful new product: Many projects do not result in technically feasible products and, of those that do, many fail to earn a commercial return. According a 2012 study by the Product Development and Management Association, only about one in nine projects that are initiated are successful, and of those that make it to the point of being launched to the market, only about half earn a profit.[7] Furthermore, many ideas are sifted through and abandoned before

Research Brief   How Long Does New Product Development Take?[a]

In a large-scale survey administered by the Product Development and Management Association (PDMA), researchers examined the length of time it took firms to develop a new product from initial concept to market introduction. The study divided new product development projects into categories representing their degree of innovativeness: "radical" projects, "more innovative" projects, and "incremental" projects. On average, *incremental* projects took only 33 weeks from concept to market introduction. *More innovative* projects took significantly longer, clocking in at 57 weeks. The development of *radical* products or technologies took the longest, averaging 82 weeks. The study also found that on average, for *more innovative* and *radical* projects, firms reported significantly shorter cycle times than those reported in the previous PDMA surveys conducted in 1995 and 2004.

[a] Adapted from Markham, SK, and Lee, H. "Product Development and Management Association's 2012 comparative performance assessment study," *Journal of Product Innovation Management* 30 (2013), issue 3: 408–429.

a project is even formally initiated. According to one study that combined data from prior studies of innovation success rates with data on patents, venture capital funding, and surveys, it takes about 3,000 raw ideas to produce one significantly new and successful commercial product.[8] The pharmaceutical industry demonstrates this well—only one out of every 5,000 compounds makes it to the pharmacist's shelf, and only one-third of those will be successful enough to recoup their R&D costs.[9] Furthermore, most studies indicate that it costs at least $1.5 billion and a decade of research to bring a new Food and Drug Administration (FDA)-approved pharmaceutical product to market![10] The innovation process is thus often conceived of as a funnel, with many potential new product ideas going in the wide end, but very few making it through the development process (see Figure 1.3).

FIGURE 1.3
The New Product Development Funnel in Pharmaceuticals

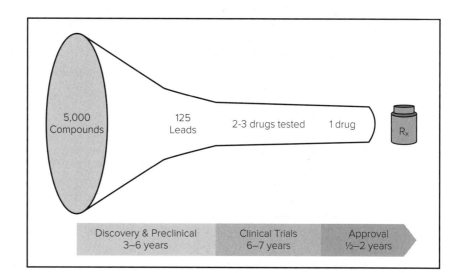

5,000 Compounds

125 Leads

2-3 drugs tested

1 drug

R_x

Discovery & Preclinical
3–6 years

Clinical Trials
6–7 years

Approval
½–2 years

The Strategic Management of Technological Innovation

Improving a firm's innovation success rate requires a well-crafted strategy. A firm's innovation projects should align with its resources and objectives, leveraging its core competencies and helping it achieve its strategic intent. A firm's organizational structure and control systems should encourage the generation of innovative ideas while also ensuring efficient implementation. A firm's new product development process should maximize the likelihood of projects being both technically and commercially successful. To achieve these things, a firm needs (*a*) an in-depth understanding of the dynamics of innovation, (*b*) a well-crafted innovation strategy, and (*c*) well-designed processes for implementing the innovation strategy. We will cover each of these in turn (see Figure 1.4).

In Part One, we will cover the foundations of technological innovation, gaining an in-depth understanding of how and why innovation occurs in an industry, and why some innovations rise to dominate others. First, we will look at the sources of innovation in Chapter Two. We will address questions such as: Where do great ideas come from? How can firms harness the power of individual creativity? What role do customers, government organizations, universities, and alliance networks play in creating innovation? In this chapter we will first explore the role of creativity in the generation of novel and useful ideas. We then look at various sources of innovation, including the role of individual inventors, firms, publicly sponsored research, and collaborative networks.

In Chapter Three, we will review models of types of innovation (such as radical versus incremental and architectural versus modular) and patterns of innovation (including s-curves of technology performance and diffusion, and technology cycles). We will address questions such as: Why are some innovations much harder to create and implement than others? Why do innovations often diffuse slowly even when they appear to offer a great advantage? What factors influence the rate at which a technology tends to improve over time? Familiarity with these types and patterns of innovation will help us distinguish how one project is different from another and the underlying factors that shape the project's likelihood of technical or commercial success.

In Chapter Four, we will turn to the particularly interesting dynamics that emerge in industries characterized by increasing returns, where strong pressures to adopt a single dominant design can result in standards battles and winner-take-all markets. We will address questions such as: Why do some industries choose a single dominant standard rather than enabling multiple standards to coexist? What makes one technological innovation rise to dominate all others, even when other seemingly superior technologies are offered? How can a firm avoid being locked out? Is there anything a firm can do to influence the likelihood of its technology becoming the dominant design?

In Chapter Five, we will discuss the impact of entry timing, including first-mover advantages, first-mover *dis*advantages, and the factors that will determine the firm's optimal entry strategy. This chapter will address such questions as: What are the advantages and disadvantages of being first to market, early but not first, and late? What determines the optimal timing of entry for a new innovation? This chapter reveals a number of consistent patterns in how timing of entry impacts innovation success, and it outlines what factors will influence a firm's optimal timing of entry, thus beginning the transition from understanding the dynamics of technological innovation to formulating technology strategy.

FIGURE 1.4
The Strategic Management of Technological Innovation

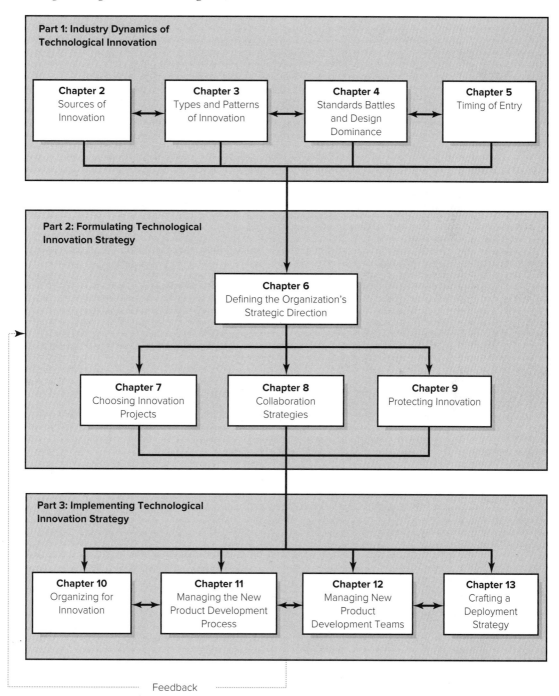

In Part Two, we will turn to formulating technological innovation strategy. Chapter Six reviews the basic strategic analysis tools managers can use to assess the firm's current position and define its strategic direction for the future. This chapter will address such questions as: What are the firm's sources of sustainable competitive advantage? Where in the firm's value chain do its strengths and weaknesses lie? What are the firm's core competencies, and how should it leverage and build upon them? What is the firm's strategic intent—that is, where does the firm want to be 10 years from now? Only once the firm has thoroughly appraised where it is currently can it formulate a coherent technological innovation strategy for the future.

In Chapter Seven, we will examine a variety of methods of choosing innovation projects. These include quantitative methods such as discounted cash flow and options valuation techniques, qualitative methods such as screening questions and balancing the research and development portfolio, as well as methods that combine qualitative and quantitative approaches such as conjoint analysis and data envelopment analysis. Each of these methods has its advantages and disadvantages, leading many firms to use a multiple-method approach to choosing innovation projects.

In Chapter Eight, we will examine collaboration strategies for innovation. This chapter addresses questions such as: Should the firm partner on a particular project or go solo? How does the firm decide which activities to do in-house and which to access through collaborative arrangements? If the firm chooses to work with a partner, how should the partnership be structured? How does the firm choose and monitor partners? We will begin by looking at the reasons a firm might choose to go solo versus working with a partner. We then will look at the pros and cons of various partnering methods, including joint ventures, alliances, licensing, outsourcing, and participating in collaborative research organizations. The chapter also reviews the factors that should influence partner selection and monitoring.

In Chapter Nine, we will address the options the firm has for appropriating the returns to its innovation efforts. We will look at the mechanics of patents, copyright, trademarks, and trade secrets. We will also address such questions as: Are there ever times when it would benefit the firm to not protect its technological innovation so vigorously? How does a firm decide between a wholly proprietary, wholly open, or partially open strategy for protecting its innovation? When will open strategies have advantages over wholly proprietary strategies? This chapter examines the range of protection options available to the firm, and the complex series of trade-offs a firm must consider in its protection strategy.

In Part Three, we will turn to implementing the technological innovation strategy. This begins in Chapter Ten with an examination of how the organization's size and structure influence its overall rate of innovativeness. The chapter addresses such questions as: Do bigger firms outperform smaller firms at innovation? How do formalization, standardization, and centralization impact the likelihood of generating innovative ideas and the organization's ability to implement those ideas quickly and efficiently? Is it possible to achieve creativity and flexibility at the same time as efficiency and reliability? How do multinational firms decide where to perform their development activities? How do multinational firms coordinate their development activities toward a common goal when the activities occur in multiple countries? This chapter examines how organizations can balance the benefits and trade-offs of flexibility, economies of scale, standardization, centralization, and tapping local market knowledge.

In Chapter Eleven, we will review a series of "best practices" that have been identified in managing the new product development process. This includes such questions as: Should new product development processes be performed sequentially or in parallel? What are the advantages and disadvantages of using project champions? What are the benefits and risks of involving customers and/or suppliers in the development process? What tools can the firm use to improve the effectiveness and efficiency of its new product development processes? How does the firm assess whether its new product development process is successful? This chapter provides an extensive review of methods that have been developed to improve the management of new product development projects and to measure their performance.

Chapter Twelve builds on the previous chapter by illuminating how team composition and structure will influence project outcomes. This chapter addresses questions such as: How big should teams be? What are the advantages and disadvantages of choosing highly diverse team members? Do teams need to be collocated? When should teams be full-time and/or permanent? What type of team leader and management practices should be used for the team? This chapter provides detailed guidelines for constructing new product development teams that are matched to the type of new product development project under way.

Finally, in Chapter Thirteen, we will look at innovation deployment strategies. This chapter will address such questions as: How do we accelerate the adoption of the technological innovation? How do we decide whether to use licensing or OEM agreements? Does it make more sense to use penetration pricing or a market-skimming price? When should we sell direct versus using intermediaries? What strategies can the firm use to encourage distributors and complementary goods providers to support the innovation? What are the advantages and disadvantages of major marketing methods? This chapter complements traditional marketing, distribution, and pricing courses by looking at how a deployment strategy can be crafted that especially targets the needs of a new technological innovation.

Summary of Chapter

1. Technological innovation is now often the single most important competitive driver in many industries. Many firms receive more than one-third of their sales and profits from products developed within the past five years.

2. The increasing importance of innovation has been driven largely by the globalization of markets and the advent of advanced technologies that enable more rapid product design and allow shorter production runs to be economically feasible.

3. Technological innovation has a number of important effects on society, including fostering increased GDP, enabling greater communication and mobility, and improving medical treatments.

4. Technological innovation may also pose some negative externalities, including pollution, resource depletion, and other unintended consequences of technological change.

5. While government plays a significant role in innovation, industry provides the majority of R&D funds that are ultimately applied to technological innovation.

6. Successful innovation requires an in-depth understanding of the dynamics of innovation, a well-crafted innovation strategy, and well-developed processes for implementing the innovation strategy.

Discussion Questions

1. Why is innovation so important for firms to compete in many industries?
2. What are some advantages of technological innovation? Disadvantages?
3. Why do you think so many innovation projects fail to generate an economic return?

Suggested Further Reading

Classics

Arrow, K. J., "Economic welfare and the allocation of resources for inventions," in *The Rate and Direction of Inventive Activity: Economic and Social Factors*, ed. R. Nelson (Princeton, NJ: Princeton University Press, 1962), pp. 609–25.

Mansfield, E., "Contributions of R and D to economic growth in the United States," *Science* CLXXV (1972), pp. 477–86.

Schumpeter, J. A., *The Theory of Economic Development* (1911; English translation, Cambridge, MA: Harvard University Press, 1936).

Stalk,G. and Hout, T.M., "Competing Against Time: How Time-Based Competition Is Reshaping Global Markets" (New York: Free Press, 1990).

Recent Work

Ahlstrom, D., "Innovation and growth: How business contributes to society," Academy of Management Perspectives, (2010) August, pp. 10–23.

Baumol, W. J., *The Free Market Innovation Machine: Analyzing the Growth Miracle of Capitalism* (Princeton, NJ: Princeton University Press, 2002).

Editors, "The top 25 innovations of the last 25 years," *Popular Science* (2012), November 15th. (www.popsci.com)

Friedman, T. L., *The World Is Flat: A Brief History of the Twenty-First Century* (New York: Farrar, Straus and Giroux, 2006).

Schilling, M.A. 2015. Towards dynamic efficiency: Innovation and its implications for antitrust. Forthcoming in *Antitrust Bulletin*.

Endnotes

1. J. P. Womack, D. T. Jones, and D. Roos, *The Machine That Changed the World* (New York: Rawson Associates, 1990).

2. W. Qualls, R. W. Olshavsky, and R. E. Michaels, "Shortening of the PLC—an Empirical Test," *Journal of Marketing* 45 (1981), pp. 76–80.

3. M. A. Schilling and C. E. Vasco, "Product and Process Technological Change and the Adoption of Modular Organizational Forms," in *Winning Strategies in a Deconstructing World*, eds. R. Bresser, M. Hitt, R. Nixon, and D. Heuskel (Sussex, England: John Wiley & Sons, 2000), pp. 25–50.

4. N. Crafts, "The First Industrial Revolution: A Guided Tour for Growth Economists," *The American Economic Review* 86, no. 2 (1996), pp. 197–202; R. Solow, "Technical Change and the Aggregate Production Function," *Review of Economics and Statistics* 39 (1957), pp. 312–20; and N. E. Terleckyj, "What Do R&D Numbers Tell Us about Technological Change?" *American Economic Association* 70, no. 2 (1980), pp. 55–61.

5. H. A. Simon, "Technology and Environment," *Management Science* 19 (1973), pp. 1110–21.

6. S. Brown and K. Eisenhardt, "The Art of Continuous Change: Linking Complexity Theory and Time-Paced Evolution in Relentlessly Shifting Organizations," *Administrative Science Quarterly* 42 (1997), pp. 1–35; K. Clark and T. Fujimoto, *Product Development Performance* (Boston: Harvard Business School Press, 1991); R. Cooper, "Third Generation New Product Processes," *Journal of Product Innovation Management* 11 (1994), pp. 3–14; D. Doughery, "Reimagining the Differentiation and Integration of Work for Sustained Product Innovation," *Organization Science* 12 (2001), pp. 612–31; and M. A. Schilling and C. W. L. Hill, "Managing the New Product Development Process: Strategic Imperatives," *Academy of Management Executive* 12, no. 3 (1998), pp. 67–81.

7. Markham, SK, and Lee, H. "Product Development and Management Association's 2012 comparative performance assessment study," *Journal of Product Innovation Management* 30 (2013), issue 3:408–429.

8. G. Stevens and J. Burley, "3,000 Raw Ideas Equals 1 Commercial Success!" *Research Technology Management* 40, no. 3 (1997), pp. 16–27.

9. Standard & Poor's Industry Surveys, Pharmaceutical Industry, 2008.

10. See Joseph A. DiMasi & Henry G. Grabowski, *The Costs of Biopharmaceutical R&D: Is Biotech Different?* 28 Managerial & Decision Econ. 469-179. (2007).

Industry Dynamics of Technological Innovation

In this section, we will explore the industry dynamics of technological innovation, including:

- The sources from which innovation arises, including the roles of individuals, organizations, government institutions, and networks.
- The types of innovations and common industry patterns of technological evolution and diffusion.
- The factors that determine whether industries experience pressure to select a dominant design, and what drives which technologies to dominate others.
- The effects of timing of entry, and how firms can identify (and manage) their entry options.

This section will lay the foundation that we will build upon in Part Two, Formulating Technological Innovation Strategy.

Industry Dynamics of Technological Innovation

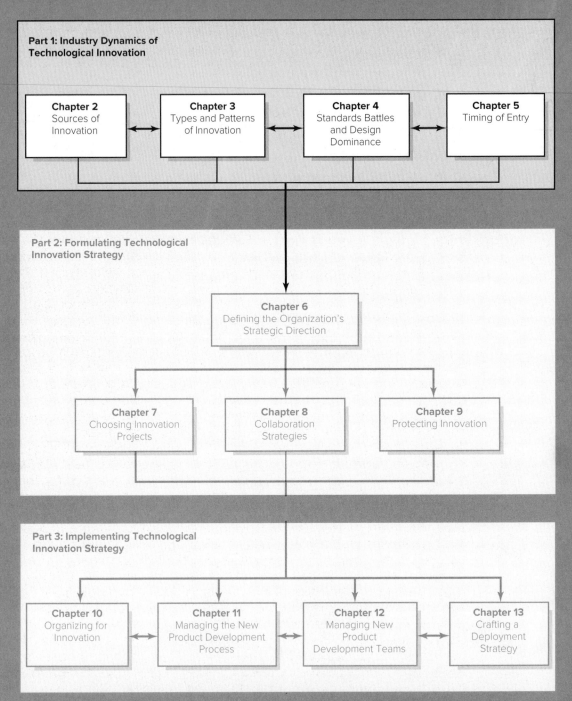

Part 1: Industry Dynamics of Technological Innovation

Chapter 2
Sources of Innovation

Chapter 3
Types and Patterns of Innovation

Chapter 4
Standards Battles and Design Dominance

Chapter 5
Timing of Entry

Part 2: Formulating Technological Innovation Strategy

Chapter 6
Defining the Organization's Strategic Direction

Chapter 7
Choosing Innovation Projects

Chapter 8
Collaboration Strategies

Chapter 9
Protecting Innovation

Part 3: Implementing Technological Innovation Strategy

Chapter 10
Organizing for Innovation

Chapter 11
Managing the New Product Development Process

Chapter 12
Managing New Product Development Teams

Chapter 13
Crafting a Deployment Strategy

Sources of Innovation

Getting an Inside Look: Given Imaging's Camera Pill[a]

Gavriel Iddan was an electro-optical engineer at Israel's Rafael Armament Development Authority, the Israeli authority for development of weapons and military technology. One of Iddan's projects was to develop the "eye" of a guided missile, which leads the missile to its target. In 1981, Iddan traveled to Boston on sabbatical to work for a company that produced X-ray tubes and ultrasonic probes. While there, he befriended a gastroenterologist (a physician who focuses on digestive diseases) named Eitan Scapa. During long conversations in which each would discuss his respective field, Scapa taught Iddan about the technologies used to view the interior lining of the digestive system. Scapa pointed out that the existing technologies had a number of significant limitations, particularly with respect to viewing the small intestine.[b] The small intestine is the locale of a number of serious disorders. In the United States alone, approximately 19 million people suffer from disorders in the small intestine (including bleeding, Crohn's disease, celiac disease, chronic diarrhea, irritable bowel syndrome, and small bowel cancer).[c]

Furthermore, the nature of the small intestine makes it a difficult place to diagnose and treat such disorders. The small intestine (or "small bowel") is about 5 to 6 meters long in a typical person and is full of twists and turns. X-rays do not enable the physician to view the lining of the intestine, and endoscopes (small cameras attached to long, thin, flexible poles) can reach only the first third of the small intestine and can be quite uncomfortable for the patient. The remaining option, surgery, is very invasive and can be impractical if the physician does not know which part of the small intestine is affected. Scapa thus urged Iddan to try to come up with a better way to view the small intestine, but at that time Iddan had no idea how to do it.

Ten years later, Iddan visited the United States again, and his old friend Scapa again inquired whether there was a technological solution that would provide a better solution for viewing the small intestine. By this time, very small image sensors—*charge-coupled devices* (CCDs)—had been developed in the quest to build small video cameras. Iddan wondered if perhaps it would be possible to create a very small missile-like device that could travel through the intestine without a lifeline leading to the outside of the body. Like the missiles Iddan developed at Rafael, this device would have a camera "eye." If the device were designed well, the body's natural peristaltic action would propel the camera through the length of the intestine.

could be transmitted through the body wall, he conducted a very rudimentary experiment with a store-bought chicken: He placed a transmitting antenna inside the chicken and a receiving antenna outside the chicken. The results indicated that it was possible to transmit a clear video image. Encouraged by this, he set about overcoming the battery life problem: The small CCD sensors consumed so much energy that their batteries were often depleted within 10 minutes. Fortunately, advances in semiconductors promised to replace CCD imagers with a new generation of *complementary metal oxide semiconductors* (CMOS) that would consume a fraction of the power of CCD imagers. Iddan began developing a prototype based on CMOS technology and applied for an initial patent on the device in 1994. In 1995, he presented his product idea to Gavriel Meron, the CEO of Applitec Ltd., a company that made small endoscopic cameras. Meron thought the project was a fascinating idea, and founded Given Imaging (**GI** for gastrointestinal, **V** for video, and **EN** for endoscopy) to develop and market the technology.[d]

Unbeknownst to Iddan or Meron, another team of scientists in the United Kingdom was also working on a method for wireless endoscopy. This team included a physician named C. Paul Swain, a bioengineer named Tim Mills, and a doctoral student named Feng Gong. Swain, Mills, and Gong were exploring applications of commercially available miniature video cameras and processors. They scouted out miniature camera technology at "spy shops" in London that supplied small video cameras and transmitters to private detectives and other users.[e] By 1994 they were developing crude devices to see if they could transmit moving images from within the gut using microwave frequencies. By 1996 they had succeeded in their first live animal trial. They surgically inserted their prototype device into a pig's stomach, and demonstrated that they could see the pylorus valve of the stomach open and close. Their next hurdle was to develop a device that could be swallowed instead of surgically inserted.

In the fall of 1997, Gavriel Meron met Dr. Swain at a conference in Birmingham, England, and they concluded that their progress would be much faster if they joined forces. Swain's team had superior expertise in anatomy and the imaging needs of diagnosing small intestine disorders, while Iddan's CMOS-based sensors enabled the production of a smaller device with lower power requirements. The teams thus had complementary knowledge that each knew would be crucial to producing a successful capsule endoscope.

In 1999, the team got permission from the ethics committee at the Royal London Hospital to conduct their first human trial. Dr. Swain would be the patient, and Dr. Scapa (whose initial urgings had motivated Iddan to develop the wireless endoscope) would be the surgeon who would oversee the procedure. In October of 1999, in Scapa's clinic near Tel Aviv, Israel, Dr. Swain swallowed the prototype capsule. The first images were of poor quality because of the team's inexperience at holding the receiving antenna in an optimal position. The team was not sure how far the capsule had traveled, so they used a radiograph to find the position of the capsule. The radiograph revealed that the device had reached Swain's colon, and thus had successfully traversed the entire length of the small intestine. The team was thrilled at this victory, and urged Swain to swallow another capsule, which he did the next morning. Now that the team was more practiced at optimizing the receiving antennas, they achieved much better quality images. Swain remarked that he "enjoyed watching the lovely sea view" of his lower intestine. Though the first capsule had transmitted for only about 2 hours before its battery life was depleted, the second capsule transmitted for more than 6 hours, and the team knew they had obtained quality images of a substantial length of small intestine.[f]

Over the next few months the team conducted several animal and human trials, and by April of 2000 they had used the device to find a small intestinal bleeding source in three patients with "obscure recurrent gastrointestinal bleeding" (a difficult problem to diagnose and treat). An article on the device was published that year in *Nature* (a prestigious scientific journal), with a header reading "The discomfort of internal endoscopy may soon be a thing of the past."[g] By August of 2001 the device had received FDA clearance, and by October of 2001 Given Imaging had gone public, raising $60 million in its initial public offering.

Given Imaging marketed its device as a system that included a workstation, proprietary software, wearable video recording packs, and the swallowable capsules (called "PillCams"). After swallowing the $450 PillCam, the patient goes about the day while the PillCam broadcasts images to a video recording pack the patient wears around the waist. When the patient returns the pack to the physician, the physician uploads the images and can both view them directly and utilize Given's computer software, which employs algorithms that examine the pixels in the images to identify possible locations of bleeding. The PillCam exits the patient naturally.

Encouraged by their success, the developers at Given Imaging began working on PillCams for the esophagus (PillCam ESO) and for the colon (PillCam COLON). Whereas Given estimated the global market potential for small bowel capsule endoscopy (PillCam SB) was $1 billion, it believed that the global market opportunity for PillCam COLON could be a multi-billion dollar opportunity due to widespread routine screening for colon cancer. By 2013, Given had also developed PillCam SB3, which offered sharper images and adaptive frame rate technology that enables it to snap more pictures, more quickly. These improvements would enable clinicians to better spot lesions indicating Crohn's disease—lesions that would go undetected by traditional endoscopic methods.[h] Crohn's disease is an auto-immune disorder in which the digestive tract attacks itself, leading to pain, diarrhea, and vomiting. More than one million people have been diagnosed worldwide, and many more cases were thought to be undiagnosed.

By 2015, numerous studies had shown that PillCams compared favorably to traditional endoscopy in terms of safety: While use of capsule endoscopy could result occasionally in the camera becoming lodged and not exiting the body naturally (roughly eight cases of this happening had been identified by 2015), traditional endoscopy bore a risk of tearing the gastrointestinal wall, which could quickly lead to deadly infections. At $500, PillCams were also less expensive than traditional gastrointestinal endoscopy procedures, which ran from $800 to $4000 or more.

A View to the Future . . .

Colonoscopy was the largest category of the endoscopy market—in the United States alone, 14 million patients undergo colonoscopy a year, and it was believed that even more people would undergo screening if screening were more comfortable. Given thus had the potential of growing market. As of 2015, the U.S. approval for the Pillcam COLON was limited to "patients who had undergone incomplete colonoscopies," citing some results that indicated that the pictures from the camera pill were less clear than traditional colonoscopy. Many in the industry, however, suspected that the camera pill would eventually supplant all traditional colonoscopy.

In February of 2014, Dublin-based medical device maker Covidien had acquired Given Imaging for roughly $860 million[i], and then in early 2015, medical equipment giant Medtronic acquired Covidien for $49.9 billion.[j] Given would now have access to much greater capital resources and larger (and more geographically distributed) salesforces—if it could continue to get its Pillcams approved for more applications and in more countries, it was positioned to transform the market for gastrointestinal endoscopy.

Discussion Questions

1. What factors do you think enabled Iddan, an engineer with no medical background, to pioneer the development of wireless endoscopy?
2. To what degree would you characterize Given's development of the camera pill as "science-push" versus "demand-pull"?
3. What were the advantages and disadvantages of Iddan and Meron collaborating with Dr. Swain's team?
4. What were the advantages and disadvantages of Given being owned by Medtronic?

[a] This case was developed through a combination of publicly available materials and documents provided by Given Imaging. The author is grateful for the valuable assistance of Sharon Koninsky of Given Imaging.

[b] G. J. Iddan and C. P. Swain, "History and Development of Capsule Endoscopy," *Gastrointestinal Endoscopy Clinics of North America* 14 (2004), pp. 1–9.

[c] Given Imaging Prospectus, 2004.

[d] "Given Imaging," 15th Annual Healthcare Special, *Wall Street Transcript*–Bear, Stearns & Co., September 2000, pp. 203–06.

[e] Iddan and Swain, "History and Development of Capsule Endoscopy."

[f] Iddan and Swain, "History and Development of Capsule Endoscopy."

[g] G. Iddan, G. Meron, A. Glukhovsky, and P. Swain, "Wireless Capsule Endoscopy," *Nature* 405 (2000), p. 417.

[h] Arnold, M. 2013. A view to a pill. *Medical Marketing & Media*, June 1: 27–30

[i] Walker, J. 2013. PillCam maker Given Imaging to Be bought by Covidien. *Wall Street Journal*, December 8th.

[j] Riley, C. 2014. Medtronic buys Covidien for $2.9 billion. *CNN Money*, June 15th.

OVERVIEW

innovation
The practical implementation of an idea into a new device or process.

Innovation can arise from many different sources. It can originate with individuals, as in the familiar image of the lone inventor or users who design solutions for their own needs. Innovation can also come from the research efforts of universities, government laboratories and incubators, or private nonprofit organizations. One primary engine of innovation is firms. Firms are well suited to innovation activities because they typically have greater resources than individuals and a management system to marshal those resources toward a collective purpose. Firms also face strong incentives to develop differentiating new products and services, which may give them an advantage over nonprofit or government-funded entities.

An even more important source of innovation, however, does not arise from any one of these sources, but rather the linkages between them. Networks of innovators that leverage knowledge and other resources from multiple sources are one of the most powerful agents of technological advance.[1] We can thus think of sources of innovation as composing a complex system wherein any particular innovation may emerge primarily from one or more components of the system or the linkages between them (see Figure 2.1).

In the sections that follow, we will first consider the role of creativity as the underlying process for the generation of novel and useful ideas. We will then consider how creativity is transformed into innovative outcomes by the separate components of the innovation system (individuals, firms, etc.), and through the linkages between different components (firms' relationships with their customers, technology transfer from universities to firms, etc.).

FIGURE 2.1
**Sources of
Innovation as
a System**

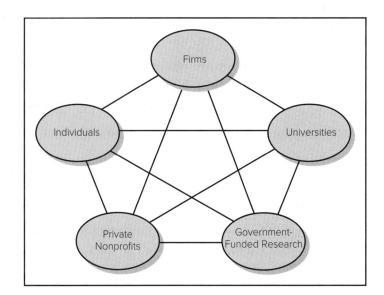

CREATIVITY

idea
Something imagined or pictured in the mind.

creativity
The ability to produce novel and useful work.

Innovation begins with the generation of new **ideas**. The ability to generate new and useful ideas is termed creativity. **Creativity** is defined as the ability to produce work that is useful and novel. Novel work must be different from work that has been previously produced and surprising in that it is not simply the next logical step in a series of known solutions.[2] The degree to which a product is novel is a function both of how different it is from prior work (e.g., a minor deviation versus a major leap) and of the audience's prior experiences.[3] A product could be novel to the person who made it, but known to most everyone else. In this case, we would call it reinvention. A product could be novel to its immediate audience, yet be well known somewhere else in the world. The most creative works are novel at the individual producer level, the local audience level, and the broader societal level.[4]

Individual Creativity

An individual's creative ability is a function of his or her intellectual abilities, knowledge, style of thinking, personality, motivation, and environment.[5] The most important intellectual abilities for creative thinking include the ability to look at problems in unconventional ways, the ability to analyze which ideas are worth pursuing and which are not, and the ability to articulate those ideas to others and convince others that the ideas are worthwhile. The impact of knowledge on creativity is somewhat double-edged. If an individual has too little knowledge of a field, he or she is unlikely to understand it well enough to contribute meaningfully to it. On the other hand, if an individual knows a field too well, that person can become trapped in the existing logic and paradigms, preventing him or her from coming up with solutions that require an alternative perspective. Thus, an individual with only a moderate degree of knowledge of a field might be able to produce more creative solutions than an individual with extensive knowledge of the field.[6] This may explain in part why a military scientist such as Gavriel Iddan came up with a significant medical innovation (as described in the opening case), despite having no formal medical training. With respect to *thinking styles*, the most creative individuals prefer to think in novel ways of their own choosing, and can discriminate between important problems and unimportant ones. The personality traits deemed most important for creativity include self-efficacy (a person's confidence in his or her own capabilities), tolerance for ambiguity, and a willingness to overcome obstacles and take reasonable risks.[7] Intrinsic motivation has also been shown to be very important for creativity.[8] That is, individuals are more likely to be creative if they work on things they are genuinely interested in and enjoy. Finally, to fully unleash an individual's creative potential often requires an environment that provides support and rewards for creative ideas.

Organizational Creativity

The creativity of the organization is a function of creativity of the individuals within the organization and a variety of social processes and contextual factors that shape the way those individuals interact and behave.[9] An organization's overall creativity level is thus not a simple aggregate of the creativity of the individuals it employs. The organization's structure, routines, and incentives could thwart individual creativity or amplify it.

The most familiar method of a company tapping the creativity of its individual employees is the suggestion box. In 1895, John Patterson, founder of National Cash Register (NCR), created the first sanctioned suggestion box program to tap the ideas of the hourly worker.[10] The program was considered revolutionary in its time. The originators of adopted ideas were awarded $1. In 1904, employees submitted 7,000 ideas, of which one-third were adopted. Other firms have created more elaborate systems that not only capture employee ideas, but incorporate mechanisms for selecting and implementing those ideas. Google, for example, utilizes an idea management system whereby employees e-mail their ideas for new products and processes to a company-wide database where every employee can view the idea, comment on it, and rate it (for more on how Google encourages innovation, see the Theory in Action on Inspiring Innovation at Google, later in this section). Honda of America utilizes an employee-driven idea system (EDIS) whereby employees submit their ideas, and if approved, the employee who submits the idea is responsible for following through on the suggestion, overseeing its progress from concept to implementation. Honda of America reports that more than 75 percent of all ideas are implemented.[11] Bank One, one of the largest holding banks in the United States, has created an employee idea program called "One Great Idea." Employees access the company's idea repository through the company's **intranet**. There they can submit their ideas and actively interact and collaborate on the ideas of others.[12] Through active exchange, the employees can evaluate and refine the ideas, improving their fit with the diverse needs of the organization's stakeholders.

intranet
A private network, accessible only to authorized individuals. It is like the Internet but operates only within ("intra") the organization.

At Bank of New York Mellon they go a step further—the company holds enterprise-wide innovation competitions where employees form their own teams and compete in coming up with innovative ideas. These ideas are first screened by judges at both the regional and business-line level. Then, the best ideas are pitched to senior management in a "Shark Tank" style competition that is webcast around the world. If a senior executive sees an idea they like, they step forward and say they will fund it and run with it. The competition both helps the company come up with great ideas and sends a strong signal to employees about the importance of innovation.[13]

Idea collection systems (such as suggestion boxes) are relatively easy and inexpensive to implement, but are only a first step in unleashing employee creativity. Today companies such as Intel, Motorola, 3M, and Hewlett-Packard go to much greater lengths to tap the creative potential embedded in employees, including investing in creativity training programs. Such programs encourage managers to develop verbal and nonverbal cues that signal employees that their thinking and autonomy are respected. These cues shape the culture of the firm and are often more effective than monetary rewards—in fact, sometimes monetary rewards undermine creativity by encouraging employees to focus on extrinsic rather than intrinsic motivation.[14] The programs also often incorporate exercises that encourage employees to use creative mechanisms such as developing alternative scenarios, using analogies to compare the problem with another problem that shares similar features or structure, and restating the problem in a new way. One product design firm, IDEO, even encourages employees to develop mock prototypes of potential new products out of inexpensive materials such as cardboard or styrofoam and pretend to use the product, exploring potential design features in a tangible and playful manner.

Google is always working on a surprising array of projects, ranging from the completely unexpected (such as autonomous self-driving cars and solar energy) to the more mundane (such as e-mail and cloud services).[a] In pursuit of continuous innovation at every level of the company, Google uses a range of formal and informal mechanisms to encourage its employees to innovate:[b]

20 percent Time: All Google engineers are encouraged to spend 20 percent of their time working on their own projects. This was the source of some of Google's most famous products (e.g., Google Mail, Google News).

Recognition Awards: Managers were given discretion to award employees with "recognition awards" to celebrate their innovative ideas.

Google Founders' Awards: Teams doing outstanding work could be awarded substantial stock grants.

Some employees had become millionaires from these awards alone.

Adsense Ideas Contest: Each quarter, the Adsense online sales and operations teams reviewed 100 to 200 submissions from employees around the world, and selected finalists to present their ideas at the quarterly contest.

Innovation Reviews: Formal meetings where managers product ideas originated in their divisions directly to founders Larry Page and Sergey Brin, as well as to CEO Eric Schmidt.[c]

[a] Bradbury, D. 2011. Google's rise and rise. *Backbone*, Oct:24–27.
[b] Groysberg, B., Thomas, D.A. & Wagonfeld, A.B. 2011. Keeping Google "Googley." *Harvard Business School Case* 9-409-039.
[c] Kirby, J. 2009. How Google really does it. *Canadian Business*, 82(18):54–58.

TRANSLATING CREATIVITY INTO INNOVATION

Innovation is more than the generation of creative ideas; it is the implementation of those ideas into some new device or process. Innovation requires combining a creative idea with resources and expertise that make it possible to embody the creative idea in a useful form. We will first consider the role of individuals as innovators, including innovation by inventors who specialize in creating new products and processes, and innovation by end users. We then will look at innovation activity that is organized by firms, universities, and government institutions.

The Inventor

The familiar image of the inventor as an eccentric and doggedly persistent scientist may have some basis in cognitive psychology. Analysis of personality traits of inventors suggests these individuals are likely to be interested in theoretical and abstract thinking, and have an unusual enthusiasm for problem solving. Their tendency toward introversion may cause them to be better at manipulating concepts than at interacting socially.[15] Such personality traits appear to suggest that the capacity to be an inventor is an innate ability of an individual. Others, however, disagree with this conclusion and argue that inventors are made, not born.[16] One 10-year study of inventors concludes that the most successful inventors possess the following traits:

1. They have mastered the basic tools and operations of the field in which they invent, but they have not specialized solely in that field; instead they have pursued two or three fields simultaneously, permitting them to bring different perspectives to each.

2. They are curious and more interested in problems than solutions.

In January 2001, an Internet news story leaked that iconoclastic inventor Dean Kamen had devised a fantastic new invention—a device that could affect the way cities were built, and even change the world. Shrouded in secrecy, the mysterious device, code-named "Ginger" and "IT," became the talk of the technological world and the general public, as speculation about the technology grew wilder and wilder. In December of that year, Kamen finally unveiled his invention, the Segway Human Transporter.[a] Based on an elaborate combination of motors, gyroscopes, and a motion control algorithm, the Segway HT was a self-balancing, two-wheeled scooter. Though to many it looked like a toy, the Segway represented a significant advance in technology. John Doerr, the venture capitalist behind Amazon.com and Netscape, predicted it would be bigger than the Internet. Though the Segway did not turn out to be a mass market success, its technological achievements were significant. In 2009, General Motors and Segway announced that they were developing a two-wheeled, two-seat electric vehicle based on the Segway that would be fast, safe, inexpensive, and clean. The car would run on a lithium-ion battery and achieve speeds of 35 miles-per-hour.

The Segway was the brainchild of Dean Kamen, an inventor with more than 150 U.S. and foreign patents, whose career began in his teenage days of devising mechanical gadgets in his parents' basement.[b] Kamen never graduated from college, though he has since received numerous honorary degrees. He is described as tireless and eclectic, an entrepreneur with a seemingly boundless enthusiasm for science and technology. Kamen has received numerous awards for his inventions, including the Kilby award, the Hoover Medal, and the National Medal of Technology. Most of his inventions have been directed at advancing health care technology. In 1988, he invented the first self-service dialysis machine for people with kidney failure. Kamen had rejected the original proposal for the machine brought to him by Baxter, one of the world's largest medical equipment manufacturers. To Kamen, the solution was not to come up with a new answer to a known problem, but to instead reformulate the problem: "What if you can find the technology that not only fixes the valves but also makes the whole thing as simple as plugging a cassette into a VCR? Why do patients have to continue to go to these centers? Can we make a machine that can go in the home, give the patients back their dignity, reduce the cost, reduce the trauma?"[c] The result was the HomeChoice dialysis machine, which won *Design News*' 1993 Medical Product of the Year award.

In 1999, Kamen's company, DEKA Research, introduced the IBOT Mobility System, an extremely advanced wheelchair incorporating a sophisticated balancing system that enabled users to climb stairs and negotiate sand, rocks, and curbs. According to Kamen, the IBOT "allowed a disabled person, a person who cannot walk, to basically do all the ordinary things that you take for granted that they can't do even in a wheelchair, like go up a curb."[d] It was the IBOT's combination of balance and mobility that gave rise to the idea of the Segway.

[a] J. Bender, D. Condon, S. Gadkari, G. Shuster, I. Shuster, and M. A. Schilling, "Designing a New Form of Mobility: Segway Human Transporter," New York University teaching case, 2003.
[b] E. I. Schwartz, "The Inventor's Play-Ground," *Technology Review* 105, no. 8 (2002), pp. 68–73.
[c] Ibid.
[d] *The Great Inventor*. Retrieved November 19, 2002, from www.cbsnews.com.

3. They question the assumptions made in previous work in the field.
4. They often have the sense that all knowledge is unified. They seek global solutions rather than local solutions, and are generalists by nature.[17]

These traits are demonstrated by Dean Kamen, inventor of the Segway Human Transporter and the IBOT Mobility System (a technologically advanced wheelchair), profiled in the Theory in Action section on Dean Kamen. They are also illustrated in the following quotes by Nobel laureates. Sir MacFarlane Burnet, Nobel Prize–winning immunologist, noted, "I think there are dangers for a research man being too well trained in the field he is going to study,"[18] and Peter Debye, Nobel Prize–winning chemist, noted, "At the beginning of the Second World War, R. R. Williams of Bell Labs came to Cornell to try to interest me in the polymer field. I said to him, 'I don't know anything about polymers. I never thought about them.' And his answer was, 'That is why we want you.' "[19] The global search for global solutions is aptly illustrated by Thomas Edison, who did not set out to invent just a lightbulb: "The problem then that I undertook to solve was . . . the production of the multifarious apparatus, methods, and devices, each adapted for use with every other, and all forming a comprehensive system."[20]

Such individuals may spend a lifetime developing numerous creative new devices or processes, though they may patent or commercialize few. The qualities that make people inventive do not necessarily make them entrepreneurial; many inventors do not actively seek to patent or commercialize their work. Many of the most well-known inventors (e.g., Alexander Graham Bell, Thomas Alva Edison, Albert Einstein, and Benjamin Franklin), however, had both inventive and entrepreneurial traits.[21]

Innovation by Users

Innovation often originates with those who create solutions for their own needs. Users often have both a deep understanding of their unmet needs and the incentive to find ways to fulfill them.[22] While manufacturers typically create new product innovations in order to profit from the sale of the innovation to customers, user innovators often have no initial intention to profit from the sale of their innovation—they create the innovation for their own use.[23] Users may alter the features of existing products, approach existing manufacturers with product design suggestions, or develop new products themselves. For example, the extremely popular small sailboat, the Laser, was designed without any formal market research or concept testing. Instead it was the creative inspiration of three former Olympic sailors, Ian Bruce, Bruce Kirby, and Hans Vogt. They based the boat design on their own preferences: simplicity, maximum performance, transportability, durability, and low cost. The resulting sailboat became hugely successful; during the 1970s and '80s, 24 Laser sailboats were produced daily.[24]

Another dramatic example is the development of Indermil, a tissue adhesive based on Super Glue. Super Glue is a powerful instant adhesive, and while its strength and speed of action were a great asset in most product applications, these features also caused a key product concern—its tendency to bond skin. Managers at Loctite, the company that developed Super Glue, wondered if this tendency could be exploited to develop an alternative to sutures for surgical applications. In the 1970s, the company experimented with developing a version of the adhesive that could be packaged and sterilized, but the project failed and funding for it was canceled. In 1980 the project was resurrected when Loctite was approached by a pharmaceutical company that wanted to collaborate on developing a wound closure product. The two companies spent three years attempting to develop special Super Glues that would degrade quickly in the body, but ultimately shelved the project again. By this point most managers in the company no longer wanted to be involved in developing an alternative to sutures—it was considered far too risky. However, in 1988, Bernie Bolger of Loctite was contacted by Professor Alan Roberts, a worldwide figure in reconstructive surgery. Roberts proceeded to give the

The first snowboards were not developed by major sports equipment manufacturers seeking to leverage their capabilities by developing a new sport. Instead, they were developed by individuals who sought new ways of fulfilling their own desires for gliding over snow.

Snowboarding traces its history to the early 1960s, when a number of individuals developed an assortment of snowboard precursors, whose designs would ultimately give rise to the modern snowboard.[a] Some of the most notable of these individuals included Tom Sims, Sherman Poppen, Jake Burton Carpenter, Dimitrije Milovich, Mike Olson, and Chuck Barfoot. In 1963, Tom Sims, an avid skier and skateboarder, made his first "ski board" in wood shop class. Sims and Bob Weber would go on to design snowboards and found the company known as Sims. Another very early developer was Sherman Poppen. In 1965, to make a toy for his daughter, Poppen attached two skis together into what he called a "snurfer." The toy turned out to be so popular that Poppen began organizing informal competitions for snurfer enthusiasts. Jake Burton Carpenter was one such enthusiast, and he began developing a version of the snurfer with rubber straps to act as bindings, giving the user greater control. This led to the founding of his Vermont-based company, Burton, which rose to become a dominant force in snowboarding. It is notable that the primary motive for most of these innovators was to develop a product for their own use; however, over time they received so many requests for their innovations from other would-be users that they subsequently founded firms.[b]

By the early 1970s, several other individuals were developing snowboards, often driven by a desire to more closely replicate the action and feel of skateboarding or surfing rather than skiing. In 1975, Dimitrije Milovich set up one of the earliest snowboard companies, Winterstick, to sell his swallow-tailed snowboards based on a surfboard design. He gained considerable exposure when *Newsweek* covered him in March of that same year, and *Powder* magazine gave him a two-page photo spread.[c] About the same time, Mike Olson and Chuck Barfoot were also developing their own snowboard prototypes, which would evolve to become the snowboard lines of Gnu and Barfoot.

By the mid-1980s, snowboarding was beginning to be allowed in major ski resorts, and ski manufacturers such as K2 and Rossignol were eyeing this growing market. The skiing industry had peaked in the 1970s and had since seen slumping demand. Snowboarding offered a way to revitalize the industry because it promised to tap a new market (largely skateboarders and surfers) rather than cannibalizing existing ski sales. By the late 1980s, K2 had a successful line of snowboards, and Rossignol was working the kinks out of its snowboarding line (early Rossignols received a lackluster response due to their more skilike feel). Even Mistral, a Swiss windsurfing company, began designing and selling snowboards.

The 1990s witnessed the rapid proliferation of new competitors in the snowboard industry. By 1995 there were approximately 300 snowboard companies. In 1998 snowboarding made its debut as an official Olympic event in Nagana, Japan, officially sealing its position in the mainstream. By 2014, there were approximately 7.3 million snowboarding participants in the United States alone and the U.S. market for snowboarding equipment was roughly $256 million.[d] What had begun as the creation of a few renegade sportsmen had developed into a significant industry.

[a] M. A. Schilling, A. Eng, and M. Velasquez, "Madd Snowboards," in *Strategic Management: Competitiveness and Globalization,* eds. M. Hitt, D. Ireland, and B. Hoskisson, 4th ed. (St. Paul, MN: West Publishing, 2000).
[b] S. K. Shah and M. Tripsas, "The Accidental Entrepreneur: The Emergent and Collective Process of User Entrepreneurship," *Strategic Entrepreneurship Journal* 1 (2007), pp. 123–40.
[c] Transworld Snowboarding, Snowboard History Timeline, www.twsnow.com.
[d] Statistics from Snowsports Industries America Fact Sheet 2015.

managers at Loctite a stunning presentation about doctors who had responded to the Bradford football stadium fire of 1983. Roberts and many other doctors had been called in to carry out surgery and skin grafting in makeshift tents around the stadium. Because stitching was too slow and skin damage was such that sutures would be ineffective, the doctors had used standard tubes of Super Glue to repair the skin and stick skin grafts in place! Roberts showed pictures of doctors in green garb standing around with Super Glue tubes stuck to their aprons, and pictures of people with large areas of skin missing and then those same people years later, with almost perfect skin repairs. Roberts begged the Loctite managers to continue their work on developing a version of Super Glue for tissue adhesion. Roberts's presentation was so compelling that the company again took up the project, this time with support from the CEO and serious funding. Approval from the United States Food and Drug Administration was won in 2002, and by 2003 the product was selling well in over 40 countries.[25]

User innovations can also blossom into new industries. For example, consider the development of snowboards, as described in the accompanying Theory in Action section.

Research and Development by Firms

One of the most obvious sources of firm innovation is the firm's own research and development efforts. Though the terms *research* and *development* are often lumped together, they actually represent different kinds of investment in innovation-related activities. *Research* can refer to both basic research and applied research. **Basic research** is effort directed at increasing understanding of a topic or field without a specific immediate commercial application in mind. This research advances scientific knowledge, which may (or may not) turn out to have long-run commercial implications. **Applied research** is directed at increasing understanding of a topic to meet a specific need. In industry, this research typically has specific commercial objectives. **Development** refers to activities that apply knowledge to produce useful devices, materials, or processes. Thus, the term *research and development* refers to a range of activities that extend from early exploration of a domain to specific commercial implementations.

Studies show that firms consider their in-house R&D (central corporate research or R&D within divisions) to be their most important source of innovation (see Figure 2.2). This perception also appears to be supported by evidence on R&D

basic research
Research targeted at increasing scientific knowledge for its own sake. It may or may not have any long-term commercial application.

applied research
Research targeted at increasing knowledge for a specific application or need.

development
Activities that apply knowledge to produce useful devices, materials, or processes.

FIGURE 2.2
Firms' Rank Ordering of the Importance of Sources for Research and Development Work, 1999

Source: E. Roberts, "Benchmarking Global Strategic Management of Technology," *Research Technology Management*. March–April 2001, pp. 25–36.

Rank Order of Sources of Research Work	Rank Order of Sources of Development Work
1 Central corporate research	Internal R&D within divisions
2 Internal R&D within divisions	Central corporate research
3 Sponsored university research	Suppliers' technology
4 Recruited students	Joint ventures/alliances
5 Continuing education	Licensing
6 University liaison programs	Customers' technology
7 Consultants/contract R&D	Continuing education
8 Joint ventures/alliances	Acquisition of products

spending and firm sales: A firm's R&D intensity (its R&D expenditures as a percentage of its revenues) has a strong positive correlation with its sales growth rate, sales from new products, and profitability.[26]

During the 1950s and 1960s, scholars of innovation emphasized a *science-push* approach to research and development.[27] This approach assumed that innovation proceeded linearly from scientific discovery, to invention, to engineering, then manufacturing activities, and finally marketing. According to this approach, the primary sources of innovation were discoveries in basic science that were translated into commercial applications by the parent firm. This linear process was soon shown to have little applicability to real-world products. In the mid-1960s, another model of innovation gained prominence: the *demand-pull* model of research and development. This approach argued that innovation was driven by the perceived demand of potential users. Research staff would develop new products in efforts to respond to customer problems or suggestions. This view, however, was also criticized as being too simplistic. Rothwell, for example, points out that different phases of innovation are likely to be characterized by varying levels of science push and demand pull.[28]

Most current research suggests that firms that are successful innovators utilize multiple sources of information and ideas, including:

- In-house research and development, including basic research.
- Linkages to customers or other potential users of innovations.
- Linkages to an external network of firms that may include competitors, complementors, and suppliers.
- Linkages to other external sources of scientific and technical information, such as universities and government laboratories.[29]

Firm Linkages with Customers, Suppliers, Competitors, and Complementors

Firms often form alliances with customers, suppliers, complementors, and even competitors to jointly work on an innovation project or to exchange information and other resources in pursuit of innovation. Collaboration might occur in the form of alliances, participation in research consortia, licensing arrangements, contract research and development, joint ventures, and other arrangements. The advantages and disadvantages of different forms of collaboration are discussed in Chapter Eight. Collaborators can pool resources such as knowledge and capital, and they can share the risk of a new product development project.

complementors
Producers of complementary goods or services (e.g., for video game console producers such as Sony or Nintendo, game developers) are complementors.

The most frequent collaborations are between firms and their customers, suppliers, and local universities (see Figure 2.3).[30] Several studies indicate that firms consider users their most valuable source of new product ideas. The use of such collaborations is consistent across North America, Europe, and Japan, though Japanese firms may be somewhat more likely to collaborate extensively with their customers (see Figure 2.3).

Firms may also collaborate with competitors and complementors. **Complementors** are organizations (or individuals) that produce complementary goods, such as lightbulbs for lamps, or DVD movies for DVD players. In some industries, firms produce a range of goods and the line between competitor and complementor can blur.

In some circumstances, firms might be bitter rivals in a particular product category and yet engage in collaborative development in that product category or

FIGURE 2.3

Percentage of Companies That Report Extensive Collaboration with Customers, Suppliers, and Universities

Source: E. Roberts, "Benchmarking Global Strategic Management of Technology," *Research Technology Management*, March–April 2001, pp. 25–36.

	North America	Europe	Japan
Collaborates with:			
Customers	44%	38%	52%
Suppliers	45	45	41
Universities	34	32	34

complementary product categories. For instance, Microsoft competes against Rockstar Games in many video game categories, yet also licenses many Rockstar Games to play on its Xbox models. Rockstar is thus both a competitor and complementor to Microsoft. This can make the relationships between firms very complex—firms may have to manage a delicate balance between its roles of competitor versus complementor, or complementors might refuse to cooperate. For example, when Google bought Motorola Mobility in 2011, makers of mobile phone handsets that used Google's Android operating system such as Samsung and HTC were watching closely to see if Google would give Motorola handsets preferential access to Google software. Many analysts speculated that Samsung and HTC would begin developing more phones based on Microsoft's mobile operating system. To avoid the ire and defection of its complementors, Google announced that Motorola would be run as a separate entity and be given no advantages over makers of other Android-powered handsets. Android was to remain an equal-opportunity platform where any handset maker had a shot at making the next great Android phone.[31]

External versus Internal Sourcing of Innovation

Critics have often charged that firms are using external sources of technological innovation rather than investing in original research. But empirical evidence suggests that external sources of information are more likely to be complements to rather than substitutes for in-house research and development. Research by the Federation of British Industries indicated firms that had their own research and development were also the heaviest users of external collaboration networks. Presumably doing in-house R&D helps to build the firm's **absorptive capacity**, enabling it to better assimilate and utilize information obtained externally.[32] Absorptive capacity refers to the firm's ability to understand and use new information (absorptive capacity is discussed in more detail in Chapter Four).

absorptive capacity
The ability of an organization to recognize, assimilate, and utilize new knowledge.

Universities and Government-Funded Research

Another important source of innovation comes from public research institutions such as universities, government laboratories, and incubators. A significant share of companies report that research from public and nonprofit institutions enabled them to develop innovations that they would not have otherwise developed.[33]

Universities

Universities in the United States performed $63.1 billion worth of R&D in 2011, making them the second largest performer of R&D in the United States after industry (see Figure 2.5 below). Of that, over $40 billion was for *basic research* (versus *applied research*), making universities the number one performer of basic research in the United States. Many universities encourage their faculty to engage in research that may lead to useful innovations. Typically the intellectual property policies of a university embrace both patentable and unpatentable innovations, and the university retains sole discretion over the rights to commercialize the innovation. If an invention is successfully commercialized, the university typically shares the income with the individual inventor(s).[34] To increase the degree to which university research leads to commercial innovation, many universities have established **technology transfer offices**.

technology transfer offices
Offices designed to facilitate the transfer of technology developed in a research environment to an environment where it can be commercially applied.

In the United States, the creation of university technology transfer offices accelerated rapidly after the Bayh-Dole Act was passed in 1980. This act allowed universities to collect royalties on inventions funded with taxpayer dollars. Before this, the federal government was entitled to all rights from federally funded inventions.[35] While the revenues from the university technology transfer activities are still quite small in comparison to university research budgets, their importance is growing rapidly. Universities also contribute significantly to innovation through the publication of research results that are incorporated into the development efforts of other organizations and individuals.

Government-Funded Research

Governments of many countries actively invest in research through their own laboratories, the formation of **science parks** and **incubators**, and grants for other public or private research entities. For example, the U.S. Small Business Administration manages two programs that enable innovative small businesses to receive funding from federal agencies such as the Department of Defense, the Department of Energy, the Department of Health and Human Services, and others. The first is the Small Business Innovation Research (SBIR) program. Under the SBIR program, agencies award grants of up to $850,000 to small businesses to help them develop and commercialize a new innovation. The second is the Small Business Technology Transfer (STTR) program, which awards grants of up to $850,000 to facilitate a partnership between a small business and a nonprofit research institution—its objective is to more fully leverage the innovation that takes place in research laboratories by connecting research scientists with entrepreneurs.

science parks
Regional districts, typically set up by government, to foster R&D collaboration between government, universities, and private firms.

incubators
Institutions designed to nurture the development of new businesses that might otherwise lack access to adequate funding or advice.

The U.S. government was the main provider of research and development funds in the United States in the 1950s and 1960s, accounting for as much as 66.5 percent in 1964. Its share has fallen significantly since then, and in 2011, U.S. government spending accounted for only 30 percent of the nation's R&D spending. However, the decline in the government share of spending is largely due to the rapid increase in industry R&D funding rather than a real decline in the absolute amount spent by the government. U.S. government funding for R&D in 2011 was close to its highest ever—$126 billion (see Figure 2.4). By contrast, about $264 billion was spent by industry on R&D.

FIGURE 2.4

U.S. R&D, by performing and funding sectors: 1953–2011[36]

Source: National Science Foundation, National Centre for Science and Engineering Statistics, National Patterns of R&D Resources (annual series). See appendix tables 4–2 and 4–6.

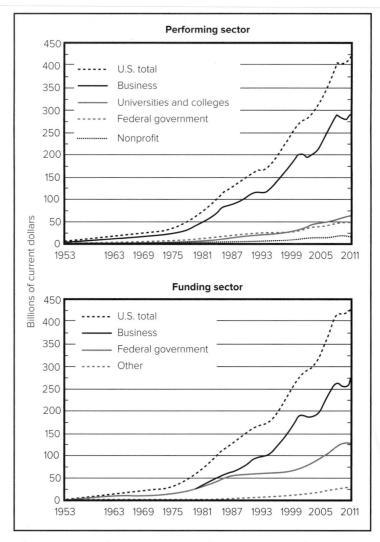

Notes: Federal performers of R&D include federal agencies and federally funded R&D centers. Other funding includes support from universities and colleges, nonfederal government, and nonprofit organizations. State and local government funding to businesses is included in business support for business R&D performance.

Science and Engineering Indicators 2014

    Figure 2.5 shows the amount spent on R&D for the top seven R&D spending countries. The figure also shows the proportions of R&D that are funded and performed by business, government, higher education, and private nonprofit. As shown, industry both funds and performs the largest share of R&D in each of the countries shown.

FIGURE 2.5

Gross expenditures on R&D for selected countries, by performing sector and funding sources: 2011 or most recent year[37]

Source: National Science Foundation, National centre for Science and Engineering Statistics, National Patterns of R&D Resources (annual series); Organisation for Economic Co-operation and development, *Main Science and Technology Indicators* (2013/1).

Country	GERD PPP ($billions)	Share of total (%) Business	Government	Higher Education	Private nonprofit
		R&D Performance			
United States (2011)[a]	429.1	68.5	12.7	14.6	4.3
China (2011)	208.2	75.7	16.3	7.9	0.0
Japan (2011)	146.5	77.0	8.4	13.2	1.5
Germany (2011)	93.1	67.3	14.7	18.0	**
South Korea (2011)	59.9	76.5	11.7	10.1	1.6
France (2011)	51.9	63.4	14.1	21.2	1.2
United Kingdom (2011)	39.6	61.5	9.3	26.9	2.4
		R&D Funding Sources			
United States (2011)[a,b]	429.1	58.6	31.2	6.4	3.8
China (2011)	208.2	73.9	21.7	NA	1.3
Japan (2011)	146.5	76.5	16.4	6.6	0.5
Germany (2010)	93.1	65.6	30.3	0.2	3.9
South Korea (2011)	59.9	73.7	24.9	1.2	0.2
France (2010)	51.9	53.5	37.0	1.8	7.6
United Kingdom (2011)	39.6	44.6	32.2	6.2	17.0

GERD = gross expenditures on R&D; PPP = purchasing power parity

One way governments support the research and development efforts in both the public and private sectors is through the formation of science parks and incubators. Since the 1950s, national governments have actively invested in developing science parks to foster collaboration between national and local government institutions, universities, and private firms. These science parks often include institutions designed to nurture the development of new businesses that might otherwise lack access to adequate funding and technical advice. Such institutions are often termed *incubators*. Incubators help overcome the market failure that can result when a new technology has the potential for important societal benefits, but its potential for direct returns is highly uncertain.[38]

Notable examples of science parks with incubators include:

- Stanford Research Park, established near Stanford University in 1951.
- Research Triangle Park, established in North Carolina in 1959.
- Sophia Antipolis Park, established in Southern France in 1969.
- Cambridge Science Park, established in Cambridge, England, in 1972.

These parks create fertile hotbeds for new start-ups and a focal point for the collaboration activities of established firms. Their proximity to university laboratories and other research centers ensures ready access to scientific expertise. Such centers also help university researchers implement their scientific discoveries in commercial applications.[39] Such parks often give rise to technology clusters that have long-lasting and self-reinforcing advantages (discussed later in the chapter).

Private Nonprofit Organizations

Private nonprofit organizations, such as private research institutes, nonprofit hospitals, private foundations, professional or technical societies, academic and industrial consortia, and trade associations, also contribute to innovation activity in a variety of complex ways. Many nonprofit organizations perform their own research and development activities, some fund the research and development activities of other organizations but do not do it themselves, and some nonprofit organizations do both in-house research and development and fund the development efforts of others.

INNOVATION IN COLLABORATIVE NETWORKS

As the previous sections indicate, there is a growing recognition of the importance of collaborative research and development networks for successful innovation.[40] Such collaborations include (but are not limited to) joint ventures, licensing and second-sourcing agreements, research associations, government-sponsored joint research programs, value-added networks for technical and scientific interchange, and informal networks.[41] Collaborative research is especially important in high-technology sectors, where it is unlikely that a single individual or organization will possess all of the resources and capabilities necessary to develop and implement a significant innovation.[42]

As firms forge collaborative relationships, they weave a network of paths between them that can act as conduits for information and other resources. By providing member firms access to a wider range of information (and other resources) than individual firms possess, interfirm networks can enable firms to achieve much more than they could achieve individually.[43] Thus, interfirm networks are an important engine of innovation. Furthermore, the structure of the network is likely to influence the flow of information and other resources through the network. For example, in a dense network where there are many potential paths for information to travel between any pair of firms, information diffusion should be fairly rapid and widespread.

Figure 2.6 provides pictures of the worldwide technology alliance network in 1995 and in 2000.[44] The mid-1990s saw record peaks in alliance activity as firms scrambled to respond to rapid change in information technologies. This resulted in a very large and dense web of connected firms. The network shown here connects 3,856 organizations, predominantly from North America, Japan, and Europe. However, there was a subsequent decline in alliance activity toward the end of the decade that caused the web to diminish in size and splinter apart into two large components and many small components. The large component on the left is primarily made up of organizations in the chemical and medical industries. The large component on the right is primarily made up of organizations in electronics-based industries. If the size and density of the collaboration network influences the amount of information available to organizations that are connected via the network, then the difference between the network shown for 1995 and the network shown for 2000 could have resulted in a substantial change in the amount of information that was transmitted between firms. (The strategic implications for a firm's position within the network are discussed in Chapter Eight.)

FIGURE 2.6
The Global Technology Collaboration Network, 1995 and 2000
1995

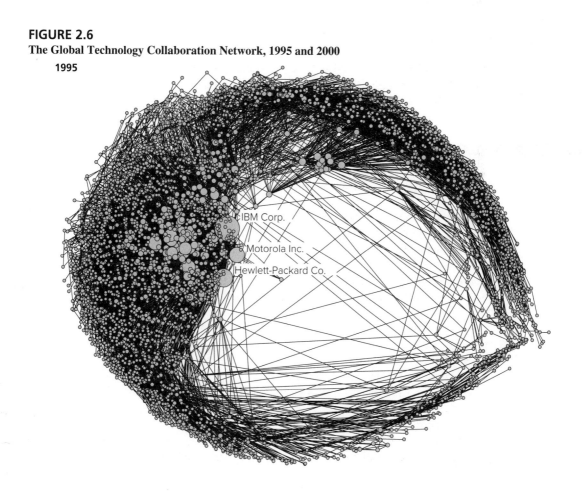

Technology Clusters

Sometimes geographical proximity appears to play a role in the formation and innovative activity of collaborative networks. Well-known regional clusters such as Silicon Valley's semiconductor firms, lower Manhattan's multimedia cluster, and the Modena, Italy, knitwear district aptly illustrate this point. This has spurred considerable interest in the factors that lead to the emergence of a cluster. City and state governments, for example, might like to know how to foster the creation of a technology cluster in their region in order to increase employment, tax revenues, and other economic benefits. For firms, understanding the drivers and benefits of clustering is useful for developing a strategy that ensures the firm is well positioned to benefit from clustering.

technology clusters
Regional clusters of firms that have a connection to a common technology, and may engage in buyer, supplier, and complementor relationships, as well as research collaboration.

Technology clusters may span a region as narrow as a city or as wide as a group of neighboring countries.[45] Clusters often encompass an array of industries that are linked through relationships between suppliers, buyers, and producers of complements. One primary reason for the emergence of regional clusters is the benefit of proximity in knowledge exchange. Though advances in information technology have made it easier, faster, and cheaper to transmit information great distances, several studies indicate that knowledge does not always transfer readily via such mechanisms.

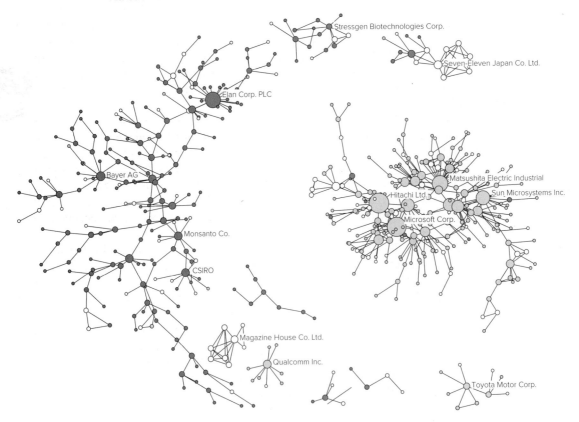

complex knowledge
Knowledge that has many underlying components, or many interdependencies between those components, or both.

tacit knowledge
Knowledge that cannot be readily codified (documented in written form).

Proximity and interaction can directly influence firms' ability and willingness to exchange knowledge. First, knowledge that is **complex** or **tacit** may require frequent and close interaction to be meaningfully exchanged.[46] Firms may need to interact frequently to develop common ways of understanding and articulating the knowledge before they are able to transfer it.[47] Second, closeness and frequency of interaction can influence a firm's *willingness* to exchange knowledge. When firms interact frequently, they can develop trust and reciprocity norms. Firms that interact over time develop greater knowledge of each other, and their repeated interactions give them information as to the likelihood of their partner's behaving opportunistically. A shared understanding of the rules of engagement emerges, wherein each partner understands its obligations with respect to how much knowledge is exchanged, how that knowledge can be used, and how the firms are expected to reciprocate.[48]

Firms that are proximate thus have an advantage in sharing information that can lead to greater innovation productivity. This can, in turn, lead to other self-reinforcing geographical advantages. A cluster of firms with high innovation productivity can lead to more new firms starting up in the immediate vicinity and can attract other firms to the area.[49] As firms grow, divisions may be spun off into new firms, entrepreneurial employees may start their own enterprises, and supplier and distributor markets emerge to service the cluster. Successful firms also attract new labor to the area and help to make the existing labor pool more valuable by enabling individuals to gain experience working with the innovative firms. The increase in employment and tax revenues in the region can lead to improvements in infrastructure (such as roads and utilities), schools, and other markets that service the population (shopping malls, grocery stores, health care providers, etc.). The benefits firms reap by locating in close geographical proximity to each other are known collectively as

agglomeration economies
The benefits firms reap by locating in close geographical proximity to each other.

agglomeration economies.

There are also some downsides to geographical clustering. First, the proximity of many competitors serving a local market can lead to competition that reduces their pricing power in their relationships with both buyers and suppliers. Second, close proximity of firms may increase the likelihood of a firm's competitors gaining access to the firm's proprietary knowledge (this is one of the mechanisms of technology spillovers, discussed in the next section). Third, clustering can potentially lead to traffic congestion, inordinately high housing costs, and higher concentrations of pollution.

A big part of the reason that technologies are often regionally localized is that technological knowledge is, to a large extent, held by people, and people are often only reluctantly mobile. In a well-known study, Annalee Saxenian found that engineers in Silicon Valley were more loyal to their craft than to any particular company, but they were also very likely to stay in the region even if they changed jobs.[50] This was due in part to the labor market for their skills in the region, and in part to the disruption in an individual's personal life if he or she were to move out of the region. Thus, if for some reason an innovative activity commences in a geographic locale, the knowledge and expertise that accumulates might not spread readily into other geographic locales, leading to a localized cluster of technological expertise.[51]

Research Brief Knowledge Brokers

Andrew Hargadon and Robert Sutton point out that some firms play a particularly pivotal role in the innovation network—that of knowledge brokers. **Knowledge brokers** are individuals or firms that transfer information from one domain to another in which it can be usefully applied. The knowledge broker puts existing information to use in new and profitable ways. Hargadon and Sutton provide the example of Robert Fulton who, after observing the use of steam engines in mines, realized this technology could be used to propel boats and subsequently developed the first successful steamboat.[a] While Fulton did not claim to have invented the steamboat (there had been at least 30 years of prior development on steamboats), Fulton's design was the first to combine existing technologies into a successful product.

In a network of firms, a knowledge broker may be a firm that connects clusters of firms that would otherwise share no connection. By serving as the bridge between two different knowledge networks, the knowledge broker is in a position to find unique combinations from the knowledge possessed by the two groups. This can enable knowledge brokers to be exceptionally prolific in generating innovation. Consider Thomas Edison's laboratory. Edison's strategy of borrowing from different industries to create products that would ultimately serve many markets resulted in innovations in telegraphs, telephones, phonographs, generators, lightbulbs, vacuum pumps, and many others.[b]

Knowledge brokers may not create breakthroughs in any single technology, but instead may exploit the potential synergies of combining existing technologies. While this might at first seem to limit the scope of a knowledge broker's potential, research suggests that most innovation is not due to the discovery of something fundamentally new, but is instead the result of novel recombinations of known concepts and materials.[c] Thus, the knowledge broker's key expertise may lie not in a particular domain of science, but instead in the ability to recognize and capture potential solutions that may be matched to problems in an unexpected way.

[a] A. Hargadon and R. Sutton, "Building an Innovation Factory," *Harvard Business Review* May–June, 2000, pp. 157–66.

[b] A. B. Hargadon, "Firms as Knowledge Brokers: Lessons in Pursuing Continuous Innovation," *California Management Review* 40, no. 3 (1998), pp. 209–27.

[c] S. C. Gilfillan, *The Sociology of Invention* (Chicago: Follett, 1935); R. R. Nelson and S. Winter, *An Evolutionary Theory of Economic Change* (Cambridge, MA: Harvard University Press, 1982); E. G. Penrose, *The Theory of the Growth of the Firm* (New York: Wiley, 1959); J. A. Schumpeter, *The Theory of Economic Development* (Cambridge, MA: Harvard University Press, 1934); and A. Usher, *A History of Mechanical Inventions* (Cambridge, MA: Harvard University Press, 1954).

knowledge brokers
Individuals or organizations that transfer information from one domain to another in which it can be usefully applied.

Studies have indicated that while many innovative activities appear to have some geographic component, the degree to which innovative activities are geographically clustered depends on things such as:

- The nature of the technology, such as its underlying knowledge base or the degree to which it can be protected by patents or copyright, and the degree to which its communication requires close and frequent interaction.
- Industry characteristics, such as the degree of market concentration or stage of the industry life cycle, transportation costs, and the availability of supplier and distributor markets.

- The cultural context of the technology, such as the population density of labor or customers, infrastructure development, or national differences in the way technology development is funded or protected.

For example, one study that examined the spatial distribution of technology sectors in different countries found that pharmaceutical development was highly clustered in the United Kingdom and France, but much more spatially diffused in Italy and Germany.[52] The same study found, however, that the manufacture of clothing demonstrated high clustering in Italy, but not in France, Germany, or the United Kingdom. While the clustering of pharmaceutical development may have been influenced by the national systems of research funding and the need to share complex technological expertise, the formation of textile clusters may have been due more to cultural factors that influenced the historical rise of industrial districts.

Technological Spillovers

technological spillovers
A positive externality from R&D resulting from the spread of knowledge across organizational or regional boundaries.

While the work on technology clusters has tended to emphasize the "stickiness" of knowledge, a related body of research has focused on explaining the spread of knowledge across organizational or regional boundaries. This topic is known as **technological spillovers**. Technological spillovers occur when the benefits from the research activities of one firm (or nation or other entity) spill over to other firms (or nations or other entities). Spillovers are thus a positive externality of research and development efforts. Evidence suggests that technology spillovers are a significant influence on innovative activity. For example, in a series of studies conducted in the 1980s and 1990s, Adam Jaffe and his coauthors found that both a firm's patenting activities and profits were influenced by the R&D spending of other firms and universities in its geographical region.[53]

Whether R&D benefits will spill over is partially a function of the strength of protection mechanisms such as patents, copyrights, and trade secrets (methods of protecting innovation are discussed in greater detail in Chapter Nine). Since the strength of protection mechanisms varies significantly across industries and countries, the likelihood of spillovers varies also.[54] The likelihood of spillovers is also a function of the nature of the underlying knowledge base (for example, as explained in the previous section, tacit knowledge may not flow readily across firm boundaries) and the mobility of the labor pool.[55]

Summary of Chapter

1. Creativity is the underlying process for innovation. Creativity enables individuals and organizations to generate new and useful ideas. Creativity is considered a function of intellectual abilities, knowledge, thinking styles, personality traits, intrinsic motivation, and environment.

2. Innovation sometimes originates with individual inventors. The most prolific inventors tend to be trained in multiple fields, be highly curious, question previously made assumptions, and view all knowledge as unified. The most well-known inventors tend to have both inventive and entrepreneurial traits.

3. Innovation can also originate with users who create solutions to their own needs. The rise of the snowboarding industry provides a rich example.

4. Firms' research and development is considered a primary driver of innovation. In the United States, firms spend significantly more on R&D than government institutions spend on R&D, and firms consider their in-house R&D their most important source of innovation.

5. Firms often collaborate with a number of external organizations (or individuals) in their innovation activities. Firms are most likely to collaborate with customers, suppliers, and universities, though they also may collaborate with competitors, producers of complements, government laboratories, nonprofit organizations, and other research institutions.

6. Many universities have a research mission, and in recent years universities have become more active in setting up technology transfer activities to directly commercialize the inventions of faculty. Universities also contribute to innovation through the publication of research findings.

7. Government also plays an active role in conducting research and development (in its own laboratories), funding the R&D of other organizations, and creating institutions to foster collaboration networks and to nurture start-ups (e.g., science parks and incubators). In some countries, government-funded research and development exceeds that of industry-funded research.

8. Private nonprofit organizations (such as research institutes and nonprofit hospitals) are another source of innovation. These organizations both perform their own R&D and fund R&D conducted by others.

9. Probably the most significant source of innovation does not come from individual organizations or people, but from the collaborative networks that leverage resources and capabilities across multiple organizations or individuals. Collaborative networks are particularly important in high-technology sectors.

10. Collaboration is often facilitated by geographical proximity, which can lead to regional technology clusters.

11. Technology spillovers are positive externality benefits of R&D, such as when the knowledge acquired through R&D spreads to other organizations.

Discussion Questions

1. What are some of the advantages and disadvantages of (*a*) individuals as innovators, (*b*) firms as innovators, (*c*) universities as innovators, (*d*) government institutions as innovators, (*e*) nonprofit organizations as innovators?

2. What traits appear to make individuals most creative? Are these the same traits that lead to successful inventions?

3. Could firms identify people with greater capacity for creativity or inventiveness in their hiring procedures?

4. To what degree do you think the creativity of the firm is a function of the creativity of individuals, versus the structure, routines, incentives, and culture of the firm? Provide an example of a firm that does a particularly good job at nurturing and leveraging the creativity of its individuals.

5. Several studies indicate that the use of collaborative research agreements is increasing around the world. What are some reasons collaborative research is becoming more prevalent?

Suggested Further Reading

Classics

Amabile, T. M., *Social Psychology of Creativity* (New York: Springer-Verlag, 1983).

Chesbrough, H., *Open Innovation: The New Imperative for Creating and Profiting from Technology* (Boston: Harvard University Press, 2003).

Jaffe, A., "Technological Opportunity and Spillovers of R&D: Evidence from Firms' Patents, Profits, and Market Value," *American Economic Review* 76 (1986), pp. 984–1001.

Usher, A. P., *A History of Mechanical Inventions* (New York/London: McGraw-Hill, 1929).

Von Hippel, E., *Sources of Innovation* (New York: Oxford University Press, 1988).

Weber, A., *Theory of Location of Industries* (Chicago: University of Chicago, 1929).

Recent Work

Kelley, T., *The Art of Innovation: Lessons in Creativity from IDEO, America's Leading Design Firm* (New York: Random House, 2007).

Sawyer, R. K., *Explaining Creativity: The Science of Human Innovation* (Oxford: Oxford University Press, 2011).

Schilling, M. A., and Phelps, C., "Interfirm Collaboration Networks: The impact of Large-scale Network Structure on Firm Innovation," *Management Science* 53 (2007), pp. 1113–1126.

Toole, A.A., "The Impact of Public Basic Research on Industrial Innovation: Evidence from the Pharmaceutical Industry," *Research Policy* 41 (2012), pp. 1–12.

Youtie, J., and Shapira, P., "Building an Innovation Hub: A Case Study of the Transformation of University Roles in Regional Technological Development," *Research Policy* 37 (2008), pp. 1188–1204.

Endnotes

1. R. Rothwell, "Factors for Success in Industrial Innovations, Project SAPPHO—A Comparative Study of Success and Failure in Industrial Innovation," SPRU, University of Sussex, Brighton, U.K., 1972; and L. Smith-Doerr, J. Owen-Smith, K. W. Koput, and W. W. Powell, "Networks and Knowledge Production: Collaboration and Patenting in Biotechnology," in *Corporate Social Capital*, eds. R. Leenders and S. Gabbay (Norwell, MA: Kluwer Academic Publishers, 1999), pp. 331–50.

2. F. Barron, *Creative Person and Creative Process* (New York: Holt, Rinehart, and Winston, 1969); D. W. MacKinnon, "Personality and the Realization of Creative Potential," *American Psychologist* 17 (1965), pp. 484–95; R. Oshse, *Before the Gates of Excellence: The Determinants of Creative Genius* (New York: Cambridge University Press, 1990); and T. I. Lubart, "Creativity," in *Thinking and Problem Solving*, ed. R. J. Sternberg (New York: Academic Press, 1994), pp. 289–332.

3. M. Boden, *The Creative Mind: Myths and Mechanisms* (New York: Basic Books, 1992).

4. Lubart, "Creativity."

5. R. J. Sternberg and T. I. Lubart, "The Concept of Creativity: Prospects and Paradigms," in *Handbook of Creativity*, ed. R. J. Sternberg (Cambridge, England: Cambridge University Press, 1999).

6. P. A. Frensch and R. J. Sternberg, "Expertise and Intelligent Thinking: When Is It Worse to Know Better?" in *Advances in the Psychology of Human Intelligence*, vol. 5, ed. R. J. Sternberg (Hillsdale, NJ: Erlbaum, 1989), pp. 157–58.

7. T. I. Lubart, "Product-Centered Self-Evaluation and the Creative Process," unpublished doctoral dissertation (New Haven, CT: Yale University Press, 1994); and Sternberg and Lubart, "The Concept of Creativity."

8. T. M. Amabile, *The Social Psychology of Creativity* (New York: Springer-Verlag, 1983); and T. M. Amabile, *Creativity in Context* (Boulder, CO: Westview, 1996).

9. R. W. Woodman, J. E. Sawyer, and R. W. Griffin, "Toward a Theory of Organizational Creativity," *Academy of Management Review* 18 (1993), pp. 293–321.

10. C. Gorski and E. Heinekamp, "Capturing Employee Ideas for New Products," in *The PDMA Toolbook for New Product Development*, eds. P. Belliveau, A. Griffin, and S. Somermeyer (New York: John Wiley & Sons, 2002).

11. Gorski and Heinekamp, "Capturing Employee Ideas for New Products;" and R. E. Mcdermott, R. J. Mikulak, and M. R. Beauregard, *Employee Driven Quality: Releasing the Creative Spirit of Your Organization through Suggestion Systems* (White Plains, NY: Quality Resource, 1993).

12. Gorski and Heinekamp, "Capturing Employee Ideas for New Products."

13. Reiss, R. 2015. "Top CEOs share how to shepherd innovation." *Forbes*, July 20th.

14. Woodman, Sawyer, and Griffin, "Toward a Theory of Organizational Creativity;" and Amabile, *The Social Psychology of Creativity*.

15. A. H. Church and J. Waclawski, "The Relationship between Individual Personality Orientation and Executive Leadership Behavior," *Journal of Occupational and Organizational Psychology* 71, no. 2 (1998), pp. 99–125.

16. R. S. Root-Bernstein, "Who Discovers and Who Invents," *Research Technology Management* 32, no. 1 (1989), pp. 43–51.

17. Ibid.

18. Sir Frank Macfarlane Burnet, *Changing Patterns, an Atypical Autobiography* (Melbourne and London: Heinemann, 1968), p. 35.

19. P. Debye, interview in *The Editors of International Science and Technology, The Way of the Scientist. Interviews from the World of Science and Technology* (New York: Simon and Schuster, 1966), p. 80.

20. T. P. Hughes, "How Did the Heroic Inventors Do It?" *American Heritage of Invention and Technology*, Fall 1985, p. 21.

21. B. Z. Khan and K. I. Sokoloff, "Schemes of Practical Utility: Entrepreneurship and Innovation among 'Great Inventors' in the United States, 1790–1865," *Journal of Economic History* 53, no. 2 (1993), p. 289.

22. E. Von Hippel, "Innovation by User Communities: Learning from Open-Source Software," *Sloan Management Review* 42, no. 4 (2001), pp. 82–86.

23. E. Von Hippel, *The Sources of Innovation* (New York: Oxford University Press, 1988); S. K. Shah, "Motivation, Governance, And The Viability of Hybrid Forms In Open Source Software Development," *Management Science* 52 (2006), pp. 1000–14.

24. R. J. Thomas, *New Product Success Stories: Lessons from Leading Innovators* (New York: John Wiley & Sons, 1995).

25. From a presentation given by Bernie Bolger of Loctite to the Masters of Science Technology Group at University College Dublin, November 21, 2003. Thanks to Brian McGrath for providing this example.

26. E. Roberts, "Benchmarking Global Strategic Management of Technology," *Research Technology Management*, March–April 2001, pp. 25–36.

27. M. Dodgson, *The Management of Technological Innovation* (New York: Oxford University Press, 2000).

28. Ibid.

29. C. Freeman, "Networks of Innovators: A Synthesis of Research Issues," *Research Policy* 20 (1991), pp. 499–514; Rothwell, "Factors for Success in Industrial Innovations, Project SAP-PHO;" and R. Rothwell, C. Freeman, A. Horseley, V. T. B. Jervis, A. B. Robertson, and J. Townsend, "SAPPHO Updated—Project SAPPHO Phase II," *Research Policy* 3 (1974), pp. 258–91.

30. Roberts, "Benchmarking Global Strategic Management of Technology."

31. "Supercharging Android: Google to Acquire Motorola Mobility," Google Press Release, August 15, 2011; Efrati, A & Anti, SE. "Google's $12.5 Billion Gamble: Web Giant Pays Big for Motorola's Phone Business, Patents; Risks Alienating Allies." *Wall Street Journal* (2011) August 16 (www.wsj.com)

32. W. M. Cohen and D. A. Levinthal, "Absorptive Capacity: A New Perspective on Learning and Innovation," *Administrative Science Quarterly*, March 1990, pp. 128–52.

33. M. Biese and H. Stahl, "Public Research and Industrial Innovations in Germany," *Research Policy* 28 (1999), pp. 397–422; and E. Mansfield, "Academic Research and Industrial Innovation," *Research Policy* 20 (1991), pp. 1–12.

34. A. Silverman, "Understanding University Patent Policies," *JOM* 55, no. 1 (2003), p. 64.

35. D. Rahm and V. Hansen, "Technology Policy 2000: University to Industry Transfer," *International Journal of Public Administration* 22, no. 8 (1999), pp. 1189–1211.

36. National Science Foundation, Science and Engineering Indicators, 2008.

37. National Science Foundation, Science and Engineering Indicators, 2008.

38. M. Colombo and M. Delmastro, "How Effective Are Technology Incubators? Evidence from Italy," *Research Policy* 31 (2001), pp. 1103–22.

39. Ibid.

40. G. Ahuja and C. M. Lampert, "Entrepreneurship in the Large Corporation: A Longitudinal Study of How Established Firms Create Breakthrough Inventions," *Strategic Management Journal* 22 (2001), pp. 521–43; T. J. Allen, *Managing the Flow of Technology: Technology Transfer and the Dissemination of Technological Information within the R&D Organization* (Cambridge, MA: MIT Press, 1977); R. S. Burt, *Structural Holes* (Cambridge, MA: Harvard University Press, 1992); C. Freeman, "Networks of Innovators: A Synthesis of Research Issues," *Research Policy* 20 (1991), pp. 499–514; S. C. Gilfillan, *The Sociology of Invention* (Chicago: Follett, 1935); and A. B. Hargadon and R. I. Sutton, "Technology Brokering and Innovation in a Product Development Firm," *Administrative Science Quarterly* 42 (1997) pp. 716–49.

41. K. Imai and Y. Baba, 1989, "Systemic Innovation and Cross-Border Networks: Transcending Markets and Hierarchies to Create a New Techno-Economic System," OECD, Conference on Science Technology and Economic Growth, Paris; and C. Freeman, "Networks of Innovators: A Synthesis of Research Issues," *Research Policy* 20 (1991), pp. 499–514.

42. J. Hagedoorn, "Inter-Firm R&D Partnerships—an Overview of Major Trends and Patterns since 1960," *Research Policy* 31 (2002), pp. 477–92.

43. Rosenkopf and Almeida, "Overcoming Local Search through Alliances and Mobility;" and Liebeskind, Oliver, Zucker, and Brewer, "Social Networks, Learning, and Flexibility."

44. This analysis is from M. A. Schilling, "The Global Technology Collaboration Network: Structure, Trends, and Implications," New York University Working Paper. In accordance with norms in network research, each snapshot shows the aggregate of alliances formed in the

previous three years (i.e., the 1995 snapshot aggregates alliances from 1993 to 1995; the 2000 snapshot aggregates alliances from 1998 to 2000). Only large components (those greater than 15 organizations) are shown.

45. M. E. Porter, "Location, Competition, and Economic Development: Local Clusters in a Global Economy," *Economic Development Quarterly* 14, no. 1 (2000), pp. 15–34.

46. P. Almeida and B. Kogut, "Localization of Knowledge and the Mobility of Engineers in Regional Networks," *Management Science* 45 (1999), pp. 905–17; P. Bourdieu, "The Forms of Capital," in *Handbook of Theory and Research for the Sociology of Education*, ed. J. G. Richardson (Westport, CT: Greenwood Press, 1986), pp. 241–58; M. S. Granovetter, "Problems of Explanation in Economic Sociology," in *Networks and Organizations: Structure, Form, and Action*, eds. N. Nohria and R. Eccles (Boston: Harvard Business School Press, 1992), pp. 25–56; and M. T. Hansen, "The Search-Transfer Problem: The Role of Weak Ties in Sharing Knowledge across Organization Subunits," *Administrative Science Quarterly* 44 (1999), pp. 82–112.

47. U. Zander and B. Kogut, "Knowledge and the Speed of the Transfer and Imitation of Organizational Capabilities: An Empirical Test," *Organization Science* 6 (1995), pp. 76–92; and G. Szulanski, "Exploring Internal Stickiness: Impediments to the Transfer of Best Practice within the Firm," *Strategic Management Journal* 17 (winter special issue) (1996), pp. 27–43.

48. J. H. Dyer and K. Nobeoka, "Creating and Managing a High-Performance Knowledge-Sharing Network: The Toyota Case," *Strategic Management Journal* 21 (2000), pp. 345–67; and E. Von Hippel, "Cooperation between Rivals: Informal Know-How Trading," *Research Policy* 16 (1987), pp. 291–302.

49. T. Stuart and O. Sorenson, "The Geography of Opportunity: Spatial Heterogeneity in Founding Rates and the Performance of Biotechnology Firms," *Research Policy* 32 (2003), p. 229.

50. A. Saxenian, *Regional Advantage: Culture and Competition in Silicon Valley and Route* 128 (Cambridge, MA/London: Harvard University Press, 1994).

51. P. Almeida and B. Kogut, "Localization of Knowledge and the Mobility of Engineers in Regional Networks," *Management Science* 45 (1999), pp. 905–17.

52. S. Breschi, "The Geography of Innovation: A Cross-Sector Analysis," *Regional Studies* 34, no. 3 (2000), pp. 213–29.

53. A. B. Jaffe, "Technological Opportunity and Spillovers of R&D: Evidence from Firms' Patents, Profits and Market Value," *American Economic Review* 76 (1986), pp. 984–1001; A. B. Jaffe, "Real Effects of Academic Research," *American Economic Review* 79 (1989), pp. 957–70; and A. B. Jaffee, M. Trajtenberg, and R. Henderson, "Geographic Localization of Knowledge Spillovers as Evidenced by Citations," *Quarterly Journal of Economics* 63 (1993), pp. 577–98.

54. W. Cohen, A. Goto, A. Nagata, R. Nelson, and J. Walsh, "R&D Spillovers, Patents and the Incentives to Innovate in Japan and the United States," *Research Policy* 31 (2002), pp. 1349–67.

55. Almeida and Kogut, "Localization of Knowledge and the Mobility of Engineers in Regional Networks."

Types and Patterns of Innovation

Tesla Motors

In 2015, Tesla Motors was a $3.2 billion company on track to set history. It had created two cars that most people agreed were remarkable. Consumer reports had rated Tesla's Model S the best car it had ever reviewed. Though it was not yet posting profits, sales were growing rapidly and analysts were hopeful that profits would soon follow. It had repaid its government loans ahead of the major auto conglomerates. Most importantly, it looked like it might *survive*. Perhaps even thrive. This was astonishing as there had been no other successful auto manufacturing start-up in the United States since the 1920s.

The road leading up to Tesla's position in 2015 had not always been smooth, and there were many doubts that still lingered. Tesla had benefited from the enthusiasm of the "eco-wealthy"—a rather narrow portion of the market. How would Tesla fare when it was in direct competition with General Motors, Ford, and Nissan for the mass market? Would it be able to turn a sustainable profit on its auto-making operations? Furthermore, some questioned whether Tesla's goals to sell to the mass market even made sense. In the niche market, it had a privileged position with customers that were relatively price-insensitive and were seeking a stylish, high-performance car that made an environmental statement. To compete for the mass market, the car would have to provide good value for the money (involving trade-offs that might conflict with Chairman Elon Musk's ideals), and the obstacles to charging would have to be overcome.

History of Tesla

In the year 2003, an engineer named Martin Eberhard was looking for his next big project. A tall, slim man with a mop of gray hair, Eberhard was a serial entrepreneur who had launched a number of start-ups, including a company called NuvoMedia, which he sold to Gemstar in a $187 million deal. Eberhard was also looking for a sports car that would be environmentally friendly—he had concerns about global warming and U.S. dependence on the Middle East for oil. When he didn't find the car of his dreams on the market he began contemplating building one himself, even though he had zero experience in the auto industry. Eberhard noticed that many of the driveways that had a Toyota Prius hybrid electric vehicle (or "dork mobile" as he called it) also had expensive sports cars in them—making Eberhard speculate that there could be a market for a high-performance environmentally friendly car. As explained by Eberhard, "It was clear that people weren't buying a Prius to save money on gas—gas was selling close to inflation-adjusted all-time lows. They were buying them to make a statement about the environment."[a]

Eberhard began to consider a range of alternative fuel options for his car: hydrogen fuel cells, natural gas, and diesel. However, he soon concluded that the highest efficiency and performance would come from a pure electric vehicle. Luckily for Eberhard, Al Cocconi (founder of AC Propulsion and one of the original engineers for GM's ill-fated EV-1) had concluded the same thing and had produced a car called the tzero. The tzero could go from zero to 60 miles per hour in 4.1 seconds, but it was powered with extremely heavy lead-acid batteries, limiting its range to about 60 miles between charges. Eberhard approached Cocconi with the idea of using the lighter lithium ion batteries, which offered six times more energy per pound. Cocconi was eager to try out the idea (he had, in fact, been experimenting with lithium ion batteries himself), and the resulting lithium ion-based tzero accelerated to 60 miles per hour in 3.6 seconds, and could travel more than 300 miles. Eberhard licensed the electric-drive-train technology from AC Propulsion, and founded his company, Tesla Motors (named after Nikola Tesla, a late nineteenth-century and early twentieth-century inventor who developed, among other things, the AC electrical systems used in the United States today).[b]

Meanwhile, there was another entrepreneur—one with much deeper pockets—also interested in developing electric vehicles based on the tzero: Elon Musk. In 2002, Elon Musk was a 31-year-old South African living in California, who had founded a company that ultimately became PayPal. After selling PayPal to eBay in 2002 for $1.5 billion, he started a company called SpaceX with the ambitious goal of developing cheap, consumer space travel. (SpaceX's Dragon spacecraft ultimately made history in May of 2012 by becoming the first commercial vehicle to launch and dock at the International Space Station.[c]) Musk was also the chairman of a high profile clean tech venture in Northern California called Solar City. Musk's assertive style, and his astonishing record of high-tech entrepreneurship, made him one of the inspirations for the Tony Stark character in Jon Favreau's Iron Man movies.

Like Eberhard, Musk thought electric cars were the key to the United States achieving energy independence, and he approached Cocconi about buying the tzero. Tom Gage, who was then AC Propulsion's CEO, suggested that Musk collaborate with Eberhard. After a two hour meeting in February of 2004, Musk agreed to fund Eberhard's plan with $6.3 million. He would be the company's chairman and Eberhard would serve as CEO.

The Roadster

The first Tesla prototype, named the Roadster, was based on the $45,000 Lotus Elise, a fast and light sports car that seemed perfect for the creation of Eberhard and Musk's grand idea. The car would have 400 volts of electric potential, liquid-cooled lithium ion batteries, and a series of silicon transistors that would give the car acceleration so powerful the driver would be pressed back against their seat.[d] It would be about as fast as a Porsche 911 Turbo, would not create a single emission, and would get about 220 miles on a single charge from the kind of outlet you would use to power a washing machine.[e]

After a series of clashes between Musk and Eberhard that led to delays in launching the Roadster, Eberhard was pushed out of the company. The Roadster missed its deadline for beginning production at the Lotus facility, triggering a penalty built into the manufacturing contract Eberhard had signed with Lotus: a $4 million fee. However, when the car finally launched in 2008, the enthusiastic response it received was astonishing—it boasted an all-star list of celebrities with reservations to buy, and everywhere the Roadster drove, people stopped to stare.[f]

The Model S

Musk's ambitions did not stop at a niche high-end car. He wanted to build a major U.S. auto company—a feat that had not been successfully accomplished since the 1920s. To do so, he knew he needed to introduce a less-expensive car that could attract a higher volume of sales, if not quite the mass market. In June of 2008, Tesla announced the Model S—a high-performance all-electric sedan that would sell for a price ranging from $57,400 to $77,400 and compete against cars like the BMW 5-series. The car would have an all-aluminum body, and a range of up to 300 miles per charge.[g] The Model S cost $500 million to develop,[h] however offsetting that cost was a $465 million loan Tesla received from the U.S. government to build the car, as part of the U.S. government's initiative to promote the development of technologies that would help the United States to achieve energy independence.

By May of 2012, Tesla reported that it already had 10,000 reservations for customers hoping to buy the Model S, and Musk confidently claimed that the company would soon be producing—and selling—20,000 Model S cars a year. Musk also noted that after ramping up production, he expected to see "at least 10,000 units a year from demand in Europe and at least 5,000 in Asia."[i] The production of the Model S went more smoothly than that of the Roadster, and by June of 2012, the first Model S cars were rolling off the factory floor. The very first went to Jeff Skoll, eBay's first president, and a major investor in Tesla. On the day of the launch, Skoll talked with Musk about whether it was harder to build a rocket or a car (referring to Musk's SpaceXcompany): "We decided it was a car. There isn't a lot of competition in space."[j]

To build the car, Tesla bought a recently closed automobile factory in Fremont, California, that had been used for the New United Motor Manufacturing Inc. (NUMMI) venture between Toyota and General Motors. The factory, which was capable of producing 1,000 cars a week, was far bigger than Tesla's immediate needs and would give the company room to grow. Furthermore, though the plant and the land it was on had been appraised at around $1 billion before NUMMI was shut down, Tesla was able to snap up the idled factory for

$42 million.[k] Tesla also used the factory to produce battery packs for Toyota's RAV4, and a charger for a subcompact Daimler AG electric vehicle. These projects would supplement Tesla's income while also helping it to build scale and learning curve efficiencies in its technologies.

In the first quarter of 2013, Tesla announced its first quarterly profit. The company had taken in $562 million in revenues and reported an $11.2 million profit. Then more good news came: The Model S had earned Consumer Reports' highest rating and had outsold similarly priced BMW and Mercedes models in the first quarter.[l] In May of 2013, the company raised $1 billion by issuing new shares and then surprised investors by announcing that it had paid back its government loan. After repaying the loan, Tesla had about $679 million in cash. Musk had announced confidently that he felt it was his obligation to pay back taxpayer money as soon as possible and that the company had sufficient funds now to develop its next generation of automobiles without the loan and without issuing further shares.[m]

The Future of Tesla

By 2015, Tesla Motors was also in the process of developing a sport utility vehicle that seats seven, the Model X, which cost $250 million to develop and would be available in 2016.[n] This car was part of Musk's longer-term ambition to tap a more mainstream market for the cars.

Though Tesla's moves had been bold and risky, its success thus far was inspiring. The company had survived its infancy, appeared to be solvent, and was meeting its sales objectives even though serious obstacles remained for electric vehicles. It was also competing against companies with far greater scale. As noted by O'Dell, a senior editor at auto information site Edmunds.com, on Tesla's success, "A lot of people have been very, very skeptical . . . when you want to be an automaker, you are competing with multibillion-dollar conglomerates . . . It's entrepreneurism on steroids . . . They had a huge learning curve but they've powered through it." Theo O'Neill, an analyst at Wunderlich Securities adds that "It's going to prove everybody in Detroit wrong . . . They all say what Tesla is doing isn't possible."[o]

Discussion Questions

1. Is the Tesla Model S a radical innovation or an incremental innovation? Competence enhancing or destroying, and from whose perspective? Is it a component or an architectural innovation?
2. What factors do you think influence the rate at which consumers have adopted (or will adopt) the Tesla Model S?
3. Where do you think electric vehicle battery technology is on the technology s curve?
4. Do you think Tesla Motors will be profitable? Why or why not?

[a] Copeland, M.V. 2008. Tesla's wild ride. *Fortune*, Vol. 158, issue 2, pg. 82–94.
[b] Copeland, M.V. 2008. Tesla's wild ride. *Fortune*, Vol. 158, issue 2, pg. 82–94.
[c] Boudreau. J. 2012. In a Silicon Valley milestone, Tesla Motors begins delivering Model S electric cars. June 24: Breaking News Section.
[d] Copeland, M.V. 2008. Tesla's wild ride. *Fortune*, Vol. 158, issue 2, pg. 82–94.
[e] Williams, A. 2009. Taking a Tesla for a status check in New York. *New York Times*, July 19th, ST.7.
[f] Williams, A. 2009. Taking a Tesla for a status check in New York. *New York Times*, July 19th, ST.7.
[g] Ramsey, M. 2011. Tesla sets 300-mile range for second electric car. *Wall Street Journal (Online)*, March 7th: n/a
[h] Vance, A. 2015. Elon Musk: Tesla, SpaceX, and the Quest for a Fantastic Future. New York: Harper Collins
[i] Sweet, C. 2013. Tesla posts its first quarterly profit. *Wall Street Journal (Online)*, May 9th: n/a.
[j] Boudreau. J. 2012. In a Silicon Valley milestone, Tesla Motors begins delivering Model S electric cars. *Oakland Tribune*, June 24: Breaking News Section.
[k] Anonymous. 2010. Idle Fremont plant gears up for Tesla. *Wall Street Journal (Online)*, October 20th: n/a
[l] Levi, M. 2013. How Tesla pulled ahead of the electric-car pack. *Wall Street Journal*, June 21:A.11.
[m] White, J.B. 2013. Corporate News: Electric car startup Tesla repays U.S. loan. *Wall Street Journal*, May 23rd:B.3.
[n] Caranddriver.com, accessed May 11, 2015.
[o] Boudreau. J. 2012. In a Silicon Valley milestone, Tesla Motors begins delivering Model S electric cars. *Oakland Tribune*, June 24: Breaking News Section.

OVERVIEW

The previous chapters pointed out that technological innovation can come from many sources and take many forms. Different types of technological innovations offer different opportunities for organizations and society, and they pose different demands upon producers, users, and regulators. While there is no single agreed-upon taxonomy to describe different kinds of technological innovations, in this chapter we will review several dimensions that are often used to categorize technologies. These dimensions are useful for understanding some key ways that one innovation may differ from another.

technology trajectory
The path a technology takes through its lifetime. This path may refer to its rate of performance improvement, its rate of diffusion, or other change of interest.

The path a technology follows through time is termed its **technology trajectory.** Technology trajectories are most often used to represent the technology's rate of performance improvement or its rate of adoption in the marketplace. Though many factors can influence these technology trajectories (as discussed in both this chapter and the following chapters), some patterns have been consistently identified in technology trajectories across many industry contexts and over many periods. Understanding these patterns of technological innovation provides a useful foundation that we will build upon in the later chapters on formulating technology strategy.

The chapter begins by reviewing the dimensions used to distinguish types of innovations. It then describes the s-curve patterns so often observed in both the rate of technology improvement and the rate of technology diffusion to the market. In the last section, the chapter describes research suggesting that technological innovation follows a cyclical pattern composed of distinct and reliably occurring phases.

TYPES OF INNOVATION

Technological innovations are often described using dimensions such as "radical" versus "incremental." Different types of innovation require different kinds of underlying knowledge and have different impacts on the industry's competitors and customers. Four of the dimensions most commonly used to categorize innovations are described here: product versus process innovation, radical versus incremental, competence enhancing versus competence destroying, and architectural versus component.

Product Innovation versus Process Innovation

Product innovations are embodied in the outputs of an organization—its goods or services. For example, Honda's development of a new hybrid electric vehicle is a product innovation. Process innovations are innovations in the way an organization conducts its business, such as in the techniques of producing or marketing goods or services. Process innovations are often oriented toward improving the effectiveness or efficiency of production by, for example, reducing defect rates or increasing the quantity that may be produced in a given time. For example, a process innovation at a biotechnology firm might entail developing a genetic algorithm that can quickly search a set of disease-related genes to identify a target for therapeutic intervention. In this instance, the process innovation (the genetic algorithm) can speed up the firm's ability to develop a product innovation (a new therapeutic drug).

New product innovations and process innovations often occur in tandem. First, new processes may enable the production of new products. For example, as discussed later in the chapter, the development of new metallurgical techniques enabled the development of the bicycle chain, which in turn enabled the development of multiple-gear bicycles. Second, new products may enable the development of new processes. For example, the development of advanced workstations has enabled firms to implement computer-aided manufacturing processes that increase the speed and efficiency of production. Finally, a product innovation for one firm may simultaneously be a process innovation for another. For example, when United Parcel Service (UPS) helps a customer develop a more efficient distribution system, the new distribution system is simultaneously a product innovation for UPS and a process innovation for its customer.

Though product innovations are often more visible than process innovations, both are extremely important to an organization's ability to compete. Throughout the remainder of the book, the term *innovation* will be used to refer to both product and process innovations.

radical innovation
An innovation that is very new and different from prior solutions.

incremental innovation
An innovation that makes a relatively minor change from (or adjustment to) existing practices.

Radical Innovation versus Incremental Innovation

One of the primary dimensions used to distinguish types of innovation is the continuum between radical versus incremental innovation. A number of definitions have been posed for **radical innovation** and **incremental innovation**, but most hinge on the degree to which an innovation represents a departure from existing practices.[1] Thus radicalness might be conceived as the combination of *newness* and the degree of *differentness*. A technology could be new to the world, new to an industry, new to a firm, or new merely to an adopting business unit. A technology could be significantly different from existing products and processes or only marginally different. The most radical innovations would be new to the world and exceptionally different from existing products and processes.

The introduction of wireless telecommunication products aptly illustrates this—it embodied significantly new technologies that required new manufacturing and service processes. Incremental innovation is at the other end of the spectrum. An incremental innovation might not be particularly new or exceptional; it might have been previously known to the firm or industry, and involve only a minor change from (or adjustment to) existing practices. For example, changing the configuration of a cell phone from one that has an exposed keyboard to one that has a flip cover or offering a new service plan that enables more free weekend minutes would represent incremental innovation.

The radicalness of innovation is also sometimes defined in terms of risk. Since radical innovations often embody new knowledge, producers and customers will vary in their experience and familiarity with the innovation, and in their judgment of its usefulness or reliability.[2] The development of third generation (3G) telephony is illustrative. 3G wireless communication technology utilizes broadband channels. This increased bandwidth gives mobile phones far greater data transmission capabilities that enable activities such as videoconferencing and accessing the most advanced Internet sites. For companies to develop and offer 3G wireless telecommunications service required a significant investment in new networking equipment and an infrastructure capable of carrying a much larger bandwidth of signals. It also required developing phones with greater display and memory capabilities, and either increasing the phone's battery power or increasing the efficiency of the phone's power utilization. Any of these technologies could potentially pose serious obstacles. It was also unknown to what degree customers would ultimately value broadband capability in a wireless device. Thus, the move to 3G required managers to assess several different risks simultaneously, including technical feasibility, reliability, costs, and demand.

Finally, the radicalness of an innovation is relative, and may change over time or with respect to different observers. An innovation that was once considered radical may eventually be considered incremental as the knowledge base underlying the innovation becomes more common. For example, while the first steam engine was a monumental innovation, today its construction seems relatively simple. Furthermore, an innovation that is radical to one firm may seem incremental to another. Although both Kodak and Sony introduced digital cameras for the consumer market within a year of each other (Kodak's DC40 was introduced in 1995, and Sony's Cyber-Shot Digital Still Camera was introduced in 1996), the two companies' paths to the introduction were quite different. Kodak's historical competencies and reputation were based on its expertise in chemical photography, and thus the transition to digital photography and video required a significant redirection for the firm. Sony, on the other hand, had been an electronics company since its inception, and had a substantial level of expertise in digital recording and graphics before producing a digital camera. Thus, for Sony, a digital camera was a straightforward extension of its existing competencies.

Competence-Enhancing Innovation versus Competence-Destroying Innovation

Innovations can also be classified as **competence enhancing** versus **competence destroying**. An innovation is considered to be competence enhancing from the perspective of a particular firm if it builds on the firm's existing knowledge base. For example, each generation of Intel's microprocessors (e.g., 286, 386, 486, Pentium, Pentium II, Pentium III, Pentium 4) builds on the technology underlying the previous

competence-enhancing (-destroying) innovation An innovation that builds on (renders obsolete) existing knowledge and skills. Whether an innovation is competence enhancing or competence destroying depends on whose perspective is being taken. An innovation can be competence enhancing to one firm, while competence destroying for another.

generation. Thus, while each generation embodies innovation, these innovations leverage Intel's existing competencies, making them more valuable.

An innovation is considered to be competence destroying from the perspective of a particular firm if the technology does not build on the firm's existing competencies or renders them obsolete. For example, from the 1600s to the early 1970s, no self-respecting mathematician or engineer would have been caught without a slide rule. Slide rules are lightweight devices, often constructed of wood, that use logarithm scales to solve complex mathematical functions. They were used to calculate everything from the structural properties of a bridge to the range and fuel use of an aircraft. Specially designed slide rules for businesses had, for example, scales for doing loan calculations or determining optimal purchase quantities. During the 1950s and 1960s, Keuffel & Esser was the preeminent slide-rule maker in the United States, producing 5,000 slide rules a month. However, in the early 1970s, a new innovation relegated the slide rule to collectors and museum displays within just a few years: the inexpensive handheld calculator. Keuffel & Esser had no background in the electronic components that made electronic calculators possible and was unable to transition to the new technology. By 1976, Keuffel & Esser withdrew from the market.[3] Whereas the inexpensive handheld calculator built on the existing competencies of companies such as Hewlett-Packard and Texas Instruments (and thus for them would be competence enhancing), for Keuffel & Esser, the calculator was a competence-destroying innovation.

Architectural Innovation versus Component Innovation

Most products and processes are hierarchically nested systems, meaning that at any unit of analysis, the entity is a system of components, and each of those components is, in turn, a system of finer components, until we reach some point at which the components are elementary particles.[4] For example, a bicycle is a system of components such as a frame, wheels, tires, seat, brakes, and so on. Each of those components is also a system of components: The seat might be a system of components that includes a metal and plastic frame, padding, a nylon cover, and so on.

component (or modular) innovation
An innovation to one or more components that does not significantly affect the overall configuration of the system.

An innovation may entail a change to individual components, to the overall architecture within which those components operate, or both. An innovation is considered a **component innovation** (or **modular innovation**) if it entails changes to one or more components, but does not significantly affect the overall configuration of the system.[5] In the example above, an innovation in bicycle seat technology (such as the incorporation of gel-filled material for additional cushioning) does not require any changes in the rest of the bicycle architecture.

architectural innovation
An innovation that changes the overall design of a system or the way its components interact with each other.

In contrast, an **architectural innovation** entails changing the overall design of the system or the way that components interact with each other. An innovation that is strictly architectural may reconfigure the way that components link together in the system, without changing the components themselves.[6] Most architectural innovations, however, create changes in the system that reverberate throughout its design, requiring changes in the underlying components in addition to changes in the ways those components interact. Architectural innovations often have far-reaching and complex influences on industry competitors and technology users.

For example, the transition from the high-wheel bicycle to the safety bicycle was an architectural innovation that required (and enabled) the change of many components of the bicycle and the way in which riders propelled themselves. In the 1800s, bicycles had extremely large front wheels. Because there were no gears, the size of the front wheel directly determined the speed of the bicycle since the circumference of the wheel was the distance that could be traveled in a single rotation of the pedals. However, by the start of the twentieth century, improvements in metallurgy had enabled the production of a fine chain and a sprocket that was small enough and light enough for a human to power. This enabled bicycles to be built with two equally sized wheels, while using gears to accomplish the speeds that the large front wheel had enabled. Because smaller wheels meant shorter shock-absorbing spokes, the move to smaller wheels also prompted the development of suspension systems and pneumatic (air-filled) tires. The new bicycles were lighter, cheaper, and more flexible. This architectural innovation led to the rise of companies such as Dunlop (which invented the pneumatic tire) and Raleigh (which pioneered the three-speed, all-steel bicycle), and transformed the bicycle from a curiosity into a practical transportation device.

For a firm to initiate or adopt a component innovation may require that the firm have knowledge only about that component. However, for a firm to initiate or adopt an architectural innovation typically requires that the firm have architectural knowledge about the way components link and integrate to form the whole system. Firms must be able to understand how the attributes of components interact, and how changes in some system features might trigger the need for changes in many other design features of the overall system or the individual components.

Using the Dimensions

Though the dimensions described above are useful for exploring key ways that one innovation may differ from another, these dimensions are not independent, nor do they offer a straightforward system for categorizing innovations in a precise and consistent manner. Each of the above dimensions shares relationships with others—for example, architectural innovations are often considered more radical and more competence destroying than component innovations. Furthermore, how an innovation is described on a dimension often depends on who is doing the describing and with what it is being compared. An all-electric vehicle, for example, might seem like a radical and competence destroying innovation to a manufacturer of internal combustion engines, but to a customer who only has to change how they fuel/charge the vehicle, it might seem like an incremental and competence-enhancing innovation. Thus, while the dimensions above are valuable for understanding innovation, they should be considered relative dimensions whose meaning is dependent on the context in which they are used.

We now will turn to exploring patterns in technological innovation. Numerous studies of innovation have revealed recurring patterns in how new technologies emerge, evolve, are adopted, and are displaced by other technologies. We begin by examining technology s-curves.

TECHNOLOGY S-CURVES

Both the rate of a technology's performance improvement and the rate at which the technology is adopted in the marketplace repeatedly have been shown to conform to an s-shape curve. Though s-curves in technology performance and s-curves in technology diffusion are related (improvements in performance may foster faster adoption, and greater adoption may motivate further investment in improving performance), they are fundamentally different processes. S-curves in technology improvement are described first, followed by s-curves in technology diffusion. This section also explains that despite the allure of using s-curves to predict when new phases of a technology's life cycle will begin, doing so can be misleading.

S-Curves in Technological Improvement

Many technologies exhibit an s-curve in their performance improvement over their lifetimes.[7] When a technology's performance is plotted against the amount of effort and money invested in the technology, it typically shows slow initial improvement, then accelerated improvement, then diminishing improvement (see Figure 3.1). Performance improvement in the early stages of a technology is slow because the fundamentals of the technology are poorly understood. Great effort may be spent exploring different paths of improvement or different drivers of the technology's improvement. If the technology is very different from previous technologies, there may be no evaluation routines that enable researchers to assess its progress or its potential. Furthermore, until the technology has established a degree of legitimacy, it may be difficult to attract other researchers to participate in its development.[8] However, as scientists or firms gain a deeper understanding of the technology, improvement begins to accelerate. The technology begins to gain legitimacy as a worthwhile endeavor, attracting other developers. Furthermore, measures for assessing the technology are developed, permitting researchers to target their attention toward those activities that reap the greatest improvement per unit of effort, enabling performance to increase rapidly. However, at some point, diminishing returns to effort begin to set in. As the technology begins to reach its inherent limits, the cost of each marginal improvement increases, and the s-curve flattens.

Often a technology's s-curve is plotted with performance (e.g., speed, capacity, or power) against time, but this must be approached with care. If the effort invested is not constant over time, the resulting s-curve can obscure the true relationship. If effort is

FIGURE 3.1
S-Curve of
Technology
Performance

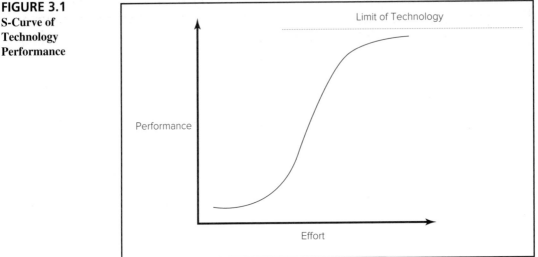

relatively constant over time, plotting performance against time will result in the same characteristic curve as plotting performance against effort. However, if the amount of effort invested in a technology decreases or increases over time, the resulting curve could appear to flatten much more quickly, or not flatten at all. For instance, one of the more well-known technology trajectories is described by an axiom that became known as Moore's law. In 1965, Gordon Moore, cofounder of Intel, noted that the density of transistors on integrated circuits had doubled every year since the integrated circuit was invented. That rate has since slowed to doubling every 18 months, but the rate of acceleration is still very steep. Figure 3.2 reveals a sharply increasing performance curve.

However, Intel's rate of investment (research and development dollars per year) has also been increasing rapidly, as shown in Figure 3.3. Not all of Intel's R&D expense goes directly to improving microprocessor power, but it is reasonable to assume that Intel's investment specifically in microprocessors would exhibit a similar pattern of increase. Figure 3.3 shows that the big gains in transistor density have come at a big cost in terms of effort invested. Though the curve does not yet resemble the traditional s-curve, its rate of increase is not as sharp as when the curve is plotted against years. Gordon Moore predicted that transistor miniaturization will reach its physical limits about 2017.

discontinuous technology

A technology that fulfills a similar market need by building on an entirely new knowledge base.

Technologies do not always get the opportunity to reach their limits; they may be rendered obsolete by new, **discontinuous technologies**. A new innovation is discontinuous when it fulfills a similar market need, but does so by building on an entirely new knowledge base.[9] For example, the switches from propeller-based planes to jets, from silver halide (chemical) photography to digital photography, from carbon copying to photocopying, and from vinyl records (or analog cassettes) to compact discs were all technological discontinuities.

FIGURE 3.2

Improvements in Intel's Microprocessor Transistor Density over Time

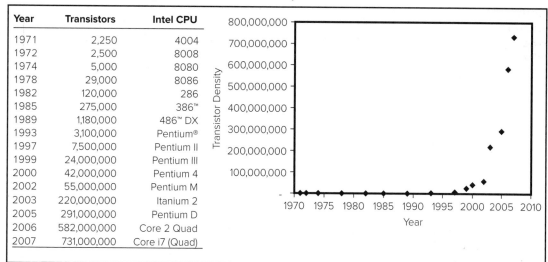

Year	Transistors	Intel CPU
1971	2,250	4004
1972	2,500	8008
1974	5,000	8080
1978	29,000	8086
1982	120,000	286
1985	275,000	386™
1989	1,180,000	486™ DX
1993	3,100,000	Pentium®
1997	7,500,000	Pentium II
1999	24,000,000	Pentium III
2000	42,000,000	Pentium 4
2002	55,000,000	Pentium M
2003	220,000,000	Itanium 2
2005	291,000,000	Pentium D
2006	582,000,000	Core 2 Quad
2007	731,000,000	Core i7 (Quad)

FIGURE 3.3
Graph of
Transistor
Density versus
Cumulative
R&D Expense,
1972–2007

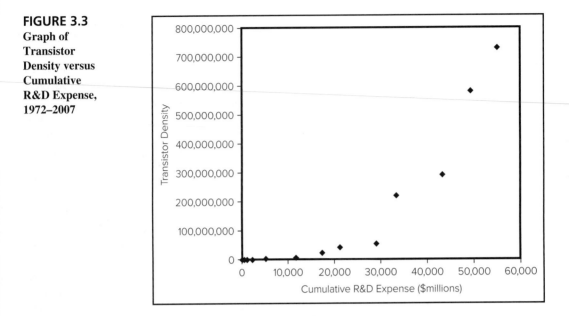

Initially, the technological discontinuity may have lower performance than the incumbent technology. For instance, one of the earliest automobiles, introduced in 1771 by Nicolas Joseph Cugnot, was never put into commercial production because it was much slower and harder to operate than a horse-drawn carriage. It was three-wheeled, steam-powered, and could travel at 2.3 miles per hour. A number of steam- and gas-powered vehicles were introduced in the 1800s, but it was not until the early 1900s that automobiles began to be produced in quantity.

In early stages, effort invested in a new technology may reap lower returns than effort invested in the current technology, and firms are often reluctant to switch. However, if the disruptive technology has a steeper s-curve (see Figure 3.4a) or an s-curve that increases to a higher performance limit (see Figure 3.4b), there may come a time when the returns to effort invested in the new technology are much higher than effort invested in the incumbent technology. New firms entering the industry are likely to choose the disruptive technology, and incumbent firms face the difficult choice of trying to extend the life of their current technology or investing in switching to the new technology. If the disruptive technology has much greater performance potential for a given amount of effort, in the long run it is likely to displace the incumbent technology, but the rate at which it does so can vary significantly.

S-Curves in Technology Diffusion

technology
diffusion
The spread of
a technology
through a
population.

S-curves are also often used to describe the diffusion of a technology. Unlike s-curves in technology performance, s-curves in **technology diffusion** are obtained by plotting the cumulative number of adopters of the technology against time. This yields an s-shape curve because adoption is initially slow when an unfamiliar technology is introduced to the market; it accelerates as the technology becomes better understood and utilized by the mass market, and eventually the market is saturated so the rate of new adoptions declines. For instance, when electronic calculators were introduced to

FIGURE 3.4
Technology
S-Curves—
Introduction of
Discontinuous
Technology

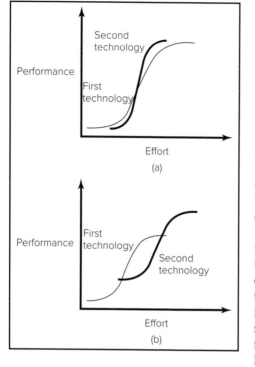

the market, they were first adopted by the relatively small pool of scientists and engineers. This group had previously used slide rules. Then the calculator began to penetrate the larger markets of accountants and commercial users, followed by the still larger market that included students and the general public. After these markets had become saturated, fewer opportunities remained for new adoptions.[10] One rather curious feature of technology diffusion is that it typically takes far more time than information diffusion.[11] For example, Mansfield found that it took 12 years for half the population of potential users to adopt industrial robots, even though these potential users were aware of the significant efficiency advantages the robots offered.[12] If a new technology is a significant improvement over existing solutions, why do some firms shift to it more slowly than others? The answer may lie in the complexity of the knowledge underlying new technologies, and in the development of complementary resources that make those technologies useful. Although some of the knowledge necessary to utilize a new technology might be transmitted through manuals or other documentation, other aspects of knowledge necessary to fully realize the potential of a technology might be built up only through experience. Some of the knowledge about the technology might be *tacit* and require transmission from person to person through extensive contact. Many potential adopters of a new technology will not adopt it until such knowledge is available to them, despite their awareness of the technology and its potential advantages.[13]

Furthermore, many technologies become valuable to a wide range of potential users only after a set of complementary resources are developed for them. For example, while the first electric light was invented in 1809 by Humphry Davy, an English chemist, it did not become practical until the development of bulbs within which the arc of light would be encased (first demonstrated by James Bowman Lindsay in 1835) and vacuum pumps to create a vacuum inside the bulb (the mercury vacuum pump was invented by Herman Sprengel in 1875). These early lightbulbs burned for only a few hours. Thomas Alva Edison built on the work of these earlier inventors when, in 1880, he invented filaments that would enable the light to burn for 1,200 hours. The role of complementary resources and other factors influencing the diffusion of technological innovations are discussed further in Chapters 4, 5, and 13.

Finally, it should be clear that the s-curves of diffusion are in part a function of the s-curves in technology improvement: As technologies are better developed, they become more certain and useful to users, facilitating their adoption. Furthermore, as learning-curve and scale advantages accrue to the technology, the price of finished goods often

FIGURE 3.5

**Average
Sales Prices
of Consumer
Electronics**

Source: Consumer
Electronics
Association.

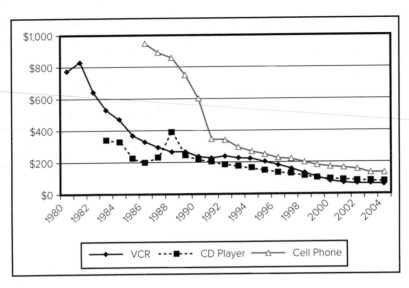

FIGURE 3.6

**Penetration
of Consumer
Electronics**

Source: Consumer
Electronics
Association.

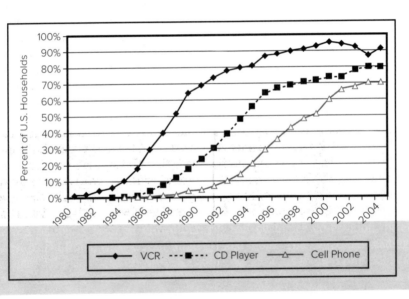

drops, further accelerating adoption by users. For example, as shown in Figures 3.5 and 3.6, drops in average sales prices for video recorders, compact disc players, and cell phones roughly correspond to their increases in household penetration.

S-Curves as a Prescriptive Tool

Several authors have argued that managers can use the s-curve model as a tool for predicting when a technology will reach its limits and as a prescriptive guide for whether and when the firm should move to a new, more radical technology.[14] Firms can use data on the investment and performance of their own technologies, or data on the overall industry investment in a technology and the average performance achieved by multiple producers. Managers could then use these curves to assess whether a technology appears to be approaching its limits or to identify new technologies that might be emerging on s-curves that will intersect the firm's technology s-curve. Managers could then switch s-curves by acquiring or developing the new technology. However, as a prescriptive tool, the s-curve model has several serious limitations.

Limitations of S-Curve Model as a Prescriptive Tool

First, it is rare that the true limits of a technology are known in advance, and there is often considerable disagreement among firms about what a technology's limits will be. Second, the shape of a technology's s-curve is not set in stone. Unexpected changes in the market, component technologies, or complementary technologies can shorten or extend the life cycle of a technology. Furthermore, firms can influence the shape of the s-curve through their development activities. For example, firms can sometimes stretch the s-curve through implementing new development approaches or revamping the architecture design of the technology.[15]

Christensen provides an example of this from the disk-drive industry. A disk drive's capacity is determined by its size multiplied by its areal recording density; thus, density has become the most pervasive measure of disk-drive performance. In 1979, IBM had reached what it perceived as a density limit of ferrite-oxide–based disk drives. It abandoned its ferrite-oxide–based disk drives and moved to developing thin-film technology, which had greater potential for increasing density. Hitachi and Fujitsu continued to ride the ferrite-oxide s-curve, ultimately achieving densities that were eight times greater than the density that IBM had perceived to be a limit.

Finally, whether switching to a new technology will benefit a firm depends on a number of factors, including (*a*) the advantages offered by the new technology, (*b*) the new technology's fit with the firm's current abilities (and thus the amount of effort that would be required to switch, and the time it would take to develop new competencies), (*c*) the new technology's fit with the firm's position in complementary resources (e.g., a firm may lack key complementary resources, or may earn a significant portion of its revenues from selling products compatible with the incumbent technology), and (*d*) the expected rate of diffusion of the new technology. Thus, a firm that follows an s-curve model too closely could end up switching technologies earlier or later than it should.

TECHNOLOGY CYCLES

The s-curve model above suggests that technological change is cyclical: Each new s-curve ushers in an initial period of turbulence, followed by rapid improvement, then diminishing returns, and ultimately is displaced by a new technological discontinuity.[16] The emergence of a new technological discontinuity can overturn the existing competitive structure of an industry, creating new leaders and new losers. Schumpeter called this process *creative destruction*, and argued that it was the key driver of progress in a capitalist society.[17]

Several studies have tried to identify and characterize the stages of the technology cycle in order to better understand why some technologies succeed and others fail, and whether established firms or new firms are more likely to be successful in introducing or adopting a new technology.[18] One technology evolution model that rose to

Research Brief   The Diffusion of Innovation and Adopter Categories

S-curves in technology diffusion are often explained as a process of different categories of people adopting the technology at different times. One typology of adopter categories that gained prominence was proposed by Everett M. Rogers.[a] Figure 3.7 shows each of Rogers's adopter categories on a technology diffusion s-curve. The figure also shows that if the non-cumulative share of each of these adopter groups is plotted on the vertical axis with time on the horizontal axis, the resulting curve is typically bell shaped (though in practice it may be skewed right or left).

INNOVATORS

Innovators are the first individuals to adopt an innovation. Extremely adventurous in their purchasing behavior, they are comfortable with a high degree of complexity and uncertainty. Innovators typically have access to substantial financial resources (and thus can afford the losses incurred in unsuccessful adoption decisions). Though they are not always well integrated into a particular social system, innovators play an extremely important role in the diffusion of an innovation because they are the individuals who bring new ideas into the social system. Rogers estimated that the first 2.5 percent of individuals to adopt a new technology are in this category.

EARLY ADOPTERS

The second category of adopters is the early adopters. Early adopters are well integrated into their social system and have the greatest potential for opinion leadership. Early adopters are respected by their peers and know that to retain that respect they must make sound innovation adoption decisions. Other potential adopters look to early adopters for information and advice; thus

early adopters make excellent missionaries for new products or processes. Rogers estimated that the next 13.5 percent of individuals to adopt an innovation (after innovators) are in this category.

EARLY MAJORITY

Rogers identifies the next 34 percent of individuals in a social system to adopt a new innovation as the early majority. The early majority adopts innovations slightly before the average member of a social system. They are typically not opinion leaders, but they interact frequently with their peers.

LATE MAJORITY

The next 34 percent of the individuals in a social system to adopt an innovation are the late majority, according to Rogers. Like the early majority, the late majority constitutes one-third of the individuals in a social system. Those in the late majority approach innovation with a skeptical air and may not adopt the innovation until they feel pressure from their peers. The late majority may have scarce resources, thus making them reluctant to invest in adoption until most of the uncertainty about the innovation has been resolved.

LAGGARDS

The last 16 percent of the individuals in a social system to adopt an innovation are termed *laggards*. They may base their decisions primarily upon past experience rather than influence from the social network, and they possess almost no opinion leadership. They are highly skeptical of innovations and innovators, and they must feel certain that a new innovation will not fail before adopting it.

[a] E. M. Rogers, *Diffusion of Innovations*, 3rd ed. (New York: Free Press, 1983).

continued

concluded
FIGURE 3.7
Technology Diffusion S-Curve with Adopter Categories

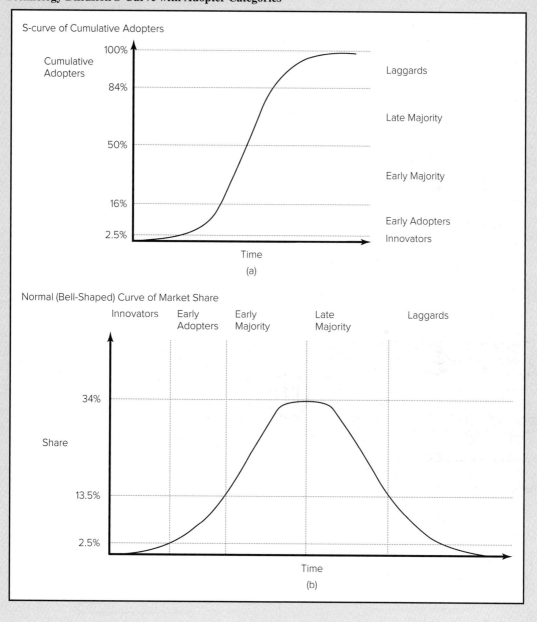

From 1980 to 2012, Microsoft was entrenched as the dominant personal computer operating system, giving it enormous influence over many aspects of the computer hardware and software industries. Though competing operating systems had been introduced during that time (e.g., Unix, Geoworks, NeXTSTEP, Linux, and the Mac OS), Microsoft's share of the personal computer operating system market held stable at roughly 85 percent throughout most of that period. In 2013, however, Microsoft's dominance in computer operating systems was under greater threat than it had ever been. A high-stakes race for dominance over the next generation of computing was well underway, and Microsoft was not even in the front pack.

"SEGMENT ZERO"

As Andy Grove, former CEO of Intel, noted in 1998, in many industries—including microprocessors, software, motorcycles, and electric vehicles—technologies improve faster than customer demands of those technologies increase. Firms often add features (speed, power, etc.) to products faster than customers' capacity to absorb them. Why would firms provide higher performance than that required by the bulk of their customers? The answer appears to lie in the market segmentation and pricing objectives of a technology's providers. As competition in an industry drives prices and margins lower, firms often try to shift sales into progressively higher tiers of the market. In these tiers, high performance and

feature-rich products can command higher margins. Though customers may also expect to have better-performing products over time, their ability to fully utilize such performance improvements is slowed by the need to learn how to use new features and adapt their work and lifestyles. Thus, while both the trajectory of technology improvement and the trajectory of customer demands are upward sloping, the trajectory for technology improvement is steeper (for simplicity, the technology trajectories are drawn in Figure 3.8 as straight lines and plotted against time in order to compare them against customer requirements).

In Figure 3.8, the technology trajectory begins at a point where it provides performance close to that demanded by the mass market, but over time it increases faster than the expectations of the mass market as the firm targets the high-end market. As the price of the technology rises, the mass market may feel it is overpaying for technological features it does not value. In Figure 3.9, the low-end market is not being served; it either pays far more for technology that it does not need, or it goes without. It is this market that Andy Grove, former CEO of Intel, refers to as segment zero.

For Intel, segment zero was the market for low-end personal computers (those less than $1,000). While segment zero may seem unattractive in terms of margins, if it is neglected, it can become the breeding ground for companies that provide lower-end versions of the technology. As Grove notes,

FIGURE 3.8
Trajectories of Technology Improvement and Customer Requirements

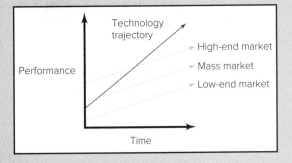

FIGURE 3.9
Low-End Technology's Trajectory Intersects Mass Market Trajectory

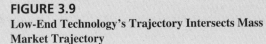
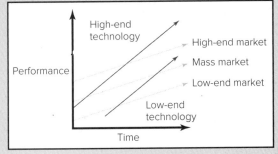

continued

"The overlooked, underserved, and seemingly unprofitable end of the market can provide fertile ground for massive competitive change."[a]

As the firms serving low-end markets with simpler technologies ride up their own trajectories (which are also steeper than the slope of the trajectories of customer expectations), they can eventually reach a performance level that meets the demands of the mass market, while offering a much lower price than the premium technology (see Figure 3.9). At this point, the firms offering the premium technology may suddenly find they are losing the bulk of their sales revenue to industry contenders that do not look so low end anymore. For example, by 1998, the combination of rising microprocessor power and decreasing prices enabled personal computers priced under $1,000 to capture 20 percent of the market.

THE THREAT TO MICROSOFT

So where was the "segment zero" that could threaten Microsoft? Look in your pocket. In 2015, Apple's iPhone operating system (iOS) and Google's Android collectively controlled over 90 percent of the worldwide market for smartphone, followed by Research in Motion's Blackberry.[b] Gartner estimates put Microsoft's share at 3 percent. The iOS and Android interfaces offered a double whammy of beautiful aesthetics and remarkable ease of use. The applications business model used for the phones was also extremely attractive to both developers and customers, and quickly resulted in enormous libraries of applications that ranged from the ridiculous to the indispensible.

From a traditional economics perspective, the phone operating system market should not be that attractive to Microsoft—people do not spend as much on the applications, and the carriers have too much bargaining power, among other reasons. However, those smartphone operating systems soon became tablet operating systems, and tablets were rapidly becoming fully functional computers. Suddenly, all of that mindshare that Apple and Google had achieved in smartphone operating systems was transforming into mindshare in personal computer operating systems. Despite years of masterminding the computing industry, Microsoft's dominant position was at risk of evaporating. The outcome was still uncertain–in 2015 Microsoft had an impressive arsenal of capital, talent, and relationships in its armory—but for the first time, it was fighting the battle from a disadvantaged position.

[a] A. S. Grove, "Managing Segment Zero," *Leader to Leader*, 1999, p. 11.
[b] Dignan, L. 2013. Android, Apple iOS flip consumer, corporate market share. Between the Lines, February 13th.

---

prominence was proposed by Utterback and Abernathy. They observed that a technology passed through distinct phases. In the first phase (what they termed the *fluid phase*), there was considerable uncertainty about both the technology and its market. Products or services based on the technology might be crude, unreliable, or expensive, but might suit the needs of some market niches. In this phase, firms experiment with different form factors or product features to assess the market response. Eventually, however, producers and customers begin to arrive at some consensus about the desired product attributes, and a **dominant design** emerges.[19] The dominant design establishes a stable architecture for the technology and enables firms to focus their efforts on process innovations that make production of the design more effective and efficient or on incremental innovations to improve components within the architecture. Utterback and Abernathy termed this phase the *specific phase* because innovations in products, materials, and manufacturing processes are all specific to the dominant design. For example, in the United States the vast majority of energy production is based on the use of fossil fuels (e.g., oil, coal), and the methods of producing energy based on these fuels are well established. On the other hand, technologies that produce energy based on renewable resources (e.g., solar, wind, hydrogen) are still in the fluid

dominant design

A product design that is adopted by the majority of producers, typically creating a stable architecture on which the industry can focus its efforts.

FIGURE 3.10
The
Technology
Cycle

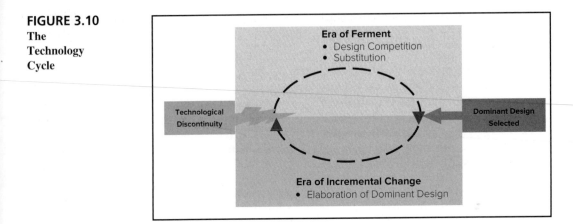

phase. Organizations such as Royal Dutch/Shell, General Electric, and Ballard Power are experimenting with various forms of solar photocell technologies, wind-turbine technologies, and hydrogen fuel cells in efforts to find methods of using renewable resources that meet the capacity and cost requirements of serving large populations.

Building on the Utterback and Abernathy model, Anderson and Tushman studied the history of the U.S. minicomputer, cement, and glass industries through several cycles of technological change. Like Utterback and Abernathy, Anderson and Tushman found that each technological discontinuity inaugurated a period of turbulence and uncertainty (which they termed the *era of ferment*) (see Figure 3.10). The new technology might offer breakthrough capabilities, but there is little agreement about what the major subsystems of the technology should be or how they should be configured together. Furthermore, as later researchers noted, during the era of ferment different stakeholders might have different concepts of what purpose the technology should serve, or how a business model might be built around it.[20] Thus, while the new technology displaces the old (Anderson and Tushman refer to this as *substitution*), there is considerable design competition as firms experiment with different forms of the technology. Just as in the Utterback and Abernathy model, Anderson and Tushman found that a dominant design always arose to command the majority of the market share unless the next discontinuity arrived too soon and disrupted the cycle, or several producers patented their own proprietary technologies and refused to license to each other. Anderson and Tushman also found that the dominant design was never in the same form as the original discontinuity, but it was also never on the leading edge of the technology. Instead of maximizing performance on any individual dimension of the technology, the dominant design tended to bundle together a combination of features that best fulfilled the demands of the majority of the market.

In the words of Anderson and Tushman, the rise of a dominant design signals the transition from the era of ferment to the *era of incremental change*.[21] In this era, firms focus on efficiency and market penetration. Firms may attempt to achieve greater market segmentation by offering different models and price points. They may also attempt to lower production costs by simplifying the design or improving the production process. This period of accumulating small improvements may account for the bulk of the technological progress in an industry, and it continues until the next technological discontinuity.

Understanding the knowledge that firms develop during different eras lends insight into why successful firms often resist the transition to a new technology, even if it provides significant advantages. During the era of incremental change, many firms cease to invest in learning about alternative design architectures and instead invest in refining their competencies related to the dominant architecture. Most competition revolves around improving components rather than altering the architecture; thus, companies focus their efforts on developing component knowledge and knowledge related to the dominant architecture. As firms' routines and capabilities become more and more wedded to the dominant architecture, the firms become less able to identify and respond to a major architectural innovation. For example, the firm might establish divisions based on the primary components of the architecture and structure the communication channels between divisions on the basis of how those components interact. In the firm's effort to absorb and process the vast amount of information available to it, it is likely to establish filters that enable it to identify the information most crucial to its understanding of the existing technology design.[22] As the firm's expertise, structure, communication channels, and filters all become oriented around maximizing its ability to compete in the existing dominant design, they become barriers to the firm's recognizing and reacting to a new technology architecture.

While many industries appear to conform to this model in which a dominant design emerges, there are exceptions. In some industries, heterogeneity of products and production processes are a primary determinant of value, and thus a dominant design is undesirable.[23] For example, art and cuisine may be examples of industries in which there is more pressure to do things differently than to settle upon a standard.

Summary of Chapter

1. Different dimensions have been used to distinguish types of innovation. Some of the most widely used dimensions include product versus process innovation, radical versus incremental innovation, competence-enhancing versus competence-destroying innovation, and architectural versus component innovation.

2. A graph of technology performance over cumulative effort invested often exhibits an s-shape curve. This suggests that performance improvement in a new technology is initially difficult and costly, but, as the fundamental principles of the technology are worked out, it then begins to accelerate as the technology becomes better understood, and finally diminishing returns set in as the technology approaches its inherent limits.

3. A graph of a technology's market adoption over time also typically exhibits an s-shape curve. Initially the technology may seem uncertain and there may be great costs or risks for potential adopters. Gradually, the technology becomes more certain (and its costs may be driven down), enabling the technology to be adopted by larger market segments. Eventually the technology's diffusion slows as it reaches market saturation or is displaced by a newer technology.

4. The rate at which a technology improves over time is often faster than the rate at which customer requirements increase over time. This means technologies that initially met the demands of the mass market may eventually exceed the needs of the market. Furthermore, technologies that initially served only low-end customers (segment zero) may eventually meet the needs of the mass market and capture the market share that originally went to the higher-performing technology.

5. Technological change often follows a cyclical pattern. First, a technological discontinuity causes a period of turbulence and uncertainty, and producers and

consumers explore the different possibilities enabled by the new technology. As producers and customers begin to converge on a consensus of the desired technological configuration, a dominant design emerges. The dominant design provides a stable benchmark for the industry, enabling producers to turn their attention to increasing production efficiency and incremental product improvements. This cycle begins again with the next technological discontinuity.

6. The first design based on the initial technological discontinuity rarely becomes the dominant design. There is usually a period in which firms produce a variety of competing designs of the technology before one design emerges as dominant.

7. The dominant design rarely embodies the most advanced technological features available at the time of its emergence. It is instead the bundle of features that best meets the requirements of the majority of producers and customers.

Discussion Questions

1. What are some reasons that established firms might resist adopting a new technology?

2. Are well-established firms or new entrants more likely to (*a*) develop and/or (*b*) adopt new technologies? Why?

3. Think of an example of an innovation you have studied at work or school. How would you characterize it on the dimensions described at the beginning of the chapter?

4. What are some reasons that both technology improvement and technology diffusion exhibit s-shape curves?

5. Why do technologies often improve faster than customer requirements? What are the advantages and disadvantages to a firm of developing a technology beyond the current state of market needs?

6. In what industries would you expect to see particularly short technology cycles? In what industries would you expect to see particularly long technology cycles? What factors might influence the length of technology cycles in an industry?

Suggested Further Reading

Classics

Anderson, P., and M. L. Tushman, "Technological discontinuities and dominant designs," *Administrative Science Quarterly* 35 (1990), pp. 604–33.

Bijker, W. E., T. P. Hughes, and T. J. Pinch, *The Social Construction of Technological Systems* (Cambridge, MA: MIT Press, 1987).

Christensen, C. M., *The Innovator's Dilemma: When New Technologies Cause Great Firms to Fail* (Boston: Harvard Business School Publishing, 1997).

Dosi, G., "Technological paradigms and technological trajectories," *Research Policy* 11 (1982), pp. 147–60.

Rogers, E., *Diffusion of Innovations*, 5th ed. (New York: Simon & Schuster Publishing, 2003).

Utterback, J. M., and W. J. Abernathy, "A dynamic model of process and product innovations," *Omega* 3 (1975), pp. 639–56.

Recent Work

Ander, R., and R. Kapoor, "Innovation Ecosystems and the Pace of Substitution: Re-examining Technology S-curves," *Strategic Management Journal* (2015), doi: 10.1002/smj.2363

Ethiraj, S., D. Levinthal, and R. R. Roy, "The dual role of modularity: Innovation and imitation," *Management Science*, 54 (2008), pp. 93–955.

Gladwell, M. *The Tipping Point: How Little Things Can Make a Big Difference* (Boston: Back Bay Paperback, 2002).

Schilling, M. A., and M. Esmundo, "Technology s-curves in renewable energy alternatives: Analysis and implications for industry and government," *Energy Policy*, 37 (2009), pp. 1767–81.

Young, H. P., "Innovation diffusion in heterogeneous populations: Contagion, social influence, and social learning," *American Economic Review* 99 (2009), pp. 1899–1924.

Endnotes

1. R. L. Daft and S. W. Becker, *Innovation in Organizations* (New York: Elsevier, 1978); T. D. Duchesneau, S. Cohn, and J. Dutton, *A Study of Innovation in Manufacturing: Determination, Processes and Methodological Issues*, vol. 1 (Social Science Research Institute, University of Maine, 1979); and J. Hage, *Theories of Organization* (New York: Wiley Interscience, 1980).

2. R. D. Dewar and J. E. Dutton, "The Adoption of Radical and Incremental Innovations: An Empirical Analysis," *Management Science* 32 (1986), pp. 1422–33; and J. Dutton and A. Thomas, "Relating Technological Change and Learning by Doing," in *Research on Technological Innovation, Management and Policy*, ed. R. Rosenbloom (Greenwich, CT: JAI Press, 1985), pp. 187–224.

3. C. Scuria-Fontana, "The Slide Rule Today: Respect for the Past; History of the Slide Rule," *Mechanical Engineering-CIME*, July 1990, pp. 122–24.

4. H. Simon, "The Architecture of Complexity," *Proceedings of the American Philosophical Society* 106 (1962), pp. 467–82.

5. L. Fleming and O. Sorenson, "Navigating the Technology Landscape of Innovation," *Sloan Management Review* 44, no. 2 (2003), p. 15; and M. A. Schilling, "Towards a General Modular Systems Theory and Its Application to Interfirm Product Modularity," *Academy of Management Review* 25 (2000), pp. 312–34.

6. R. Henderson and K. Clark, "Architectural Innovation: The Reconfiguration of Existing Product Technologies and the Failure of Established Firms," *Administrative Science Quarterly* 35 (1990), pp. 9–30.

7. R. Foster, *Innovation: The Attacker's Advantage* (New York: Summit Books, 1986).

8. R. Garud and M. A. Rappa, "A Socio-Cognitive Model of Technology Evolution: The Case of Cochlear Implants," *Organization Science* 5 (1994), pp. 344–62; and W. E. Bijker, T. P. Hughes, and T. J. Pinch, *The Social Construction of Technological Systems* (Cambridge, MA: MIT Press, 1987).

9. Foster, *Innovation*.

10. R. Brown, "Managing the 's' Curves of Innovation," *Journal of Consumer Marketing* 9 (1992), pp. 61–72.

11. E. Rogers, *Diffusion of Innovations*, 4th ed. (New York: Free Press, 1995).

12. E. Mansfield, "Industrial Robots in Japan and the USA," *Research Policy* 18 (1989), pp. 183–92.

13. P. A. Geroski, "Models of Technology Diffusion," *Research Policy* 29 (2000), pp. 603–25.

14. Foster, *Innovation;* and E. H. Becker and L. M. Speltz, "Putting the S-curve Concept to Work," *Research Management* 26 (1983), pp. 31–33.

15. C. Christensen, *Innovation and the General Manager* (New York: Irwin/McGraw-Hill, 1999).

16. P. Anderson and M. Tushman, "Technological Discontinuities and Dominant Designs: A Cyclical Model of Technological Change," *Administrative Science Quarterly* 35 (1990), pp. 604–34.

17. J. Schumpeter, *Capitalism, Socialism and Democracy* (New York: Harper Brothers, 1942).

18. See, for example, J. M. Utterback and W. J. Abernathy, "A Dynamic Model of Process and Product Innovation," *Omega, the International Journal of Management Science* 3 (1975), pp. 639–56; and D. Sahal, *Patterns of Technological Innovation* (Reading, MA: Addison-Wesley Publishing Co., 1981).

19. Utterback and Abernathy, "A Dynamic Model of Process and Product Innovation"; F. F. Suarez and J. M. Utterback, "Dominant Designs and the Survival of Firms," *Strategic Management Journal* 16 (1995), pp. 415–30; and J. M. Utterback and F. F. Suarez, "Innovation, Competition and Industry Structure," *Research Policy* 22 (1993), pp. 1–21.

20 Kaplan, S. and Tripsas, M. "Thinking about Technology: Applying a Cognitive Lens to Technical Change," *Research Policy*, 37 (2008):790–805.

21. P. Anderson and M. Tushman, "Technological Discontinuities and Dominant Designs: A Cyclical Model of Technological Change," *Administrative Science Quarterly* 35 (1990), pp. 604–34.

22. R. Henderson and K. Clark, "Architectural Innovation: The Reconfiguration of Existing Product Technologies and the Failure of Established Firms," *Administrative Science Quarterly* 35 (1990), pp. 9–30.

23. M. E. Porter, "The Technological Dimension of Competitive Strategy," in *Research on Technological Innovation, Management and Policy*, ed. R. S. Rosenbloom (Greenwich, CT: JAI Press, 1983); and S. Klepper, "Entry, Exit, Growth, and Innovation over the Product Life Cycle," *American Economic Review* 86 (1996), pp. 562–83.

Standards Battles and Design Dominance

A Battle Emerging in Mobile Payments

By 2014, there were 6.6 billion mobile phone subscriptions in the world, and of those, 2.3 billion had active mobile broadband subscriptions that would enable users to access the mobile web.[a] Mobile payment systems offered the potential of enabling all of these users to perform financial transactions on their phones, similar to how they would perform those transactions using personal computers. However, in 2015, there was no dominant mobile payment system, and a battle among competing mobile payment mechanisms and standards was unfolding.

In the United States, several large players, including Apple, Samsung, and a joint venture called Softcard between Google, AT&T, T-Mobile, and Verizon Wireless, had developed systems based on Near Field Communication (NFC) chips in smartphones. NFC chips enable communication between a mobile device and a point-of-sale system just by having the devices in close proximity.[b] The systems being developed by Apple, Samsung, and Softcard transferred the customer's information wirelessly and then used merchant banks and credit card systems such as Visa or MasterCard to complete the transaction. These systems were thus very much like existing ways of using credit cards but enabled completion of the purchase without contact.

Other competitors, such as Square (with Square Wallet) and PayPal, did not require a smartphone with an NFC chip but instead used a downloadable application and the Web to transmit a customer's information. Square had gained early fame by offering small, free, credit card readers that could be plugged into the audio jack of a smartphone. These readers enabled vendors that would normally only take cash (street vendors, babysitters, etc.) to accept major credit cards.[c] Square processed $30 billion in payments in 2014, making the company one of the fastest growing tech start-ups in Silicon Valley.[d] Square takes about 2.75 to 3 percent from each transaction it processes but must split that with credit card companies and other financial institutions. In terms of installed base, however, PayPal had the clear advantage, with over 161 million active registered accounts. With PayPal, customers could complete purchases simply by entering their phone numbers and a pin number or use a PayPal-issued magnetic stripe cards linked to their PayPal accounts. Users could opt to link their PayPal accounts to their credit cards or directly to their bank accounts. PayPal also owned a service called Venmo that enabled peer-to-peer exchanges with a Facebook-like interface that was growing in popularity as a way to exchange money without carrying cash. Venmo charged a 3 percent fee if the transaction used a major credit card but was free if the consumer used it with a major bank card and debit card.

As noted above, some of the systems being developed did not require involvement of the major credit card companies—which potentially meant that billions of dollars in transaction fees might be avoided or captured by a new player. PayPal, and its peer-to-peer system Venmo, for instance, did not require credit cards. A group of large merchants that included Wal-Mart, Old Navy, Best Buy, 7-eleven, and more had also developed their own payment system—"Current-C"—a downloadable application for a smartphone that enabled purchases to be deducted directly from the customer's bank accounts. This would enable the merchants to avoid the 2–4 percent charges that merchants paid on credit card transactions—amounting to billions of dollars in savings for the participating merchants.[e]

For consumers, the key dimensions that influenced adoption were convenience (e.g., would the customer have to type in a code at the point of purchase? Was it easily accessible on a device the individual already owned?), risk of fraud (e.g., was the individual's identity and financial information at risk?), and ubiquity (e.g., could the system be used everywhere? Did it enable peer-to-peer transactions?). For merchants, fraud was also a big concern—especially in situations where the transaction was not guaranteed by a third party, and cost (e.g., what were the fixed costs and transaction fees of using the system?). Apple Pay had a significant convenience advantage in that a customer could pay with their fingerprint.[f] Current-C, by contrast had a serious convenience disadvantage because consumers would have to open the application on their phone and get a QR code that would need to be scanned at the checkout aisle. Both Apple Pay and Current-C had also experienced fraud problems, with multiple reports of hacked accounts emerging by early 2015.

In the United States, almost half of all consumers had used their smartphones to make a payment at a merchant location by early 2015. Mobile payments accounted for $52 billion in transactions in 2014 and were expected to be $67 billion in 2015.

In other parts of the world, intriguing alternatives for mobile banking were gaining traction even faster. In India and Africa, for example, there are enormous populations of "unbanked" or "underbanked" people (individuals who do not have bank accounts or make limited use of banking services). In these regions, the proportion of people with mobile phones vastly exceeds the proportion of people with credit cards. In Africa, for example, less than 3 percent of the population was estimated to have a credit card, whereas 69 percent of the population was estimated to have mobile phones. Notably, the maximum fixed-line phone penetration ever achieved in Africa was 1.6 percent—reached in 2009—demonstrating the power of mobile technology to "leapfrog" land-based technology in the developing world. The opportunity, then, of giving such people access to fast and inexpensive funds transfer is enormous.

The leading system in India is the Inter-bank Mobile Payment Service developed by National Payments Corporation of India (NPCI).[g] NPCI leveraged its ATM

FIGURE 1
Financial Inclusion around the World

Source: Data from 2011 World Bank survey.

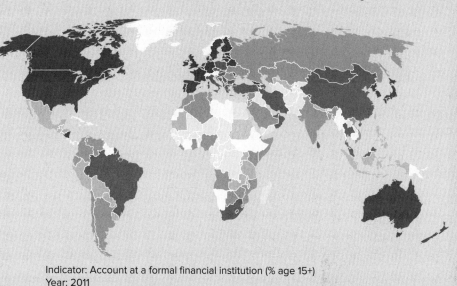

Indicator: Account at a formal financial institution (% age 15+)
Year: 2011

| | No data | 0–16.5 | 16.5–28.5 | 28.5–50.3 | 50.3–81.2 | 81.2–99.8 |

network (connecting more than 65 large banks in India) to create a person-to-person mobile banking system that works on mobile phones. The system uses a unique identifier for each individual that links directly to his or her bank account. In parts of Africa, where the proportion of people who are unbanked is even larger, a system called M-Pesa ("M" for mobile and "pesa," which is kiswahili for money) enables any individual with a passport or national ID card to deposit money into his or her phone account, and transfer money to other users using short message service (SMS).[h] By 2015, the M-Pesa system had roughly 12.2 million active users. The system enabled the percent of Kenyans with access to banking to rise from 41 percent in 2009 to 67 percent in 2014.[i]

FIGURE 2
Mobile phone penetration around the world, 2005–2014

Source: United Nations Telecommunications, ICT Report 2014

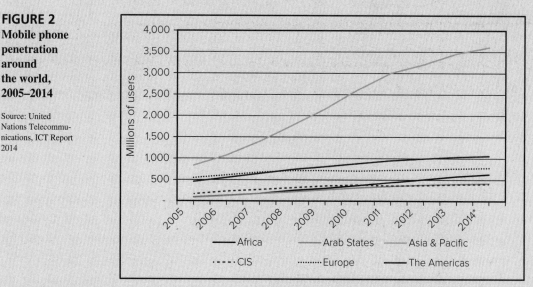

By early 2015, it was clear that mobile payments represented a game-changing opportunity that could accelerate e-commerce, smartphone adoption, and the global reach of financial services. However, lack of compatibility between many of the mobile payment systems and uncertainty over what type of mobile payment system would become dominant still posed significant obstacles to consumer and merchant adoption.

Discussion Questions

1. What are some of the advantages and disadvantages of mobile payment systems in (a) developed countries and (b) developing countries?
2. What are the key factors that differentiate the different mobile payment systems? Which factors do consumers care most about? Which factors do merchants care most about?
3. Are there forces that are likely to encourage one of the mobile payment systems to emerge as dominant? If so, what do you think will determine which becomes dominant?
4. Is there anything the mobile payment systems could do to increase the likelihood of them becoming dominant?
5. How do these different mobile systems increase or decrease the power of a) banks, b) credit cards?

[a] *United Nations Telecommunications Development Sector*, ICT Report, 2014.

[b] J. Kent, "Dominant Mobile Payment Approaches and Leading Mobile Payment Solution Providers: A Review," *Journal of Payments Strategy & Systems* 6:4 (2012): 315–324.

[c] Helft, M. "The Death of Cash," *Fortune* 166:2 (2012): 118–128.

[d] Isaac, M. 2015. "Square expands its reach into small-business services." *New York Times*, March 8th.

[e] Isaac, M. 2015. "Square expands its reach into small-business services." *New York Times*, March 8th; Pogue, D. 2015. "How mobile payments are failing and credit cards are getting better," in *Scientific American*, January 20th.

[f] Pogue, D. 2015. "How mobile payments are failing and credit cards are getting better," in *Scientific American*, January 20th.

[g] V. Govindarajan and M. Balakrishnan, "Developing Countries Are Revolutionizing Mobile Banking," *Harvard Business Review* Blog Network, April 30, 2012.

[h] V. Govindarajan and M. Balakrishnan, "Developing Countries Are Revolutionizing Mobile Banking," *Harvard Business Review* Blog Network, April 30, 2012.

[i] McKay, C & Mazer, R. 2014. "10 Myths about M-PESA: 2014 Update." *Consultative Group to Assist the Poor*, October 1st.

OVERVIEW

The previous chapter described recurrent patterns in technological innovation, and one of those patterns was the emergence of a dominant design. As Anderson and Tushman pointed out, the technology cycle almost invariably exhibits a stage in which the industry selects a **dominant design**. Once this design is selected, producers and customers focus their efforts on improving their efficiency in manufacturing, delivering, marketing, or deploying this dominant design, rather than continue to develop and consider alternative designs. In this chapter, we first will examine why industries experience strong pressure to select a single technology design as dominant. We then will consider the multiple dimensions of value that will shape which technology designs rise to dominance.

WHY DOMINANT DESIGNS ARE SELECTED

dominant design

A single product or process architecture that dominates a product category—usually 50 percent or more of the market. A dominant design is a "de facto standard," meaning that while it may not be officially enforced or acknowledged, it has become a standard for the industry.

Why do many markets coalesce around a single dominant design rather than support a variety of technological options? One primary reason is that many industries exhibit increasing returns to adoption, meaning that the more a technology is adopted, the more valuable it becomes.[1] Complex technologies often exhibit increasing returns to adoption in that the more they are used, the more they are improved. A technology that is adopted usually generates revenue that can be used to further develop and refine the technology. Furthermore, as the technology is used, greater knowledge and understanding of the technology accrue, which may then enable improvements both in the technology itself and in its applications. Finally, as a technology becomes more widely adopted, complementary assets are often developed that are specialized to operate with the technology. These effects can result in a self-reinforcing mechanism that increases the dominance of a technology regardless of its superiority or inferiority to competing technologies. Two of the primary sources of increasing returns are (1) learning effects and (2) network externalities.

Learning Effects

Ample empirical evidence shows that the more a technology is used, the more it is developed and the more effective and efficient it becomes.[2] As a technology is adopted, it generates sales revenues that can be reinvested in further developing and refining the technology. Furthermore, as firms accumulate experience with the technology, they find ways to use the technology more productively, including developing an organizational context that improves the implementation of the technology. Thus, the more a technology is adopted, the better it should become.

One example of learning effects is manifest in the impact of cumulative production on cost and productivity—otherwise known as the *learning curve*. As individuals and producers repeat a process, they learn to make it more efficient, often producing new technological solutions that may enable them to reduce input costs or waste rates. Organizational learning scholars typically model the learning curve as a function of cumulative output: Performance increases, or cost decreases, with the number of units of production, usually at a decreasing rate (see Figure 4.3). For example, in studies of industries as diverse as aircraft production and pizza franchises, researchers have consistently found that the cost of producing a unit (for example, a pizza or an airplane) falls as the number of units produced increases.

The standard form of the learning curve is formulated as $y = ax^{-b}$, where y is the number of direct labor hours required to produce the xth unit, a is the number of direct labor hours required to produce the first unit, x is the cumulative number of units produced, and b is the learning rate. This pattern has been found to be consistent with production data on a wide range of products and services, including the production of automobiles, ships, semiconductors, pharmaceuticals, and even heart surgery techniques.[3] Learning curves have also been identified by using a variety of performance measures, including productivity, total costs per unit, accidents per unit, and waste per unit.[4]

FIGURE 4.3
Standard Learning-Curve Forms

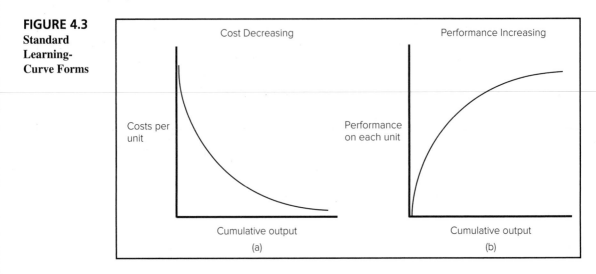

Cost Decreasing

Performance Increasing

Costs per unit

Performance on each unit

Cumulative output
(a)

Cumulative output
(b)

Though learning curves are found in a wide range of organizational processes, there are substantial differences in the rates at which organizations learn.[5] Both managers and scholars are very interested in understanding why one firm reaps great improvement in a process while another exhibits almost no learning. Many studies have examined reasons for this variability, including looking at how the firm's learning rate is affected by process-improvement projects, intentional innovation, or contact with customers and suppliers.[6] The results suggest the learning rate can be influenced by factors such as the nature of the task, firm strategy, and the firm's prior experience.

Prior Learning and Absorptive Capacity

A firm's investment in prior learning can accelerate its rate of future learning by building the firm's absorptive capacity.[7] **Absorptive capacity** refers to the phenomenon whereby as firms accumulate knowledge, they also increase their future ability to assimilate information. A firm's prior related experience shapes its ability to recognize the value of new information, and to utilize that information effectively. For example, in developing a new technology, a firm will often try a number of unsuccessful configurations or techniques before finding a solution that works well. This experimentation builds a base of knowledge in the firm about how key components behave, what alternatives are more likely to be successful than others, what types of projects the firm is most successful at, and so on. This knowledge base enables the firm to more rapidly assess the value of related new materials, technologies, and methods. The effects of absorptive capacity suggest that firms that develop new technologies ahead of others may have an advantage in staying ahead. Firms that forgo investment in technology development may find it very difficult or expensive to develop technology in a subsequent period. This explains, in part, why firms that fall behind the technology frontier find it so difficult to catch up.

At the aggregate level, the more firms that are using a given technology and refining it, the more absorptive capacity that is being generated related to that technology, making development of that technology (and related technologies) more effective and efficient. Furthermore, as firms develop complementary technologies to improve the productivity or ease of utilization of the core technology, the technology becomes more attractive to other firms. In sum, learning effects suggest that early technology

absorptive capacity
The ability of an organization to recognize, assimilate, and utilize new knowledge.

offerings often have an advantage because they have more time to develop and become enhanced than subsequent offerings. (However, as we shall discuss in Chapter Five, it is also possible to be *too early* to a market!)

Network Externalities

network externalities
Also termed *positive consumption externalities*, this is when the value of a good to a user increases with the number of other users of the same or similar good.

Many markets are characterized by **network externalities**, or positive consumption externalities.[8] In a market characterized by network externalities, the benefit from using a good increases with the number of other users of the same good. The classic examples of markets demonstrating network externality effects are those involving physical networks, such as railroads or telecommunications. Railroads are more valuable as the size of the railroad network (and therefore the number of available destinations) increases. Similarly, a telephone is not much use if only a few people can be called with it—the amount of utility the phone provides is directly related to the size of the network.

installed base
The number of users of a particular good. For instance, the installed base of a particular video game console refers to the number of those consoles that are installed in homes worldwide.

Network externalities can also arise in markets that do not have physical networks. For example, a user's benefit from using a good may increase with the number of users of the same good when compatibility is important. The number of users of a particular technology is often referred to as its **installed base**. A user may choose a computer platform based on the number of other users of that platform, rather than on the technological benefits of a particular platform, because it increases the ease of exchanging files. For example, many people choose a computer that uses the Windows operating system and an Intel microprocessor because the "Wintel" (*Windows* and *Intel*) platform has the largest installed base, thus maximizing the number of people with which the user's files will be compatible. Furthermore, the user's training in a particular platform becomes more valuable as the size of the installed base of the platform increases. If the user must invest considerable effort in learning to use a computer platform, the user will probably choose to invest this effort in learning the format he or she believes will be most widely used.

complementary goods
Additional goods and services that enable or enhance the value of another good. For example, the value of a video game console is directly related to the availability of complementary goods such as video games, peripheral devices, and services such as online gaming.

Network externalities also arise when **complementary goods** are important. Many products are only functional or desirable when there is a set of complementary goods available for them (videotapes for VCRs, film for cameras, etc.). Some firms make both a good and its complements (e.g., Kodak produced both cameras and film), whereas others rely on other companies to provide complementary goods or services for their products (e.g., computer manufacturers often rely on other vendors to supply service and software to customers). Products that have a large installed base are likely to attract more developers of complementary goods. This is demonstrated in the Theory in Action about Microsoft: Once the Windows operating system had the largest installed base, most producers of complementary software applications chose to design their products to be optimized to work with Windows. Since the availability of complementary goods will influence users' choice among competing platforms, the availability of complementary goods influences the size of the installed base. A self-reinforcing cycle ensues (see Figure 4.4).

The effect of this cycle is vividly demonstrated by Microsoft's dominance of the operating system market, and later the graphical user interface market, as discussed in the Theory in Action on the rise of Microsoft. Microsoft's early advantage in installed base led to an advantage in the availability of complementary goods. These network externality advantages enabled Windows to lock several would-be contenders such as Geoworks and NeXT (and, some would argue, Apple) out of the market.

From the early 1980s to the decade beginning in 2010, Microsoft's Windows controlled an overwhelming share of the personal computer operating system market. An operating system is the main program on a computer, which enables it to run other programs. Operating systems are responsible for recognizing the input from a keyboard, sending output to the display, tracking files and directories on the disk drives, and controlling peripheral devices. Because the operating system determines how other software applications must be designed, Microsoft's dominance in the operating system market made it extraordinarily powerful in the software industry. However, Microsoft's emergence as a software superpower was due largely to the unfolding of a unique set of circumstances. Had these events played out differently, Microsoft's dominance might have never been.

In 1980, the dominant operating system for personal computers was CP/M. CP/M was invented by Gary Kildall and marketed by Kildall's company, Digital Research. Kildall had been retained by Intel in 1972 to write software for Intel's 4004, the first true microprocessor in that it could be programmed to do custom calculations. Later that year, Intel began to sell the 8008 to designers who would use it as a computer, and Kildall was hired to write a programming language for the chip, called PL/M (Programming Language/Microcomputers).[a]

Then Memorex and Shugart began offering floppy disks (which IBM had invented) as a replacement for punch cards, and Kildall acquired one of these drives. However, no existing program would make the disk drive communicate with Intel's microprocessor, so he wrote a disk operating system that he called Control Program/Microprocessor (CP/M).[b] CP/M could be adapted to any computer based on Intel microprocessors.

Before 1980, IBM, the world's largest computer producer, had not been interested in developing a personal computer. IBM managers could not imagine the personal computer market ever amounting to more than a small niche of hobbyists. However, when businesses began adopting Apple computers to do basic accounting or word processing, IBM began to get nervous. IBM suddenly realized that the personal computer market might become a significant industry, and if it wanted to be a major player in that market it needed to act fast. IBM's managers did not believe they had time to develop their own microprocessor and operating system, so they based their personal computer on Intel microprocessors and planned to use Kildall's CP/M operating system. There are many stories of why Kildall did not sign with IBM. One story is that Kildall was out flying his plane when IBM came around, and though the IBM managers left their names with Kildall's wife, Dorothy McEwen, they did not state the nature of their business, and Kildall did not get back to them for some time. Another version of the story posits that Kildall was reluctant to become tied into any long-term contracts with the massive company, preferring to retain his independence. Yet a third version claims that Kildall was simply more interested in developing advanced technologies than in the strategic management of the resulting products. Whatever the reason, Kildall did not sign with IBM.

Pressed for time, IBM turned to Bill Gates, who was already supplying other software for the system, and asked if he could provide an operating system as well. Though Gates did not have an operating system at that time, he replied that he could supply one. Gates bought a 16-bit operating system (basically a clone of CP/M) from Seattle Computer Company, and reworked the software to match IBM's machines. The product was called Microsoft DOS. With DOS bundled on every IBM PC (which sold more than 250,000 units the first year), the product had an immediate and immense installed base. Furthermore, the companies that emerged to fulfill the unmet demand for IBM PCs with clones also adopted Microsoft DOS to ensure that their products were IBM PC–compatible. Because it replicated CP/M, Microsoft DOS was compatible with the range of software that had been developed for the CP/M operating system. Furthermore, after it was bundled with the IBM PC, more software was developed for the operating system, creating an even wider availability of complementary goods. Microsoft DOS was soon entrenched as the industry standard, and Microsoft was the world's fastest-growing software company.

"We were able to get the technology out into the market early to develop a standard. We were effective in soliciting software vendors to write to that platform to solidify the standard," said B. J. Whalen, Microsoft product manager. "Once you get it going, it's a snowball effect. The more applications you have available for a platform, the more people will want to use that platform. And of course, the more people

continued

that want to use that platform, the more software vendors will want to write to that platform."

Later Microsoft would develop a graphical interface named Windows that closely replicated the user-friendly functionality of Apple computers. By bundling Windows with DOS, Microsoft was able to transition its base of DOS customers over to the Windows system. Microsoft also worked vigorously to ensure that compatible applications were developed for DOS and Windows, making applications itself and also encouraging third-party developers to support the platform. Microsoft was able to leverage its dominance with Windows into a major market share in many other software markets (e.g., word processing, spreadsheet programs, presentation programs) and influence over many aspects of the computer software and hardware industries. However, had Kildall signed with IBM, or had Compaq and other computer companies been unable to clone the IBM personal computer, the software industry might look very different today.

[a] P. Korzeniowski, "DOS: Still Thriving after All These Years," *Software Magazine* 10, no. 6 (1990), pp. 83–112.
[b] S. Veit, "What Ever Happened to . . . Gary Kildall?" *Computer Shopper* 14, no. 11 (1994), pp. 608–14.

Firms can also attempt to influence the selection of a dominant design by building coalitions around a preferred technology.[9] This is aptly illustrated in the opening case. While the preceding has emphasized the emergence of dominant designs through market forces, occasionally a dominant design is put in place through government regulation.

Government Regulation

In some industries, the consumer welfare benefits of having compatibility among technologies have prompted government regulation, and thus a legally induced adherence to a dominant design. This has often been the case for the utilities, telecommunications, and television industries, to name a few.[10] For example, in 1953 the U.S. Federal Communications Commission (FCC) approved the National Television Systems Committee (NTSC) color standard in television broadcasting to ensure that individuals with monochrome television sets would be able to receive the color television programs broadcast by networks (though they would see them in black and white). That standard was still in place in 2003. Similarly, in 1998, while a battle was being fought in the United States over wireless technology formats, the European Union (EU) adopted a single wireless telephone standard (the general standard for mobile communications, or GSM). By choosing a uniform standard, the EU could avoid the proliferation of incompatible

FIGURE 4.4
The Self-Reinforcing Cycle of Installed Base and Availability of Complementary Goods

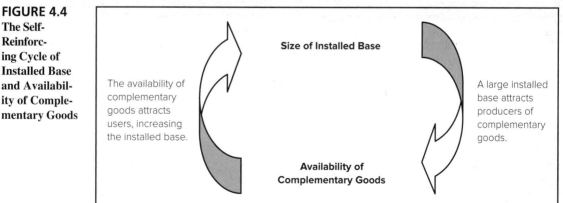

Size of Installed Base

The availability of complementary goods attracts users, increasing the installed base.

A large installed base attracts producers of complementary goods.

Availability of Complementary Goods

standards and facilitate exchange both within and across national borders. Where government regulation imposes a single standard on an industry, the technology design embodied in that standard necessarily dominates the other technology options available to the industry. The consumer welfare impact of dominant designs is explored further in the Theory in Action section.

The Result: Winner-Take-All Markets

All these forces can encourage the market toward natural monopolies. While some alternative platforms may survive by focusing on niche markets, the majority of the market may be dominated by a single (or few) design(s). A firm that is able to lock in its technology as the dominant design of a market usually earns huge rewards and may dominate the product category through several product generations. When a firm's technology is chosen as a dominant design, not only does the firm have the potential to earn near-monopoly rents in the short run, but the firm also is in a good position to shape the evolution of the industry, greatly influencing what future generations of products will look like. However, if the firm supports a technology that is not chosen as the dominant design, it may be forced to adopt the dominant technology, effectively forfeiting the capital, learning, and brand equity invested in its original technology. Even worse, a firm may find itself locked out of the market if it is unable to adopt the dominant technology. Such standards battles are high-stakes games—resulting in big winners and big losers.

path dependency
When end results depend greatly on the events that took place leading up to the outcome. It is often impossible to reproduce the results that occur in such a situation.

Increasing returns to adoption also imply that technology trajectories are characterized by **path dependency**, meaning that relatively small historical events may have a great impact on the final outcome. Though the technology's quality and technical advantage undoubtedly influence its fate, other factors, unrelated to the technical superiority or inferiority, may also play important roles.[11] For instance, timing may be crucial; early technology offerings may become so entrenched that subsequent technologies, even if considered to be technically superior, may be unable to gain a foothold in the market. How and by whom the technology is sponsored may also impact adoption. If, for example, a large and powerful firm aggressively sponsors a technology (perhaps even pressuring suppliers or distributors to support the technology), that technology may gain a controlling share of the market, locking out alternative technologies.

The influence of a dominant design can also extend beyond its own technology cycle. As the dominant design is adopted and refined, it influences the knowledge that is accumulated by producers and customers, and it shapes the problem-solving techniques used in the industry. Firms will tend to use and build on their existing knowledge base rather than enter unfamiliar areas.[12] This can result in a very "sticky" technological paradigm that directs future technological inquiry in the area.[13] Thus, a dominant design is likely to influence the nature of the technological discontinuity that will eventually replace it.

Such winner-take-all markets demonstrate very different competitive dynamics than markets in which many competitors can coexist relatively peacefully. These markets also require very different firm strategies to achieve success. Technologically superior products do not always win—the firms that win are usually the ones that know how to manage the multiple dimensions of value that shape design selection.

MULTIPLE DIMENSIONS OF VALUE

The value a new technology offers a customer is a composite of many different things. We first consider the value of the stand-alone technology, and then show how the stand-alone value of the technology combines with the value created by the size of the installed base and availability of complementary goods.[14] In industries characterized by **increasing returns**, this combination will influence which technology design rises to dominance.

increasing returns
When the *rate of return* (not just gross returns) from a product or process increases with the size of its installed base.

A Technology's Stand-Alone Value

The value a new technology offers to customers can be driven by many different things, such as the functions it enables the customer to perform, its aesthetic qualities, and its ease of use. To help managers identify the different aspects of utility a new technology offers customers, W. Chan Kim and Renee Mauborgne developed a "Buyer Utility Map."[15] They argue that it is important to consider six different utility levers, as well as six stages of the buyer experience cycle, to understand a new technology's utility to a buyer.

The stages they identify are *purchase, delivery, use, supplements, maintenance,* and *disposal*. The six utility levers they consider are *customer productivity, simplicity, convenience, risk, fun and image,* and *environmental friendliness*. Creating a grid with stages and levers yields a 36-cell utility map (see Figure 4.5). Each cell provides an opportunity to offer a new value proposition to a customer.

A new technology might offer a change in value in a single cell or in a combination of cells. For example, when retailers establish an online ordering system, the primary new value proposition they are offering is greater *simplicity* in the *purchase* stage. On the other hand, as shown in Figure 4.5, the introduction of the Toyota Prius hybrid-electric vehicle offered customers greater productivity (in the form of gas savings), image benefits, and environmental friendliness in the customer's use, supplements, and maintenance stages, while providing the same simplicity and convenience of regular gasoline-only–powered vehicles.

Kim and Mauborgne's model is designed with an emphasis on consumer products, but their mapping principle can be easily adapted to emphasize industrial products or different aspects of buyer utility. For example, instead of having a single entry for customer productivity, the map could have rows for several dimensions of productivity such as speed, efficiency, scalability, and reliability. The map provides a guide for managers to consider multiple dimensions of technological value and multiple stages of the customer experience. Finally, the new benefits have to be considered with respect to the cost to the customer of obtaining or using the technology—it is the ratio of benefits to cost that determines value.

Network Externality Value

In industries characterized by network externalities, the value of a technological innovation to users will be a function not only of its stand-alone benefits and cost, but also of the value created by the size of its installed base and the availability of complementary goods (see Figure 4.6(a)).[16] Thus, the value to consumers of using the Windows operating system is due in part to the technology's stand-alone value (for example, the

FIGURE 4.5
The Buyer Utility Map with Toyota Prius Example

Source: Adapted from *Harvard Business Review*. Exhibit from "Knowing a Winning Business Idea When You See One," by W. C. Kim and R. Mauborgne, September–October 2000. Copyright © 2000 by the Harvard Business School Publishing Corporation; all rights reserved.

	Purchase	Delivery	Use	Supplements	Maintenance	Disposal
Customer productivity	Price of Prius slightly higher than comparable nonhybrid models		Offers speed and power comparable to nonhybrid models	Can stop less often for gas, saving money and time		
Simplicity	Buyer may feel less able to assess value of vehicle		Operates like a regular combustion engine vehicle	Refuels like a regular combustion engine vehicle		Hybrids have larger batteries that would have to be recycled and disposed of at end of life
Convenience		Will be sold through traditional dealer channels	Does not have to be plugged into electrical outlet	Can purchase fuel at regular gas stations	Maintenance is similar to regular combustion engine vehicle	
Risk			Buyer might face a higher risk of product failure because it embodies a new technology		Buyer might have difficulty finding replacement parts because of new technology	Prius might be more difficult to resell or have lower resell value
Fun and image		Connotes image of environmental responsibility				
Environmental friendliness	Buyers feel they are helping support the development of more environmentally friendly cars		Emits lower levels of pollutants	Requires less use of fossil fuels		

ability of the operating system to make it easy for consumers to use the computer), the installed base of the operating system (and thus the number of computers with which the user can easily interact), and the availability of compatible software. Visualizing the value of technological innovations in this way makes it clear why even innovations that offer significant improvements in technological functionality often fail to displace existing technologies that are already widely adopted: Even if a new innovation has a significant advantage in functionality, its overall value may be significantly less than the incumbent standard. This situation is poignantly illustrated in the case of NeXT computers. In 1985, Steve Jobs and five senior managers of Apple Computer founded NeXT Incorporated. They unveiled their first computer in 1988. With a 25-MHz

FIGURE 4.6
Components of Value

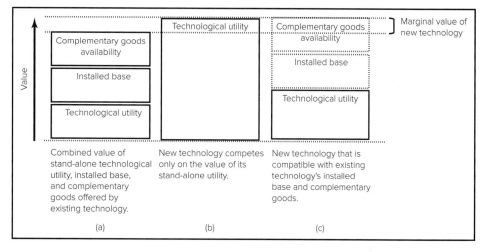

Motorola 68030 and 8 MB of RAM, the machine was significantly more powerful than most other personal computers available. It offered advanced graphics capability and even ran an object-oriented operating system (called NextStep) that was considered extremely advanced. However, the machine was not compatible with the IBM-compatible personal computers (based on Intel's microprocessors and Microsoft's operating system) that had become the dominant standard. The machine thus would not run the vast majority of software applications on the market. A small contingent of early adopters bought the NeXT personal computers, but the general market rejected them because of a dire lack of software and uncertainty about the company's viability. The company discontinued its hardware line in 1993 and ceased development of NextStep in 1996.

A similar battle was playing out in 2015 between smartphone operating systems, though in this case there were two contenders who were more evenly matched: Apple's iOS and Google's Android. Both companies offered smartphone operating systems with intuitive, powerful, and aesthetically pleasing interfaces (technological utility). Both were aggressively building communities of applications providers that provided large ranges of interesting and/or useful applications (complementary goods). Both were also trying to build installed base through aggressive marketing and distribution. Market share estimates of the two systems varied widely based on the timing of the data announcements, the geographical scope considered, and the product scope considered, but in early 2015 it was clear that Apple and Google were in a head-to-head battle for dominance, whereas Rim's Blackberry and Microsoft's mobile operating systems were barely in the race (for more on this, see the section on the "Segment Zero" threat to Microsoft in Chapter 3).

As shown in Figure 4.6(b), it is not enough for a new technology's stand-alone utility to exceed that of the incumbent standard. The new technology must be able to offer greater overall value. For the new technology to compete on its stand-alone utility alone, that utility must be so great that it eclipses the combined value of an existing technology's stand-alone utility, its installed base, and its complementary goods.

In some cases, the new technology may be made compatible with the existing technology's installed base and complementary goods as in Figure 4.6(c). In this case, a new technology with only a moderate functionality advantage may offer greater overall value to users. Sony and Philips employed this strategy with their high-definition audio format, Super Audio CD (SACD), a high-density multichannel audio format based on a revolutionary "scalable" bit-stream technology known as Direct Stream Digital (DSD). Anticipating that users would be reluctant to replace their existing compact disc players and compact disc music collections, Sony and Philips made the new Super Audio CD technology compatible with existing compact disc technology. The Super Audio CD players included a feature that enables them to play standard CDs, and the recorded Super Audio CDs included a CD audio layer in addition to the high-density layer, enabling them to be played on standard CD systems. Customers can thus take advantage of the new technology without giving up the value of their existing CD players and music libraries.

When users are comparing the value of a new technology to an existing technology, they are weighing a combination of objective information (e.g., actual technological benefits, actual information on installed base or complementary goods), subjective information (e.g., perceived technological benefits, perceived installed base or complementary goods), and expectations for the future (e.g., anticipated technological benefits, anticipated installed base and complementary goods). Thus, each of the primary value components described above also has corresponding perceived or anticipated value components (see Figure 4.7). In Figure 4.7(a), the perceived and anticipated value components map proportionately to their corresponding actual components. However, as depicted in Figure 4.7(b), this need not be the case. For instance, perceived installed base may greatly exceed actual installed base, or customers may expect that a technology will eventually have a much larger installed base than competitors and thus the value accrued from the technology's installed base is expected to grow much larger than it is currently.

Firms can take advantage of the fact that users rely on both objective and subjective information in assessing the combined value offered by a new technology. For example, even a technology with a small installed base can achieve a relatively large mind share through heavy advertising by its backers. Producers can also shape users' expectations of the future installed base and availability of complements through announcements of preorders, licensing agreements, and distribution arrangements. For example, when Sega and Nintendo were battling for dominance in the 16-bit video game console market, they went to great lengths to manage impressions of their installed base and market share, often to the point of deception. At the end of 1991, Nintendo claimed it had sold 2 million units of the Super Nintendo Entertainment System in the U.S. market. Sega disagreed, arguing that Nintendo had sold 1 million units at most. By May 1992, Nintendo was claiming a 60 percent share of the 16-bit market, and Sega was claiming a 63 percent share![17] Since perceived or expected installed base may drive subsequent adoptions, a large perceived or expected installed base can lead to a large actual installed base.

Such a tactic also underlies the use of "vaporware"—products that are not actually on the market and may not even exist but are advertised—by many software vendors. By building the impression among customers that a product is ubiquitous, firms can prompt rapid adoption of the product when it actually is available. Vaporware may also buy a firm valuable time in bringing its product to market. If other vendors beat the firm to market and the firm fears that customers may select a dominant design before its offering is introduced, it can use vaporware to attempt to persuade customers to delay purchase until the firm's product is available. The video game console industry also provides an excellent example here. When Sega and Sony introduced their 32-bit video game consoles (the Saturn and PlayStation, respectively), Nintendo

FIGURE 4.7
Actual, Perceived, and Expected Components of Value

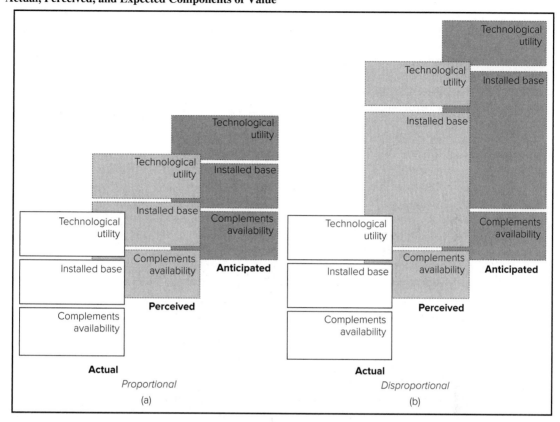

was still a long way from introducing its next-generation console. In an effort to forestall consumer purchases of 32-bit systems, Nintendo began aggressively promoting its development of a 64-bit system (originally named Project Reality) in 1994, though the product would not actually reach the market until September 1996. The project underwent so many delays that some industry observers dubbed it "Project Unreality."[18] Nintendo was successful in persuading many customers to wait for its Nintendo 64, and the system was ultimately relatively successful.

Nintendo, however, was never able to reclaim dominance over the video game industry. By the time the Nintendo 64 had gained significant momentum, Sony was developing its even more advanced PlayStation2. Sony's experience in VCRs and compact discs had taught it to manage the multiple dimensions of value very well: Sony's PlayStation2 offered more than double the processing power of the Nintendo 64, it was backward compatible (helping the PlayStation2 tap the value of customers' existing PlayStation game libraries), and Sony sold it for a price that many speculated was less than the cost of manufacturing the console ($299). Sony also invested heavily to ensure that many game titles would be available at launch, and it used its distribution leverage and advertising budget to ensure the product would seem ubiquitous at its launch.

Competing for Design Dominance
in Markets with Network Externalities

Graphs illustrate how differing technological utilities and network externality returns to installed base or market share impact the competition for design dominance. The following figures examine whether network externalities create pressure for a single dominant design versus a few dominant designs by considering the rate at which value increases with the size of the installed base, and how large of an installed base is necessary before most of the network externality benefits are achieved. As explained earlier, when an industry has network externalities, the value of a good to a user increases with the number of other users of the same or similar good. However, it is rare that the value goes up linearly—instead, the value is likely to increase in an s-shape as shown in Figure 4.8(a). Initially, the benefits may increase slowly. For example, whether a cell phone can reach 1 percent of the population or 5 percent is fairly insignificant—the reach of the phone service has to become much wider before the phone has much value. However, beyond some threshold level, the network externality returns begin to increase rapidly, until at some point, most of the benefits have been obtained and the rate of return decreases. Consider the example of operating systems at the beginning of the chapter: If an operating system has too small of an installed base, few software developers will write applications for it and thus it will be of little value to consumers. An increase from a 1 percent market share to a 2 percent market share makes little difference—developers are still unlikely to be attracted to the platform. Once the operating system exceeds some threshold level of adoption, however, it becomes worthwhile to develop software applications for it, and the value of the operating system begins to increase rapidly. Once the operating system achieves a large share of the market, the user has probably obtained most of the network externality value. There is likely to be a large range of quality software available for the operating system, and incremental increases in available software have less marginal impact on the value reaped by the customer.

Next we consider the stand-alone functionality of the technology. In Figure 4.8(b), a base level of technological utility has been added to the graph, which shifts the

FIGURE 4.8
Network Externality Returns to Market Share

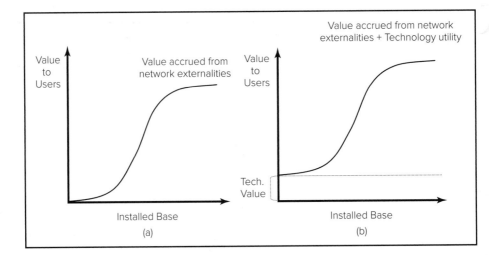

entire graph up. For example, an operating system that has an exceptionally easy-to-use interface makes the technology more valuable at any level of installed base. This becomes relevant later when two technologies that have different base levels of technological utility are considered.

When two technologies compete for dominance, customers will compare the overall value yielded (or expected) from each technology, as discussed in the previous section. In Figure 4.9, two technologies, A and B, each offer similar technological utility, and have similarly shaped network externality returns curves. To illustrate the competitive effects of two technologies competing for market share, the graphs in Figure 4.9 are drawn with market share on the horizontal axis instead of installed base. Furthermore, the curve for B is drawn with the market share dimension reversed so that we can compare the value offered by the two different technologies at different market share splits, that is, when A has a 20 percent market share, B has an 80 percent market share, and so on. This graph shows that at every point where A has less than 50 percent market share (and thus B has greater than 50 percent market share), B will yield greater overall value, making B more attractive to customers. On the other hand, when A has greater than 50 percent market share (and B thus has less than 50 percent market share), A yields more overall value. When each technology has exactly 50 percent market share, they yield the same overall value and customers will be indifferent between them. However, if both technologies earn similar network externality returns to market share, but one technology offers greater stand-alone utility, the indifference point will be shifted in its favor. In the right-hand graph in Figure 4.9, technology B offers a greater level of stand-alone technological utility, shifting its overall value curve up. In this graph, technology A must have greater than 60 percent market share (and B must have less than 40 percent market share) for A to offer more overall value than B.

Another interesting scenario arises when customers attain their desired level of network externality benefits at lower levels of market share, depicted graphically in Figure 4.10. In this graph, the curves flatten out sooner, implying that the maximum

FIGURE 4.9
Network Externality Returns and Technological Utility: Competing Designs

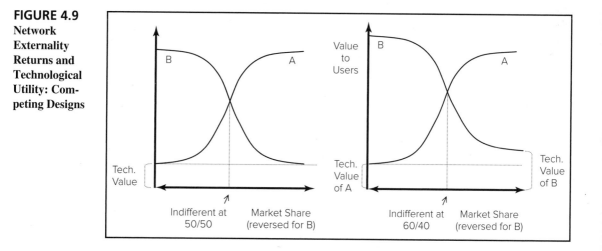

FIGURE 4.10

Network Externality Value Is Fully Tapped at Minority Market Share Levels

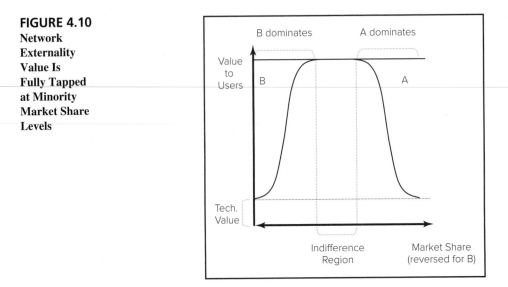

amount of network externality value is obtained by customers at lower levels of market share. In this case, customers may face a relatively large indifference region within which neither technology clearly dominates. This may be the case with the video game console industry: While customers may experience some network externality benefits to a console having significant share (more game titles, more people to play against), those benefits might be achieved by a console without attaining a majority of the market. For example, even with Sony, Microsoft, and Nintendo splitting the game console market, there is still an abundance of game titles for all three consoles and a significant pool of people to play games against. Such markets may not experience great pressure to select a single dominant design; two or more platforms may successfully coexist.

Are Winner-Take-All Markets Good for Consumers?

Traditionally, economics has emphasized the consumer welfare benefits of competitive markets; however, increasing returns make this a complicated issue. This is exemplified by the antitrust suits brought against Microsoft. While some analysts argued that Microsoft had clearly engaged in anticompetitive behavior and had damaged consumers in its quest to dominate the personal computer operating system market, others argued that Microsoft had behaved appropriately, and that its overwhelming share of the personal computer operating system market was good for consumers since it created greater compatibility among computers and more software applications. So how does a regulatory body decide when a firm has become too dominant? One way to think about this is to compare the value customers reap from network externalities at different levels of market share with the corresponding monopoly costs. Network externality returns refers to the value customers reap as a larger portion of the market adopts the same good (e.g., there is likely to be greater availability of complementary goods, more compatibility among users, and more revenues can be channeled into further developing the technology). Monopoly costs refer to the costs users bear as

FIGURE 4.11
Network
Externality
Benefits and
Monopoly
Costs

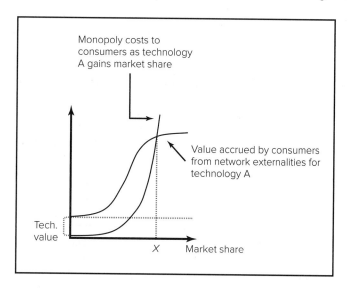

a larger portion of the market adopts the same good (e.g., a monopolist may charge higher prices, there may be less product variety, and innovation in alternative technologies may be stifled). Network externality returns to market share often exhibit the s-shape described in the previous section. Monopoly costs to market share, however, are often considered to be exponentially increasing. Plotting them on the same graph (as in Figure 4.11) reveals how network externality benefits and monopoly costs trade off against each other.

In Figure 4.11, so long as technology A's market share remains less than X, the combination of technological utility and network externality benefits exceeds the monopoly costs, even if X represents a very large share of the market. However, as technology A's market share climbs beyond X, the monopoly costs now exceed the value of the technology utility and network externality benefits. A number of factors can shift where these two curves cross. If the technology utility for A were higher, the curves would cross at a point greater than X. If the network externality returns curve began to flatten at a lower market share (as was demonstrated earlier with the video game console industry), then the curves would cross at a market share less than X.

The steepness of the monopoly cost curve is largely a function of the firm's discretionary behavior. A firm can choose not to exploit its monopoly power, thus flattening the monopoly costs curve. For instance, one of the most obvious assertions of monopoly power is typically exhibited in the price charged for a good. However, a firm can choose not to charge the maximum price that customers would be willing to pay for a good. For example, many people would argue that Microsoft does not charge the maximum price for its Windows operating system that the market would bear. However, a firm can also assert its monopoly power in more subtle ways, by controlling the evolution of the industry through selectively aiding some suppliers or complementors more than others, and many people would argue that in this respect, Microsoft has taken full advantage of its near-monopoly power.

Summary of Chapter

1. Many technologies demonstrate increasing returns to adoption, meaning that the more they are adopted, the more valuable they become.

2. One primary source of increasing returns is learning-curve effects. The more a technology is produced and used, the better understood and developed it becomes, leading to improved performance and reduced costs.

3. Another key factor creating increasing returns is network externality effects. Network externality effects arise when the value of a good to a user increases with the size of the installed base. This can be due to a number of reasons, such as need for compatibility or the availability of complementary goods.

4. In some industries, the consumer welfare benefits of having a single standard have prompted government regulation, such as the European Union's mandate to use the GSM cellular phone standard.

5. Increasing returns can lead to winner-take-all markets where one or a few companies capture nearly all the market share.

6. The value of a technology to buyers is multidimensional. The stand-alone value of a technology can include many factors (productivity, simplicity, etc.) and the technology's cost. In increasing returns industries, the value will also be significantly affected by the technology's installed base and availability of complementary goods.

7. Customers weigh a combination of objective and subjective information. Thus, a customer's perceptions and expectations of a technology can be as important as (or more important than) the actual value offered by the technology.

8. Firms can try to manage customers' perceptions and expectations through advertising and public announcements of preorders, distribution agreements, and so on.

9. The combination of network externality returns to market share and technological utility will influence at what level of market share one technology will dominate another. For some industries, the full network externality benefits are attained at a minority market share level; in these industries, multiple designs are likely to coexist.

Discussion Questions

1. What are some of the sources of increasing returns to adoption?

2. What are some examples of industries not mentioned in the chapter that demonstrate increasing returns to adoption?

3. What are some of the ways a firm can try to increase the overall value of its technology and its likelihood of becoming the dominant design?

4. What determines whether an industry is likely to have one or a few dominant designs?

5. Are dominant designs good for consumers? Competitors? Complementors? Suppliers?

Suggested Further Reading

Classics

Arthur, W. B., *Increasing Returns and Path Dependency in the Economy* (Ann Arbor, MI: University of Michigan Press, 1994).

Gawer, A., and M. A. Cusumano, *Platform Leadership* (Boston: Harvard Business School Publishing, 2002).

Katz, M., and C. Shapiro, "Technology adoption in the presence of network externalities," *Journal of Political Economy* 94 (1986), pp. 822–41.

Schilling, M. A., "Technological leapfrogging: Lessons from the U.S. video game console industry," *California Management Review* 45, no. 3 (2003), pp. 6–32.

Shapiro, C., and Varian, H. *Information Rules: A Strategic Guide to the Network Economy* (1999), Boston: Harvard Business Review Press.

Recent Work

Bollinger, B., and K. Gillingham, "Peer effects in the diffusion of solar photovoltaic panels," *Marketing Science* 31 (2012), pp. 900–912.

Casadesus-Masanell, R., and D. B. Yoffie, "Wintel: Cooperation and conflict," *Management Science* 53 (2007), pp. 584–598.

Jacobides, M., "Blackberry forgot to manage the ecosystem," *Business Strategy Review* 24 (2013), p. 8.

Kaplan, S., and M. Tripsas, "Thinking about technology: Applying a cognitive lens to technical change," *Research Policy*, 37 (2008), pp. 790–805.

Sterman, J. D., R. Henderson, E. D. Beinhocker, and L. I. Newman, "Getting big too fast: Strategic dynamics with increasing returns and bounded rationality," *Management Science* 53 (2007), pp. 683–696.

Seamans, R., and F. Zhu, "Responses to entry in multi-sided markets: The impact of craigslist on local newspapers," *Management Science* 60 (2013), pp. 476–493.

Endnotes

1. W. B. Arthur, *Increasing Returns and Path Dependency in the Economy* (Ann Arbor, MI: University of Michigan Press, 1994).

2. For examples of this, see M. Lapre, A. S. Mukherjee, and L. N. Van Wassenhove, "Behind the Learning Curve: Linking Learning Activities to Waste Reduction," *Management Science* 46 (2000), pp. 597–611; F. K. Levy, "Adaptation in the Production Process," *Management Science* 11 (1965), pp. B136–54; and L. E. Yelle, "The Learning Curve: Historical Review and Comprehensive Survey," *Decision Sciences* 10 (1979), pp. 302–28.

3. L. Argote, *Organizational Learning: Creating, Retaining and Transferring Knowledge* (Boston: Kluwer Academic Publishers, 1999); N. W. Hatch and D. C. Mowery, "Process Innovation and Learning by Doing in Semiconductor Manufacturing," *Management Science* 44, no. 11 (1998), pp. 1461–77; and M. A. Schilling, P. Vidal, R. Ployhart, and A. Marangoni, "Learning by Doing Something Else: Variation, Relatedness, and the Learning Curve," *Management Science* 49 (2003), pp. 39–56.

4. For examples, see L. Argote, "Group and Organizational Learning Curves: Individual, System and Environmental Components," *British Journal of Social Psychology* 32 (1993), pp. 31–52; Argote, *Organizational Learning;* N. Baloff, "Extensions of the Learning Curve—Some Empirical Results," *Operations Research Quarterly* 22, no. 4 (1971), pp. 329–40; E. D. Darr, L. Argote, and D. Epple, "The Acquisition, Transfer and Depreciation of Knowledge in Service Organizations: Productivity in Franchises," *Management Science* 41 (1995), pp. 1750–62; L. Greenberg, "Why the Mine Injury Picture Is Out of Focus," *Mining Engineering* 23 (1971), pp. 51–53; Hatch and Mowery, "Process Innovation and Learning by Doing in Semiconductor Manufacturing"; A. Mukherjee, M. Lapre, and L. Wassenhove, "Knowledge Driven Quality Improvement," *Management Science* 44 (1998), pp. S35–S49; and Yelle, "The Learning Curve."

5. Argote, *Organizational Learning.*

6. J. Dutton and A. Thomas, "Treating Progress Functions as a Managerial Opportunity," *Academy of Management Review* 9 (1984), pp. 235–47; Levy, "Adaptation in the Production Process"; and Mukherjee, Lapre, and Wassenhove, "Knowledge Driven Quality Improvement."

7. W. M. Cohen and D. A. Levinthal, "Absorptive Capacity: A New Perspective on Learning and Innovation," *Administrative Science Quarterly*, March 1990, pp. 128–52.

8. M. Katz and C. Shapiro, "Technology Adoption in the Presence of Network Externalities," *Journal of Political Economy* 94 (1986), pp. 822–41; M. Schilling, "Technological Lock Out: An Integrative Model of the Economic and Strategic Factors Driving Technology Success and Failure," *Academy of Management Review* 23 (1998), pp. 267–84; and M. Thum, "Network Externalities, Technological Progress, and the Competition of Market Contracts," *International Journal of Industrial Organization* 12 (1994), pp. 269–89.

9. J. Wade, "Dynamics of Organizational Communities and Technological Bandwagons: An Empirical Investigation of Community Evolution in the Microprocessor Market," *Strategic Management Journal* 16 (1995), pp. 111–34.

10. Schilling, "Technological Lock Out"; and F. F. Suarez, "Battles for Technological Dominance: An Integrative Framework," *Research Policy* 33, pp. 271–86.

11. W. B. Arthur, "Competing Technologies, Increasing Returns, and Lock-In by Historical Events," *The Economic Journal*, March 1989, pp. 116–31; R. W. England, "Three Reasons for Investing Now in Fossil Fuel Conservation: Technological Lock-In, Institutional Inertia, and Oil Wars," *Journal of Economic Issues*, September 1994, pp. 755–76; and Katz and Shapiro, "Technology Adoption in the Presence of Network Externalities."

12. G. Dosi, "Sources, Procedures, and Microeconomic Effects of Innovation," *Journal of Economic Literature* 26 (1988), p. 1130.

13. Ibid., pp. 1120–71.

14. M. A. Schilling, "Technological Leapfrogging: Lessons from the U.S. Video Game Console Industry," *California Management Review* 45, no. 3 (2003), pp. 6–32; and Suarez, "Battles for Technological Dominance."

15. W. C. Kim and R. Mauborgne, "Knowing a Winning Business Idea When You See One," *Harvard Business Review*, September–October 2000, pp. 129–38.

16. Schilling, "Technological Leapfrogging."

17. A. Brandenberger, 1995b. "Power Play (B): Sega in 16-Bit Video Games," Harvard Business School case no. 9-795-103.

18. A. Brandenberger, 1995c. "Power Play (C): 3DO in 32-Bit Video Games," Harvard Business School case no. 9-795-104; and Schilling, "Technological Leapfrogging."

Chapter **Five**

Timing of Entry

From SixDegrees.com to Facebook: The Rise of Social Networking Sites

In the 1960s, Stanley Milgram addressed a number of letters to a friend of his, a stockbroker in Boston. Milgram then distributed these letters to a random selection of people in Nebraska. He instructed the individuals to pass the letters to the addressee by sending them to a person they knew on a first-name basis who seemed in some way closer (socially, geographically, etc.) to the stockbroker. This person would then do the same, until the letters reached their final destination. Many of the letters did eventually reach the stockbroker, and Milgram found that on average, the letters had passed through six individuals en route. Milgram had demonstrated that the world was indeed small, and dubbed this finding "six degrees of separation."[a] This finding, which inspired both the John Guare play "Six Degrees of Separation" and the 1993 film by the same name, also inspired one of the very first social networking sites. Started in 1997 by Andrew Weinrech, SixDegrees.com sought to leverage both the growing popularity of the Internet and people's curiosity about to whom they might be connected—or connectable. The site enabled users to create profiles and invite their friends to join.[b] SixDegrees attracted three million members, but many users felt that not enough of their friends were members to make it an interesting destination, and there was little to do on the site beyond inviting and accepting friend requests.[c] The company soon ran out of money, and it shut down in 2000.

Friendster was launched in March of 2003 by former Netscape engineer Jonathan Abrams with $400,000 in seed money and a similar concept to SixDegrees.com. In fact, Friendster would even show you a network map of you and your acquaintances, lending imagery to the "six degrees of separation" concept. It also used this map to determine who had permission to view which pages—dramatically increasing the computer time required for users to access pages. In its first six months Friendster attracted about 1.5 million users and Google offered to acquire it for $30 million. Abrams declined the offer, and instead raised $13 million in venture capital.[d] Later that year *Time* magazine declared Friendster was one of the "coolest inventions of 2003." Like Six Degrees, though the site was very popular, the infrastructure for social networking (and the knowledge about what was required to efficiently manage a social networking site) was in its infancy. The number of members rapidly grew to seven million, but the company did not have sufficient servers to support the traffic, causing severe page load delays. The company began to receive thousands of customer service complaints, and soon members (and would-be members) were fleeing to other sites that had learned from Friendster's mistakes. One of those sites was MySpace.

Also founded in 2003 (by Brad Greenspan, Chris DeWolfe, and Tom Anderson of community website conglomerate eUniverse), MySpace mimicked some of the more popular features of Friendster, but also leveraged the 20 million subscribers and e-mail users of eUniverse to jumpstart its membership. Unlike Friendster, MySpace made all members' profiles viewable by any user, which reduced the computational burden of figuring out who was able to look at which profile. MySpace also made user profiles very customizable, and offered spaces for blogs, places to display photos, and the ability to play music. MySpace was acquired in July of 2005 by media conglomerate New Corporation for $580 million, and from 2005 to 2008 was the most popular social networking site in the world. A three-year advertising deal with Google for $900 million was a cash windfall, but it also lead to heavy amounts of advertising on the site, which annoyed many users.

Meanwhile, in 2004, college students Mark Zuckerberg, Eduardo Saverin, Dustin Moskovitz, and Chris Hughes had launched Facebook, initially as a service available only to Harvard University students, but later as a service for the general public in 2006. A growing awareness of social networking (and the large News Corp. acquisition of MySpace) made it relatively easy to find investors for the company, and Facebook quickly raised nearly $50 million in venture capital. This enabled the company to avoid advertising sales in its early years, helping the site to retain a cleaner looking design. Facebook also had a reputation for better security than MySpace, and had a platform that allowed outside developers to create features for the site. While MySpace was being run by corporate managers who attempted to develop all of its applications in-house, Facebook was letting the marketplace determine what it would become, leading to a huge proliferation of social games, product reviews, and self-created groups. Facebook also made it easy for users to restrict who could see their information, which (according to Zuckerberg) made them more likely to share more personal information on the site. Whereas MySpace had been the social networking site of choice for teenagers, Facebook began to dominate the 18–30 year old crowd, rapidly becoming the number one site in the world for exchanging photos and information. Corporations began setting up their own Facebook pages, and the site began to be an important vehicle for developing brands. In 2007, Facebook began offering advertising sales, which it could closely target to users based on demographics, geographical location, and other preferences. In the spring of 2008, Facebook overtook MySpace in terms of overall number of users. From that point on, MySpace suffered a rapid decline in users. By 2010, MySpace had all but conceded defeat and announced that it would focus on the niche of "social entertainment." After losing a reported $350 million in 2010, it laid off half its staff in early 2011.[e] Facebook, on the other hand, continued to grow at a staggering pace, accumulating 901 million users by 2012[f], and more than 1.4 billion active users by mid-2015.

Twitter was launched in 2006 in Jack Dorsey with a somewhat different angle— it was a "microblogging" site where users were restricted to posting short messages (known as "tweets") of up to 140 characters. Users could then subscribe to view other users' messages (this is known as "following"). The messages were visible to the public by default, but users could restrict the messages to only their followers if they chose. According to popular lore, Twitter's tipping point in adoption came at the 2007 South by Southwest Interactive Conference (an important film, interactive media, and music conference held in Austin, Texas, every Spring) where two large plasma screens had been placed in the hallways to stream twitter messages exclusively. The tweets were captivating, and soon the entire conference was buzzing about this new social medium. Twitter's revenue model was based on paid advertising by organizations that wanted to purchase "promoted tweets" based on search terms (similar to Google's Adwords). By 2012, Twitter had 112 million active users, and by the first quarter of 2015, it had 288 million average users per month.[g] Though Twitter's growth had been impressive, many observers did not believe it posed a serious threat to Facebook as its reliance on the "tweeting" model meant that it appealed only to a subset of Facebook users (other Facebook users were more motivated to maintain pages with photos, group memberships, etc.), and Facebook had countered the Twitter threat by incorporating similar features (such as status updates with real-time updating) in its "news feed" application. Making matters worse for Twitter, a new entrant, Instagram, threatened to usurp Twitter's role in microblogging. Launched in late 2010, Instagram (from "instant camera" and "telegram") focused on enabling users to share photos and videos with short comments. It took off rapidly with a young audience, and had accrued 30 million users by 2012. Worried that it might miss out on a new social networking demographic, Facebook acquired Instagram in 2012 for about $1 billion. Instagram grew to 300 million active users by 2015, making it a solid rival to Twitter.[h]

There were dozens of other social networking sites that emerged over this time period, including several that gained wide popularity within more narrowly defined markets. Hi5, for example, was founded in 2003, growing out of a matchmaking site for South Asian singles. This would become a very popular social networking site in Asia, attracting nearly 5 million users by 2007. LinkedIn took a more serious approach and positioned itself more as a professional networking site. Though never gaining popularity among the young people that drove the huge traffic on sites such as Myspace and Facebook, it grew steadily and reached 332 million users by 2015.

Analysts speculated that a bigger threat could be posed by Google. From 2007 to 2012, Google introduced a number of would-be competing social network platforms, including a Friendster-like site called Orkut, a social networking site development platform called OpenSocial, and a tool for social networking sites called Friend Connect. None of these gained much traction, however. Google then developed a product to compete more directly with Twitter, called Google Buzz. However, by default this program made users' e-mail addresses publicly visible, leading a scandal in which the Electronic Privacy Information Center filed a complaint with the Federal Trade Commission claiming that that Buzz "violated user expectations, diminished user privacy, contradicted Google's privacy policy, and may have violated federal wiretap laws."[i] Google's settlement with the FTC subjected Google to privacy audits for the next 20 years.

Undeterred, in 2011, Google launched a product to compete directly against Facebook called Google+. Google+ enabled users to share photos and status

FIGURE 5.1
A Timeline of Social Networking Site Growth

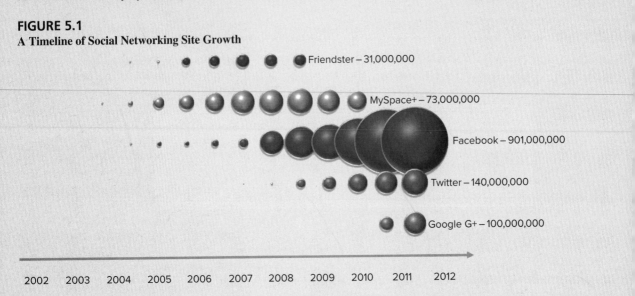

Friendster – 31,000,000

MySpace+ – 73,000,000

Facebook – 901,000,000

Twitter – 140,000,000

Google G+ – 100,000,000

2002 2003 2004 2005 2006 2007 2008 2009 2010 2011 2012

updates like Facebook; however, it also offered video chatting and stronger functionality to enable users to organize their contacts into groups—a move that was considered important to enhance users' privacy. By 2015, Google+ had 2.2 billion profiles posted online, but only 300 million users were active. Figure 5.1 provides a timeline of the growth of social networking sites.

Discussion Questions

1. Why did the first social networking sites fail? Is there anything they could have done to survive?
2. What factors made MySpace more successful than Friendster and SixDegrees.com? What factors enabled Facebook to overtake MySpace?
3. Are there significant switching costs that lock users into a particular social networking site?
4. What will determine if Google+ can overtake Facebook?

[a] Schilling, M. A. and Phelps, C. 2007. Interfirm collaboration networks: The impact of large-scale network structure on firm innovation, *Management Science*, 53: 1113–26.
[b] Anonymous, 2008. The social networking story. In *Technology Review*, July/August, p. 40.
[c] Piskorski, M. K., Eisenmann, T. R., Chen, D., and Feinstein, B. 2011. Facebook. Harvard Business School case 9-808-128.
[d] Anonymous, 2008. The social networking story. In *Technology Review*, July/August, p. 40.
[e] Hartung, A. 2011. How Facebook beat MySpace. *Forbes*, January 14.
[f] Data from Techcrunch.com and Comscore and www.venturebeat.com.
[g] Data from Techcrunch.com and Comscore and money.cnn.com.
[h] Primack, D. HYPERLINK http://fortune.com/2012/04/09/breaking-facebook-buying-instagram-for-1-billion/ "Breaking: Facebook buying Instagram for $1 billion." "CNNMoney.com" CNNMoney.com (2012), April 9th. "Instagram now bigger than twitter," Instagram Blog, (2014), BBC Newsbeat, December 11th.
[i] Piskorski, M. K., Eisenmann, T. R., Chen, D., and Feinstein, B. 2011. Facebook. Harvard Business School case 9-808-128.

OVERVIEW

The previous chapter pointed out that some industries are characterized by increasing returns to adoption, meaning that the more a technology is adopted, the more valuable it becomes. In such industries, timing can be crucial—a technology that is adopted earlier than others may reap self-reinforcing advantages such as greater funds to invest in improving the technology, greater availability of complementary goods, and less customer uncertainty. On the other hand, the same factors that cause increasing returns to adoption may make very early technologies unattractive: If there are few users of the technology or availability of complementary goods is poor, the technology may fail to attract customers. A number of other first-mover advantages, and disadvantages, can shape how timing of entry is related to likelihood of success.

first movers
The first entrants to sell in a new product or service category.

early followers
Entrants that are early to market, but not first.

late entrants
Entrants that do not enter the market until the time the product begins to penetrate the mass market or later.

Entrants are often divided into three categories: **first movers** (or pioneers), which are the first to sell in a new product or service category; **early followers** (also called early leaders), which are early to the market *but not first*; and **late entrants**, which enter the market when or after the product begins to penetrate the mass market. The research on whether it is better to be a first mover, early follower, or late entrant yields conflicting conclusions. Some studies that contrast early entrants (lumping first movers and early followers together) with late entrants find that early entrants have higher returns and survival rates, consistent with the notion of first-mover (or at least early-mover) advantage.[1] However, other research has suggested the first firm to market is often the first to fail, causing early followers to outperform first movers.[2] Still other research contends the higher returns of being a first mover typically offset the survival risk.[3] A number of factors influence how timing of entry affects firm survival and profits. In this chapter, we will first examine first-mover advantages and disadvantages. We will then look more closely at what factors determine the optimal timing of entry, and its implications for a firm's entry strategy.

FIRST-MOVER ADVANTAGES

Being a first mover may confer the advantages of brand loyalty and technological leadership, preemption of scarce assets, and exploitation of buyer switching costs.[4] Furthermore, in industries characterized by increasing returns, early entrants may accrue learning and network externality advantages that are self-reinforcing over time.[5]

Brand Loyalty and Technological Leadership

The company that introduces a new technology may earn a long-lasting reputation as a leader in that technology domain. Such a reputation can help sustain the company's image, brand loyalty, and market share even after competitors have introduced comparable products. The organization's position as technology leader also enables it to shape customer expectations about the technology's form, features, pricing, and other characteristics. By the time later entrants come to market, customer requirements may be well established. If aspects that customers have come to expect in a technology are difficult for competitors to imitate (e.g., if they are protected by patent or copyright, or arise from the first mover's unique capabilities), being the technology leader can yield sustained

monopoly rents
The additional returns (either higher revenues or lower costs) a firm can make from being a monopolist, such as the ability to set high prices, or the ability to lower costs through greater bargaining power over suppliers.

monopoly rents. Even if the technology characteristics are imitable, the first mover has an opportunity to build brand loyalty before the entry of other competitors.

Preemption of Scarce Assets

Firms that enter the market early can preemptively capture scarce resources such as key locations, government permits, patents, access to distribution channels, and relationships with suppliers.

For example, companies that wish to provide any wireless communication service must license the rights to broadcast over particular radio frequencies from the government. In the United States, the Federal Communications Commission (FCC) is primarily responsible for allotting rights to use bands of radio frequencies (known as the spectrum) for any wireless broadcasting. The FCC first allocates different portions of the spectrum for different purposes (digital television broadcasting, third-generation wireless telecommunication, etc.) and different geographic areas. It then auctions off rights to use these segments to the highest bidders. This means that early movers in wireless services can preemptively capture the rights to use portions of the wireless spectrum for their own purposes, while effectively blocking other providers. By 2003, the proliferation of wireless services had caused the spectrum to become a scarce commodity, and the FCC was under pressure to allow the holders of wireless spectrum rights to sublet unused portions of their spectrum to other organizations.

Exploiting Buyer Switching Costs

Once buyers have adopted a good, they often face costs to switch to another good. For example, the initial cost of the good is itself a switching cost, as is the cost of complements purchased for the good. Additionally, if a product is complex, buyers must spend time becoming familiar with its operation; this time investment becomes a switching cost that deters the buyer from switching to a different product. If buyers face switching costs, the firm that captures customers early may be able to keep those customers even if technologies with a superior value proposition are introduced later. This is often the reason given for the dominance of the QWERTY typewriter keyboard. In 1867, Christopher Sholes began experimenting with building a typewriter. At that time, letters were struck on paper by mechanical keys. If two keys were struck in rapid succession, they often would jam. Key jamming was a particularly significant problem in the 1800s, because typewriters then were designed so that keys struck the back side of the paper, making it impossible for users to see what they were typing. The typist thus might not realize he or she had been typing with jammed keys until after removing the page. Scholes designed his keyboard so that commonly used letter combinations were scattered as widely as possible over the keyboard. The QWERTY keyboard also puts a disproportionate burden on the left hand (3,000 English words can be typed with the left hand alone, while only 300 can be typed with the right hand alone). This positioning of keys would slow the typing of letter combinations, and thus reduce the likelihood of jamming the keys.[6]

Over time, many competing typewriter keyboards were introduced that boasted faster typing speeds or less-tiring typing. For example, the Hammand and Blickensderfer "Ideal" keyboard put the most commonly used letters in the bottom row for easy access, and used only three rows total. Another example, the Dvorak keyboard, placed all five vowels and the three most commonly used consonants in the home row, and common letter combinations required alternating hands frequently, reducing fatigue. However, QWERTY's early dominance meant typists were trained only on QWERTY keyboards. By the time Dvorak keyboards were introduced in 1932, tens of millions of typists were committed to QWERTY keyboards—the switching costs of learning how to type all over again were more than people were willing to bear.[7] Even after daisy-wheel keys (and later, electronic typewriters) removed all possibility of jamming keys, the QWERTY keyboard remained firmly entrenched. August Dvorak is said to have died a bitter man, claiming, "I'm tired of trying to do something worthwhile for the human race. They simply don't want to change!"[8]

Reaping Increasing Returns Advantages

In an industry with pressures encouraging adoption of a dominant design, the timing of a firm's investment in new technology development may be particularly critical to its likelihood of success. For example, in an industry characterized by increasing returns to adoption, there can be powerful advantages to being an early provider; a technology that is adopted early may rise in market power through self-reinforcing positive feedback mechanisms, culminating in its entrenchment as a dominant design. Intel is an apt example of this.

Intel's Ted Hoff invented the first microprocessor in 1971, and in 1975, Bill Gates and Paul Allen showed that it could run a version of BASIC that Gates had written. Gates's BASIC became widely circulated among computer enthusiasts, and as BASIC was adopted and applications developed for it, the applications were simultaneously optimized for Intel's architecture. IBM's adoption of Intel's 8088 microprocessor in its PC introduction secured Intel's dominant position, and each of Intel's subsequent generations of products has set the market standard.[9]

FIRST-MOVER DISADVANTAGES

Despite the great attention that first-mover advantages receive, there are also arguments for not entering a market too early. In a historical study of 50 product categories, Gerard Tellis and Peter Golder found that market pioneers have a high failure rate—roughly 47 percent—and that the mean market share of market pioneers is 10 percent.[10] By contrast, early leaders (firms that enter after market pioneers but assume market leadership during the early growth phase of the product life cycle) averaged almost three times the market share of market pioneers.[11] Tellis and Golder point out that the market may often perceive first movers to have advantages because it has misperceived who the first mover really was. For example, while today few people would dispute Procter & Gamble's claim that it "created the disposable diaper market,"[12] in actuality, Procter & Gamble entered the disposable market almost 30 years after Chux, a brand owned by a subsidiary of Johnson & Johnson. In the mid-1960s, *Consumer Reports* ranked both products as best buys. However, over time Pampers became very successful and Chux disappeared, and eventually people began to reinterpret history.

Other studies have found that first movers earn greater revenues than other entrants, but that they also face higher costs, causing them to earn significantly lower profits in the long run.[13] First movers typically bear the bulk of the research and development expenses for their product or service technologies, and they must also often pay to develop suppliers and distribution channels, plus consumer awareness. A later entrant often can capitalize on the research and development investment of the first mover, fine-tune the product to customer needs as the market becomes more certain, avoid any mistakes made by the earlier entrant, and exploit **incumbent inertia**.[14] Later entrants can also adopt newer and more efficient production processes while early movers are either stuck with earlier technologies or must pay to rebuild their production systems.[15]

incumbent inertia

The tendency for incumbents to be slow to respond to changes in the industry environment due to their large size, established routines, or prior strategic commitments to existing suppliers and customers.

Research and Development Expenses

Developing a new technology often entails significant research and development expenses, and the first to develop and introduce a technology typically bears the brunt of this expense. By the time a firm has successfully developed a new technology, it may have borne not only the expense of that technology but also the expense of exploring technological paths that did not yield a commercially viable product. This firm also typically bears the cost of developing necessary production processes and complementary goods that are not available on the market. Since the new product development failure rate can be as high as 95 percent, being the first to develop and introduce an unproven new technology is expensive and risky.

By contrast, later entrants often do not have to invest in exploratory research. Once a product has been introduced to the market, competitors can often ascertain how the product was created. The later entrant can also observe the market's response to particular features of the technology and decide how to focus its development efforts. Thus, the later entrant can both save development expense and produce a product that achieves a closer fit with market preferences.

Undeveloped Supply and Distribution Channels

When a firm introduces a new-to-the-world technology, often no appropriate suppliers or distributors exist. The firm may face the daunting task of developing and producing its own supplies and distribution service, or assisting in the development of supplier and developer markets. For example, when DEKA Research began developing its self-balancing IBOT wheelchair, it needed a type of ball bearing for which there were no suppliers. DEKA was forced to develop a machine to mold the bearings. According to Dean Kamen, the company's founder, "Nobody here planned to invent new ball bearings, but in order to make this engine practical we have to develop a bearing technology that doesn't exist."[16]

Immature Enabling Technologies and Complements

enabling technologies

Component technologies that are necessary for the performance or desirability of a given innovation.

When firms develop technologies, they often rely on other producers of **enabling technologies**. For instance, the opening vignette demonstrated that even though producers of personal digital assistants (PDAs) had created palm-size devices with significant computing power, the potential of these devices would be delivered only if battery and modem technologies were further developed. Since few PDA manufacturers were actually involved in the development of batteries or modems, they were reliant on the development efforts of other firms.

Fuel cells create electricity from a reaction between hydrogen and oxygen, and are much more efficient than internal combustion gasoline engines. Whereas a typical internal combustion engine converts less than 20 percent of the energy potential of gasoline into power for the automobile, fuel cells capture 40 percent to 60 percent of the energy potential of their fuel source, which can be any hydrogen-rich liquid or gas.[a] Hydrogen is one of the most abundant elements on earth and can be obtained in a number of ways, including electrolysis of water or steam conversion of methanol. Furthermore, the only waste products of hydrogen fuel cells are water vapor and carbon dioxide. Hydrogen thus offers an inexhaustible and environmentally friendly fuel source.[b] Utilizing hydrogen to power vehicles (among other things) offers the promise of reducing reliance on dwindling fossil fuel reserves while dramatically decreasing the environmental impact of automobiles. Many of the key players in fuel cell development envision a "hydrogen economy" whereby automobiles with hydrogen fuel cells are used to supply power to homes and offices, eventually replacing the existing electrical power grids.

Fuel cells were developed more than 150 years ago, but were initially too bulky and expensive to be used in automobiles. In the 1970s, however, the energy crisis sparked a resurgence in fuel cell development, and a number of prototypes emerged through the late 1970s and 1980s. By the 1990s, several auto manufacturers, including Toyota and Daimler had developed automobiles powered by fuel cells and were planning commercial production. A number of serious obstacles, however, stood in the way of fuel cell adoption by the mass market. The most serious of these was the lack of a complementary refueling infrastructure. Before fuel cell vehicles could be promoted to the mass market, refueling options had to be developed that would be convenient and easy for consumers to use. This was no small feat—the existing fuel stations that were ubiquitous in almost every corner of the globe could not handle a gaseous fuel such as hydrogen. While liquid gasoline can be stored in almost any type of container, hydrogen gas is liquid only under very high pressure and has very small molecules. It would rapidly leak out of existing gasoline storage containers. Both fueling stations and automobiles would need to be able to keep compressed hydrogen in a pressurized tank. Furthermore, many of the existing gasoline stations were owned or otherwise connected to oil companies. Since it was not yet clear what role oil companies would play in the hydrogen economy, many suspected that oil companies would use their resources and lobbying power to resist the adoption of hydrogen fuel cells. To unleash the power of the "hydrogen economy" vision would not only require heavy investment in new infrastructure, but also require resolving or overcoming the conflicting interests of numerous stakeholders, including government, utilities, auto manufacturers, oil producers, and consumers.

[a] www.doe.gov.
[b] J. Rifkin, "The Hydrogen Economy," *E Magazine*, January–February 2003, pp. 26–37.

As discussed in Chapter Four, many products also require complementary goods to be useful or valuable. Computers need software, cameras need film, automobiles need service, gasoline, and roads. When new technologies are introduced to a market, important complements may not yet be fully developed, thus hindering adoption of the innovation. The development of vehicles powered by hydrogen fuel cells (see the above Theory in Action) provides an excellent example of how a lack of complementary technologies and infrastructure can pose serious obstacles for early movers.

Uncertainty of Customer Requirements

A first mover to the market may face considerable uncertainty about what product features customers will ultimately desire and how much they will be willing to pay for them. For a very new product technology, market research may be of little help.

Customers may have little idea of the value of the technology or the role it would play in their lives. As a consequence, first movers may find that their early product offerings must be revised as the market begins to reveal customer preferences.

For instance, when Kodak introduced the 8-mm video camera in the late 1980s, it expected that customers would flock to the design's smaller size and superior recording ability. Instead, consumers rejected the product. The 8-mm video cameras were more expensive, and consumers had not yet recognized a need for this product and were unsure of what value it could provide. Kodak decided to withdraw from the market. However, by the early 1990s, consumers had become more comfortable with the concept of 8-mm video camera technology, and several competitors (most notably Sony) successfully entered this market.

First movers have an opportunity to shape customer preferences by establishing the precedent for product design in the newly emerging market and by investing in customer education. Customer education efforts are expensive, however. If the product is slow to begin to reap revenues for the sponsoring firm, it may collapse under the weight of its R&D and marketing expenses. Figure 5.2 provides a number of product categories with their first movers, prominent followers, and which of these were ultimately more successful.

FIGURE 5.2
First Movers and Followers— Who Wins?

Source: R. M. Grant, *Contemporary Strategy Analysis* (Malden, MA: Blackwell Publishers, 1998); D. Teece, *The Competitive Challenge: Strategies for Industrial Innovation and Renewal* (Cambridge, MA: Ballinger, 1987); and M. A. Schilling, "Technology Success and Failure in Winner-Take-All Markets: Testing a Model of Technological Lock Out," *Academy of Management Journal* 45 (2002), pp. 387–98.

Product	First Mover	Notable Follower(s)	The Winner
8-mm video camera	Kodak	Sony	Follower
Disposable diaper	Chux	Pampers Kimberly Clark	Followers
Float glass	Pilkington	Corning	First mover
Groupware	Lotus	AT&T	First mover
Instant camera	Polaroid	Kodak	First mover
Microprocessors	Intel	AMD Cyrix	First mover
Microwave	Raytheon	Samsung	Follower
Personal computer	MITS (Altair)	Apple IBM	Followers
Personal computer operating system	Digital Research	Microsoft (MS-DOS)	Follower
Smartphones	IBM (Simon)	Apple Nokia	Followers
Social networking sites	SixDegrees.com	MySpace Facebook	Followers
Spreadsheet software	VisiCalc	Microsoft (Excel) Lotus	Followers
Video game console	Magnavox	Atari Nintendo	Followers
Web browser	NCSA Mosaic	Netscape Microsoft (Internet Explorer)	Followers
Word processing software	MicroPro (WordStar)	Microsoft (MS Word) WordPerfect	Followers
Workstation	Xerox Alto	Sun Microsystems Hewlett-Packard	Followers

FACTORS INFLUENCING OPTIMAL TIMING OF ENTRY

In very early market stages, a technology may be underdeveloped and its fit with customer needs unknown. In late market stages, a technology may be well understood, but competitors may have already captured controlling shares of the market. How does a firm decide whether to attempt to pioneer a technology category or to wait while others do so? The answer will depend on several factors, including customer certainty, the margin of improvement offered by the new technology, the state of enabling technologies and complementary goods, the threat of competitive entry, the degree to which the industry exhibits increasing returns, and the firm's resources.

1. How certain are customer preferences?

When new-to-the-world technologies are first developed, customers may have difficulty understanding the technology and its role in their life. Both producers and customers may face considerable ambiguity about the importance of various features of the technology. As producers and customers gain experience with the technology, features that initially seemed compelling may turn out to be unnecessary, and features that had seemed unimportant may turn out to be crucial. For example, many of the companies that raced to establish an online presence in the e-commerce frenzy of the late 1990s believed that their Web sites needed exciting graphics and sounds to be competitive. Graphics and sound, however, turned out to be the downfall of many early Web sites. Many customers did not have high-speed Internet access or computers with enough processing power to quickly download the Web sites, making multimedia Web sites an annoyance rather than an attraction.

The reverse scenario is demonstrated in Sony's introduction of the Play-Station2. When Sony introduced its multifeatured PlayStation2, many industry analysts believed that Sony had overestimated consumer interest in having a game console that would play music CDs or DVD movies. It turned out, however, that Sony may have *underestimated* the desirability of these features. Video game consoles are typically sold at cost (or at a loss) in order to rapidly build an installed base. Profits are then made on game royalties. However, when consumers realized that the PlayStation2 was a very affordable combination of game console and high-quality DVD player, many consumers bought the system for its DVD capabilities first and game capabilities second. Many of these consumers bought very few games, causing Sony's strategy of subsidizing the console with the intention of making money on the games to backfire. Observing this, Microsoft disabled DVD playback on its Xbox unless consumers purchased an add-on DVD playback kit.

Not all pioneers face customer uncertainty—some innovations are developed in response to well-understood customer needs. Customer requirements may have been long known even if the method of meeting them was not. For example, the developers of Tagamet (a medication for patients with chronic heartburn or ulcers) faced very little customer uncertainty. Customers wanted an affordable, easy-to-use solution to their stomach discomfort. Once a method of achieving this objective had been developed, tested, and approved, its developers raced the product to market in hopes of patenting it and securing market share ahead of competing products. Other things being equal, less customer uncertainty favors earlier timing of entry.

2. How much improvement does the innovation provide over previous solutions?

The degree to which the technology represents an improvement over previous technologies increases a firm's likelihood of successful early entry. That is, when a technology makes a dramatic improvement over previous generations or different technologies that serve similar functions, it will more rapidly gain customer acceptance. There will be less ambiguity about the value of the technology and more early adoptions (as well as more support by complementary goods providers); as a consequence, customer expectations should become known sooner, and adoptions should be more rapid.[17]

3. Does the innovation require enabling technologies, and are these technologies sufficiently mature?

As mentioned earlier, many innovations rely on crucial enabling technologies to ensure their performance. A high-definition television set is of little value if networks are incapable of broadcasting in high definition; cellular phones or portable stereos would have little value if small and long-lasting batteries were unavailable. A developer must identify which enabling technologies will affect the performance of the new innovation and assess the degree to which those technologies are mature enough (or *will be* mature enough) to deliver the desired performance. More mature enabling technologies allow earlier entry; less mature enabling technologies may favor waiting for enabling technologies to be further developed.

4. Do complementary goods influence the value of the innovation, and are they sufficiently available?

If the value of an innovation hinges critically on the availability and quality of complementary goods, then the state of complementary goods determines the likelihood of successful entry. Not all innovations require complementary goods, and many more innovations can utilize existing complementary goods. For example, though numerous innovations in 35-mm cameras have been introduced in the last few decades, almost all have remained compatible with standard rolls of 35-mm film; thus availability of that complementary good was ensured. If, on the other hand, the innovation requires the development of new complementary goods, then a pioneer must find a way to ensure their availability. Some firms have the resources and capabilities to develop both a good and its complements, while others do not. If the firm's innovation requires complementary goods that are not available on the market, and the firm is unable to develop those complements, successful early entry is unlikely.

5. How high is the threat of competitive entry?

If there are significant entry barriers or few potential competitors with the resources and capabilities to enter the market, the firm may be able to wait while customer requirements and the technology evolve. Over time, one would expect customer expectations to become more certain, enabling technologies to improve, and support goods and services to be developed, thus increasing the likelihood that sponsored technologies will possess a set of attributes that meet consumer demands. However, if the technology proves to be valuable, other firms are also likely to be attracted to the market. Thus, if entry barriers are low, the market could quickly become quite competitive, and entering a market that has already become highly competitive can be much more challenging than entering an emerging market.[18] Margins may already have been

Research Brief Whether and When to Enter?

In a study of 30 years of data on entry into the medical diagnostic imaging industry, Will Mitchell examined the factors that drive whether and when a firm that is an incumbent in one subfield of an industry chooses to enter a newly emerging subfield of the industry.[a] For instance, what determines whether and when a manufacturer of conventional X-ray machines decides to go into magnetic resonance imaging (MRI) equipment? While new goods offer opportunities for growth, they can cannibalize existing products, and they also require an investment in new skills. Incumbents often are slow to enter new technical subfields.[b] They may be intentionally waiting for industry turbulence to subside, or they may be unintentionally slowed by factors that create inertia, such as the difficulty in altering well-established routines and strategic commitments to the firm's existing supplier and customer base.

Mitchell pointed out that entry barriers and imitability of a new product (for example, whether it can be effectively protected by patents) interact to create different incentives for timing. First, if only one firm can produce an inimitable good, it can enter if and when it wants. However, if several firms could produce a good that will subsequently be inimitable, they may race to do so to capture the market. In such a circumstance, being early confers a significant advantage. Finally, if the good is expected to be highly imitable (for example, if it would be difficult to effectively protect with patents because competitors could easily invent around the patent), then firms will prefer to wait while others bear the expense of developing and introducing the good. There are disincentives to being early to market.[c]

Mitchell found that firms that had more specialized assets that would be useful in the new subfield (for example, a well-established distribution system that could be used for the new imaging equipment) were more likely to enter the new subfield. A firm was also more likely to enter if the products it currently produced were threatened by the new products (i.e., if the new technology was likely to displace the firm's current technology as the dominant choice in the market). Furthermore, the incumbent was likely to enter *earlier* if its core products were threatened and there were several potential rivals.

[a] W. Mitchell, "Whether and When? Probability of Incumbent's Entry into Emerging Technical Subfields," *Administrative Science Quarterly* 38 (1989), pp. 208–30.
[b] F. M. Scherer, *Industrial Market Structure and Economic Performance*, 2nd ed. (Chicago: Rand McNally, 1980).
[c] M. Katz and C. Shapiro, "Technology Adoption in the Presence of Network Externalities," *Journal of Political Economy* 94 (1986), pp. 822–41.

driven down to levels that require competitors to be highly efficient, and access to distribution channels may be limited. If the threat of competitive entry is high, the firm may need to enter earlier to establish brand image, capture market share, and secure relationships with suppliers and distributors. This is discussed further in the Research Brief "Whether and When to Enter?"

6. Is the industry likely to experience increasing returns to adoption?

In industries that have increasing returns to adoption due to strong learning curve effects or network externalities, allowing competitors to get a head start in building an installed base can be very risky. If a competitor's offering builds a significant installed base, the cycle of self-reinforcing advantages could make it difficult for the firm to ever catch up. Furthermore, if there are forces encouraging adoption of a single dominant design, a competitor's technology may be selected. If protection mechanisms such as patents prevent the firm from offering a compatible technology, the firm may be locked out.[19]

7. Can the firm withstand early losses?

As was discussed earlier, a first mover often bears the bulk of the expense and risk of developing and introducing a new innovation. First movers thus often need significant amounts of capital that either is available internally (in the case of large firms) or can be accessed externally (e.g., through the debt or equity markets). Furthermore, the first mover must be able to withstand a significant period with little sales revenue from the product. Even in the case of successful new technologies, often a considerable period elapses between the point at which a first mover introduces a new innovation and the point at which the innovation begins to be adopted by the mass market. The s-curve shape of technology diffusion (discussed in Chapter Three and Chapter Thirteen) illustrates this aptly. New innovations tend to be adopted very slowly at first, while innovators and early adopters try the technology and communicate their experience to others. This slow initial takeoff of new innovations has caused the demise of many start-up firms. For example, in the personal digital assistant (PDA) industry—the pre-cursor to smartphones—start-ups such as GO Corporation and Momenta had received accolades for their technology designs, but were unable to withstand the long period of market confusion about PDAs and ultimately ran out of capital. Companies such as IBM and Compaq survived because they were large and diversified, and thus not reliant on PDA revenues. Palm was a relatively late mover in the PDA industry so it did not have to withstand as long of a takeoff period, but even Palm was forced to seek external capital and was acquired by U.S. Robotics, which was later bought by 3COM.

On the other hand, firms with significant resources also may be able to more easily catch up to earlier entrants.[20] By spending aggressively on development and advertising, and leveraging relationships with distributors, a late entrant may be able to rapidly build brand image and take market share away from earlier movers. For example, though Nestlé was very late to enter the freeze-dried coffee market with Taster's Choice, the company was able to use its substantial resources to both develop a superior product and rapidly build market awareness. It was thus able to quickly overtake the lead from General Foods' Maxim.[21]

8. Does the firm have resources to accelerate market acceptance?

A firm with significant capital resources not only has the capability to withstand a slow market takeoff, but also can invest such resources in accelerating market take-off. The firm can invest aggressively in market education, supplier and distributor development, and development of complementary goods and services. Each of these strategies can accelerate the early adoption of the innovation, giving the firm much greater discretion over entering early.[22] These strategies are discussed in more detail in Chapter Thirteen. Thus, a firm's capital resources can give it some influence on the shape of the adoption curve.

9. Is the firm's reputation likely to reduce the uncertainty of customers, suppliers, and distributors?

In addition to capital resources, a firm's reputation and credibility can also influence its optimal timing of entry.[23] A firm's reputation can send a strong signal about its likelihood of success with a new technology. Customers, suppliers, and distributors will use the firm's track record to assess its technological expertise and market prowess. Customers may use the firm's reputation as a signal of the innovation's quality, and thus face less ambiguity about adopting the innovation. A firm with a well-respected reputation for successful technological leadership is also more likely to attract suppliers and distributors.[24] This was aptly demonstrated in Microsoft's entry into the videogame console industry: Despite having little experience in producing hardware, suppliers and distributors eagerly agreed to work with Microsoft because of its track record in personal computing. Other things being equal, an entrant with a strong reputation can attract adoptions earlier than entrants without strong reputations.

STRATEGIES TO IMPROVE TIMING OPTIONS

As should now be clear, managing the timing of entry into the market is a complex matter. If the technology has a clear advantage to consumers, entering the market early may give the entrant a path-dependent advantage that is nearly impossible for competitors to overcome. If, on the other hand, a firm enters a market very early and the advantages of the technology are not very clear to consumers, there is a strong possibility that the technology will receive a tepid welcome. Confounding this risk is the fact that watchful competitors may be able to use the firm's failure to their advantage, refining the technology the firm has introduced to the market and making any corrections necessary to improve the technology's market acceptance. The later entrant may be able to enter at a lower cost because it can capitalize on the research and development of the early firm, and use knowledge of the market gained from observing the early entrant's experience.

In the above, it is assumed that timing of entry is a matter of *choice* for the firm. However, implicit in this assumption is a corollary assumption that the firm is capable of producing the technology at any point in the time horizon under consideration. For this to be true, the firm must possess the core capabilities required to produce the technology to consumer expectations, or be able to develop them quickly. Furthermore, if the firm intends to refine an earlier entrant's technology and beat the earlier entrant to market with a new version of this technology, it must have *fast-cycle development processes*. If a firm has very fast cycle development processes, the firm not only has a better chance at being an early entrant, but it can also use experience gained through customers' reactions to its technology to quickly introduce a refined version of its technology that achieves a closer fit with customer requirements. In essence, a firm with very fast development deployment processes should be able to take advantage of both first- and second-mover advantages. The research on new product development cycle time indicates that development time can be greatly shortened by using strategic alliances, cross-functional new product development teams, and **parallel development processes**. Chapter Eleven will deal specifically with how firms can ensure that their innovations are deployed rapidly to the market.

parallel development process
When multiple stages of the new product development process occur simultaneously.

Summary of Chapter

1. A first mover may be able to build brand loyalty and a reputation for technological leadership, preemptively capture scarce resources, and exploit buyer switching costs.

2. First movers may also benefit from increasing returns to adoption due to learning curve effects and network externalities.

3. Some studies, however, argue that first movers may have higher failure rates. First movers have to bear the brunt of R&D expenses and may face considerable consumer ambiguity. Second movers can capitalize on the R&D and marketing efforts of the first mover, producing a technology that costs less to develop and that corrects for any of the first mover's mistakes.

4. First movers may also face poorly developed supplier markets, distribution channels, and availability of complementary goods, all of which can increase the challenge of successfully launching their new product or service. Enabling technologies may also be immature, hindering the new technology's performance.

5. The biggest disadvantage many first movers face is uncertainty over customer requirements. Customers themselves may be uncertain about what features or form they desire in a new innovation. A firm may have to withstand significant losses before customer preferences become more certain.

6. The optimal timing of entry is thus a function of several factors, including the margin of advantage offered by the new innovation, the state of enabling technologies and complements, the state of customer expectations, the threat of competitive entry, whether the industry faces increasing returns, and a firm's resources.

7. Firms that have fast-cycle development processes have more options when it comes to timing. Not only does a fast-cycle developer have an advantage in introducing innovations earlier, but it also can be its own fast follower by quickly introducing refined versions of its own technology.

Discussion Questions

1. What are some advantages of entering a market early? Are there any advantages to entering a market late?

2. Name a successful (*a*) first mover, (*b*) early follower, and (*c*) late entrant. Identify unsuccessful examples of each.

3. What factors might make some industries harder to pioneer than others? Are there industries in which there is no penalty for late entry?

Suggested Further Reading

Classics

David, P. A., "Clio and the economics of QWERTY," *American Economic Review* 75 (1985), pp. 332–38.

Lieberman, M. B., and D. B. Montgomery, "First-mover (dis)advantages: Retrospective and link with the resource-based view," *Strategic Management Journal* 19 (1998):1111–25.

Spence, M., "The learning Curve and Competition," *Bell Journal of Economics* 12 (1981), pp. 49–70.

Tellis, G. J., and P. N. Golder, "First to Market, First to Fail? Real Causes of Enduring Market Leadership," *Sloan Management Review* 37, no. 2 (1996), pp. 65–75.

Recent Work

Argyres, N., L. Bigelow, and J. A. Nickerson, "Dominant Designs, Innovation Shocks and the Follower's Dilemma," *Strategic Management Journal* 36 (2015), pp. 216–234.

DiMasi, J. A., and L. B. Faden, "Competitiveness in follow-on drug R&D: A race or imitation?" *Nature Reviews Drug Discovery* 10 (2011), pp. 23–27.

Katila, R., and E. L. Chen, "Effects of search timing on innovation: The value of not being in sync with rivals," *Administrative Science Quarterly* 53 (2008), pp. 593–625.

Suarez, F. F., S. Grodal, S., and A. Gotsopoulos, "Perfect timing? Dominant category, dominant design, and the window of opportunity for firm entry," *Strategic Management Journal* 36 (2015), pp. 437–448.

Endnotes

1. R. Agarwal, "Technological Activity and Survival of Firms," *Economics Letters* 52 (July 1996), pp. 101–8; R. Agarwal, "Survival of Firms over the Product Life Cycle," *Southern Economic Journal* 63, no. 3 (1997), pp. 571–84; and R. Agarwal and G. Michael, "The Evolution of Markets and Entry, Exit, and Survival of Firms," *Review of Economics and Statistics* 78 (November 1996), pp. 489–98.

2. P. Golder and G. Tellis, "Pioneer Advantage: Marketing Logic or Marketing Legend?" *Journal of Marketing Research* 30 (May 1993), pp. 158–70.

3. W. Robinson and M. Sungwook, "Is the First to Market the First to Fail? Empirical Evidence for Industrial Goods Businesses," *Journal of Marketing Research* 39 (2002), pp. 120–28.

4. M. Lieberman and D. Montgomery, "First Mover Advantages: A Survey," *Strategic Management Journal* 9 (1988), pp. 41–58.

5. Ibid.; and M. Spence, "The Learning Curve and Competition," *Bell Journal of Economics* 12 (1981), pp. 49–70.

6. Diamond, "The Curse of QWERTY," *Discover* 18, no. 4 (1997), pp. 34–42.

7. P. A. David, "Clio and the Economics of QWERTY," *American Economic Review* 75 (1985), pp. 332–38.

8. Diamond, "The Curse of QWERTY."

9. C. Ferguson and C. Morris, *Computer Wars* (New York: Random House, 1993).

10. P. N. Golder and G. Tellis, "Pioneer Advantage: Marketing Logic or Marketing Legend," *Journal of Marketing Research* 20 (1993), pp. 158–70.

11. G. Tellis and P. Golder, "First to Market, First to Fail? Real Causes of Enduring Market Leadership," *Sloan Management Review*, Winter 1996, pp. 65–75.

12. Procter & Gamble Annual Report, 1977.

13. W. Boulding and M. Christen, "First-Mover Disadvantage," *Harvard Business Review*, October 2001.

14. M. Lieberman and D. Montgomery, "First Mover Advantages: A Survey," *Strategic Management Journal* 9 (1988), pp. 41–58.

15. Boulding and Christen, "First-Mover Disadvantage."

16. E. I. Schwartz, "The Inventor's Play-Ground," *Technology Review* 105, no. 8 (2002), p. 69.

17. A counterargument to this is made in S. Min, M. U. Kalwani, and W. T. Ronson, "Market Pioneer and Early Follower Survival Risks: A Contingency Analysis of Really New versus Incrementally New Product Markets," *Journal of Marketing* 70, no. 1 (2006), pp. 15–33.

18. G. L. Lilien and E. Yoon, "The Timing of Competitive Market Entry: An Exploratory Study of New Industrial Products," *Management Science* 36 (1990), pp. 568–85; R. Makadok, "Can First-Mover and Early-Mover Advantages Be Sustained in an Industry with Low Barriers

to Entry/Imitation?" *Strategic Management Journal* 19 (1998), pp. 683–96; and R. W. Shaw and S. A. Shaw, "Late Entry, Market Shares and Competitive Survival: The Case of Synthetic Fibers," *Managerial and Decision Economics* 5 (1984), pp. 72–79.

19. W. B. Arthur, "Competing Technologies, Increasing Returns, and Lock-In by Historical Events," *The Economic Journal*, March 1989, pp. 116–31; and M. Schilling, "Technological Lock Out: An Integrative Model of the Economic and Strategic Factors Driving Technology Success and Failure," *Academy of Management Review* 23 (1998), pp. 267–84.

20. J. Shamsie, C. Phelps, and J. Kuperman, "Better Late than Never: A Study of Late Entrants in Household Electrical Equipment," *Strategic Management Journal* 25 (2003), pp. 69–84.

21. D. A. Aaker and G. S. Day, "The Perils of High-Growth Markets," *Strategic Management Journal* 7 (1986), pp. 409–21; Shamsie, Phelps, and Kuperman, "Better Late than Never;" V. Shankar, G. S. Carpenter, and L. Krishnamurthi, "Late Mover Advantage: How Innovative Late Entrants Outsell Pioneers," *Journal of Marketing Research* 35, no. 1 (1998), pp. 54–70; and G. L. Urban, T. Carter, S. Gaskin, and Z. Mucha, "Market Share Rewards to Pioneering Brands: An Empirical Analysis and Strategic Implications," *Management Science* 32 (1986), pp. 645–59.

22. M. A. Schilling, "Technological Leapfrogging: Lessons from the U.S. Video Game Console Industry," *California Management Review* 45, no. 3 (2003), pp. 6–32.

23. D. A. Shepherd and M. Shanley, *New Venture Strategy: Timing, Environmental Uncertainty and Performance* (London: Sage, 1998).

24. Schilling, "Technological Leapfrogging."

Part Two

Formulating Technological Innovation Strategy

In this section, we will cover the key aspects of formulating a technological innovation strategy, including:

- Assessing the firm's position and defining its strategic direction.
- Choosing innovation projects in which to invest, including both quantitative and qualitative valuation techniques.
- Deciding whether and how the firm will collaborate on development activities, choosing a collaboration mode, and choosing and monitoring partners.
- Crafting a strategy for protecting—or diffusing—a technological innovation through such methods as patents, trademarks, copyrights, and trade secrets.

Formulating Technological Innovation Strategy

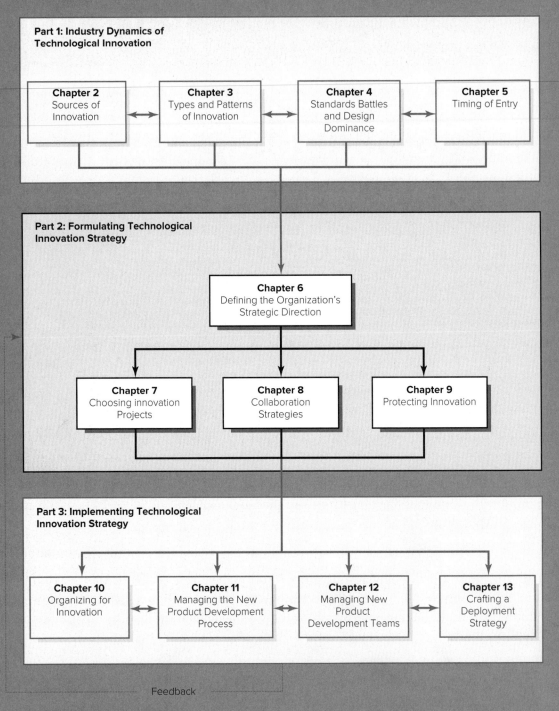

Part 1: Industry Dynamics of Technological Innovation

Chapter 2
Sources of Innovation

Chapter 3
Types and Patterns of Innovation

Chapter 4
Standards Battles and Design Dominance

Chapter 5
Timing of Entry

Part 2: Formulating Technological Innovation Strategy

Chapter 6
Defining the Organization's Strategic Direction

Chapter 7
Choosing innovation Projects

Chapter 8
Collaboration Strategies

Chapter 9
Protecting Innovation

Part 3: Implementing Technological Innovation Strategy

Chapter 10
Organizing for Innovation

Chapter 11
Managing the New Product Development Process

Chapter 12
Managing New Product Development Teams

Chapter 13
Crafting a Deployment Strategy

Feedback

Chapter **Six**

Defining the Organization's Strategic Direction

Reinventing Hotels: citizenM

In 2008, Michael Levie, Rattan Chadha, and Robin Chadha set out to create a new kind of hotel chain. Convinced that innovation in the hotel industry had stagnated, they believed that there was an opportunity to create more value for customers that were frequent travelers, or "Mobile Citizens of the World." They named their new hotel chain "citizenM," and they set out to rethink what dimensions customers really cared about, and which they didn't really value.

First, the founders concluded that frequent travelers wanted to be in stylish and modern hotels that reflected their own identities, but they did not really care about front desks and porters—after all, who wants to wait in line after a long flight, and why would they need a porter to get the luggage to the room if they had already managed to get it from the airport? Instead, the chain could greatly reduce both costs and waiting lines by having self-service check-in machines that dispensed keys (similar to the self-service machines that dispense boarding passes at airports) and eliminating porters.[a]

Second, in cosmopolitan cities such as London or New York, Levie and the Chadhas did not believe that it made sense to try to compete with the local bars and restaurants by offering premium service inside the hotel. Instead they created a stylish and comfortable space with an open-plan round-the-clock kitchen, where customers can help themselves to a quick meal whenever they wanted by simply using their credit card.

Third, the founders reasoned that most travelers do not want to hang out in their hotel rooms. They thus made the bedrooms small and pod-like—similar to those offered in cruise ships.[b] A typical citizenM room is 172 square feet, significantly smaller than the average 280 square feet of a London hotel room or the average 250 square feet of a Manhattan hotel room.[c] However, they outfitted the rooms with king-sized beds and the kind of high quality bedding, upscale fixtures, big fluffy towels, and free Internet service that frequent travelers would be likely to have at home. The rooms also had "mood pads"—electronic tablets that guests could use to control the television, lighting, and temperature. The idea was to create "affordable luxury."[d]

By eliminating many of the costly features of a typical hotel, citizenM's construction and staffing costs averaged 40 percent less than other four-star hotels. This resulted in nightly prices that were roughly $50 less than those of other four-star hotels in its major markets. The combination of the comfortable and stylish ambiance with affordable prices resulted in occupancy rates that were consistently higher than industry averages—over 95 percent compared to 85 percent. As noted by Robin Chadha, "We've started from scratch, looked at the behavior of this new generation of travelers and built our company accordingly . . . . We're an online company with no reservations team—everything on the Internet—and we use technology to offset staff costs. All the savings, we pass on to our guests."[e] Within a year after opening, citizenM was ranked by the *Sunday Times*, CNBC, and *Fortune* as the best business hotel. It went on to win the "Trendiest Hotel in the World" from TripAdvisor (2010 & 2011), Fodor's 100 Hotel awards (2011), and "Best New Hotel Concept" from Entrepreneur (2013). By 2015, the chain had hotels in Amsterdam, Glasgow, London, New York, Paris, and Rotterdam.

Discussion Questions

1. What are some of the challenges and opportunities of competing in the hotel industry? How do you think the hotel industry (or travel industry more generally) has changed over time?

2. Can you identify different customer groups in the hotel industry? What are some of the ways that hotels attract these different groups?

3. What are the advantages and disadvantages of targeting a narrower niche of customers rather than trying to appeal to a wide range of hotel customers?

4. What are some of the ways that citizenM has substituted technology for labor? What are some of the benefits/risks of this approach?

5. Can you think of other ways to dramatically re-envision how a hotel might operate and attract guests? What are the advantages and disadvantages of your approach?

[a] Vermeulen, F. 2015. "Innovation: Stop doing obsolete things." *Forbes*, May 29th. (www.forbes.com)
[b] Anonymous. 2014. "robin, noreen, and rattan chadha." *Hospitality Design*, 36(5):126–127; Vermeulen, F. 2015. "Innovation: Stop doing obsolete things." *Forbes*, May 29th. (www.forbes.com)
[c] Bourke, J. 2013. "Going DUTCH." *Estates Gazette*, September 14th, pp. 72–74.
[d] www.citizenM.com (retrieved July 30, 2015)
[e] Schoenfeld, B. 2013. 2013 Business Travel Awards. Entrepreneur, May 2013, pp. 44–53.

OVERVIEW

The first step in formulating a company's technological innovation strategy is to assess its current position and define its strategic direction for the future. This chapter reviews some of the basic tools used in strategic analysis to assess the firm's current position and help chart its direction for the future. These tools help the manager answer such questions as:

- What threats and opportunities are most pressing in the firm's environment?
- What are the firm's key strengths and weaknesses?
- Does the firm have any sources of sustainable competitive advantage?
- What are the firm's core competencies, and what kind of value propositions do those core competencies offer to customers? How do managers want those value propositions to evolve?
- What key resources and capabilities does the firm need to develop or acquire to meet its long-term objectives?

The outputs of the analytical tools in this chapter are crucial inputs for the tools used in Chapter Seven, Choosing Innovation Projects. A coherent technological innovation strategy both leverages and enhances the firm's existing competitive position, and it provides direction for the future development of the firm. Formulating a technological innovation strategy first requires an accurate appraisal of where the firm currently is. It then requires articulating an ambitious strategic intent—one that creates a gap between a company's existing resources and capabilities and those required to achieve its intent.[1] The ability of the firm to cohesively leverage all its resources around a unified vision can enable it to create a competitive advantage that is very difficult for competitors to imitate.[2]

ASSESSING THE FIRM'S CURRENT POSITION

To assess the firm's current position in the marketplace, it is useful to begin with some standard tools of strategic analysis for analyzing the external and internal environment of the firm.

External Analysis

The two most commonly used tools for analyzing the external environment of the firm include Porter's five-force model and stakeholder analysis.

Porter's Five-Force Model

In this model, the attractiveness of an industry and a firm's opportunities and threats are identified by analyzing five forces (see Figure 6.1).[3]

While the five-force model was originally developed to assess industry attractiveness (i.e., "Is this a desirable industry in which to compete?"), in practice the model is often used to assess a specific firm's external environment (i.e., "What factors in the firm's external environment create threats and opportunities for the firm?"). The difference between these two approaches is subtle but important. In the former approach, the analysis focuses on the industry level, treating all competitors as roughly the

FIGURE 6.1
**Porter's Five-
Force Model**

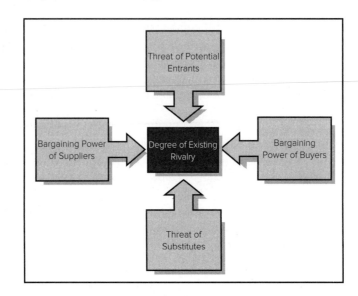

same, and its objective is to ascertain whether the industry as a whole will tend to be profitable. In the latter approach, the analysis may take the perspective of a particular firm, often identifying ways in which the external forces differentially affect the firm vis-à-vis its competitors, and its objective is to identify threats and opportunities for the firm.[4] For example, an external analysis of the discount retailing industry that is focused only on industry attractiveness might conclude that the industry is relatively unattractive given high price competition and limited opportunities to differentiate. An external analysis of the discount retailing industry focused on Walmart, on the other hand, might conclude that while the industry is a difficult one in which to be profitable, Walmart is likely to be more profitable than its competitors because its scale, its use of advanced technology for inbound and outbound logistics, and its location strategies give it considerable bargaining power over both suppliers and buyers. The latter approach will be emphasized here because it better suits our purpose of helping a particular firm to chart its strategic direction.

The five forces are:

1. **The degree of existing rivalry.** An industry's degree of rivalry is influenced by a number of factors. First, the number and relative size of competitors will shape the nature of rivalry. In general, the more firms competing that are of comparable size, the more competitive the industry will be. There are, however, exceptions to this generality. For example, **oligopolistic industries** (those that have a few large competitors) can be fiercely competitive if firms choose to engage in price wars (as happened in the personal digital assistant industry). On the other hand, oligopolistic industries can have a low degree of rivalry if the competitors choose to avoid competing head-to-head in the same market segments, or if they engage in tacit price collusion. Rivalry is also influenced by the degree to which competitors are differentiated from each other. For example, if competitors are highly differentiated, they will experience less direct rivalry because their products are likely to appeal

**oligopolistic
industries**
Highly consoli-
dated industries
with a few large
competitors.

to different market segments. For example, even though Genzyme operated in the extremely competitive biotech industry, its unique focus on orphan drugs meant that it typically was not competing head-on with other rivals for its customers. This enabled it to charge much higher margins on its products. Demand conditions also influence degree of rivalry. When demand is increasing, there are more revenues to go around and firms will experience less competitive pressure. On the other hand, when demand is declining, firms have to compete for a shrinking pool of revenues, and competition can become very aggressive. In declining industries, high **exit barriers** (fixed capital investments, emotional attachment to the industry, etc.) can also intensify rivalry by making firms reluctant to abandon the industry.

exit barriers
Costs or other commitments that make it difficult for firms to abandon an industry (large fixed-asset investments, emotional commitment to the industry, etc.).

entry barriers
Conditions that make it difficult or expensive for new firms to enter an industry (government regulation, large start-up costs, etc.).

2. **Threat of potential entrants.** The threat of potential entrants is influenced by both the degree to which the industry is likely to attract new entrants (i.e., is it profitable, growing, or otherwise alluring?) and the height of **entry barriers**. Entry barriers can include such factors as large start-up costs, brand loyalty, difficulty in gaining access to suppliers or distributors, government regulation, threat of retaliation by existing competitors, and many others. While profitability and growth may attract new entrants, entry barriers will deter them. For example, while high projected growth in the smart phone market attracts potential entrants to this market, the challenge of competing against large, well-established, and efficient competitors such as Nokia and Ericsson deters many entrants. To effectively compete against these companies requires that an entrant be able to manufacture, advertise, and distribute on a large scale, suggesting significant start-up costs for an entrant to achieve a competitive position. However, some of these capabilities could be obtained through partnerships with other firms, such as having contract manufacturers handle production and having mobile phone service providers handle distribution, thereby lowering start-up costs.

3. **Bargaining power of suppliers.** The degree to which the firm relies on one or a few suppliers will influence its ability to negotiate good terms. If there are few suppliers or suppliers are highly differentiated, the firm may have little choice in its buying decision, and thus have little leverage over the supplier to negotiate prices, delivery schedules, or other terms. On the other hand, if suppliers are very abundant and/or are not highly differentiated, the firm may be able to force the suppliers to bid against one another for the sale. The amount the firm purchases from the supplier is also relevant. If the firm's purchases constitute the bulk of a supplier's sales, the supplier will be heavily reliant upon the firm and the supplier will have little bargaining power. Likewise, if the supplier's sales constitute a large portion of the firm's purchases, the firm will be heavily reliant upon the supplier and the supplier will have more bargaining power. For example, manufacturers that sell to Walmart often have little bargaining power because Walmart's enormous volume often makes its purchases a significant portion of a manufacturer's yearly sales. Walmart's suppliers typically have little bargaining power. When Intel sells to personal computer manufacturers, on the other hand, it typically wields considerable supplier bargaining power. When computer manufacturers consider potential suppliers for microprocessors, they often have little choice but to go with Intel—many consumers demand that their systems include Intel microprocessors, and the majority of personal computer hardware

switching costs
Factors that make it difficult or expensive to change suppliers or buyers, such as investments in specialized assets to work with a particular supplier or buyer.

vertical integration
Getting into the business of one's suppliers (backward vertical integration) or one's buyers (forward vertical integration). For example, a firm that begins producing its own supplies has practiced backward vertical integration, and a firm that buys its distributor has practiced forward vertical integration.

complements
Products or services that enhance the usefulness or desirability of another product.

and software has been optimized for the Intel architecture. If the firm faces **switching costs** that make it difficult or expensive to change suppliers, this will also increase the supplier's bargaining power. Finally, if the firm can backward **vertically integrate** (i.e., produce its own supplies), this will lessen supplier bargaining power, and if the supplier can threaten to forward vertically integrate into the firm's business, this will increase the supplier's bargaining power.

4. **Bargaining power of buyers.** Many of the same factors that influence the bargaining power of suppliers have an analogous role with the bargaining power of buyers. The degree to which the firm is reliant on a few customers will increase the customer's bargaining power, and vice versa. If the firm's product is highly differentiated, buyers will typically experience less bargaining power, and if the firm's product is undifferentiated, buyers will typically experience greater bargaining power. If buyers face switching costs, this is likely to lower their bargaining power, and if the firm faces switching costs to work with other buyers, this will increase the buyer's bargaining power. Finally, if the buyers can threaten to backward vertically integrate, this will increase their bargaining power, and if the firm can threaten to forward vertically integrate, it will lower customer bargaining power.

5. **Threat of substitutes.** Substitutes are products or services that are not considered competitors, but fulfill a strategically equivalent role for the customer. For example, Starbucks may consider other coffeehouses as competitors, but other social destinations (such as bars or restaurants) or beverages (such as soft drinks or beer) as substitutes. The more potential substitutes there are, and the closer they are in function to the firm's product or service, the greater the threat of substitution. Furthermore, the threat of substitutes will also be shaped by the relative price. For example, while traveling by bus versus air is not particularly comparable in terms of speed, traveling by bus is often considerably less expensive; thus, it poses a threat of substitution, particularly for shorter distances to be traveled. Note that distinguishing between a competitor and a substitute depends on how the industry is defined. For example, if one considers the *airline* industry as the unit of analysis, then bus service is a substitute for airlines. However, if one were considering the *transportation* industry as the unit of analysis, then bus services would be competitors of airlines.

Recently, Porter has acknowledged the role of **complements**.[5] As has been discussed in several of the earlier chapters, complements are products that enhance the usefulness or desirability of a good. For example, software is an important complement for computers, and gasoline is an important complement for automobiles. The availability, quality, and price of complements will influence the threats and opportunities posed by the industry. It is important to consider (1) how important complements are in the industry, (2) whether complements are differentially available for the products of various rivals (impacting the attractiveness of their goods), and (3) who captures the value offered by the complements. For example, desktop printer manufacturers such as Hewlett Packard and Lexmark make a considerable portion of their desktop printing profits from the ink cartridges that consumers have to replace when empty. The printer manufacturers thus design the printer cartridges to be specific to each printer model, avoiding standardized designs that would facilitate consumers purchasing printer cartridges from other vendors for their Hewlett Packard and Lexmark printers. The market for ink cartridges is so lucrative, however, that a number of third-party vendors have emerged that either clone Hewlett Packard and Lexmark cartridges or offer to refill the consumer's empty cartridges with ink.

Stakeholder Analysis

stakeholder
Any entity that
has an interest
("stake") in the
organization.

Stakeholder models are often used for both strategic and normative purposes. A strategic *stakeholder analysis* emphasizes the stakeholder management issues that are likely to impact the firm's financial performance, while a *normative stakeholder analysis* emphasizes the stakeholder management issues the firm ought to attend to due to their ethical or moral implications.[6] Typically, the first step of a stakeholder analysis is to identify all the parties that will be affected by the behavior of the firm (and thus have a "stake" in the firm). For each party, the firm identifies what that stakeholder's interests are, what resources they contribute to the organization, what claims they are likely to make on the organization, and which will be most important from the firm's perspective. Stakeholders include (but are not limited to) stockholders, employees, customers, suppliers, lenders, the local community, government, and rivals (see Figure 6.2).

Internal Analysis

The analysis of the internal environment of the firm most often begins with identifying the firm's strengths and weaknesses. Sometimes this task is organized by examining each of the activities of the value chain (see Figure 6.3).[7] In Michael Porter's model of a value chain, activities are divided into primary activities and support activities. Primary activities include *inbound logistics* (all activities required to receive, store, and disseminate inputs), *operations* (activities involved in the transformation of inputs into outputs), *outbound logistics* (activities required to collect,

FIGURE 6.2
Stakeholder
Analysis

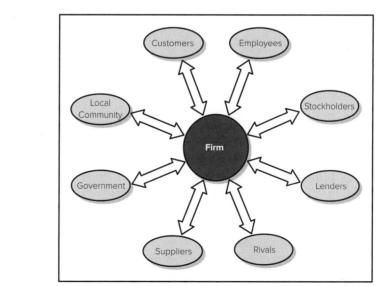

FIGURE 6.3
Porter's Value Chain

Source: Adapted with the permission of The Free Press, a Division of Simon & Schuster Adult Publishing Group, from *Competitive Advantage: Creating and Sustaining Superior Performance*, by Michael E. Porter. Copyright © 1985, 1998 by Michael E. Porter.

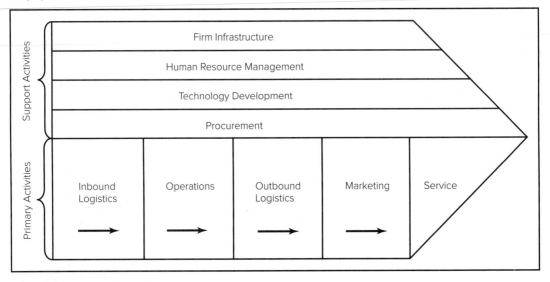

store, and distribute outputs), *marketing and sales* (activities to inform buyers about products and services and to induce their purchase), and *service* (after-sales activities required to keep the product or service working effectively). Support activities include *procurement* (the acquisition of inputs, but not their physical transfer, as that would be covered in inbound logistics), *human resource management* (activities such as recruiting, hiring, training, and compensating personnel), *technology development* (activities involved in developing and managing equipment, hardware, software, procedures, and knowledge necessary to transform inputs into outputs), and *infrastructure* (functions such as accounting, legal counsel, finance, planning, public affairs, government relations, quality assurance, and general management necessary to ensure smooth functioning of the firm). This generic model can be adapted to better fit a particular firm's needs. For example, for a biotechnology firm or software developer, research and development is likely to be a primary activity and inbound logistics may be insignificant.

Each activity can then be considered from the point of view of how it contributes to the overall value produced by the firm, and what the firm's strengths and weaknesses are in that activity. For example, Figure 6.4 illustrates what a value-chain analysis might look like for Take2 Interactive Software, which produces the Grand Theft Auto video game. In the figure, research and development is considered a primary activity, but the support activity of the technology development is not considered. Because all the game manufacturing is performed by the console producers rather than by Take2, its primary technology activities center on design of the games, which is covered in the research and development section.

FIGURE 6.4

Example of Value-Chain Analysis for Take2 Interactive Software

Value-Chain Activity	Strengths	Weaknesses
Inbound Logistics Insignificant; few inputs necessary.		
Research & Development Ability to incorporate state-of-the-art graphics capabilities, sound, and innovative themes significantly differentiates the product in the eyes of the consumer.	Take2's game maximized the polygon processing potential of the video game console, making play more lifelike. Parallel development processes kept the development cycles short.	Lack of experience in developing online games could become major liability if the market for playing games over the Internet takes off.
Operations Company focuses on producing a few very high-quality games, introducing a new version every year. Once designed, games are manufactured by the video game console producers (e.g., Sony).	Concentrating on a few games enables firm to focus significant resources on ensuring that the game is a hit.	Concentrating on a few games could be risky—if a game fails, the company may have no revenues to support operations. Take2 is completely reliant on console manufacturers for the right to develop compatible games and for manufacture of games.
Outbound Logistics Products are sold through game retailers (e.g., Gamestop), general merchandisers (e.g., Best Buy), and occasionally through bundling arrangements with video console producers, avoiding expense of maintaining the company's own retail stores. On initial launch, Take2 had signed an exclusive deal with Sony to offer Grand Theft Auto exclusively for PlayStation2.	Existing retailers already have excellent market penetration, providing rapid and wide deployment of the games. Since Sony PlayStation2 was the No. 1 video game console, signing an exclusive with Sony enabled Take2 to tap a large market.	Using retailers gives company little discretion over store placement, promotion, and pricing.
Marketing Helps build customer awareness of products, builds brand image, accelerates sales. Uses Web sites, advertisements in gaming magazines, billboards. Grand Theft Auto is targeted toward the adult market.	GTA had successfully established an image as being leading edge, and was the No. 1 game in 2002. In 2008, Grand Theft Auto: San Andreas made the "Top 20 console games of all times" list by selling 12 million copies.	Some consumers, retailers, and regulatory agencies criticized Grand Theft Auto's violence and sexual images, potentially tarnishing the company's image.
Service Phone line for technical support helps customers resolve problems in using the product.	Take2 has had relatively few returns or warranty problems.	

continued

concluded

Firm Infrastructure		Copyright infringement suits by other game producers are becoming more frequent.
Legal department negotiates license rights for games.		
Human Resource Management		
Hiring and retaining skilled and creative developers is crucial for the production of high-quality games. Company had 2,002 full-time employees in 2007.	Employees are not unionized. Employee stock option plan improves loyalty and morale.	
Procurement		
Necessary to acquire rights to use copyright-protected characters and music.	Thus far, Take2 has been very successful in obtaining rights to use copyrighted materials.	

Sources: S. Balasubramanian, A. Kim, L. Lei, and S. Singh, "Beyond the Mayhem: Take-Two Interactive Software," New York University teaching case, 2003; www.Take2games.com.

tacit resources
Resources of an intangible nature (such as knowledge) that cannot be readily codified.

socially complex resources
Resources or activities that emerge through the interaction of multiple individuals.

causal ambiguity
The relationship between a resource and the outcome it produces is poorly understood (the *causal* mechanism is *ambiguous*).

Once the key strengths and weaknesses are identified, the firm can assess which strengths have the potential to be a source of sustainable competitive advantage. This helps the firm gain valuable perspective on which of its activities and resources should be further leveraged in its articulation of its strategic intent for the future.

To be a potential source of sustainable competitive advantage, resources must be *rare, valuable, durable*, and *inimitable*.[8] Resources that are rare and valuable may yield a competitive advantage, but that advantage will not be sustainable if the firm is incapable of keeping the resources, or if other firms are capable of imitating them. For example, a positive brand image can be a rare and valuable resource, but it requires ongoing investment to sustain. If a firm lacks the capital to reinvest in its brand image, it will erode. Furthermore, many valuable resources are quickly imitated by other firms. Technological advances are reverse-engineered, skillful marketing campaigns are copied, innovative human resource practices are adopted by imitators, and so on. Some resources, however, are not readily imitable. For example, if valuable resources are **tacit** (i.e., they cannot be readily codified in written form), path dependent (i.e., they are dependent on a particular historical sequence of events), **socially complex** (i.e., they arise through the complex interaction of multiple people), or **causally ambiguous** (i.e., it is unclear how the resource gives rise to value), they will be extremely difficult to imitate.[9] For example, *talent* is typically considered to be a tacit and causally ambiguous resource. It is thought to be an inherent trait that cannot be trained, and the mechanisms by which individuals acquire it or tap it are poorly understood. A first-mover advantage is a path-dependent advantage that cannot be copied—once a firm has become the first mover in a category, other firms no longer have the opportunity to be first. Once the firm has established a baseline internal analysis, it can move on to identifying its core competencies and formulate its strategic intent.

IDENTIFYING CORE COMPETENCIES AND DYNAMIC CAPABILITIES

Core Competencies

A company's core competencies are typically considered to be those that differentiate it strategically. A core competency is more than just a core technology. A core competency arises from a firm's ability to combine and harmonize multiple primary abilities in which the firm excels into a few key building blocks of specialized expertise. Competencies often combine different kinds of abilities, such as abilities in managing the market interface (e.g., advertising, distribution), building and managing an effective infrastructure (e.g., information systems, logistics management), and technological abilities (e.g., applied science, process design).[10] This combination and harmonization of multiple abilities make core competencies difficult to imitate. Consider, for example, Sony's core competency in miniaturization.[11] This competency arises from the harmonization of multiple technologies (liquid crystal displays, semiconductors, etc.) and is leveraged into multiple markets (televisions, radios, personal digital assistants, etc.). A firm's core competencies also depend on building high-quality relationships across different functions and business units.

Prahalad and Hamel compare core competencies to roots, from which grow core products such as major components or subassemblies. Core products, in turn, give rise to business units, whose fruits are the various end products of the company (see Figure 6.5).

Several core competencies may underlie an individual business unit, and several business units may draw upon the same core competency. This indicates the organization's structure and incentives must encourage cooperation and exchange of resources across strategic business unit boundaries. If managers or resources are wed too closely to their business units, there will be underinvestment in the development and leverage of core competencies.[12] Prahalad and Hamel go so far as to argue that strategic business units should be expected to bid for people in the firm who have particular skills to contribute to a project. Instead of viewing individuals as being employed by a particular strategic business unit, individuals should be considered corporate assets that can be redeployed across the organization.

Prahalad and Hamel offer the following tests to identify the firm's core competencies:

1. Is it a significant source of competitive differentiation? Does it provide a unique signature to the organization? Does it make a significant contribution to the value a customer perceives in the end product? For example, Sony's skills in miniaturization have an immediate impact on the utility customers reap from its portable products.

2. Does it transcend a single business? Does it cover a range of businesses, both current and new? For example, Honda's core competence in engines enables the company to be successful in businesses as diverse as automobiles, motorcycles, lawn mowers, and generators.

3. Is it hard for competitors to imitate? In general, competencies that arise from the complex harmonization of multiple technologies will be difficult to imitate. The competence may have taken years (or decades) to build. This combination of resources and embedded skills will be difficult for other firms to acquire or duplicate.

FIGURE 6.5

Visualizing the Firm's Core Competencies, Core Products, Business Units, and End Products

Source: Reprinted by permission of *Harvard Business Review*. Exhibit from "The Core Competence of the Corporation," by C. K. Prahalad and G. Hamel, May–June 1990. Copyright © 1990 by the Harvard Business School Publishing Corporation; all rights reserved.

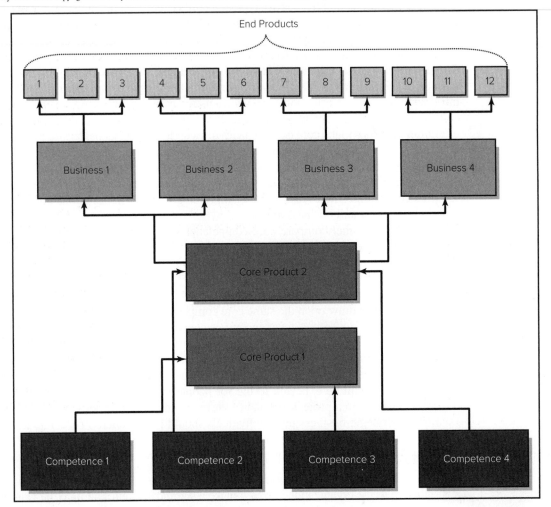

According to Prahalad and Hamel, few firms are likely to be leaders in more than five or six core competencies. If a company has compiled a list of 20 to 30 capabilities, it probably has not yet identified its true core competencies. By viewing the business as a portfolio of core competencies, managers are better able to focus on value creation and meaningful new business development, rather than cost cutting or opportunistic expansion.[13]

The Risk of Core Rigidities

Sometimes the very things that a firm excels at can enslave it, making the firm rigid and overly committed to inappropriate skills and resources.[14] Incentive systems may evolve that favor activities that reinforce the firm's core competencies. The organizational culture may reward employees who are most closely connected to core competencies with higher status and better access to other organizational resources. While these systems and norms can prove beneficial in reinforcing and leveraging the firm's existing core competencies, they can also inhibit the development of new core competencies. For example, a firm's emphasis on a scientific discipline that is central to its core competency can make the firm less attractive to individuals from other disciplines. Rewards for engaging in core competency activities can discourage employees from pursuing more exploratory activities. Finally, as noted in Chapter Four, knowledge accumulation tends to be very path dependent. Firms that have well-developed knowledge sets along a particular trajectory may find it very hard to assimilate or utilize knowledge that appears unrelated to that trajectory, potentially limiting the firm's flexibility.[15]

Dynamic Capabilities

dynamic capabilities
A set of abilities that make a firm more agile and responsive to change.

In fast-changing markets, it can be extremely useful for a firm to develop a core competency in responding to change. Whereas in Prahalad and Hamel's model, core competencies relate to sets of specific core products, it is also possible for a firm to develop core competencies that are not specific to any set of technologies or products, but rather to a set of abilities that enable it to quickly reconfigure its organizational structure and routines in response to new opportunities.[16] Such competencies are termed **dynamic capabilities**. Dynamic capabilities enable firms to quickly adapt to emerging markets or major technological discontinuities. For example, Corning has made its own evolvability one of its most important core competencies. It invests heavily in research in areas likely to provide scientific breakthroughs (such as opal glasses and their solvents). It develops pilot plants to experiment with new products and production processes.[17] It even manages its relationships with alliance partners not as individual relationships focused on particular projects, but rather as an integrative and flexible system of capabilities that extend the firm's boundaries.[18]

STRATEGIC INTENT

A firm's purpose is to create value. This entails more than just improving operations or cutting costs; it means leveraging corporate resources to create more performance for customers, more well-being for employees, and more returns for shareholders. This is accomplished through developing new businesses and markets, and leveraging corporate resources, all guided by the firm's *strategic intent*.[19]

A company's strategic intent is a long-term goal that is ambitious, builds upon and stretches the firm's existing core competencies, and draws from all levels of the organization. Hamel and Prahalad's examples include Canon's obsession with overtaking Xerox in copiers, Apple's mission of ensuring that every individual has a personal computer, and Yahoo's goal of becoming the world's largest Internet shopping mall. Typically a strategic intent looks 10 to 20 years ahead and establishes clear milestones for employees to target.[20] This forward-looking orientation is crucial;

Research Brief Blue Ocean Strategy

In a series of articles and their 2005 book[a], Renée Mauborgne and W. Chan Kim describe firms who crafted what they call "blue ocean" strategies by innovating in a way that allowed them to enter untapped market space. In most industries, the rules of the game are well-understood and accepted, and firms compete by trying to outdo each other on the accepted dimensions of competition. Each firm hopes to capture a greater share of existing demand, and as the industry becomes crowded, the likelihood of firm profits or growth diminishes. Cutthroat competition turns the ocean bloody (also known as "red ocean"). Blue oceans refer to untapped market space that firms create by redefining the dimensions of competition. They are uncharted, and there are no (or few) competitors. Blue ocean strategies are thus fundamentally about differentiation through innovation.

Mauborgne and Chan suggest that firms can identify "blue ocean" strategies by first using a visualization tool, the "strategy canvas," to help them understand how different players are competing in an industry, and how they might choose to compete differently. The horizontal axis lists the factors that the industry competes on/invests in, and the vertical axis indicates "high" or "low." Managers can then plot **"value curves"** for different product offerings. For example, comparing one and two star hotels you might draw the following:

RedOcean Strategy	BlueOcean Strategy
Compete in existing market space	Create uncontested market space
Beat the competition	Make the competition irrelevant
Exploit existing demand	Create and capture new demand
Make the value-cost trade-off	Break the value-cost trade-off
Align the whole system of a firm's activities with its strategic choice of differentiation *or* low cost.	Align the whole system of a firm's activities in pursuit of differentiation *and* low cost.

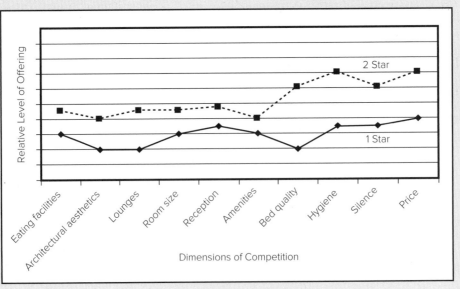

continued

concluded

Managers can then challenge the industry's strategic logic by asking the following four questions:

1. Which of the factors that the industry takes for granted should be *eliminated*?
2. Which factors should be *reduced well below* the industry's standard?
3. Which factors should be *raised well above* the industry's standard?
4. Which factors should be *created* that the industry has never offered?

For example, returning to the hotel example Formule 1 found a successful market space by rejecting the idea that all hotel customers need eating facilities, lounges, and large rooms. Instead, some customers would prefer a hotel that skimped on these things and instead provided very quiet and clean rooms with high-quality beds at a moderate price:

Mauborgne and Chan argue that the NIntendo Wii, Cirque du Soleil and Southwest Airlines' business model are all examples of successful "blue ocean" strategies.

[a] Adapted from Kim, W.C. & Mauborgne, R. 2005. *Blue ocean strategy.* Boston: Harvard Business School Press.

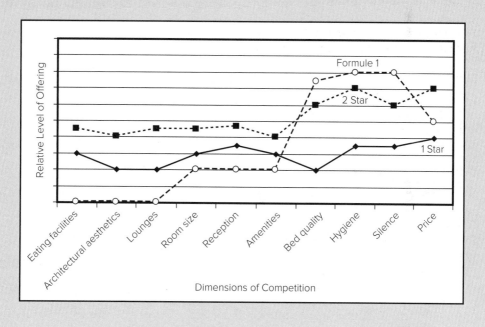

without it companies can easily become focused on markets they have served in the past. Focusing on the firm's existing markets results in the development of products and services that meet current market requirements, rather than future market requirements. Successful and innovative firms question existing price-performance assumptions. They lead customers by developing and introducing products that extend well beyond current market requirements and help mold the market's expectations for the future.[21]

Robert Kaplan and David Norton point out that a firm's methods of measuring performance will strongly influence whether and how the firm pursues its strategic objectives. They argue that effective performance measurement must be more than simple reliance on financial indicators; it must be a coherent and integral part of the management process. They proposed a method, the "balanced scorecard," that they argue can motivate breakthrough improvements in product, process, customer, and market development.[a] The balanced scorecard (see Figure 6.6) emphasizes four perspectives the firm should take in formulating goals that target critical success factors and in defining measures:

1. **Financial perspective.** Goals might include such things as "meet shareholder's expectations" or "double our corporate value in seven years." Measures might include return on capital, net cash flow, and earnings growth.

2. **Customer perspective.** Goals might be to "improve customer loyalty," "offer best-in-class customer service," or "increase customer satisfaction." Measures might include market share, percentage of repeat purchases, customer satisfaction surveys, and so on.

3. **Internal perspective.** Goals might include such things as "reduce internal safety incidents," "build best-in-class franchise teams," or "improve

FIGURE 6.6
The Balanced Scorecard

Source: Reprinted by permission of *Harvard Business Review*. Exhibit from "Putting the Balanced Scorecard to Work," by R. Kaplan and D. Norton, September–October 1993. Copyright © 1993 by the Harvard Business School Publishing Corporation; all rights reserved.

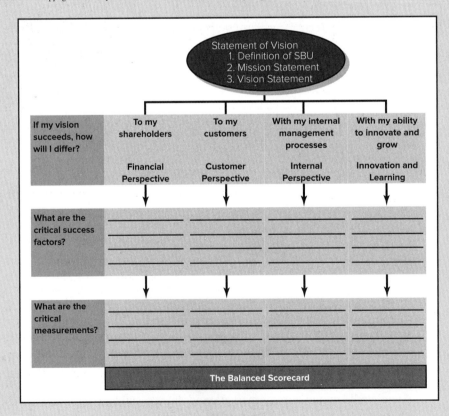

continued

concluded

inventory management." Measures might include the number of safety incidents per month, franchise quality ratings, stockout rates, and inventory costs.

4. **Innovation and learning perspective.** Goals might include such things as "accelerate and improve new product development" or "improve employee skills." Measures might include the percentage of sales from products developed within the past five years, average length of the new product development cycle, or employee training targets.

Kaplan and Norton acknowledge that the balanced scorecard model often has to be adapted to fit different markets and businesses, but many firms (including IBM, Philips Electronics, Apple, and Advanced Micro Electronics) in many different industries (including electronics, petrochemicals, and health care) are finding the balanced scorecard useful.[b] In fact, a 2002 survey by Bain & Company found that approximately 50 percent of Fortune 1,000 companies in the United States and 40 percent in Europe use some version of the balanced scorecard.[c]

[a] R. Kaplan and D. Norton, "Putting the Balanced Scorecard to Work," *Harvard Business Review,* September–October 1993, pp. 134–47; and R. Kaplan and D. Norton, "The Balanced Scorecard—Measures That Drive Performance," *Harvard Business Review,* January–February 1992, pp. 71–80.
[b] Kaplan and Norton, "Putting the Balanced Scorecard to Work."
[c] A. Gumbus and B. Lyons, "The Balanced Scorecard at Philips Electronics," *Strategic Finance* 84, no. 5 (2002), pp. 45–49.

FIGURE 6.7

Identifying the Resource and Capability Gap

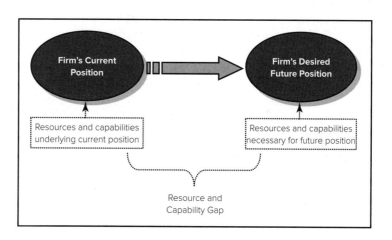

Once the strategic intent has been articulated, the company should be able to identify the resources and capabilities required to close the gap between the strategic intent and the current position (see Figure 6.7). This includes identifying any technological gap. Articulating the company's strategic intent enables the company to focus its development efforts and choose the investments necessary to develop strategic technologies and incorporate them into the company's new products.[22] Many companies are now pairing the articulation of their strategic intent with a multidimensional performance measurement system, such as the balanced scorecard, as discussed in the Theory in Action section.

Summary of Chapter

1. The first step in establishing a coherent strategy for the firm is assessing the external environment. Two commonly used models of external analysis are Porter's five-force model and stakeholder analysis.

2. Porter's five-force model entails assessing the degree of existing rivalry, threat of potential entrants, bargaining power of suppliers, bargaining power of customers, and threat posed by substitutes. Recently Porter added a sixth force, the role of *complements.*

3. Stakeholder analysis involves identifying any entity with an interest in the firm, what it wants from the company, and what claims it can make on the company.

4. To analyze the internal environment, firms often begin by identifying strengths and weaknesses in each activity of the value chain. The firm can then identify which strengths have the potential to be a source of sustainable competitive advantage.

5. Next the firm identifies its core competencies. Core competencies are integrated combinations of abilities that distinguish the firm in the marketplace. Several core competencies may underlie each business unit, and several business units may draw upon the same core competency.

6. Sometimes core competencies can become core rigidities that limit the firm's ability to respond to a changing environment.

7. Dynamic capabilities are competencies that enable a firm to quickly reconfigure the firm's organizational structure or routines in response to change in the firm's environment or opportunities.

8. A firm's strategic intent is the articulation of an ambitious long-term (10 to 20 years out) goal or set of goals. The firm's strategic intent should build upon and stretch its existing core competencies.

9. Once the firm articulates its strategic intent, managers should identify the resources and capabilities that the firm must develop or acquire to achieve its strategic intent.

10. The balanced scorecard is a measurement system that encourages the firm to consider its goals from multiple perspectives (financial, customer, business process, and innovation and learning), and establish measures that correspond to each of those perspectives.

Discussion Questions

1. What is the difference between a strength, a competitive advantage, and a sustainable competitive advantage?

2. What makes an ability (or set of abilities) a core competency?

3. Why is it necessary to perform an external and internal analysis before the firm can identify its true core competencies?

4. Pick a company you are familiar with. Can you identify some of its core competencies?

5. How is the idea of "strategic intent" different from models of strategy that emphasize achieving a fit between the firm's strategies and its current strengths, weaknesses, opportunities, and threats (SWOT)?

6. Can a strategic intent be too ambitious?

Suggested Further Reading

Classics

Barney, J., "Firm Resources and Sustained Competitive Advantage," *Journal of Management* 17 (1994), pp. 99–120.

Hamel, G., and C. K. Prahalad, "Strategic Intent," *Harvard Business Review*, May–June 1991, pp. 63–76.

Penrose, E. T., *The Theory of the Growth of the Firm* (New York: Wiley, 1959).

Porter, M. E., *Competitive Advantage* (New York: Free Press, 1985).

Brandenburger, A. M., and B. J. Nalebuff, *Co-opetition* (New York: Doubleday, 1996).

Recent Work

Kim, W. C., and R. Mauborgne, Blue Ocean Strategy: *How to Create Uncontested Market Space and Make Competition Irrelevant* (Boston: Harvard Business School Press, 2005).

Rothaermel, F., and A. M. Hess, "Building Dynamic Capabilities: Innovation Driven By Individual-, Firm-, and Network-level Effects," *Organization Science* 18 (2007), pp. 898–921.

Salunke, S., J. Weerawardena, and J. R. McColl-Kennedy, "Towards a Model of Dynamic Capabilities in Innovation-based Competitive Strategy: Insights from Project-oriented Service Firms," *Industrial Marketing Management* 40 (2011), pp. 1251–1263.

Tushman, M. L., W. K. Smith, and A. Binns, "The Ambidextrous CEO," *Harvard Business Review* (2011), pp. 74–80.

Endnotes

1. G. Hamel and C. K. Prahalad, "Strategic Intent," *Harvard Business Review*, May–June 1991, pp. 63–76.
2. C. K. Prahalad, "The Role of Core Competencies in the Corporation," *Research Technology Management*, November–December 1993, pp. 40–47.
3. M. A. Porter, *Competitive Strategy.* (New York: Free Press, 1980).
4. Michael Porter is fully supportive of both ways of applying the five-force model. Personal communication with Michael Porter, March 25, 2006.
5. M. A. Porter, "Strategy and the Internet," *Harvard Business Review* 79, no. 3 (2001), pp. 62–78; and personal communication, March 13, 2006.
6. S. L. Berman, A. Wicks, S. Kotha, and T. M. Jones, "Does Stakeholder Orientation Matter? The Relationship between Stakeholder Management Models and Firm Financial Performance," *Academy of Management Journal* 42 (1999), pp. 488–507; T. Donaldson, and L. Preston, "The Stakeholder Theory of the Corporation: Concepts, Evidence, and Implications," *Academy of Management Review* 20 (1995), pp. 65–91; and W. Evan and R. E. Freeman, "A Stakeholder Theory of the Modern Corporation: Kantian Capitalism," in *Ethical Theory in Business*, eds. T. Beauchamp and N. Bowie (Englewood Cliffs, NJ: Prentice Hall, 1983), pp. 75–93.
7. M. A. Porter, *Competitive Advantage* (New York: Free Press, 1985).
8. J. Barney, "Firm Resources and Sustained Competitive Advantage," *Journal of Management* 17 (1991), pp. 99–120.
9. R. Reed and R. J. DeFillippi, "Causal Ambiguity, Barriers to Imitation, and Sustainable Competitive Advantage," *Academy of Management Review* 15, no. 1 (1990), pp. 88–102.

10. M. Gallon, H. Stillman, and D. Coates, "Putting Core Competency Thinking into Practice," *Research Technology Management*, May–June 1995, pp. 20–28.

11. Prahalad, "The Role of Core Competencies in the Corporation."

12. Prahalad and Hamel, "The Core Competence of the Corporation."

13. Prahalad, "The Role of Core Competencies in the Corporation."

14. Leonard-Barton, "Core Capabilities and Core Rigidities."

15. G. Dosi, "Sources, Procedures, and Microeconomic Effects of Innovation," *Journal of Economic Literature*, September 26, 1988, p. 1130; and M. Tripsas and G. Gavetti, "Capabilities, Cognition, and Inertia: Evidence from Digital Imaging," *Strategic Management Journal* 21 (2000), p. 1147.

16. A. King and C. Tucci, "Incumbent Entry into New Market Niches: The Role of Experience and Managerial Choice in the Creation of Dynamic Capabilities," *Management Science* 48 (2002), pp. 171–86; and K. M. Eisenhardt and J. A. Martin, "Dynamic Capabilities: What Are They?" *Strategic Management Journal* 21 (2000), pp. 1105–21.

17. M. B. Graham and A. T. Shuldiner, *Corning and the Craft of Innovation* (New York: Oxford University Press, 2001); and C. L. Tucci, "Corning and the Craft of Innovation," *Business History Review* 75 (2001), pp. 862–65.

18. C. A. Bartlett and A. Nanda, "Corning, Inc.: A Network of Alliances," Harvard Business School case no. 9-391-102, 1990.

19. Prahalad, "The Role of Core Competencies in the Corporation."

20. Hamel and Prahalad, "Strategic Intent."

21. Prahalad, "The Role of Core Competencies in the Corporation."

22. K. Marino, "Developing Consensus on Firm Competencies and Capabilities," *Academy of Management Executive* 10, no. 3 (1996), pp. 40–51.

Choosing Innovation Projects

The Mahindra Shaan: Gambling on a Radical Innovation

Mahindra Tractors, the Farm Equipment Sector of the Mahindra & Mahindra Group in India is one of the world's largest producers of tractors.[a] In the late 1990's, over 20 percent of Indian's gross domestic product came from agriculture and nearly 70 percent of Indian workers were involved in agriculture in some way.[b] However, seasonal rainfall meant that Indian farmers only used tractors for farming purposes about one-third of the year. The rest of the year they would use the tractors for personal transportation and to haul goods to earn extra income. Many farmers made modifications to their tractors to make them more useful as transporters. Furthermore, a large number of farmers had plots so small—perhaps 1–3 hectares—that it was difficult to raise enough funds to buy any tractor at all. Managers at Mahindra & Mahindra sensed that there might be an opportunity for a new kind of tractor that better served this market.

R.N. Nayak, R&D Manager at Mahindra & Mahindra (and a person well-known as a maverick that tended to break with company norms) began developing a prototype for a radical product concept he called the "Sactor"—a hybrid between a transporter and a tractor that farmers could use on and off the farm. Nayak believed that innovators should always start out with an attempt to gain deep insight into a customer problem through extensive observation rather than financial or technical analysis—too much analysis would stifle innovation. As he stated it, "start with the pictures not with the numbers."[c]

In just over a year, he had developed a prototype of the futuristic looking vehicle. It had smaller tires than a typical tractor that would be better for driving on roads. It also drew from the aesthetics of the Jeeps Mahindra & Mahindra made in their automotive division. No marketing studies had been conducted and sales people were reluctant to support the new vehicle, particularly since Indian farm equipment market was in a deep downturn due to repeated droughts and excess tractor inventory. Nayak himself was unsure of how customers would react to the trade-offs that had been required to produce the economically priced hybrid—after all, it would have lower farming performance than Mahindra & Mahindra's other tractors. To make matters worse, even after 15 production prototypes had been built, the Sactor had technical problems that needed to be resolved. Frustrated with the project's slow progress, Nayak left Mahindra & Mahindra.

Nayak's departure could have meant the death of the project, however Sanjeev Goyle, Head of Mahindra & Mahindra's Farm Equipment Sector was intrigued by the project, deeming it the "perfect confluence of M&M's two core strengths: Jeeps and tractors." His prior experience at American Home Products (healthcare) and Piaggio (motor scooters) made him realize how important dramatic innovation could be for a company. He felt that the company's existing farm equipment lines were too similar to those of competitors; innovation had been too incremental and the products appealed primarily to older farmers. He wanted a way to invigorate the product line up and the brand. As he noted, "My background in fast-moving consumer goods and motor scooters makes me a firm believer that new products and innovation can create a new aura in brands and make the brands appear to be on the move."

Goyle decided to send Sactor prototypes out to 14 dealers so that they could be used in customer trials. Feedback from the trails revealed that customers were primarily using the hybrid for hauling materials. Goyle also believed that the aesthetics of the Sactor needed some work. He overhauled the exterior of the vehicle to make it more "macho" and Jeep-like. The new vehicle, renamed the "Shaan" (Hindi for "pride"), had a 23.5 horsepower engine and a built in trolley capable of lifting up to 750 kilograms. It could run standard farm implements such as cultivators, rotators, and harrows, but it was also capable of traveling at about 40 kilometers per hour on the road. Its small turning radius (3.2 meters) made it especially maneuverable. To make the vehicle more comfortable for personal transportation, it had a spring leaf suspension (for fewer bumps and a more comfortable ride), a soft top canopy, and a windscreen with wipers.[d] The target market would include lower income farmers and semi-urban youth.

Producing the vehicle would require building a new assembly line, and engineering that turned out to be necessary to increase its reliability led to higher production costs—this meant that the Shaan would have to be priced at 2.95 lakh (295,000) rupees to be profitable (a price that would buy a conventional 35 horsepower tractor). There was great uncertainty about how many of the vehicles could be sold at that price. Mahindra & Mahindra's management, however, was swayed by Goyle's argument that "even if we made small margins, we would be pioneers, be distinctive: innovative."

The Shaan was launched in mid-2006 and won an award from the American Society of Agricultural and Biological Engineers as one of the 50 outstanding innovations of the year. Though many consumers were perplexed by its "funny looks"[e] The Shaan turned out to be extremely useful for several specialty applications.[f] For example, in the brick kiln industry, its small turning radius was a huge advantage (before the Shaan, workers were reliant on donkeys for moving the bricks due to the small spaces in which they had to work). By 2008, Mahindra & Mahindra's senior management considered the Shaan a "runaway success."[g]

Discussion Questions:

1. Why does Nayak say it's important to "start with the pictures not with the numbers"?
2. What are the challenges with doing a quantitative analysis of the value of the Shaan project?
3. What are the different sources of value that Mahindra's management appears to think will arise from developing the Shaan?

[a] www.Mahindra.com

[b] Thomke, S. and Luthra, BD. "Innovation at Mahindra & Mahindra," Harvard Business School Case (2009), May 5th.

[c] Thomke, S. and Luthra, BD. "Innovation at Mahindra & Mahindra," Harvard Business School Case (2009), May 5th.

[d] Mahindra brochure, accessed at www.pakwheels.com, retrieved August 1, 2015.

[e] www.pakwheels.com/forums/

[f] www.superbrandsindia.com, retrieved August 1, 2015.

[g] Stewart, TA and Raman, AP. "Finding a higher gear," *Harvard Business Review* (2008), July-August, pg. 69–76.

OVERVIEW

capital rationing
The allocation of a finite quantity of resources over different possible uses.

Developing innovative new products and services is expensive and time-consuming. It is also extremely risky—most studies have indicated that the vast majority of development projects fail. Firms have to make difficult choices about which projects are worth the investment, and then they have to make sure those projects are pursued with a rigorous and well-thought-out development process. In this chapter, we will explore the various methods used to evaluate and choose innovation projects. The methods range from informal to highly structured, and from entirely qualitative to strictly quantitative. We will start by considering the role of **capital rationing** in the R&D investment decision, and then we will cover various methods used to evaluate projects including strictly quantitative methods, qualitative methods, and approaches that combine quantitative and qualitative techniques.

THE DEVELOPMENT BUDGET

R&D intensity
The ratio of R&D expenditures to sales.

While many project valuation methods seem to assume that all valuable projects will be funded, most firms face serious constraints in capital and other resources, forcing them to choose between multiple valuable projects (or obtain external financing as discussed in the Theory in Action section). Many firms use a form of *capital rationing* in formulating their new product development plans. Under capital rationing, the firm sets a fixed research and development budget (often some percentage of the previous year's sales), and then uses a rank ordering of possible projects to determine which will be funded. Firms might establish this budget on the basis of industry benchmarks or historical benchmarks of the firm's own performance. To provide a sense of what firms in different industries spend on R&D, Figure 7.1 shows the ten industries with the highest **R&D intensity** (R&D expenditures as a percentage

FIGURE 7.1
Top Ten Industries (three digit SIC) by R&D Intensity, 2013

Based on Compustat data for North American publicly held firms; only industries with greater than ten or more publicly listed firms were included. Data for sales and R&D were aggregated to the industry level prior to calculating the industry-level ratio to minimize the effect of exceptionally large outliers for firm-level RDI.

Rank	Three Dig. SIC Code	Industry description	Number of publicly held firms	Industry revenues ($millions)	Industry R&D spend ($millions)	R&D intensity (R&D/Sales)
1	2830	Drugs, biological products, and diagnostics	730	$693,674	$112,984	16%
2	3550	Special industry machinery	42	$ 27,111	$ 3,955	15%
3	3670	Semiconductors and electronic components	233	$428,554	$ 46,349	11%
4	7370	Software and computer programming services	724	$789,878	$ 67,461	9%
5	3840	Medical equipment	241	$121,758	$ 9,721	8%
6	3820	Measuring equipment and instruments	102	$126,821	$ 9,149	7%
7	3660	Communications equipment	106	$319,869	$ 22,526	7%
8	3570	Computers and peripherals	91	$406,678	$ 28,215	7%
9	3940	Toys and games	18	$ 20,216	$ 1,245	6%
10	3650	Household audio and video equipment	22	$111,986	$ 6,124	5%

of sales), based on North American publicly held firms in 2013. Some industries (notably drugs, special industry machinery, and semiconductors and electronic components) spend considerably more of their revenues on R&D than other industries, on average.

There is also considerable variation within each of the industries in the amount that individual firms spend. For example, as shown in Figure 7.2, Roche Holding's R&D intensity is significantly higher than the average for drug producers (19% versus 16%), whereas Pfizer's is somewhat lower than the industry average (13% versus 16%). Figure 7.2 also reveals the impact of firm size on R&D budgets: Whereas the absolute amount spent on R&D at Volkswagen surpasses the R&D spend at other firms by a large amount, Volkswagen's R&D intensity is relatively low due its very large sales base.

The rank ordering used in capital rationing may be established by any number of methods, including quantitative methods, such as discounted cash flow analysis or options analysis, or qualitative methods, such as screening questions and portfolio mapping, or a combination of multiple methods. Knowing the requirements, strengths, and weaknesses of each method helps managers make sound decisions about which valuation techniques to employ.

FIGURE 7.2
Top 20 Global R&D Spenders, 2013

Data from Compustat

Company	R&D ($millions)	R&D intensity (R&D/sales)
Volkswagen	$14,035	5%
Intel	$10,611	20%
Roche Holding	$10,411	19%
Microsoft	$10,411	13%
Novartis	$ 9,852	17%
Toyota	$ 8,842	4%
Johnson & Johnson	$ 8,763	12%
Google	$ 7,952	13%
Merck	$ 7,503	17%
General Motors	$ 7,200	5%
Pfizer	$ 6,678	13%
Sanofi	$ 6,573	14%
Amazon.com	$ 6,565	9%
GlaxoSmithKline	$ 6,502	14%
Ford	$ 6,400	4%
Honda	$ 6,158	5%
IBM	$ 5,959	6%
Cisco Systems	$ 5,942	12%
Siemens	$ 5,808	6%
Daimler	$ 5,651	3%

QUANTITATIVE METHODS FOR CHOOSING PROJECTS

net present value (NPV)
The discounted cash inflows of a project minus the discounted cash outflows.

Quantitative methods of analyzing new projects usually entail converting projects into some estimate of future cash returns from a project. Quantitative methods enable managers to use rigorous mathematical and statistical comparisons of projects, though the quality of the comparison is ultimately a function of the quality of the original estimates. The accuracy of such estimates can be questionable—particularly in highly uncertain or rapidly changing environments. The most commonly used quantitative methods include discounted cash flow methods and real options.

Discounted Cash Flow Methods

internal rate of return (IRR)
The rate of return yielded by a project, normally calculated as the discount rate that makes the net present value of an investment equal zero.

Many firms use some form of discounted cash flow analysis to evaluate projects. Discounted cash flows are quantitative methods for assessing whether the anticipated future benefits are large enough to justify expenditure, given the risks. Discounted cash flow methods take into account the payback period, risk, and time value of money. The two most commonly used forms of discounted cash flow analysis for evaluating investment decisions are **net present value (NPV)** and **internal rate of return (IRR)**. Both methods rely on the same basic discounted cash flow mechanics, but they look at the problem from different angles. NPV asks, "Given

While large firms can fund innovation projects internally, new technology start-ups must often obtain external financing. This can sometimes be daunting. Because technology start-ups often have both an unproven technology and an unproven business concept (and sometimes an unproven management team), they typically face a much higher cost of capital than larger competitors, and their options for obtaining capital can be very limited. In the first few stages of start-up and growth, entrepreneurs may have to turn to friends, family, and personal debt. Start-ups might also be able to obtain some initial funding through government agencies. If the idea and the management team seem promising enough, the entrepreneur can tap "angel investors" and venture capitalists as sources of both funds and mentoring.

FAMILY, FRIENDS, AND CREDIT CARDS

When a new venture is starting out, often the technology and/or management is unproven, making the venture appear very risky. In this stage, entrepreneurs must often rely on friends and family members who are willing to provide initial funding either in the form of a loan or an exchange for equity in the company. Alternatively, the entrepreneur may try to obtain debt financing from a local bank. A very large number of start-ups are actually funded with credit cards, resulting in a very high rate of interest!

GOVERNMENT GRANTS AND LOANS

Some new ventures obtain start-up funds from government sources. In the United States, the Small Business Administration (SBA) is designed to foster entrepreneurship and innovation by administering grants, loans, and venture capital programs from many different federal agencies including the Department of Commerce, Department of Agriculture, Department of Energy, NASA, and others. Similarly, in the United Kingdom, the Enterprise Fund administers a series of programs designed to fund small- to medium-size technology firms, and in Germany there are more than 800 federal and state government programs established to finance new firms.[a]

ANGEL INVESTORS

Angel investors are private investors who fund projects without utilizing a venture capital limited partnership structure. They are often wealthy individuals who have been very successful in business, and who enjoy the thrill of vicarious entrepreneurship afforded by investing in—and sometimes mentoring—start-up firms. Angels typically fund projects that are $1 million or less. While angel investors lose money in a significant share of their investments, those investments that pay off can earn very high returns. Angels are usually not listed in public directories, but are identified through professional networks (through one's former colleagues, professors, or lawyers, for example). A large number of start-ups obtain "seed-stage" (before there is a real product or company organized) financing from angel investors. While it is difficult to get data on angel investing because most of the transactions are not publicly reported, estimates from the Center for Venture Research, indicate that angel investors funded 73,400 entrepreneurial ventures in 2014 for a total of $24.1 billion (an average of $328,500 per deal).

VENTURE CAPITAL

For projects that require more than $1 million, entrepreneurs often turn to venture capital, either from independent venture capital firms or corporate venture capital sources.

Independent venture capital firms manage a pool of funds that they invest in projects they believe to have rapid growth potential. Many venture capital firms specialize in particular industries, making them better able to evaluate the potential of start-ups in that industry. The venture capital funds are likely to be provided in a complex debt-equity hybrid contract that essentially looks more like equity if the firm performs well, or debt if the firm performs poorly.[b] If and when the business is successful, the venture capitalist can cash out of the investment by negotiating an initial public offering or a buyout of the company by another firm. Venture capitalists are very selective, and reject the vast majority of proposals considered. However, for those projects that are funded, the support of the venture capitalist provides a number of valuable benefits including credibility among other investors (and thus better access to capital) and mentoring. While some venture capitalists specialize in providing seed-stage funding, venture capitalists are more likely to provide funding during

continued

early stages—after the company has been organized and the product has shown early signs of success, but before it is able to sustain its development activities and growth through its own revenues. According to the U.S.-based National Venture Capital Association, in 2014 venture capitalists invested about $49.3 billion in 4,356 deals, of which 1,409 received funding for the first time.

Corporate venture capital is provided by firms that wish to take a minority equity stake in another firm's technology development, often to gain access to cutting-edge technology that they may wish to develop further should it prove technically and commercially promising. Such firms may establish an internal venturing group that is closely tied to the firm's own development operations, or they may create a dedicated external fund that has more independence from the firm's own operations.[c] The benefit of the former structure is that the firm should be better able to use its own expertise and resources to help the new venture succeed. However, under this structure, the entrepreneur may have concerns about the larger firm expropriating the entrepreneur's proprietary technology. Under the latter structure, the independence of the external venture fund provides some reassurance that the entrepreneur's technology will not be stolen, but it also limits the ability of the entrepreneur to leverage any of the larger firm's nonfinancial resources.[d] According to the National Venture Capital Association, there were 775 corporate venture capital deals totaling $5.4 billion (averaging almost $7 million per deal) in 2011. Examples of such programs include Google Ventures, Intel Capital, Johnson & Johnson Development Corporation, Dow Venture Capital, Siemens Venture Capital, Geisinger Ventures, and Ascension Health Ventures. These programs tend to invest in sectors that closely mirror those invested in by independent venture capital firms.[e]

[a] B. Hall, "The Financing of Research and Development," *Oxford Review of Economic Policy* 18 (2002), pp. 35–51.
[b] Hall, "The Financing of Research and Development."
[c] P. A. Gompers, "Corporations and the Financing of Innovation: The Corporate Venturing Experience," *Economic Review—Federal Reserve Bank of Atlanta* 87, no. 4 (2002), pp. 1–18.
[d] G. Dushnitsky, "Limitations to External Knowledge Acquisition: The Paradox of Corporate Venture Capital," doctoral dissertation, New York University, 2003.
[e] M. Sheahan, "Corporate Spin Can't Mask the VC Units' Blunders," *Venture Capital Journal*, March 1, 2003.

a particular level of expenditure, particular level(s) and rate of cash inflows, and a discount rate, what is this project worth today?" IRR asks instead, "Given a particular level of expenditure and particular level(s) and rate of cash inflows, what rate of return does this project yield?" For either method, managers must use estimates of the size and timing of expenditures and cash inflows. Both methods enable the decision maker to incorporate some basic measure of risk. For example, riskier projects may be examined by using a higher discount factor in NPV analysis. Managers also often calculate discounted cash flow measures using best-case and worst-case cash flow estimates.

Net Present Value (NPV)

To calculate the NPV of a project, managers first estimate the costs of the project and the cash flows the project will yield (often under a number of different "what if" scenarios). Costs and cash flows that occur in the future must be discounted back to the current period to account for risk and the time value of money. The present value of cash inflows can then be compared to the present value of cash outflows:

$$NPV = \text{Present value of cash inflow} - \text{Present value of cash outflows}$$

FIGURE 7.3
**Example of
Present Value
of Future Cash
Flows**

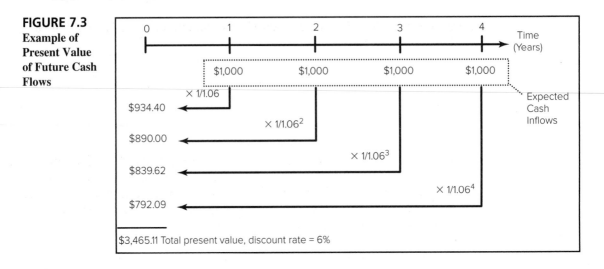

If this value is greater than 0, then the project generates wealth, given the assumptions made in calculating its costs and cash inflows.

To find the present value of cash inflow and outflows, each cash flow must be discounted back to the current period using a discount rate (see Figure 7.3). If there is a single expenditure at the beginning of the project (year 0), the original expenditure can be compared directly to the present value of the future expected cash flows. In the example in Figure 7.3, the present value of the future cash flows (given a discount rate of 6%) is $3,465.11. Thus, if the initial cost of the project were less than $3,465.11, the net present value of the project is positive. If there are cash outflows for multiple periods (as is common with most development projects), those cash outflows would have to be discounted back to the current period.

If the cash inflows from the development project were expected to be the same each year (as they were in Figure 7.3), we can use the formula for calculating the present value of an annuity instead of discounting each of the cash inflows individually. This is particularly useful when cash inflows are expected for many years. The present value of C dollars per period, for t periods, with discount rate r is given by the following formula:

$$\text{Annuity present value} = C \times \frac{1 - \{1/(1 + r)^t\}}{r}$$

**discounted
payback
period**
The time
required to break
even on a project
using discounted
cash flows.

This amount can then be compared to the initial investment. If the cash flows are expected in perpetuity (forever), then a simpler formula can be used:

$$\text{Perpetuity present value} = C \times 1/r$$

The present value of the costs and future cash flows can also be used to calculate the **discounted payback period** (that is, the time required to break even on the project using discounted cash flows). Suppose for the example above, the initial investment required was $2,000. Using the discounted cash inflows, the cumulative discounted cash flows for each year are:

Year	Cash Flow
1	$ 934.40
2	1,833.40
3	2,673.02
4	3,465.11

Thus, the investment will be paid back sometime between the end of year 2 and the end of year 3. The accumulated discounted cash flows by the end of year 2 are $1,833.40, so we need to recover $166.60 in year 3. Since the discounted cash flow expected for year 3 is $839.62, we will have to wait $166.60/$839.61 ≈ .20 of a year. Thus, the payback period is just over two years and two months.

Internal Rate of Return (IRR)

The internal rate of return of a project is the discount rate that makes the net present value of the investment zero. Managers can compare this rate of return to their required return to decide if the investment should be made. Calculating the IRR of a project typically must be done by trial and error, substituting progressively higher interest rates into the NPV equation until the NPV is driven down to zero. Calculators and computers can perform this trial and error. This measure should be used cautiously, however; if cash flows arrive in varying amounts per period, there can be multiple rates of return, and typical calculators or computer programs will often simply report the first IRR that is found.

Both net present value and internal rate of return techniques provide concrete financial estimates that facilitate strategic planning and trade-off decisions. They explicitly consider the timing of investment and cash flows, and the time value of money and risk. They can make the returns of the project seem unambiguous, and managers may find them very reassuring. However, this minimization of ambiguity may be deceptive; discounted cash flow estimates are only as accurate as the original estimates of the profits from the technology, and in many situations it is extremely difficult to anticipate the returns of the technology. Furthermore, such methods discriminate heavily against projects that are long term or risky, and the methods may fail to capture the strategic importance of the investment decision. Technology development projects play a crucial role in building and leveraging firm capabilities, and creating options for the future. Investments in new core technologies are investments in the organization's capabilities and learning, and they create opportunities for the firm that might otherwise be unavailable.[1] Thus, standard discounted cash flow analysis has the potential to severely undervalue a development project's contribution to the firm. For example, Intel's investment in DRAM technology might have been considered a total loss by NPV methods (Intel exited the DRAM business after Japanese competitors drove the price of DRAM to levels Intel could not match). However, the investment in DRAM technology laid the foundation for Intel's ability to develop microprocessors—and this business has proved to be enormously profitable for Intel. To better incorporate strategic implications in the new product development investment decision, some managers and scholars have recently begun promoting the idea of treating new product development decisions as real options, as described below.

Real Options

When a firm develops new core technologies, it is simultaneously investing in its own learning and in the development of new capabilities. Thus, development projects can create valuable future opportunities for the firm that would otherwise be unavailable.[2] Even development projects that appear unsuccessful (as Intel's DRAM discussed above) may prove to be very valuable when they are considered from the perspective of the options they create for the future of the firm. Some managers and scholars have begun arguing that new product development decisions should be evaluated as "**real options**."

real options
The application of stock option valuation methods to investments in nonfinancial assets.

To understand real options, it is first useful to consider the financial model upon which they are based—stock options. A call option on a stock enables an investor to purchase the right to buy the stock at a specified price (the "exercise price") in the future. If, in the future, the stock is worth more than the exercise price, the holder of the option will typically exercise the option by buying the stock. If the stock is worth more than the exercise price plus the price paid for the original option, the option holder makes money on the deal. If the stock is worth less than the exercise price, the option holder will typically choose not to exercise the option, allowing it to expire. In this case, the option holder loses the amount of money paid for the initial option. If, at the time the option is exercised, the stock is worth more than the exercise price but not more than the exercise price plus the amount paid for the original option, the stockholder will typically exercise the option. Even though the stockholder loses money on the deal (some portion of the price paid for the original option), he or she loses less than if he or she allowed the option to expire (the entire price paid for the original option).

In "real options," the assets underlying the value of the option are nonfinancial resources.[3] An investor who makes an initial investment in basic R&D or in breakthrough technologies is, it is argued, buying a real call option to implement that technology later should it prove to be valuable.[4] Figure 7.4 provides examples of investment decisions that can be viewed as real call options. With respect to research and development:

- The cost of the R&D program can be considered the price of a call option.
- The cost of future investment required to capitalize on the R&D program (such as the cost of commercializing a new technology that is developed) can be considered the exercise price.
- The returns to the R&D investment are analogous to the value of a stock purchased with a call option.[5]

As shown in Figure 7.5, the value of a call stock option is zero as long as the price of the stock remains less than the exercise price. If the value of the stock rises above the exercise price, however, the value of the call rises with the value of the stock, dollar for dollar (thus the value of the call rises at a 45-degree angle).[6]

Options are valuable when there is uncertainty, and because technology trajectories are uncertain, an options approach may be useful. Though there has not yet been much empirical work in the area, several authors have developed methodologies and applications of options analysis to valuing technology development investments.[7] Also, some evidence shows that an options approach results in better technology investment decisions than a cash flow analysis approach.[8]

FIGURE 7.4
Examples of Real Call Options

Source: From K. D. Miller and T. B. Folta, "Options Value and Entry Timing," *Strategic Management Journal*, Vol. 23, pp. 655–665. Copyright © 2002 John Wiley & Sons Limited. Reproduced with permission.

Investment Providing the Option	Nature of Option	Benefits from Exercising the Option	Exercise Price	Factors Affecting the Duration
License to commercialize technology	Right to commercialize a technology	• Stream of cash flows from commercialization • Manufacturing experience • Marketing and distribution experience	Cost of manufacturing, marketing, and distribution	• Patent time limit • Availability of substitutes
Equity stake in a partner	Right to acquire partner	• Cash flows • Capabilities of partner	Cost of acquiring partner	• Takeover bid by another partner or outside firm
R&D capability	Right to develop and commercialize technology	• Cash flows • Technological expertise	Cost of implementing the technology	• Competitors' replication or substitution of R&D capabilities

FIGURE 7.5
The Value of a Call Option at Expiration

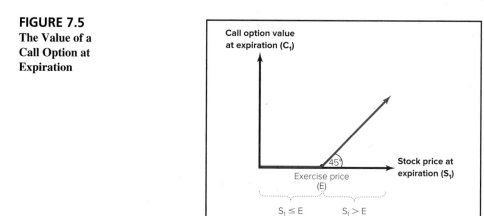

Call option value at expiration (C₁)

Other authors, however, warn against liberal application of the approach, pointing out that technology investment scenarios often do not conform to the same capital market assumptions upon which the approach is based.[9] For instance, implicit in the value of options is the assumption that one can acquire or retain the option for a small price, and then wait for a signal to determine if the option should be exercised.[10] While this assumption might hold true for an outside firm investing venture capital in another firm's innovation effort, it would be rare for this assumption to hold for a company investing in its own development efforts. In the case of a firm undertaking solo new product development, it may not be possible to secure this option at a small price; it may require full investment in the technology before a firm can determine if the technology will be successful.[11] Furthermore, while the value of a stock is independent of the call holder's behavior (that is, the call holder can simply wait and observe whether the value of the stock rises or falls), the value of an R&D investment is not independent of the investor's behavior. A firm's degree of investment, its development capabilities, its complementary assets, and its strategies can all significantly influence the future returns of the development project.[12] Therefore, rather than simply waiting and observing the value of the investment, the investor is an active driver of the value of the investment.

DISADVANTAGES OF QUANTITATIVE METHODS

Quantitative methods for analyzing potential innovation projects can provide concrete financial estimates that facilitate strategic planning and trade-off decisions. They can explicitly consider the timing of investment and cash flows and the time value of money and risk. They can make the returns of the project seem unambiguous, and managers may find them very reassuring. However, this minimization of ambiguity may be deceptive; discounted cash flow estimates are only as accurate as the original estimates of the profits from the technology, and in many situations, it is extremely difficult to anticipate the returns of the technology. As noted by Professor Freek Vermeulen, author of *Business Exposed*, one of the most common mistakes managers make in their innovation strategy is to insist on "seeing the numbers"—for truly innovative products, it is impossible to reliably produce any numbers. It is very difficult to compute the size of a market that does not yet exist.[13] Furthermore, such methods discriminate heavily against projects that are long term or risky, and the methods may fail to capture the strategic importance of the investment decision. Technology development projects play a crucial role in building and leveraging firm capabilities and creating options for the future. Investments in new core technologies are investments in the organization's capabilities and learning, and they create opportunities for the firm that might otherwise be unavailable. Thus, standard discounted cash flow analysis has the potential to severely undervalue a development project's contribution to the firm. For example, Intel's investment in DRAM technology might have been considered a total loss by NPV methods (Intel exited the DRAM business after Japanese competitors drove the price of DRAM to levels Intel could not match). However, the investment in DRAM technology laid the foundation for Intel's ability to develop microprocessors—and this business has proved to be enormously profitable for Intel.

QUALITATIVE METHODS FOR CHOOSING PROJECTS

Most new product development projects require the evaluation of a significant amount of qualitative information. Many factors in the choice of development projects are extremely difficult to quantify, or quantification could lead to misleading results.

Almost all firms utilize some form of qualitative assessment of potential projects, ranging from informal discussions to highly structured approaches.

Screening Questions

As a starting point, a management team is likely to discuss the potential costs and benefits of a project, and the team may create a list of screening questions that are used to structure this discussion. These questions might be organized into categories such as the role of the customer, the role of the firm's capabilities, and the project's timing and cost.[14] Some examples are provided below:

Role of Customer

Market

- Who are the most likely customers of the new product?
- How big is this market? Are there other likely markets for the product?
- What type of marketing will be required to create customer awareness?

Use

- How will customers use the product?
- What new benefits will the product provide the customer?
- What other products are customers likely to consider as substitutes for this product?

Compatibility and Ease of Use

- Will the product be compatible with the customer's existing complements?
- Will the product require significant new learning on the part of the customer?
- How will the customer perceive the product's ease of use?
- Will the product require the customer to bear other costs?

Distribution and Pricing

- Where will the customer buy the product?
- Will the product require installation or assembly?
- How much are customers likely to be willing to pay for the product?

Role of Capabilities

Existing Capabilities

- Does the new project leverage the firm's core competencies or sources of sustainable competitive advantage?
- Will the project render some of the firm's existing competencies obsolete or cannibalize existing products? If so, does the firm have a transition strategy to handle possible cash-flow implications?
- Does the firm have the necessary manufacturing capabilities, and if not, will those capabilities be developed in-house or acquired externally (e.g., outsourcing)?
- Will the firm need to hire employees with new skills?

Competitors' Capabilities

- Do one or more competitors have better capabilities for developing this project?
- If the company does not develop this technology, are competitors likely to?
- Will the company be able to protect its intellectual property through patents, copyright, trademarks, or trade secrets?
- Should the firm seek to form a collaboration with a potential competitor?

Future Capabilities

- Will the project help the firm build new capabilities that will allow it to achieve its strategic intent?
- What other products/markets will the new capabilities enable the firm to develop?
- Is this project a platform that will lead to a family of new products?

Project Timing and Cost

Timing

- How long will the project take to complete?
- Is the firm likely to be first to market? Is pioneering the technology a desirable strategy?
- Is the market ready for the product? (For example, are enabling and complementary technologies well developed? Will customers perceive the value of the technology?)
- If the firm misses its target deadlines, what impact will this have on the potential value of the project?
- Are there already appropriate suppliers and distribution channels?

Cost Factors

- How much will the project cost? What is the potential variability in these costs?
- What will the manufacturing costs be? At what rate are these costs expected to decline with experience?
- Will the firm need to bear other costs related to customer adoption (e.g., production of complements, installation, technical support, etc.)?

After creating a list of questions, managers can use the questions to structure debate about a project, or they can create a scoring mechanism (such as a scaled response to each question such as "Project fits closely with existing competencies" to "Project fits poorly with existing competencies") that can then be weighted according to importance and used in subsequent analysis.

While screening questions such as the one above do not always provide concrete answers about whether or not to fund a project, they enable a firm to consider a wider range of issues that may be important in the firm's development decisions. Consider Boeing's development of the Sonic Cruiser, a supersonic jet that was designed by Boeing, but never made it off the drawing board. Boeing continued designing the aircraft even after it became clear that the jet would not be profitable because Boeing considered the project necessary for preserving the company's development capabilities. As noted

FIGURE 7.6
The Project Map

Source: Adapted with the permission of The Free Press, a Division of Simon & Schuster Adult Publishing Group, from *Revolutionizing Product Development: Quantum Leaps in Speed, Efficiency, and Quality* by Steven C. Wheelwright and Kim B. Clark. Copyright © 1992 by Steven C. Wheelwright and Kim B. Clark. All rights reserved.

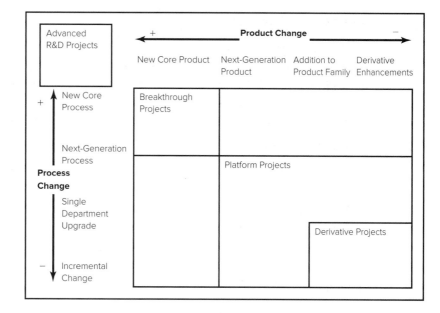

by Walt Gillette, Boeing's development program manager, "If the company doesn't create a new airplane every 12 to 15 years, the needed skills and experience will be gone. Too many of the people who created the last new airplane will have retired or moved on to other companies, and their skills and experience will not have been passed on to the next generation of Boeing employees."[15] Thus, Boeing's development of the Sonic Cruiser is expected to be valuable to the firm even if the only return from the project is the enhancement of the firm's development capabilities. Such value would be difficult to assess via quantitative methods, but is revealed clearly by qualitative analysis.

The Aggregate Project Planning Framework

Many companies find it valuable to map their R&D portfolio according to levels of risk, resource commitment, and timing of cash flows. Managers can use this map to compare their desired balance of projects with their actual balance of projects.[16] It can also help them to identify capacity constraints and better allocate resources.[17] Companies may use a project map (similar to that depicted in Figure 7.6) to aid this process. Four types of development projects commonly appear on this map—advanced R&D, breakthrough, platform, and derivative projects. Over time, a particular technology may migrate through these different types of projects. Advanced R&D projects are the precursor to commercial development projects and are necessary to develop cutting-edge strategic technologies. Breakthrough projects involve development of products that incorporate revolutionary new product and process technologies. For example, while Honda's work on hydrogen fuel cells might be considered an advanced R&D project since it is still a significant distance from a commercial application, the company's development of its original hybrid-electric vehicle, the Insight, would be considered a breakthrough project. The Honda Insight incorporated revolutionary new technology in a commercialized application.

Platform projects typically offer fundamental improvements in the cost, quality, and performance of a technology over preceding generations. Derivative projects involve incremental changes in products and/or processes. A platform project is designed to serve a core group of consumers, whereas derivative projects represent modifications of the basic platform design to appeal to different niches within that core group. For example, Hunter's Care Free humidifier is a platform that offers several derivative versions to appeal to different customer segments. The water storage tank comes in different sizes (e.g., 2.0 gallon, 2.5 gallon, 3.0 gallon); some models include a digital humidistat; and some also include Nite Glo lights. However, all of the models are based on the same Permawick filter design and fan system. Similarly, Toyota's Camry is a platform for a family of car models that includes the Camry LE, Camry SE, and Camry XLE. While all the models are based on the same basic design, each offers a different combination of features to appeal to different market segments. These variations on the Camry theme are derivative products.

Companies that use the project map categorize all their existing projects and projects under consideration by the resources they require (e.g., engineers, time, capital, etc.) and by how they contribute to the company's product line. The company can then map the project types and identify gaps in the development strategy.[18] Managers can also use the map to identify their desired mix of projects, and allocate resources accordingly. The mix of projects represented on such a map should be consistent both with the company's resources, strategic position, and with its strategic intent (as analyzed in Chapter Six). For example, a typical firm experiencing moderate growth might allocate 10 percent of its R&D budget to breakthrough innovation, 30 percent to platform projects, and 60 percent to derivative projects. A firm pursuing more significant growth might allocate higher percentages to breakthrough and platform projects, while a firm that needs to generate more short-term profit might allocate a higher percentage to derivative projects.[19] Respondents to a recent survey administered by the Product Development and Management Association indicated that roughly 8 percent of their projects were breakthrough or advanced R&D projects, 17 percent were platform projects, and 75 percent were derivative projects.

Mapping the company's R&D portfolio encourages the firm to consider both short-term cash flow needs and long-term strategic momentum in its budgeting and planning. For instance, a firm that invests heavily in derivative projects that may be immediately commercialized with little risk may appear to have good returns on its R&D investment in the short run, but then be unable to compete when the market shifts to a newer technology. On the other hand, a firm that invests heavily in advanced R&D or breakthrough projects may be on the leading edge of technology, but run into cash flow problems from a lack of revenues generated from recently commercialized platform or derivative projects. As once noted by Jack Welch, former CEO of General Electric, "You can't grow long term if you can't eat short term. Anyone can manage short. Anyone can manage long. Balancing those two things is what management is."[20]

This is poignantly illustrated in the pharmaceutical industry, where high project failure rates, long product development cycles, and reliance on patent protection can cause a firm to suddenly find it has a devastating gap in its product pipeline. Studies indicate that developing a new drug takes an average of twelve years, and costs about $359 million. In 2011, many of the world's largest pharmaceutical companies were facing a "patent cliff" as the patents began to expire on their blockbuster drugs, exposing the firms to much heavier competition from generics. This situation creates intense volatility in the revenues of a firm, which creates enormous pressures on the firm (including managing staffing, manufacturing capacity, managing R&D funds, and more). As a result, many pharmaceutical firms have begun shifting their emphasis to lower volume, specialty drugs that could potentially be more profitable because they would require less marketing investment and face less competition.

Q-Sort

Q-sort is a simple method for ranking objects or ideas on a number of different dimensions. The Q-sort method has been used for purposes as diverse as identifying personality disorders to establishing scales of customer preferences. Individuals in a group are each given a stack of cards with an object or idea on each card. In the case of new product development, each card could identify a potential project. Then a series of project selection criteria are presented (e.g., technical feasibility, market impact, fit with strategic intent), and for each criterion, the individuals sort their cards in rank order (e.g., best fit with strategic intent) or in categories (e.g., technically feasible versus infeasible) according to that criterion. Individuals then compare their rank orderings and use these comparisons to structure a debate about the projects. After several rounds of sorting and debating, the group is expected to arrive at a consensus about the best projects.[21]

COMBINING QUANTITATIVE AND QUALITATIVE INFORMATION

As demonstrated above, both quantitative methods and qualitative methods offer a number of benefits to managers in choosing development projects. Thus, many firms use a combination of methods to arrive at an investment decision.[22] For example, a firm might have screening questions that require quantitative analysis in addition to qualitative responses. Firms might also use quantitative methods to estimate the cash flows anticipated from a project when balancing their R&D portfolio on a project map. There are also valuation techniques that attempt to translate qualitative assessments into quantitative measures, such as conjoint analysis and data envelopment analysis, as discussed below.

Conjoint Analysis

conjoint analysis
A family of techniques that enables assessment of the weight individuals put on different attributes of a choice.

Conjoint analysis is a family of techniques (including discrete choice, choice modeling, hierarchical choice, trade-off matrices, and pairwise comparisons) used to estimate the specific value individuals place on some attribute of a choice, such as the relative value of features of a product or the relative importance of different outcomes of a development project. While individuals may find it very difficult to accurately assess the weight they put on individual attributes of a decision, conjoint analysis enables these weights to be derived statistically. Conjoint analysis enables a subjective assessment of a complex decision to be decomposed into quantitative scores of the relative importance of different criteria.

The most common use of conjoint analysis is to assess the relative importance to customers of different product attributes—these values can then be used in development and pricing decisions. For example, potential customers might be given a series of cards describing different models of a camera with different features and prices. The individuals are then asked to rate each in terms of its desirability (e.g., on a scale of 1 to 10) or asked to order the models in terms of which they would most likely buy. Multiple regression is then used to assess the degree to which each attribute influences the overall rating, resulting in the assignment of specific weights to individual criteria.

In the mid-1980s, Marriott was facing a nearly saturated market for full-service, upscale hotels. Marriott's managers knew that the only way to sustain the company's 20 percent annual sales growth rate was to expand its product line. Marriott's management believed there was a market opportunity in the moderately priced ($35 to $60 a night) hotel category. The dominant chains in this category (e.g., Holiday Inn, Howard Johnson) tended to receive poor marks for customer satisfaction, and Marriott's managers believed that a chain that provided newer facilities and more consistent service would be enthusiastically received by customers. They also knew, however, that the company's most valuable resource was its well-established brand name, and they were reluctant to hastily affix the Marriott name to a scaled-down version of its hotels.

The company constructed a carefully structured plan for evaluating potential designs for a mid-price hotel line. The company first conducted focus groups to identify different customer segments and the major factors that influenced their purchase decisions. The factors identified included external surroundings, room, food, lounge, services, leisure activities, and security. Within each major factor, there were several specific attributes that could take on multiple levels of product or service quality. For example, within the "services" factor, one of the attributes was "reservations," and the company had two levels: "call the hotel directly" or "call an 800 reservation number." A sample of hotel customers was selected to participate in a research group whereby each participant was given a fictional $35 with which to build his or her own hotel. Each participant was given seven cards (one card for each

of the major factors identified above). On the card was listed each of the specific attributes and their possible levels, along with a price for each level. The participants would evaluate one card at a time, selecting the features they desired. If participants went over the $35 budget, they were required to eliminate some features or choose a less expensive level of service. This technique helped management understand customer priorities and the trade-offs made by different customer segments. On the basis of these priorities, the managers then developed a series of hotel profiles offering different combinations of features and levels of service. Participants were then asked to rate each of these profiles. The managers could then use regression to assess how different levels of service within a specific attribute influenced customer ratings of the hotel overall. For example, as illustrated in Figure 7.7, after the hotel profiles are rated by the participants, the values for the levels in the profiles and the participant ratings can be entered into a spreadsheet. The ratings can then be regressed on the attribute levels, yielding a model that estimates the relative importance of each attribute.

On the basis of their conjoint analysis, Marriott's managers came up with the Courtyard concept: relatively small hotels (about 150 rooms) with limited amenities, small restaurants, small meeting rooms, enclosed courtyards, high-security features, well-landscaped exteriors, and rates of $40 to $60 a night. Courtyard by Marriott turned out to be very successful. By the end of 2002, there were 533 Courtyard hotels (508 of those were in the United States), and their average occupancy rate of 72 percent was well above the industry average.

continued

These weights provide a quantitative assessment of the trade-offs that customers implicitly consider in their evaluation of products. The firm can then use these weights in a series of "what if" scenarios to consider the implications of different product configurations. For example, Marriott used conjoint analysis to determine what features customers would most value in a moderately priced hotel. This analysis enabled Marriott to develop its very successful line of Courtyard by Marriott hotels (see the accompanying Theory in Action).

concluded

FIGURE 7.7
Hotel Profiles and Ratings for Conjoint Analysis

Hotel Profile 1	Hotel Profile 2	Hotel Profile 3	...
Reservations			
1-800 number (1)	Call hotel directly (0)	1-800 number (1)	
Room Service			
Full-menu, 24 hours a day (5)	Limited menu, offered 6 A.M. to midnight (3)	No room service (1)	
Newspaper Delivery			
None (0)	Daily (1)	None (0)	
Etc.			

Attributes	Reservations	Room Service	Newspaper Delivery	Etc.	Overall Rating (1–10)
Participant 1					
Hotel Profile 1	1	5	0		8
Hotel Profile 2	0	3	1		7
Hotel Profile 3	1	1	0		5
Participant 2					
Hotel Profile 1	1	5	0		7
Hotel Profile 2	0	3	1		9
Hotel Profile 3	1	1	0		4
Etc.					

Source: Adapted from R. J. Thomas, *New Product Success Stories* (New York: John Wiley & Sons, 1995).

Data Envelopment Analysis

data envelopment analysis (DEA)
A method of ranking projects based on multiple decision criteria by comparing them to a hypothetical efficiency frontier.

Data envelopment analysis (DEA) is a method of assessing a potential project (or other decision) using multiple criteria that may have different kinds of measurement units.[23] For instance, for a particular set of potential projects, a firm might have cash flow estimates, a ranking of the project's fit with existing competencies, a ranking of the project's potential for building desired future competencies, a score for its technical feasibility, and a score for its customer desirability. Each of these measures captures something that is qualitatively different, and the numbers assigned to them are based on different units of measure. While the first measure is in dollars and is a nearly continuous measure, the second two measures are rank orders and thus are categorical measures with little information about what the difference is between one level of rank and another. The last two measures are scores that might be based on a ranking system or scaling system (e.g., a Likert measure that goes from one to seven).

FIGURE 7.8
DEA Ranking of the Advanced Technologies Group's 10 Most Attractive Projects and Every 50th Project Thereafter

Source: Adapted from J. D. Linton, S. T. Walsch, and J. Morabito, "Analysis, Ranking and Selection of R&D Projects in a Portfolio," *R&D Management* 32, no. 2 (2002), pp. 139–48.

Rank	Intellectual Property	Product Market	Investment	Cash Flow (most likely)	Cash Flow (optimistic)	Cash Flow (pessimistic)
1	2.25	1.5	$4,322	$1,296,700	$1,353,924	$1,184,192
2	1.5	1.5	850	525,844	551,538	493,912
3	1.5	1.5	1	4	4	3
4	2.25	2.25	478	545,594	822,164	411,082
5	1.5	1.5	1	15	15	11
6	1.5	2.25	65	89,144	178,289	0
7	1.5	1.5	1,068	685,116	1,027,386	342,558
8	1.5	1.5	4	3,766	4,707	2,824
9	1.5	1.5	20	4,800	4,800	−96
10	1.5	2.25	2	23	27	18
50	1.5	2.25	9	116	139	93
100	1.5	1.5	15	60	72	48
150	2.25	2.25	40	5,531	13,829	2,766
200	2.25	1.5	38	90	135	45

efficiency frontier
The range of hypothetical configurations that optimize a combination of features.

Data envelopment analysis uses linear programming to combine these different measures from the projects to create a hypothetical **efficiency frontier** that represents the best performance on each measure. It can also consider which measures are inputs (such as costs) versus outputs (expected benefits). It then measures the distance of each project from this frontier to give it an efficiency value. These values can then be used to rank-order the projects or identify projects that clearly dominate others.[24] For example, Figure 7.8 shows a DEA ranking of projects evaluated by the Advanced Technologies Group of Bell Laboratories. The Advanced Technologies Group chose to evaluate projects in terms of three measures of discounted cash flows expected from the project (most likely, optimistic scenario, pessimistic scenario), the investment required, and each project's desirability from the perspective of intellectual property benefits and product market benefits. For the latter two measures, projects were given a score of 1, 1.5, or 2.25 based on the group's model for intellectual property and product market benefits. These scores reflect this particular group's scoring system—it would be just as appropriate to use a scaled measure (e.g., 1 = very strong intellectual property benefits, to 7 = no intellectual property benefits), or other type of measure used by the firm. As shown, the DEA method enabled Bell Laboratories to rank-order different projects, despite the fact that they offered different kinds of benefits and risks.

The biggest advantage of DEA is that it enables comparisons of projects using multiple kinds of measures. However, just as with several of the methods described previously, the results of DEA are only as good as the data utilized. Managers bear the responsibility of determining which measures are most important to include and of ensuring that the measures are accurate.

Summary of Chapter

1. Firms often use a combination of quantitative and qualitative methods to evaluate which projects should be funded. Though some methods assume that all valuable projects will be funded, resources are typically constrained and firms must use capital rationing.

2. The most commonly used quantitative methods of evaluating projects are discounted cash flow methods such as net present value (NPV) or internal rate of return (IRR). While both methods enable the firm to create concrete estimates of returns of a project and account for the time value of money, the results are only as good as the cash flow estimates used in the analysis (which are often unreliable). Both methods also tend to heavily discount long-term or risky projects, and can undervalue projects that have strategic implications that are not well reflected by cash flow estimates.

3. Some firms now use a real options approach to assessing projects. Real options better account for the long-run strategic implications of a project. Unfortunately, many new product development investment decisions do not conform to the assumptions inherent in an options valuation approach.

4. One commonly used qualitative method of assessing development projects is to subject the project to a series of screening questions that consider the project from multiple angles. These questions may be used merely to structure the discussion of a project or to create rating scales that are then utilized in an approach that combines qualitative and quantitative assessment.

5. A company's portfolio of projects typically includes projects of different types (e.g., advanced R&D, breakthrough, platform, and derivative projects) that have different resource requirements and different rates of return. Companies can use a project map to assess what their balance of projects is (or should be) and allocate resources accordingly.

6. Q-sort is a qualitative method of assessing projects whereby individuals rank each project under consideration according to a series of criteria. Q-sort is most commonly used to provide a format for discussion and debate.

7. Conjoint analysis is a method of converting qualitative assessments of a choice into quantitative weights of the different criteria underlying the choice. It is most often used for assessing how customers value different product attributes.

8. Data envelopment analysis (DEA) is another method that combines qualitative and quantitative measures. DEA enables projects that have multiple criteria in different measurement units to be ranked by comparing them to a hypothetical efficiency frontier.

Discussion Questions

1. What are the advantages and disadvantages of discounted cash flow methods such as NPV and IRR?

2. For what kind of development projects might a real options approach be appropriate? For what kind of projects would it be inappropriate?

3. Why might a firm use both qualitative and quantitative assessments of a project?

4. Identify a development project you are familiar with. What methods do you believe were used to assess the project? What methods do you believe *should have been* used to assess the project?

5. Will different methods of evaluating a project typically yield the same conclusions about whether to fund its development? Why or why not?

<table>
<tr><td rowspan="3">**Suggested Further Reading**</td></tr>
</table>

Suggested Further Reading

Classics

Amram, M., and N. Kulatilaka, Real Options: Managing Strategic Investment in an Uncertain World (Boston, MA: Harvard Business School Press, 1999).

Danneels, E., and E. J. Kleinschmidtb, " Product Innovativeness from the Firm's Perspective: Its Dimensions and Their Relation with Project Selection and Performance," *Journal of Product Innovation Management 18* (2001), pp. 357–373.

Ding, M., and J. Eliashberg, "Structuring the New Product Development Pipeline," *Management Science* 48 (2002), pp. 343–63.

Wheelwright, S. C., and K. B. Clark, "Creating Project Plans to Focus Product Development," *Harvard Business Review*, March–April 1992, pp. 67–82.

Recent Work

Bessant, J,. B. von Stamm, K. M. Moeslein, and A. Neyer, "Backing Outsiders: Selection Strategies for Discontinuous Innovation," *R&D Management* 40 (2010) pp. 345–356.

Brunner, D., L. Fleming, A. MacCormack, and D. Zinner, "R&D Project Selection and Portfolio Management: A Review of the Past, a Description of the Present, and a Sketch of the Future," in Shane, S. *Handbook of Technology and Innovation Management* (West Sussex, England: Wiley & Sons, 2008).

Nagji, B., and G. Tuff, "Managing Your Innovation Portfolio," *Harvard Business Review*, May (2012).

Endnotes

1. B. Kogut and N. Kulatilaka, "Options Thinking and Platform Investments: Investing in Opportunity," *California Management Review* 36, no. 2 (1994), pp. 52–72.

2. Ibid.

3. M. Amram and N. Kulatilaka, *Real Options: Managing Strategic Investment in an Uncertain World* (Boston: Harvard Business School Press, 1999); and K. D. Miller and T. B. Folta, "Option Value and Entry Timing," *Strategic Management Journal* 23 (2002), pp. 655–65.

4. D. Hurry, A. T. Miller, and E. H. Bowman, "Calls on High-Technology: Japanese Exploration of Venture Capital Investments in the United States," *Strategic Management Journal* 13 (1992), pp. 85–101.

5. G. Mitchell and W. Hamilton, "Managing R&D as a Strategic Option," *Research Technology Management* 31, no. 3 (1988), pp. 15–23.

6. S. A. Ross, R. W. Westerfield, and B. D. Jordan, *Fundamentals of Corporate Finance* (Boston: Irwin, 1993).

7. M. Amran and N. Kulatilaka, *Real Options* (Boston: Harvard Business School Press, 1999); F. P. Boer, "Valuation of Technology Using Real Options," *Research Technology Management*

43 (2000), pp. 26–31; and R. T. McGrath, "Assessing Technology Projects Using Real Options Reasoning," *Research Technology Management* 43 (July–August, 2000), pp. 35–50.

8. M. Benaroch and R. Kauffman, "Justifying Electronic Banking Network Expansion Using Real Options Analysis," *MIS Quarterly* 24 (June 2000), pp. 197–226.

9. M. Perlitz, T. Peske, and R. Schrank, "Real Options Valuation: The New Frontier in R&D Evaluation?" *R&D Management* 29 (1999), pp. 255–70.

10. E. H. Bowman and D. Hurry, "Strategy through the Option Lens: An Integrated View of Resource Investments and the Incremental-Choice Process," *Academy of Management Review* 18 (1993), pp. 760–82.

11. M. A. Schilling, "Technological Lock Out: An Integrative Model of the Economic and Strategic Factors Driving Success and Failure," *Academy of Management Review* 23 (1998), pp. 267–85.

12. T. Chan, J. A. Nickerson, and H. Owan, "Strategic Management of R&D Pipelines," Washington University working paper, 2003.

13. Vermeulen, F. 2011. "Five mistaken beliefs business leaders have about innovation." *Forbes*, May 30th. (www.forbes.com)

14. K. R. Allen, *Bringing New Technology to Market* (Upper Saddle River, NJ: Prentice Hall, 2003).

15. L. Gunter, 2002, "The Need for Speed," Boeing Frontiers. Retrieved November 20, 2002, from www.boeing.com/news/frontiers/archive/2002/july/i_ca2.html.

16. Y. Wind and V. Mahajan, "New Product Development Process: A Perspective for Reexamination," *Journal of Product Innovation Management* 5 (1988), pp. 304–10.

17. C. Christenson, "Using Aggregate Project Planning to Link Strategy, Innovation, and the Resource Allocation Process," Note no. 9-301-041 (2000), Harvard Business School.

18. S. C. Wheelwright and K. B. Clark, "Creating Project Plans to Focus Product Development," *Harvard Business Review,* March–April 1992.

19. C. Christenson, "Using Aggregate Project Planning to Link Strategy, Innovation, and the Resource Allocation Process."

20. J. A. Byrne, "Jack," *BusinessWeek,* June 8, 1998, p. 90.

21. Allen, *Bringing New Technology to Market;* and A. I. Helin and W. B. Souder, "Experimental Test of a Q-Sort Procedure for Prioritising R&D Projects," *IEEE Transactions on Engineering Management* EM-21 (1974), pp. 159–64.

22. R. G. Cooper, S. J. Edgett, and E. J. Kleinschmidt, "New Product Portfolio Management: Practices and Performance," *Journal of Product Innovation Management* 16 (1999), pp. 333–51.

23. A. W. Charnes, W. Cooper, and E. Rhodes, "Measuring the Efficiency of Decision Making Units," *European Journal of Operational Research* 2 (1978), pp. 429–44.

24. J. D. Linton, S. T. Walsch, and J. Morabito, "Analysis, Ranking and Selection of R&D Projects in a Portfolio," *R&D Management* 32, no. 2 (2002), pp. 139–48.

Collaboration Strategies

Ending HIV? Sangamo Biosciences and Gene Editing

In 1995, Edward Lanphier founded Sangamo Biosciences for the purpose of developing zinc-finger nucleases (ZFNs), a new technology that offered potential for "editing" the genetic code of a living individual to correct genetically based diseases (e.g., hemophilia, sickle cell anemia, Huntington's disease, and many others) or to confer genetic resistance to non-genetically based diseases.

ZFNs work by cutting the DNA in a chosen spot. The cell then typically attempts to repair the cut by either by polishing the two ends of DNA and sealing them back together or by copying the corresponding section of DNA in the other half of the chromosome pair. Since many diseases occur because of a gene on a single half of the chromosome pair, this "homologous substitution" from the other chromosome corrects the faulty gene. Alternatively, scientists can even provide a template gene sequence that they want to use to substitute for the cleaved portion of the DNA (see Figure 8.1).

Gene editing offered a radical new way to cure or prevent diseases, but it required a significant amount of R&D work both to develop ZFNs that were precise and reliable enough to safely edit human genes and to develop a delivery mechanism that would ensure the ZFNs penetrated enough of an individual's cells to make a difference. Clinical trials to establish the treatment's safety and efficacy to get FDA approval would also be a huge hurdle to overcome.

Since none of Sangamo's products were commercially available yet, the company was entirely reliant upon grants and funding from partners for its survival. Though Sangamo had signed big collaboration agreements with Shire AG and Biogen IDEC for several of its treatment areas, it had ambitions to develop its revolutionary treatment for HIV on its own, establishing itself as a fully integrated biopharmaceutical company.

Correcting Monogenic Diseases

Monogenic diseases are diseases that are caused by a defect in a single gene. One example is hemophilia. People with hemophilia lack sufficient clotting factors in

FIGURE 8.1
Gene editing with nucleases

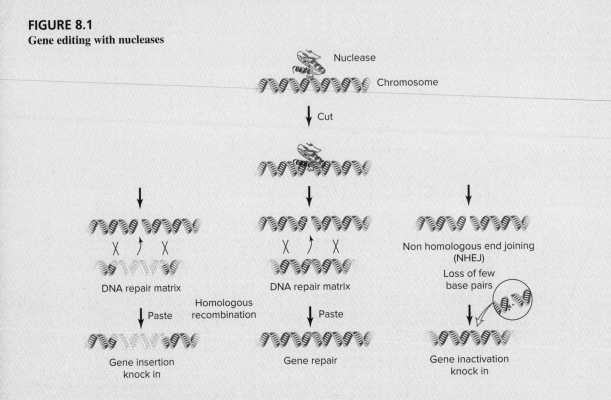

their blood, resulting in them bleeding longer after an injury. Internal bleeding, in particular, can cause significant damage and be life threatening. Individuals with hemophilia need regular infusions to replace the clotting factor in their blood. Sangamo's ZFN treatment offered the hope of a cure, rather than lifelong treatment.[a] Sangamo had already demonstrated that its ZFN method for treating hemophilia worked in mice and was preparing to file an application to begin clinical trials. Sangamo also had developed treatments for sickle cell anemia and beta-thalassemia, also monogenic diseases. Normally patients with sickle cell anemia or beta-thalassemia require lifelong care or bone marrow transplants, at great expense and risk. Sangamo, however, had shown in the laboratory that its treatment could knock out the BCL11A gene causing these diseases.

Another example of a monogenic disease is Huntington's Disease (HD). HD is a devastating neurologic disease in which people lose their motor coordination, cognition, and memory. The disease is progressive and usually fatal within 10–20 years of onset. The disease is a result of a mutation in a single gene, the Huntingtin gene that results in a greater-than-usual number of repeats of the CAG DNA sequence, resulting in a mutant form of the Huntingtin protein accumulating in cells. Most individuals inherit only one copy of the faulty gene, and it only takes one copy to produce the disease. Furthermore, 50 percent of the children of an HD sufferer also inherit the disease. Though previous research had explored ways to decrease the Huntingtin protein in cells, it turned out that the normal form of the protein is essential, and mice lacking the normal Huntingtin protein died before birth. Sangamo, however, developed a ZFN method to identify and "turn off" only the faulty gene.

This meant that an individual would have only one operational copy of the gene which would continue to produce the normal form of the Huntingtin protein.

Whereas there were treatments available that could at least stop or slow the progression of hemophilia, sickle cell anemia, and beta-thalassemia, there were no such treatments for Huntington's—nothing had been found that could halt its progression. Thus, Sangamo's presentation of promising results for its HD treatment was big news—its success could mean the difference between life and death for sufferers of HD.

Drug Development and Clinical Trials

Drug development is hugely expensive and risky. Most studies indicate that it costs at least $1.5 billion and a decade of research to bring a new Food and Drug Administration (FDA)-approved pharmaceutical product to market.[b] The statistics on drug development costs are, in fact, an understatement because they do not fully account for the costs of the many failed drugs that are abandoned earlier in the development process. In the pharmaceutical industry, only one out of every 5,000 compounds tested makes it to the pharmacist's shelf, and only one-third of those will be successful enough to recoup the investment in researching and developing the original 5,000 compounds. Accounting for investment in failed drug efforts suggests that the cost of drug development is much higher than is typically reported. A study of R&D spending and new drug approvals published in Forbes in 2012, for example, found that firms spent over $6 billion per approved drug (see Table 8.1).[c,d]

Most studies suggested that the biggest cost in drug development was the cost of clinical trials—a cost that is borne by the sponsoring organization (usually the company that developed the drug). To be approved by the FDA in the United States, most drugs have to go through several phases of trials. First, in

TABLE 8.1
Research Spending and New Drug Approvals[e]

Company	Number of drugs approved	Total R&D Spending 1997–2011 ($Mil)	R&D Spending Per Drug ($Mil)
AstraZeneca	5	58,955	11,790.93
GlaxoSmithKline	10	81,708	8,170.81
Sanofi	8	63,274	7,909.26
Roche Holding	11	85,841	7,803.77
Pfizer	14	108,178	7,727.03
Johnson & Johnson	15	88,285	5,885.65
Eli Lilly & Co	11	50,347	4,577.04
Abbott Laboratories	8	35,970	4,496.21
Merck & Co Inc	16	67,360	4,209.99
Bristol-Myers Squibb Co	11	45,675	4,152.26
Novartis	21	83,646	3,983.13
Amgen Inc	9	33,229	3,692.14
AVERAGE:	**11.58**	**66,872.33**	**6,199.85**

Sources: InnoThink Center For Research In Biomedical Innovation; Thomson Reuters Fundamentals via FactSet Research Systems

preclinical studies, the company will usually assess the safety and efficacy of the drug using animals. In **Phase 0** trials, a single dose (smaller than what would be used to provide the therapeutic treatment) is given to a small number (10–15) of human subjects to evaluate what the drug does to the body. If successful, the drug may be entered into **Phase 1** clinical trials, whereby the drug is given to a somewhat larger group of people (20–80) to evaluate its safety, determine dosage ranges, and identify side effects. Phase 1 trials are primarily to assess the safety of the drug. In **Phase 2** trials, the drug is given to larger groups of people (100–300) to evaluate its effectiveness and further evaluate its safety and side effects. Finally, in **Phase 3**, the drug is given to very large groups of subjects (1,000–3,000) to confirm its effectiveness compared to alternatives and gather still further information on its safety.

Finally, if the drug successfully makes it through Phase 3 clinical trials, the sponsoring organization can apply for a New Drug Approval from the FDA. The entire process typically takes at least 10 to 12 years, costs hundreds of millions of dollars, and as shown in the funnel above, the vast majority of new drug projects do not make it through the process successfully.

Competing Technologies

As if drug development was not risky enough, Sangamo also faced the threat that its ZFN technology would be rendered obsolete by other gene editing alternatives. In early 2015, two other gene editing alternatives were gaining traction: TALENs (transcription activator-like effector nucleases), and CRISPRs (clustered regularly interspaced short palindromic repeats). TALENs are like ZFNs in that they are special nucleases that identify and bind to a specific part of the DNA and cut the genome at a desired spot. The main difference between the two is how they identify the right DNA binding location. By 2015, ZFN technology was more mature and better developed, but TALEN technology was considered more straightforward to design treatments with, and thus many considered it to have an advantage in the longer term.[f] According to Stephen Ekker, director of the Mayo Addiction Research Center at the Mayo Clinic Cancer Center, while ZFNs had established the proof of principle for genome-editing technology, "TALENs . . . do most of what ZFNs do, but cheaper, faster and better."[g] On the other hand, TALEN molecules were larger, which made them more difficult to deliver to chosen regions of the body (a particular challenge was getting gene editing nucleases past the blood–brain barrier for treatment of diseases such as Huntington's). Since both technologies had advantages and disadvantages, their sponsors would have to race to get effective treatments to market ahead of each other.

CRISPRs were somewhat different. CRISPR technology harnessed a natural defense system of bacteria that has evolved to recognize and eliminate foreign DNA, giving bacteria "adaptive immunity." CRISPRs were even more simple and efficient than TALENS, fueling enormous excitement over their potential. However, because CRISPRs used a very short RNA sequence to guide their activity, some people worried that their effects wouldn't be precise enough—that is, they could result in "off target" cleavages—a highly undesirable result!

As of early 2015, there remained great uncertainty about which of the gene editing technologies would pay off. This uncertainty, unfortunately, dampened investor support for all three technologies.

Sangamo's Partnerships

Biotechnology firms could spend years earning only losses while they developed their treatments. Sangamo was no exception—it had yet to make any money from sale of its products. All of its revenues came from research grants and collaboration agreements (see financials in exhibit 1), and it outspent those revenues in R&D, accumulating losses in each year. This highlights the challenging nature of drug development: Though the company had developed ground breaking treatments that could radically improve the lives of several different patient populations, it was financially quite vulnerable.

As of 2015, Sangamo had only 84 full-time employees; it did not have the resources to do its own clinical testing, manufacturing, or marketing. For these stages of drug development, Sangamo would be reliant on partnerships with much larger firms.

Biogen Idec. Biogen Idec was a Cambridge, Massachusetts based biotech giant, with almost $10 billion in revenues for 2014. Most of its treatments focused on immunology and neurology, and it was probably best known for its best-selling Avonex (for multiple sclerosis), Tysabri (for multiple sclerosis and Crohn's disease), and Rituxan (a monoclonal antibody treatment for non-Hodgkin's lymphoma and rheumatoid arthritis). Biogen earned the majority (70%) of its revenues in North America and had direct sales operations in about 30 countries and used distribution partners to reach another 60 countries.

Biogen was excited by Sangamo's prospects with its zinc-finger technology and entered into a partnership with the company to develop treatments for sickle cell anemia and beta-thalassemia. Under the terms of the deal, Biogen would give Sangamo $20 million upfront and Sangamo would be responsible for performing all of the R&D on the treatments until they could be proven to work on humans. Then Biogen would take over with clinical trials, manufacturing and marketing, and Sangamo would get milestone payments of up to $300 million and double digit royalties if the products earned sales.

Shire AG. Shire was one of the UK's largest specialty biopharmaceutical companies with almost $5 billion in revenues in 2013 and operated in three main segments: specialty pharmaceuticals, human genetic therapies, and regenerative medicine. The company had a large and well-established global marketing and sales infrastructure. Though the company earned the majority (70%) of its sales in North America, it had direct operations in about 30 countries and sold products to more than 50 countries. Shire was known for being a highly acquisitive company, having acquired NPS pharmaceuticals, ViroPharma, Janssen Pharmaceuticals, and Advanced BioHealing just in the last few years. Its two most well-known drugs were treatments for Attention Deficit Disorder (ADD): Vyvanse and Adderall.

In January 2012, Sangamo entered into an agreement with Shire AG to further develop its ZNF treatments for hemophilia, Huntington's disease, and other

FIGURE 8. 2
HIV/AIDS Worldwide, 2013

Source: *UNAIDS*

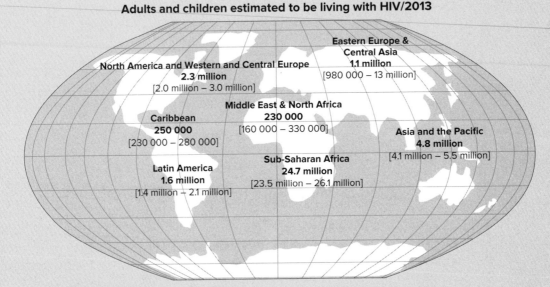

Adults and children estimated to be living with HIV/2013

Eastern Europe & Central Asia
1.1 million
[980 000 – 13 million]

North America and Western and Central Europe
2.3 million
[2.0 million – 3.0 million]

Middle East & North Africa
230 000
[160 000 – 330 000]

Caribbean
250 000
[230 000 – 280 000]

Asia and the Pacific
4.8 million
[4.1 million – 5.5 million]

Latin America
1.6 million
[1.4 million – 2.1 million]

Sub-Saharan Africa
24.7 million
[23.5 million – 26.1 million]

Total: 35.0 million [33.2 million – 37.2 million]

diseases. Like the Biogen deal, Shire agreed to pay Sangamo an upfront fee, plus milestone fees of up to $213.5 million for each of seven targets.[h]

A World-Changing Opportunity: Creating Immunity to HIV

One of the most exciting potential applications of ZFNs was creating a treatment that could cure HIV. In 2013, approximately 35 million people were living with HIV/AIDS worldwide (see Figure 8.2). However, a small percentage of people have a mutation in their CCR5 gene—a gene that makes a protein found on the surface of cells. The mutation makes it difficult for HIV to enter their cells. Individuals receive their genes in pairs—one on a specific chromosome from one parent, and another on the paired chromosome from the other parent. Individuals with one copy of the mutated gene have some protection against HIV infection and experience a less severe form of the disease if infection occurs. Individuals with two copies of the mutated CCR5 gene are typically immune to HIV. These gene mutations appear in up to 20 percent of people of European descent (scientists hypothesize that the gene mutation conferred resistance to the Bubonic plague or smallpox epidemics, leading this gene to be more prevalent in populations of people that survived such epidemics). People with the mutation appear to suffer no health problems from the mutation.

The potential for exploiting the CCR5 mutation gained widespread attention when a study published in 2011 revealed that an AIDS patient with leukemia had received a bone marrow stem cell transplant from a donor with the CCR5 mutation and subsequently appeared to be cured of AIDS. After the bone marrow

FIGURE 8.3
Summary of Sangamo's Research Programs and Drug Pipeline

Source: www.sangamo.com

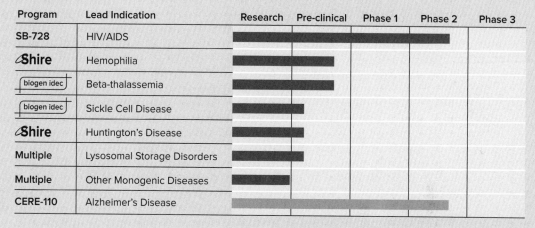

Program	Lead Indication	Research	Pre-clinical	Phase 1	Phase 2	Phase 3
SB-728	HIV/AIDS					
⟋Shire	Hemophilia					
biogen idec	Beta-thalassemia					
biogen idec	Sickle Cell Disease					
⟋Shire	Huntington's Disease					
Multiple	Lysosomal Storage Disorders					
Multiple	Other Monogenic Diseases					
CERE-110	Alzheimer's Disease					

transplant, the patient was able to discontinue all antiretroviral therapy and the virus did not reappear in his blood.[i]

Finding a bone marrow match with a CCR5 mutation is extremely unlikely, and getting a bone marrow transplant is risky. Sangamo thus decided to use its ZFN gene editing technology to develop a simpler method by which individuals could be given the mutation. Early results released by Sangamo in 2014 were promising: The treatment appeared to be well-tolerated and reduced the viral load of several patients who had been taken off of their antiretroviral therapy for 12 weeks during the study.[j] However, the percent of cells showing the mutation declined over time, which meant further work needed to be done to find a way to modify enough of the patients' genes for the therapy to be a reliable and permanent treatment.

The Future...

Sangamo clearly had a lot on its plate. It had revolutionary treatments in clinical trials for several major diseases, including the potential to create a cure for HIV. In the short term, its business was focused on developing treatments through early-stage clinical trials that it would hand over to partners who had deeper pockets and were better positioned to conduct late stage clinical trials, production, and marketing. However, in the long run, Sangamo wanted to be able to do all of its own clinical testing, production and marketing, to better capture the value of its innovative technologies. Currently, Sangamo had no revenues from actual products—only grants from research foundations and cash from upfront fees paid by its licensing partners. It was also spending over $30 million a year on R&D, and posting huge losses, year after year. Sangamo thus had to carefully weigh the pros and cons of developing its HIV treatment alone.

Discussion Questions

1. What were the pros and cons of Sangamo pursuing its gene editing programs alone versus working with a partner?
2. Does the HIV program offer any special opportunities or challenges?
3. What do you think Sangamo should do regarding the HIV program? Should it license the technology to a large pharmaceutical? Should it form a joint venture with another biotech or pharma company? If so, who?

[a] Hersher, R. 2012. A whole clot of hope for new hemophilia therapies. *Nature Medicine*. February 2.

[b] *See* Joseph A. DiMasi & Henry G. Grabowski, *The Costs of Biopharmaceutical R&D: Is Biotech Different?* 28 Managerial & Decision Econ. 469, 469 (2007).

[c] M Herper, *The Truly Staggering Costs of Inventing New Drugs*. Forbes, February 10th (2012).

[d] According to a study by the Manhattan Institute for Policy Research, the majority of the drug development expense is due to the extremely costly and time-consuming process of clinical trials: If analysis is limited to drugs that are ultimately approved by the FDA, phase 3 clinical trials represented over 90 percent of the total cost of development. (*Project FDA Report*, Manhattan Institute for Policy Research, No. 5 April 2012)

[e] Herper, M. 2012. *The Truly Staggering Costs of Inventing New Drugs*. Forbes, February 10th.

[f] Gaj, T, Gersbach, CA, Barbas CF III, "ZFN, TALEN, and CRISPR/Cas-based methods for genome engineering," *Trends Biotechnol*, 31:397–405, July 2013; Pennisi, E, "The CRISPR Craze," *Science*, 341:833–6, August 23, 2013.

[g] J.M. Perkel. 2013. Genome editing with CRISPRs, TALENs, and ZFNs. *Biocompare*, August 27th.

[h] Renauer, C. 2014. How Sangamo BioSciences, Inc. is partnering to success. *The Motley Fool*, January 29th.

[i] Allers, K, Hugger, G, Hoffman, J, Loddenkemper, C, Riger, K, Thiel, E & Schneider, T. 2011. Evidence for the cure of HIV infection by CCR5Δ32/Δ32 stem cell transplantation. *Blood*, 117:2791–9.

[j] 2014. Gene editing of CCR5 in autologous CD4 T-cells of persons infected with HIV. *New England Journal of Medicine*, 370:897–906.

OVERVIEW

Firms frequently face difficult decisions about the scope of activities to perform in-house, and whether to perform them alone as a solo venture or to perform them collaboratively with one or more partners. As mentioned in Chapter Two, a significant portion of innovation arises not from any single individual or organization, but instead from the collaborative efforts of multiple individuals or organizations. Collaboration can often enable firms to achieve more, at a faster rate, and with less cost or risk than they can achieve alone. However, collaboration also often entails relinquishing some degree of control over development and some share of the expected rewards of innovation, plus it can expose the firm to risk of malfeasance by its partner(s). In this chapter, we will first consider the reasons that a firm might choose to engage in collaborative development or might choose to avoid it. We will then review some of the most common types of collaborative arrangements and their specific advantages and disadvantages.

REASONS FOR GOING SOLO

A firm might choose to engage in solo development of a project for a number of reasons. First, the firm may perceive no need to collaborate with other organizations—it may possess all the necessary capabilities and resources for a particular development project in-house. Alternatively, the firm may prefer to obtain complementary skills or resources from a partner, but there may be no available partner that is appropriate or willing to collaborate. A firm might also choose to develop a project as a solo venture if it is concerned that collaborating would put its proprietary technologies at risk, or if it seeks to have full control over the project's development and returns. Furthermore, a firm's solo development of a technological innovation might give it more opportunities to build and renew its capabilities.

1. Availability of Capabilities

Whether a firm chooses to partner on a project is largely determined by the degree to which it possesses all of the necessary capabilities in-house and the degree to which one or more potential partners have necessary capabilities. If a firm has all of the necessary capabilities for a project, it may have little need to collaborate with others and may opt to go it alone. Furthermore, if a firm finds that it lacks certain required capabilities but there are also no potential partners with such capabilities, it may be forced to develop the capabilities on its own.

For example, in the late 1970s Monsanto was interested in developing food crop seeds that were genetically modified to survive strong herbicides. Monsanto's Roundup, a powerful herbicide, had been introduced in 1974 and had been remarkably successful. However, Roundup killed almost all plants that it came into contact with and thus had to be applied with great care. If crops could be developed that were genetically modified to resist Roundup, the herbicide could be used more easily and in larger quantities. The biotechnology industry was still quite young, so there were no appropriate partners from which to acquire the necessary technologies. Monsanto decided to pursue the opportunity as a solo internal venture and declared that biotechnology was its new strategic focus.[1] In 1983, Monsanto successfully developed its first transgenic plant, but it would not be until 1995 that it would have its first genetically modified crop seed, Roundup Ready soybeans, approved for commercialization.[2] Though many environmental groups opposed both Roundup and the genetically modified Roundup Ready crops, the combination was enormously successful. By 2002, more than 130 million acres worldwide were planted with Monsanto's Roundup Ready soybean, corn, cotton, and canola seed.[3]

2. Protecting Proprietary Technologies

Firms sometimes avoid collaboration for fear of giving up proprietary technologies. Working closely with a partner might expose the company's existing proprietary technologies to the prying eyes of a would-be competitor. Furthermore, the firm may wish to have exclusive control over any proprietary technologies created during the development project. Consider Sangamo's decision about whether to collaborate in its development of a gene editing approach to curing HIV as described in the opening case. While collaborating would give Sangamo needed cash and access to valuable testing, manufacturing, and marketing capabilities, it did not possess, collaborating also meant that it would have to share the profit, control, and reputational effects from developing the treatment.

3. Controlling Technology Development and Use

alliance
Alliance is a general term that can refer to any type of relationship between firms. Alliances may be short or long term and may include formally contracted agreements or be entirely informal in nature.

Sometimes firms choose not to collaborate because they desire to have complete control over their development processes and the use of any resulting new technologies. This desire might be for pragmatic reasons (e.g., the new technology is expected to yield high margins and the firm does not wish to share rents with collaborators) or cultural reasons (e.g., a company's culture may emphasize independence and self-reliance). Both of these reasons are demonstrated by Honda in the development of its hybrid-electric vehicle, the Insight. While other auto manufacturers were enthusiastically forming **alliances** to collaborate on automobile design and the development of more efficient manufacturing processes, Honda was very cautious about forming collaborative relationships. Honda's decision not to join the Alliance of Automobile Manufacturers, the industry trade group that leads the fight against tougher fuel and emissions standards, had both pragmatic and cultural reasons. From a pragmatic standpoint, Honda worried that participating in the trade group would limit its discretion over its development of environmentally friendly automobiles, an area where Honda intended to be the market leader. This decision was reinforced by Honda's culture that emphasized retaining complete control over the firm's technology development and direction. This is illustrated by Honda President Hiroyuki Yoshino's statement, "It's better for a person to decide about his own life rather than having it decided by others."[4]

4. Building and Renewing Capabilities

Firms may also choose to engage in solo development even when partnering could save time or money because they believe that development efforts are key to building and renewing their capabilities. Solo development of a technological innovation challenges the firm to develop new skills, resources, and market knowledge. As noted in Chapter Seven, the potential for creating and enhancing the organization's capabilities may be more valuable than the innovation itself. This is aptly demonstrated in a quote from Walt Gillette of Boeing about the development of the Sonic Cruiser: "Industry experience indicates that if the company doesn't create a new airplane every 12 to 15 years, the needed skills and experience will be gone. Too many of the people who created the last new airplane will have retired or moved on to other companies, and their skills and experience will not have been passed on to the next generation of Boeing employees."[5]

Though there are several reasons a firm might choose to stick with solo development, there are also many reasons for firms to engage in collaborative development, and collaboration appears to be on the rise. In the next sections, we will discuss the advantages of collaboration and the strengths and weaknesses of various types of collaboration.

ADVANTAGES OF COLLABORATING

Collaborating on development projects can offer a firm a number of advantages. First, collaborating can enable a firm to obtain necessary skills or resources more quickly than developing them in-house.[6] It is not unusual for a company to lack some of the complementary assets required to transform a body of technological knowledge into a commercial product. Given time, the company can develop such complementary assets internally. However, doing so extends cycle time. Instead, a company may be able to gain rapid access to important complementary assets by entering into strategic alliances or licensing arrangements.[7] For example, when Apple was developing its LaserWriter, a high-resolution laser printer, it did not possess the technological expertise to produce the printer's engine, and developing such capabilities in-house would have taken a long time. Apple persuaded Canon, the market leader in printer engines, to collaborate on the project.[8] With Canon's help, Apple was able to bring the high-quality printer to market quickly.

Second, obtaining some of the necessary capabilities or resources from a partner rather than building them in-house can help a firm reduce its asset commitment and enhance its flexibility. This can be particularly important in markets characterized by rapid technological change. High-speed technological change causes product markets to rapidly transform. Product life cycles shorten, and innovation becomes the primary driver of competition. When technology is progressing rapidly, firms may seek to avoid committing themselves to fixed assets that may rapidly become obsolete. They may choose to become more narrowly specialized and to use linkages with other specialized firms to access resources they do not possess in-house.

Third, collaboration with partners can be an important source of learning for the firm. Close contact with other firms can facilitate both the transfer of knowledge between firms and the creation of new knowledge that individual firms could not have created alone.[9] By pooling their technological resources and capabilities, firms may be able to expand their knowledge bases and do so more quickly than they could without collaboration.

Fourth, one primary reason firms collaborate on a development project is to share the costs and risks of the project. This can be particularly important when a project is very expensive or its outcome highly uncertain.[10]

Finally, firms may also collaborate on a development project when such collaboration would facilitate the creation of a shared standard. Collaboration at the development stage can be an important way of ensuring cooperation in the commercialization stage of a technology, and such cooperation may be crucial for technologies in which compatibility and complementary goods are important. For example, in 1997 Nokia, Motorola, and Ericsson formed a nonprofit corporation called the WAP Forum to establish a common wireless telecommunication format. WAP stands for Wireless Application Protocol. It is an open, global communication standard that is intended to enable users of mobile devices such as cell phones, pagers, and smart phones to easily and quickly access information from the Internet. By establishing the WAP Forum, the companies hoped to prevent the emergence of multiple competing standards. In 2002, the WAP Forum merged with the Open Mobile Architecture initiative to form the Open Mobile Alliance (OMA). By early 2003, more than 200 mobile operators, equipment producers, and software developers had signed on to the standard.[11]

FIGURE 8.4
Worldwide Formation of New Technology or Research Alliances, 1990–2011

Source: Data from Thomson's SDC Platinum Database.

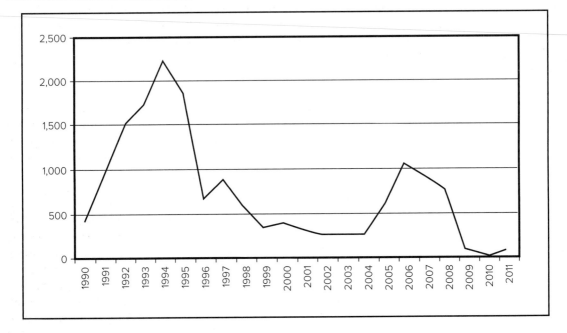

joint venture
A partnership
between two
or more firms
involving a sig-
nificant equity
stake by the part-
ners and often
resulting in the
creation of a new
business entity.

Not all such ventures are so successful, however. For example, in 1992, IBM, Apple, and Hewlett-Packard formed a **joint venture** called Taligent to jointly develop and promote an operating system that could overthrow Microsoft's Windows as the dominant standard in personal computer operating systems. After spending three years and $50 million developing and promoting the new operating system standard, the venture had failed to meet expectations and was ultimately dissolved.

Worldwide, use of technology or research alliances (joint R&D agreements, cross-technology transfer, or cross licensing) climbed to a sharp peak in the mid-1990s (see Figure 8.4), driven in large part by dramatic increases in alliance activity by firms in the information technology industries (computers, communication equipment, and software). Alliance activity then subsequently declined to very low levels at the turn of the decade, but began to climb again in the mid 2000s.[12]

TYPES OF COLLABORATIVE ARRANGEMENTS

Collaboration can include partnering with suppliers, customers, competitors, complementors, organizations that offer similar products in different markets, organizations that offer different products in similar markets, nonprofit organizations, government organizations, universities, or others. Collaboration can also be used for many different purposes, including manufacturing, services, marketing, or technology-based objectives.

In North America, as many as 23 percent of all alliances are for research and development activities, compared to 14 percent in Western Europe and 12 percent in Asia.[13]

Collaboration arrangements can also take many forms, from very informal alliances to highly structured joint ventures or technology exchange agreements (**licensing**). The most common forms of collaborative arrangements used in technological innovation include strategic alliances, joint ventures, licensing, outsourcing, and collective research organizations.

licensing
A contractual arrangement whereby one organization or individual (the licensee) obtains the rights to use the proprietary technology (or trademark, or copyright, etc.) of another organization or individual (the licensor).

Strategic Alliances

Firms may use strategic alliances to access a critical capability that is not possessed in-house or to more fully exploit their own capabilities by leveraging them in another firm's development efforts. Firms with different capabilities necessary for developing a new technology or penetrating a new market might form alliances to pool their resources so that collectively they can develop the product or market faster or less expensively. Even firms that have similar capabilities may collaborate in their development activities in order to share the risk of a venture or to speed up market development and penetration. Large firms might form alliances with small firms in order to take a limited stake in the smaller firm's development efforts, while small firms might form alliances with large firms to tap the larger firm's greater capital resources, distribution and marketing capabilities, or credibility.[14] For example, many large pharmaceutical firms have allied with small biotechnology firms for their mutual benefit: The pharmaceutical firms gain access to the drug discoveries of the biotechnology companies, and the biotechnology companies gain access to the capital resources, manufacturing, and distribution capabilities of the pharmaceutical firms.

capability complementation
Combining ("pooling") the capabilities and other resources of partner firms, but not necessarily transferring those resources between the partners.

Alliances can enhance a firm's overall level of flexibility.[15] Through an alliance, firms can establish a limited stake in a venture while maintaining the flexibility to either increase their commitment later or shift these resources to another opportunity.[16] Firms can use alliances to gain an early window on emerging opportunities that they may want to commit to more fully in the future. Alliances also enable a firm to rapidly adjust the type and scale of capabilities the firm can access, which can be very valuable in rapidly changing markets.

Alliances are also used to enable partners to learn from each other and develop new competencies. Alliance partners may hope to transfer knowledge between the firms or to combine their skills and resources to jointly create new knowledge. However, alliance relationships often lack the shared language, routines, and coordination that facilitate the transfer of knowledge—particularly the complex and tacit knowledge that is most likely to lead to sustainable competitive advantages.[17] To use alliances for learning requires a serious commitment of resources, such as a pool of dedicated people willing to travel between the home firm and partner firm, test-bed facilities, and active procedures for internalizing what has been learned.[18]

capability transfer
Exchange of capabilities across firms in such a manner that partners can internalize the capabilities and use them independently of the particular development project.

Yves Doz and Gary Hamel argue that it is useful to categorize a firm's alliance strategy along two dimensions.[19] The first dimension is the degree to which alliances practice **capability complementation** versus **capability transfer**. The second dimension is whether the firm manages each alliance individually or manages a collective network of alliances (see Figure 8.5).

FIGURE 8.5
Technology Alliance Strategies

Source: From Y. Doz and G. Hamel, 1997, "The Use of Alliances in Implementing Technology Strategies." In M. L. Tushman and P. Anderson, *Managing Strategic Innovation and Change*, 1997. By permission of Oxford University Press, Inc.

	Individual Alliance	**Network of Alliances**
Capability Complementation	A GE-SNECMA alliance	B Corning Glass alliances
Capability Transfer	C Thomson-JVC alliance	D Aspla

In quadrant A are firms that forge an individual alliance to combine complementary technologies or skills needed for a project. For example, in the mid-1970s, General Electric (GE) and SNECMA (a French jet engine producer) formed a joint venture called CFM International to develop a new jet engine. The venture would combine GE's F101 turbojet with SNECMA's low-pressure fan expertise to create a powerful and fuel-efficient engine. Because the F101 was considered a sensitive military technology by the U.S. Air Force, the venture was set up to carefully avoid the exchange of proprietary technology between the firms. GE would build the F101 portion as a sealed "black box," which could then be shipped to a separate assembly location. The resulting engine, the CFM-56, became the most successful jet engine in the history of aviation.[20]

In quadrant B are firms that use a network of alliances to combine complementary skills and resources. For example, Corning, known primarily as a producer of glass products, has created a web of alliances with partners that have complementary skills in order to extend its glass technology into fields as diverse as medical products, computer products, and fiber optics. Instead of attempting to internalize its partners' technologies, Corning views its relationships with its partners as a form of extended enterprise that forms a flexible and egalitarian network of independent businesses.[21]

In quadrant C are firms that use individual alliances to transfer capabilities between them. Doz and Hamel provide the example of the alliance between JVC and Thomson. While both companies produce VCRs, Thomson wanted to glean product technology and manufacturing expertise from JVC, whereas JVC needed to learn how to penetrate the European market from Thomson. Both sides perceived an equitable opportunity for gain from exchanging capabilities.

In quadrant D are firms that use a network of alliances to exchange capabilities and jointly develop new capabilities. The collective research organizations described later in the chapter (including Aspla and the National Center for Manufacturing Sciences) are examples of alliance networks in which a formal body has been created to govern the network. These organizations are designed to enable their member organizations to collectively create, share, and utilize knowledge. In building an alliance portfolio, managers should think carefully about competitive effects, complementing effects, and network structure effects. First, if multiple alliances are serving the same strategic needs, there is a risk of redundant resources investment, or competitive conflict between partners. The costs and benefits of this should be carefully weighed as alliance partners could become adversaries. Second, complementary alliances can be super-additive if carefully managed. For example, a pharmaceutical firm might be using an alliance to develop a drug target with one partner, and another alliance to develop a delivery method for that same drug, enabling it to bring the product to market faster.[22] In this situation, the benefits of each alliance are accentuated by the benefits of the other. Finally, managers should consider how their portfolio of alliances positions them in the web of relationships that connects their firm, their partners, and their partners' partners.[23] Such networks can be very influential in the diffusion of information and other resources, and being positioned well in an alliance network can confer significant advantages (see the Research Brief on "Strategic Positions in Collaborative Networks" later in this chapter).

The opportunities and flexibility that can be gained through using alliances can come at a cost. The potential for opportunism and self-interest exists for all parties of an alliance due to limited levels of mutual commitment.[24] Studies suggests that between 30 percent to 70 percent of alliances fail by neither meeting the goals of the partners, nor delivering the operational or strategic benefits for which they were intended.[25] Firms need to be constantly on guard to ensure that the alliance does not inadvertently result in giving too much away to a potential competitor. According to Doz and Hamel, while collegiality between partners can facilitate trust and communication, *too much* collegiality may be a warning sign that information gatekeepers within the firm are not being sufficiently vigilant.[26] Employees at all levels should be regularly informed about what information and resources are off-limits to the partner, and the firm should stringently monitor what information the partner requests and receives.[27]

Joint Ventures

Joint ventures are a particular type of strategic alliance that entails significant structure and commitment. While a strategic alliance can be any type of formal or informal relationship between two or more firms, a joint venture involves a significant equity investment from each partner and often results in establishment of a new separate entity. The capital and other resources to be committed by each partner are usually specified in carefully constructed contractual arrangements, as is the division of any profits earned by the venture.

For example, in 2005, New Life Scientific (of the United States) and InvaPharm LLC (of the Ukraine) announced that they would form a joint venture called Invamed Pharma Incorporated to manufacture prescription pharmaceuticals for the United States market. New Life Scientific would provide funding for the project while InvaPharm would supply technical know-how and intellectual property. Each party would have a 50 percent stake in the venture.

Licensing

Licensing is a contractual arrangement whereby one organization or individual (the *licensee*) obtains the rights to use the proprietary technology (or trademark, copyright, etc.) of another organization or individual (the *licensor*). Licensing enables a firm to rapidly acquire a technology (or other resource or capability) it does not possess.

For example, when Microsoft realized it had lost precious time to Netscape and needed to get a Web browser to market fast, it licensed the software it needed to produce Internet Explorer from Spyglass Inc. Microsoft also bought several companies (including Vermeer Technologies, Colusa Software, and eShop Inc.) to provide other Internet utilities.

For the licensor, licensing can enable the firm's technology to penetrate a wider range of markets than it could on its own. For example, Delphi Automotive, a supplier to the automotive industry, had developed a software program that can simulate various aspects of machining, including turning, milling, and drilling. The software enabled manufacturers that do high-volume machining to identify ways of improving their machining processes. Delphi had developed the software for its own use, but then realized it could make more money by licensing the software to others.[28]

Licensing a technology from another firm is typically much less expensive for a licensee than developing a new technology in-house. As discussed in earlier chapters, new product development is both expensive and risky; through licensing, a firm can obtain a technology that is already technically or commercially proven. Though it is often presumed that a technology available for license is an unlikely source of advantage (because it is typically available to many potential licensees), Procter & Gamble's experience shows that this need not be the case. Through its "Connect and Develop" program, it focuses on sourcing ideas and technologies external to the firm that it can then add value to in its labs. Thus while a licensed technology provides the foundation for a new product, the product that arrives to market typically draws on the deep (and difficult to imitate) expertise and other resources P&G possesses.[29] This approach is emblematic of the "Open Innovation" approach now being used by many firms.[30]

Licensing agreements typically impose many restrictions on the licensee, enabling the licensor to retain control over how the technology is used. However, over time, licensees may gain valuable knowledge from working with the licensed technology that can enable them to later develop their own proprietary technologies. In the long run, the licensor's control over the technology may erode.

Sometimes firms license their technologies to preempt their competitors from developing their own competing technologies. This can be particularly important if competitors are likely to be able to imitate the primary features of the technology or if the industry has strong pressures for the adoption of a single dominant design (see Chapter Four). By licensing out the technology to potential competitors, the licensor gives up the ability to earn monopoly rents on the technology. However, doing so may prevent potential competitors from developing their own proprietary technologies. Thus, licensing enables a firm to opt for a steady stream of royalties rather than gambling on the big gain—or big loss—of having its technology compete against others for market dominance.

Outsourcing

Firms that develop new technological innovations do not always possess the competencies, facilities, or scale to perform all the value-chain activities for the new innovation effectively or efficiently. Such firms might outsource activities to other firms.

contract manufacturing
When a firm hires another firm (often a specialized manufacturer) to manufacture its products.

One common form of outsourcing is the use of contract manufacturers. **Contract manufacturing** allows firms to meet the scale of market demand without committing to long-term capital investments or an increase in the labor force, thus giving the firm greater flexibility.[31] It also enables firms to specialize in those activities central to their competitive advantage while other firms provide necessary support and specialized resources the firm does not possess. Contract manufacturing further enables a firm to tap the greater economies of scale and faster response time of a dedicated manufacturer, thereby reducing costs and increasing organizational responsiveness to the environment.[32] For example, when Apple redesigned a screen for its iPhone just weeks before it was due on the shelves, it was able to call a foreman at a Chinese factory it was working with, who woke up the 8,000 workers sleeping in dormitories. The workers were given biscuits and tea, and immediately started a twelve-hour shift fitting glass screens into beveled frames. Within 96 hours, the plant was manufacturing more than 10,000 iPhones a day. "The speed is breathtaking," an Apple executive noted. "There's no American plant that can match that." Whereas Apple directly employs 43,000 people in the United States and 20,000 people in other countries, an additional 700,000 people work for Apple's contractors, engineering, building, and assembling Apple products. In response to a query from U.S. President Barack Obama of "What would it take to make iPhones in the United States?" Steve Jobs replied, "Those jobs aren't coming back." Apple executives noted that the vast scale of overseas factories, and the flexibility, diligence, and industrial skills of their workers had outpaced American counterparts. But in response to criticisms about what this had done to employment in the United States, the executives explained, "We sell iPhones in over a hundred countries . . . . Our only obligation is making the best product possible."[33]

Other activities, such as product design, process design, marketing, information technology, or distribution can also be outsourced from external providers. For example, large contract manufacturers such as Flextronics and Solectron now often help firms design products in addition to manufacturing them. Companies such as IBM or Siemens will provide a company with a complete information technology solution, while United Parcel Service will take care of a company's logistics and distribution needs. Outsourcing can have a number of downsides, however. Reliance on outsourcing may cause the firm to forfeit important learning opportunities, potentially putting it at a disadvantage in the long run.[34] By not investing in development of in-house capabilities, a firm might not develop many of the skills and resources related to its products that enable the development of future product platforms. The firm risks becoming hollow.[35] In fact, Prahalad and Hamel argue that Korean firms such as Goldstar, Samsung, and Daewoo have explicit missions to capture investment initiative away from potential competitors by serving as contract manufacturers for them. This allows the Korean firms to use would-be competitors' funds to accelerate their own competence development, while the competitors' competencies erode.[36]

Outsourcing can also impose significant transaction costs for a firm.[37] Contract manufacturing, for example, requires a well-specified contract: Product design, cost, and quantity requirements must be clearly communicated and generally specified up front. The contracting firm may also have to go to great lengths to protect itself from having any proprietary technology expropriated by the contract manufacturer. In addition, the contract manufacturer may bear significant costs in ramping up production for a particular firm, and must therefore specify the contract to avoid being held up by the contracting firm after the manufacturer has made investments specific to the contract.[38]

Collective Research Organizations

In some industries, multiple organizations have established cooperative research and development organizations such as the Semiconductor Research Corporation or the American Iron and Steel Institute.[39] Collective research organizations may take a number of forms, including trade associations, university-based centers, or private research corporations.

Many of these organizations are formed through government or industry association initiatives. For example, the National Center for Manufacturing Sciences (NCMS) was formed in 1986 by the U.S. Defense Department, the Association for Manufacturing Technology, the Manufacturing Studies Board, General Motors, and 20 other manufacturing companies. Its purpose was to promote collaborations among industry, government, and academic organizations. By 2012, the center had 175 U.S., Canadian, and Mexican corporate members. Typical NCMS projects involve 15 to 20 organizations and run for two to four years.[40]

Other collective research organizations have been formed solely through the initiative of private companies. For example, in 2002, six Japanese electronics manufacturers (Fujitsu, Hitachi, Matsushita Electric Industrial, Mitsubishi Electric, NEC, and Toshiba) set up a collective research company called Aspla to develop designs for more advanced computer chips. Global competition had driven down margins on chips, resulting in major losses for many of the major Japanese electronics makers. Furthermore, research in advanced chip designs had become extremely expensive. The collaborative research organization would enable the companies to share the development expense and help the Japanese semiconductor industry retain its competitive edge. Each of the companies initially invested 150 million yen ($1.3 million) in the organization, and plans were for each to contribute about $85 million annually toward joint research.[41] The Japanese government also agreed to contribute $268 million.

CHOOSING A MODE OF COLLABORATION

Figure 8.6 summarizes some of the trade-offs between solo internal development and various modes of collaboration. Solo internal development is, on average, a relatively slow and expensive way of developing a technology. The firm bears all the costs and risks, and may spend considerable time learning about the new technology, refining its designs, and developing production or service processes to implement the new technology. However, a firm that engages in solo internal development retains total control over how the technology is developed and used. Solo internal development also offers great potential for the firm to leverage its existing competencies and to develop new competencies, but offers little to no potential for accessing another firm's competencies. Therefore, solo internal development might make sense for a firm that has strong competencies related to the new technology, has access to capital, and is not under great time pressure.

Because strategic alliances can take many forms, the speed, cost, and degree of control they offer vary considerably. Some strategic alliances may enable a firm to relatively quickly and cheaply gain access to another firm's technology, but give the firm

FIGURE 8.6
Summary of Trade-offs between Different Modes of Development

	Speed	Cost	Control	Potential for Leveraging Existing Competencies	Potential for Developing New Competencies	Potential for Accessing Other Firms' Competencies
Solo Internal Development	Low	High	High	Yes	Yes	No
Strategic Alliances	Varies	Varies	Low	Yes	Yes	Sometimes
Joint Ventures	Low	Shared	Shared	Yes	Yes	Yes
Licensing In	High	Medium	Low	Sometimes	Sometimes	Sometimes
Licensing Out	High	Low	Medium	Yes	No	Sometimes
Outsourcing	Medium/High	Medium	Medium	Sometimes	No	Yes
Collective Research Organizations	Low	Varies	Varies	Yes	Yes	Yes

a low level of control over that technology. Other strategic alliances might be aimed at utilizing the firm's own technology in a broader range of markets, which can be fast and cost-effective, and still enable the firm to retain a considerable amount of control. Most alliances offer opportunities for leveraging existing competencies or developing new competencies. Strategic alliances may or may not offer potential for accessing another firm's competencies, depending on the alliance's purpose and structure.

By comparison, a joint venture is much more structured. While a joint venture typically involves developing a new technology and can take almost as long as solo internal development, it may be slightly faster due to the combination of the capabilities of multiple firms. Joint ventures enable partners to share the cost of the development effort, but they must also share control. Because joint ventures typically entail a long-term relationship between two or more firms that results in the development of a new product or business, joint ventures offer great potential for leveraging a firm's existing competencies, developing new competencies, and accessing its partners' competencies. Joint ventures may be more appropriate than a strategic alliance or solo internal development when the firm places great importance on access to other firms' competencies.

Licensing in technology offers a fast way to access a new technology that is typically lower in cost than developing it internally. The firm typically has limited discretion over what it can do with the technology, however, and thus has a low degree of control. Depending on the firm's capability mix and the nature of what it has licensed, licensing can sometimes offer the potential of leveraging a firm's existing competencies, developing new competencies, and accessing another organization's competencies. For example, many potential drugs or medical therapies are first developed in university research centers or medical schools. Pharmaceutical and biotechnology firms then license the right to explore whether the discovery has potential as a commercially viable medical treatment using their own drug development, testing, and manufacturing capabilities. Licensing the promising compounds or therapies enables the pharmaceutical and biotechnology firms to obtain drug targets quickly, thus helping them keep their pipelines full. It also helps the firms focus their development efforts on projects that have already demonstrated some treatment potential.

Licensing can also be a good way for a firm to obtain enabling technologies that are necessary for its products or services, but that are not central to the firm's competitive advantage. For example, while producers of digital cameras need to be able to incorporate batteries that are long-lasting, light, and affordable in their camera designs, most camera producers do not perceive battery power as being central to their competitive advantage, and thus rely on externally sourced technology to meet this need. Licensing can also be an effective way for a firm that lacks technological expertise to gain initial market entry and experience that it can later build upon in developing its own technological capabilities.

Licensing out a technology offers a fast way for a firm to extend the reach of its technology that is nearly free and offers the potential for royalties. The firm relinquishes some control over the technology, but also retains a moderate amount of control through restrictions in the license agreement. Licensing out a technology explicitly leverages the firm's existing competencies by enabling the technology to be deployed in a wider range of products or markets than the firm participates in itself. It offers little opportunity for developing new competencies, however. Sometimes licensing out a technology is a way of accessing another firm's competencies, as when a firm uses licensing to expand its technology into products or markets in which it has little expertise.

When a firm outsources design, production, or distribution of its technology, it is intentionally giving up a moderate amount of control to rapidly gain access to another firm's expertise and/or lower cost structure. While the firm pays to outsource activities, it typically pays less than it would to develop the capability of performing those activities in-house, and it gains access to those activities more quickly than it could develop them in-house. While outsourcing offers little opportunity for building new competencies, it can leverage the firm's existing competencies by enabling it to focus on those activities in which it earns its greatest returns. For example, Nike's strategy of outsourcing nearly all its athletic shoe production to contract manufacturers in Asia enables Nike to focus on its competitive advantages in design and marketing while tapping the lower labor and capital costs of its manufacturers. Thus, outsourcing might sometimes be appropriate for (*a*) firm activities that are not central to its competitive advantage, (*b*) activities that would cause the firm to give up crucial flexibility if performed in-house, or (*c*) activities in which the firm is at a cost or quality disadvantage.

Participation in a collective research organization is typically a long-term commitment rather than an effort to rapidly access capabilities or technology. As with strategic alliances, the nature of a firm's participation in a collective research organization can take many forms; thus, cost and control can vary significantly. Collective research organizations can be very valuable ways for the firm to leverage and build upon its existing competencies, as well as to learn from other participating organizations. Though collective research organizations may not yield immediate returns in the form of new products or services, participating in collective research organizations can be extremely useful in industries that have complex technologies and require considerable investment in basic science. By pooling their knowledge and effort, firms in collective research organizations can share the cost and risk of basic research, while accelerating the rate at which it yields useful new solutions.

CHOOSING AND MONITORING PARTNERS

Gaining access to another firm's skills or resources through collaboration is not without risks.[42] It may be difficult to determine if the resources provided by the partner are a good fit, particularly when the resource gained through the collaboration is something as difficult to assess as experience or knowledge. It is also possible that a collaboration partner will exploit the relationship, expropriating the company's knowledge while giving little in return. Furthermore, since managers can monitor and effectively manage only a limited number of collaborations, the firm's effectiveness at managing its collaborations will decline with the number of collaborations to which it is committed. This raises the possibility of not only diminishing returns to the number of collaborations, but also negative returns as the number of collaborations grows too large.[43] These risks can be minimized if the company limits the number of collaborations in which it engages, chooses its partners very carefully, and establishes appropriate monitoring and governance mechanisms to limit opportunism.[44]

Partner Selection

The success of collaborations will depend in large part on the partners chosen. A number of factors can influence how well suited partners are to each other, including their relative size and strength, the complementarity of their resources, the alignment of their objectives, and the similarity of their values and culture.[45] These factors can be boiled down to two dimensions: resource fit and strategic fit.[46]

Resource fit refers to the degree to which potential partners have resources that can be effectively integrated into a strategy that creates value.[47] Such resources may be either complementary or supplementary. Most collaborations are motivated by the need to access resources the firm does not possess; such collaborations are based on the combination of complementary resources. Most of the examples in this chapter have entailed complementary resources, such as the combination of Apple's computer technology with Canon's printer engine technology, or the combination of Sangamo's gene editing technology with the clinical testing and manufacturing expertise of larger biotechnology and pharmaceutical firms. Other collaborations seek supplementary stocks of resources that are similar to those possessed by the firm. The pooling of supplementary resources can enable partners to achieve market power or economies of scale. For example, British Petroleum and Mobil consolidated many of their operations in Europe to gain economies of scale and lower their cost structure.[48]

Strategic fit refers to the degree to which partners have compatible objectives and styles. The objectives of the partners need not be the same as long as the objectives can be achieved without harming the alliance or the partners. Not knowing a partner's true objectives or forging an alliance with a partner with incompatible objectives can result in conflict, wasted resources, and forfeited opportunities. Das and Teng provide an example of an alliance forged between General Motors and South Korea's Daewoo. While GM desired to use the alliance to drive down costs on its existing automobile models, Daewoo's objective was to develop new technologies and design new models. The alliance ultimately failed because of the incompatibility of GM's cost orientation and Daewoo's R&D orientation.[49]

Firms can also evaluate potential partners using many of the same tools used to evaluate the firm's own position and strategic direction (for a review of these, see

Chapter Six). This includes assessing how collaboration with the partner is likely to impact the firm's opportunities and threats in its external environment; its internal strengths, weaknesses, or potential for sustainable competitive advantage; and the firm's ability to achieve its strategic intent.

Impact on Opportunities and Threats in the External Environment

Assessing the collaboration's impact on the firm's opportunities and threats includes asking such questions as:

- How would the collaboration change the bargaining power of customers or suppliers?
- Would the collaboration impact the threat of entry? For example, is the partner likely to become a new competitor? Does the partnership raise barriers to entry for other potential entrants?
- Would the collaboration impact the firm's position vis-à-vis its rivals?
- Would the collaboration influence the availability of complementary goods or the threat of substitutes?

Impact on Internal Strengths and Weaknesses

Assessing the collaboration's impact on the firm's strengths and weaknesses includes asking such questions as:

- How would the collaboration leverage or enhance the firm's strengths? Does the collaboration put any of those strengths at risk?
- How would the collaboration help the firm overcome its weaknesses?
- Is the collaboration likely to yield a position of competitive advantage that is difficult for competitors to imitate? Is such a competitive advantage achievable without collaborating?
- Would the collaboration leverage or enhance the firm's core capabilities?
- Is the collaboration likely to impact the firm's financial strengths or weaknesses?

Impact on Strategic Direction

Assessing the fit of the collaboration with the firm's strategic direction includes asking such questions as:

- How does this collaboration fit with the firm's statement of strategic intent?
- Is the collaboration likely to help the firm close any resource or technology gap between where it is now and where it would like to be?
- Are the objectives of the collaboration likely to change over time? How are such changes likely to be compatible or incompatible with the firm's strategic direction?

Partner Monitoring and Governance

governance
The act or
process of exerting
authority and/or
control.

Successful collaboration agreements typically have clear, yet flexible, monitoring and **governance** mechanisms.[50] Not surprisingly, the more resources put at risk by the collaboration (for example, the greater the upfront investment or the more valuable the intellectual property contributed to the collaboration), the more governance structure partner firms are likely to impose on the relationship.[51] There are three main types of

Research Brief Strategic Positions in Collaborative Networks[a]

A growing body of research suggests that a firm's position within a collaborative network influences its access to information and other resources, and its influence over desired outcomes. For example, a firm with a highly central position in the network is typically expected to have access to a greater amount of information and to be able to access that information more quickly than a firm in a more peripheral role. A firm that occupies a key brokerage role in a network (e.g., a firm that serves as a bridge between two otherwise disconnected groups of firms) is thought to benefit both by having exposure to diverse information (assuming the two groups of firms have quite distinct information resources) and by occupying a key gatekeeping position that controls the flow of information between the two groups. A firm's position within the network may also serve as a valuable signal to other potential partners about the value of its resources. For example, if a firm is young or small but has alliances with important and innovative firms, these alliances can serve as reputation endorsements when the quality of the firm is otherwise difficult to assess.[b] Such endorsements may enhance the firm's likelihood of receiving financing or attracting other important alliances.

Consider Figure 8.7, which shows the "main component" (the largest connected group) of the global technology collaboration network in 1998 (based on R&D alliances, cross-technology transfer agreements, and cross-licensing agreements formed from 1996 to 1998, as reported by SDC's alliance database).[c] The large group on the top of the network is mostly composed of organizations in industries whose underlying technology is electronics-based (computer hardware and software, communication equipment and service, transportation equipment, etc.), and the group on the bottom is dominated by organizations in the chemical and medical-based industries (pharmaceuticals, chemicals, health services, medical equipment, etc.). This grouping also includes a large concentration of educational organizations

(primarily universities). As can be seen, some firms (e.g., IBM, Toshiba, Eli Lilly) have significantly more alliances than others. The number of links an organization has in a network is known as its "degree centrality." In general, the degree centrality of an organization tends to be strongly related to its size and prominence. The size and prominence of an organization help to determine how attractive it is to potential partners, and only large organizations typically have the resources necessary to manage a large number of alliances. An organization does not, however, have to be large or prominent to occupy a key brokerage position. Brokerage refers to how crucial an organization is to the transmission of information or other resources through the network. It is often measured with "betweenness centrality," which is the number of times an organization lies on the shortest path between other pairs of organizations. The three organizations with the highest betweenness centrality scores in this network are IBM, Eli Lilly, and PPD (Pharmaceutical Product Development Inc., a contract research organization). PPD had only three alliances during the 1996–1998 time period, but Figure 8.7 shows just how important those alliances were to the overall connectivity of the network. IBM's link to PPD and PPD's link to Eli Lilly provide a bridge from the center of the electronics group to the center of the chemical/medical group. This link is one of only three observed bridges between the two groups, and is the most central of those three.

There is still considerable debate about the relative benefits of centrality and brokerage. While many scholars argue that highly central firms have the greatest access to information and influence over information transmission, others argue that highly central firms are constrained by their many relationships to other organizations and suggest that it is better to occupy a brokerage role. There are similar debates about brokerage—while a broker is likely to have access to diverse information and serves as a key gatekeeper for the transmission

continued

concluded

FIGURE 8.7
The Global Technology Collaboration Network (Main Component) in 1998[d]

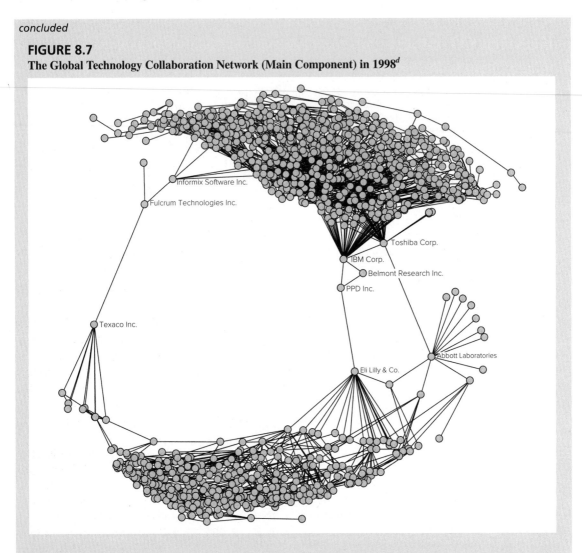

of information between otherwise disconnected groups, it is unclear to what degree brokers typically benefit from this position. Some have argued that brokers can have difficulty assimilating and utilizing such diverse information, and that it might be better to be fully embedded in one group rather than be the only bridge between multiple groups. In other words, it might be better to have a relationship with a broker than to be the broker. There generally is consensus, however, that it is less desirable to be isolated (i.e., not connected to the network) or in a "pendulum" position (i.e., have only one link, and thus hang from the network like a pendulum).

[a] Adapted from M. A. Schilling, "The Global Technology Collaboration Network: Structure, Trends, and Implications," New York University working paper, 2009.
[b] T. Stuart, "Interorganizational Alliances and the Performance of Firms: A Study of Growth and Innovation Rates," *Strategic Management Journal* 21 (2000), pp. 791–811.
[c] Adapted from Schilling, "The Global Technology Collaboration Network: Structure, Trends, and Implications."
[d] Ibid.

alliance contracts
Legally binding contractual arrangements to ensure that partners (a) are fully aware of their rights and obligations in the collaboration and (b) have legal remedies available if a partner should violate the agreement.

equity ownership
When each partner contributes capital and owns a specified right to a percentage of the proceeds from the alliance.

relational governance
Self-enforcing norms based on goodwill, trust, and reputation of the partners. These typically emerge over time through repeated experiences of working together.

governance mechanisms organizations use to manage their collaborative relationships: alliance contracts, equity ownership, and relational governance.[52] **Alliance contracts** are legally binding contractual arrangements to ensure that partners (a) are fully aware of their rights and obligations in the collaboration and (b) have legal remedies available if a partner should violate the agreement. Such contracts typically include:

- What each partner is obligated to contribute to the collaboration, including money, services, equipment, intellectual property, and so on.
- How much control each partner has in the arrangement. For example, the contract may stipulate whether partners have the right to admit new partners to the relationship or change the terms of the agreement. It may also stipulate the rights partners will have over any proprietary products or processes developed in the course of the collaboration.
- When and how proceeds of the collaboration will be distributed. For example, the collaboration agreement may stipulate whether cash, intellectual property rights, or other assets will be distributed and the schedule of such distribution.

Such contracts also often include mechanisms for monitoring each partner's adherence to the agreement, such as through regular review and reporting requirements.[53] Some collaboration agreements include provisions for periodic auditing either by the partner organizations or a third party. Many agreements also include provisions for terminating the relationship if the need for the alliance ends (for example, if the mission of the alliance is completed or the goals of the partner firms have changed) or partners encounter disputes they cannot resolve.[54] Markets and strategies change over time, and effective collaboration agreements should be flexible enough to be adapted in the event of change and provide a graceful exit strategy for members that no longer wish to participate in the collaboration.

Many alliances involve shared **equity ownership**, i.e., each partner contributes capital and owns a share of the equity in the alliance. Equity ownership helps to align the incentives of the partners (because the returns to their equity stake are a function of the success of the alliance), and provides a sense of ownership and commitment to the project that can facilitate supervision and monitoring of the alliance.

Finally, many alliances also rely on **relational governance**. Relational governance is the self-enforcing governance based on the goodwill, trust, and reputation of the partners that is built over time through shared experiences of repeatedly working together. Research suggests that relational governance can help to reduce contracting and monitoring costs of managing an alliance, and facilitate more extensive cooperation, sharing, and learning by alliance partners.[55]

Summary of Chapter

1. A number of factors will influence whether a firm chooses to collaborate on an innovation. Some of the most important include whether the firm (or a potential partner) has the required capabilities or other resources, the degree to which collaboration would make proprietary technologies vulnerable to expropriation by a potential competitor, the importance the firm places on controlling the development process and any innovation produced, and the role of the development project in building the firm's own capabilities or permitting it to access another firm's capabilities.

2. Firms may choose to avoid collaboration when they already possess the necessary capabilities and other resources in-house, they are worried about protecting proprietary technologies and controlling the development process, or they prefer to build capabilities in-house rather than access a partner firm's capabilities.

3. Some of the advantages of collaboration include sharing costs and risks of development, combining complementary skills and resources, enabling the transfer of knowledge between firms and the joint creation of new knowledge, and facilitating the creation of shared standards.

4. The term *strategic alliances* refers to a broad class of collaboration activities that may range from highly structured (e.g., joint ventures) to informal. Strategic alliances can enable simple pooling of complementary resources for a particular project, or they may enable the transfer of capabilities between partners. The transfer of capabilities often requires extensive coordination and cooperation.

5. A joint venture is a partnership between firms that entails a significant equity investment and often results in the creation of a new separate entity. Joint ventures are usually designed to enable partners to share the costs and risks of a project, and they have great potential for pooling or transferring capabilities between firms.

6. Licensing involves the selling of rights to use a particular technology (or other resource) from a licensor to a licensee. Licensing is a fast way of accessing (for the licensee) or leveraging (for the licensor) a technology, but offers little opportunity for the development of new capabilities.

7. Outsourcing enables a firm to rapidly access another firm's expertise, scale, or other advantages. Firms might outsource particular activities so that they can avoid the fixed asset commitment of performing those activities in-house. Outsourcing can give a firm more flexibility and enable it to focus on its core competencies. Overreliance on outsourcing, however, can make the firm hollow.

8. Groups of organizations may form collective research organizations to jointly work on advanced research projects that are particularly large or risky.

9. Each form of collaboration mode poses a different set of trade-offs in terms of speed, cost, control, potential for leveraging existing competencies, potential for developing new competencies, or potential for accessing another firm's competencies. An organization should evaluate these trade-offs in formulating a collaboration strategy.

10. Successful collaboration requires choosing partners that have both a resource fit and a strategic fit.

11. Successful collaboration also requires developing clear and flexible monitoring and governance mechanisms to ensure that partners understand their rights and obligations, and have methods of evaluating and enforcing each partner's adherence to these rights and obligations.

Discussion Questions

1. What are some advantages and disadvantages of collaborating on a development project?

2. How does the mode of collaborating (e.g., strategic alliance, joint venture, licensing, outsourcing, collective research organization) influence the success of a collaboration?

3. Identify an example of collaboration between two or more organizations. What were the advantages and disadvantages of collaboration versus solo development? What collaboration mode did the partners choose? What were the advantages and disadvantages of the collaboration mode?

4. If a firm decides it is in its best interest to collaborate on a development project, how would you recommend the firm choose a partner, a collaboration mode, and governance structure for the relationship?

Suggested Further Reading

Classics

Hagedoorn, J., "Understanding the Rationale of Strategic Technology Partnering: Interorganizational Modes of Cooperation and Sectoral Differences," *Strategic Management Journal* 14 (1993), pp. 371–86.

Powell, W. W., K. W. Koput, and L. Smith-Doerr, "Interorganizational Collaboration and the Locus of Innovation: Networks of Learning in Biotechnology," *Administrative Science Quarterly* 41 (1966), pp. 116–45.

Chesbrough, H., Open Innovation: The New Imperative for Creating and Profiting from Technology (Boston: Harvard Business School Press, 2003).

Recent Work

Rothaermel, F. T., Hitt, M. A., and Jobe, L.A. "Balancing Vertical Integration and Strategic Outsourcing: Effects on Product Portfolio, Product Success, and Firm Performance," *Strategic Management Journal* 27 (2006), pp. 1033–56.

Sampson, R., "The Cost of Misaligned Governance in R&D Alliances," *Journal of Law, Economics, and Organization* 20 (2004), pp. 484–526.

Schilling, M. A., and C. Phelps, "Interfirm Collaboration Networks: The Impact of Large-Scale Network Structure on Firm Innovation," *Management Science* 53 (2007), pp. 1113–26.

Schilling, M.A., "Technology Shocks, Technological Collaboration, and Innovation Outcomes," *Organization Science* 26 (2015):668–86.

Endnotes

1. C. W. L. Hill, "Monsanto: Building a Life Sciences Company," in *Cases in Strategic Management,* eds. C. W. L. Hill and G. Jones (Boston: Houghton Mifflin, 2004); and S. Brooks, M. A. Schilling, and J. Scrofani, "Monsanto: Better Living through Genetic Engineering?" in *Strategic Management, Competitiveness and Globalization,* 5th ed., eds. M. Hitt, R. Hoskisson, and R. D. Ireland (Minneapolis/St. Paul: West Publishing, 2002).

2. R. T. Fraley, S. B. Rogers, and R. B. Horsch, "Use of a Chimeric Gene to Confer Antibiotic Resistance to Plant Cells. Advances in Gene Technology: Molecular Genetics of Plants and Animals," *Miami Winter Symposia* 20 (1983a), pp. 211–21.

3. R. Melcer, "Monsanto Wants to Sow a Genetically Modified Future," *St. Louis Post Dispatch,* February 24, 2003.

4. M. Takanashi, J. Sul, J. Johng, Y. Kang, and M. A. Schilling, "Honda Insight: Personal Hybrid," New York University teaching case, 2003; and "Toyota, Honda Forge Ahead in Hybrid Vehicle Development," *AP Newswire,* March 13, 2002.

5. L. Gunter, "The Need for Speed," *Boeing Frontiers*. Retrieved November 20, 2002, from www .boeing.com/news/frontiers/archive/2002/july/i_ca2.html.

6. Su Han Chan, W. John Kensinger, J. Arthur Keown, and D. John Martin, "Do Strategic Alliances Create Value?" *Journal of Financial Economics* 46 (1997), pp. 199–221.

7. G. Hamel, Y. L. Doz, and C. K. Prahalad, "Collaborate with Your Competitors—and Win," *Harvard Business Review,* January–February 1989, pp. 133–39; W. Shan, "An Empirical Analysis of Organizational Strategies by Entrepreneurial High-Technology," *Strategic Management Journal* 11 (1990), pp. 129–39; G. P. Pisano, "The R&D Boundaries of the Firm: An Empirical Analysis," Administrative Science Quarterly 35 (1990), pp. 153–76; and R. Venkatesan, "Strategic Sourcing: To Make or Not to Make," *Harvard Business Review* 70, no. 6 (1992), pp. 98–107.

8. D. Teece, "Profiting from Technological Innovation: Implications for Integration, Collaboration, Licensing and Public Policy," *Research Policy* 15 (1986), pp. 285–305.

9. D. C. Mowery, J. E. Oxley, and B. S. Silverman, "Technological Overlap and Interfirm Cooperation: Implications for the Resource-Based View of the Firm," *Research Policy* 27 (1998), pp. 507–24; J. A. C. Baum, T. Calabrese, and B. S. Silverman, "Don't Go It Alone: Alliance Network Composition and Startups' Performance in Canadian Biotechnology," *Strategic Management Journal* 21 (2000), p. 267; J. P. Liebeskind, A. L. Oliver, L. Zucker, and M. Brewer, "Social Networks, Learning, and Flexibility: Sourcing Scientific Knowledge in New Biotechnology Firms," *Organization Science* 7 (1996), pp. 428–44; and L. Rosenkopf and P. Almeida, "Overcoming Local Search through Alliances and Mobility," *Management Science* 49 (2003), p. 751.

10. J. Hagerdoon, A. N. Link, and N. S. Vonortas, "Research Partnerships," *Research Policy* 29 (2000), pp. 567–86.

11. "More Cohesive Industry Standards Ahead?" *Frontline Solutions* 3, no. 9 (2002), p. 58; and B. Smith, "OMA Starts Ringing in the Future," *Wireless Week* 8, no. 42 (2002), pp. 1, 46.

12. M. A. Schilling, "Understanding the Alliance Data," *Strategic Management Journal* 30 (2009), pp. 233–60.

13. N. H. Kang and K. Sakai, "International Strategic Alliances: Their Role in Industrial Globalisation," Paris, Organisation for Economic Co-operation and Development, Directorate for Science, Technology, and Industry, working paper 2000/5.

14. Teece, "Profiting from Technological Innovation."

15. M. A. Schilling and K. Steensma, "The Use of Modular Organizational Forms: An Industry Level Analysis," *Academy of Management Journal* 44 (2001), pp. 1149–69.

16. R. McGrath, "A Real Options Logic for Initiating Technology Positioning Investments," *Academy of Management Review* 22 (1997), pp. 974–96.

17. S. Ghoshal and P. Moran, "Bad for Practice: A Critique of the Transaction Cost Theory," *Academy of Management Review* 21 (1996), pp. 13–47.

18. C. K. Prahalad and G. Hamel, "The Core Competence of the Corporation," *Harvard Business Review,* May–June 1990, pp. 79–91; and Hamel, Doz, and Prahalad, "Collaborate with Your Competitors—and Win."

19. Y. Doz and G. Hamel, "The Use of Alliances in Implementing Technology Strategies," in *Managing Strategic Innovation and Change,* eds. M. L. Tushman and P. Anderson (Oxford, U.K.: Oxford University Press, 1997).

20. G. W. Weiss, "The Jet Engine That Broke All the Records: The GE-SNECMA CFM-56," *Case Studies in Technology Transfer and National Security;* and P. Siekman, "GE Bets Big on Jet Engines," *Fortune,* December 19, 2002.

21. A. Nanda and C. A. Bartlett, "Corning Incorporated: A Network of Alliances," Harvard Business School case no. 9-391-102, 1990.

22. P. Kale and H. Singh, "Managing Strategic Alliances: What Do We Know Now, and Where Do We Go From Here?" *Academy of Management Perspectives* (2009) August, pp. 45–62.

23. M.A. Schilling and C. Phelps, "Interfirm Collaboration Networks: The Impact of Large-scale Network Structure on Firm Innovation," *Management Science* 53 (2007), pp. 1113–26.

24. K. R. Harrigan, "Strategic Alliances: Their New Role in Global Competition," *Columbia Journal of World Business* 22, no. 2 (1987), pp. 67–70.

25. P. Kale and H. Singh, "Managing Strategic Alliances: What Do We Know Now, and Where Do We Go From Here?" *Academy of Management Perspectives* (2009) August, pp. 45–62. See also Bamford, J, Gomes-Casseres, B, and Robinson, M. "Envisioning collaboration: Mastering alliance strategies." San Francisco: Jossey-Bass.

26. Hamel, Doz, and Prahalad, "Collaborate with Your Competitors—and Win."

27. Ibid.

28. P. E. Teague, "Other People's Breakthroughs," *Design News* 58, no. 2 (2003), pp. 55–56.

29. L. Huston and N. Sakkab, "Connect and Develop: Inside Procter & Gamble's New Model for Innovation," *Harvard Business Review,* (2006), March 1st.

30. H.W. Chesbrough, Open Innivation: The New Imperative for Creating and Profiting From Technology. (2003) Boston: Harvard Business School Press.

31. J. Holmes, "The Organization and Locational Structure of Production Subcontracting," in *Production, Work, Territory: The Geographical Anatomy of Industrial Capitalism,* eds. M. Storper and A. J. Scott (Boston: Allen and Unwin, 1986), pp. 80–106; and Teece, "Profiting from Technological Innovation."

32. Schilling and Steensma, "The Use of Modular Organizational Forms."

33. C. Duhigg and K. Bradsher, "How U.S. Lost Out on IPhone Work," *The New York Times,* January 22, 2012, pp. 1, 20–21.

34. D. Lei and M. A. Hitt, "Strategic Restructuring and Outsourcing: The Effect of Mergers and Acquisitions and LBOs on Building Firm Skills and Capabilities," *Journal of Management* 21 (1995), pp. 835–60.

35. Prahalad and Hamel, "The Core Competence of the Corporation."

36. Ibid.

37. Pisano, "The R&D Boundaries of the Firm."

38. Schilling and Steensma, "The Use of Modular Organizational Forms."

39. V. K. Narayanan, *Managing Technology and Innovation for Competitive Advantage* (Upper Saddle River, NJ: Prentice Hall, 2001).

40. C. Pellerin, "Consortia: Free Enterprise Meets Cooperation and the Results Can Be Good for Robotics," *The Industrial Robot* 22, no. 1 (1995), p. 31.

41. Associated Press, July 11, 2002.

42. C. W. L. Hill, "Strategies for Exploiting Technological Innovations: When and When Not to License," *Organization Science* 3 (1992), pp. 428–41; W. Shan, "An Empirical Analysis of Organizational Strategies by Entrepreneurial High-Technology," *Strategic Management Journal* 11 (1990), pp. 129–39; and Teece, "Profiting from Technological Innovation."

43. M. A. Schilling and C. W. L. Hill, "Managing the New Product Development Process: Strategic Imperatives," *Academy of Management Executive* 12, no. 3 (1998), pp. 67–81.

44. O. E. Williamson, *The Economic Institutions of Capitalism* (New York: Free Press, 1985).

45. J. Bleeke and D. Ernst, "Is Your Strategic Alliance Really a Sale?" Harvard Business Review 73, no. 1 (1995), pp. 97–105; T. K. Das and B. Teng, "Between Trust and Control: Developing Confidence in Partner Cooperation in Alliances," *Academy of Management Review* 23 (1998b), pp. 491–512; R. M. Kanter, "Collaborative Advantage: The Art of Alliances," Harvard Business Review 72, no. 4 (1994), pp. 96–108; and B. Uzzi, "Social Structure and Competition in Interfirm Networks: The Paradox of Embeddedness," *Administrative Science Quarterly* 42 (1997), pp. 35–67.

46. T. K. Das and B. S. Teng, "Managing Risks in Strategic Alliances," *Academy of Management Executive* 13, no. 4 (1999), pp. 50–62.

47. Ibid.

48. J. G. Crump, "Strategic Alliances Fit Pattern of Industry Innovation," *Oil & Gas Journal*, March 31, 1997, p. 59; and Das and Teng, "Managing Risks in Strategic Alliances."

49. Das and Teng, "Managing Risks in Strategic Alliances."

50. T. Pietras and C. Stormer, "Making Strategic Alliances Work," *Business and Economic Review* 47, no. 4 (2001), pp. 9–12.

51. R. Gulati and H. Singh, "The Architecture of Cooperation: Managing Coordination Costs and Appropriation Concerns in Strategic Alliances," *Administrative Science Quarterly* 43 (1998), pp. 781–814.

52. P. Kale and H. Singh, "Managing Strategic Alliances: What Do We Know Now, and Where Do We Go From Here?" *Academy of Management Perspectives* (2009) August, pp. 45–62.

53. L. Segil, "Strategic Alliances for the 21st Century," *Strategy & Leadership* 26, no. 4 (1998), pp. 12–16.

54. Pietras and Stormer, "Making Strategic Alliances Work."

55. I. Filatotchev, J. Stephan, and B. Jindra. "Ownership Structure, Strategic Controls and Export Intensity of Foreign Invested Firms in Emerging Economies." *Journal of International Business Studies* 39 (2008), pp. 1133–48. See also R. Gulati, "Does familiarity breed trust? The implications of repeated ties for contractual choice in alliances," *Academy of Management Journal* 38 (1995), pp. 85–112; and B. Uzzi. "Social Structure and Competition in Interfirm Networks: The Paradox of Embeddedness," *Administrative Science Quarterly* 42 (1997), pp. 35–67.

Protecting Innovation

The Digital Music Distribution Revolution[a]

Fraunhofer and MP3

In 1991, Fraunhofer IIS of Germany developed an algorithm that would set in motion a revolution in how music was distributed, stored, and consumed. The algorithm (commonly referred to as a codec) allowed compression of digital audio to approximately one-tenth of its original size with minimal compromise in audible quality. The format also enabled song information such as the song title and artist to be embedded within the file. This format for compressed audio files was later dubbed MPEG-1 layer 3—a.k.a. MP3. By 1995, software programs were available that enabled consumers to convert tracks from compact discs to MP3 files. This technology transformed how music could be manipulated—a song was now a file that could be kept on a hard drive, and the file was small enough to be shared over the Internet. The MP3 format became wildly popular by users sharing their music online, and software companies began releasing many variants of MP3 encoders (utilities that compress files into MP3s) and decoders (utilities that play back MP3s). Hardware manufacturers decided to capitalize on this new trend and several hardware MP3 players began appearing on the market.

With the growing popularity of the file format, Fraunhofer was faced with a dilemma—should it enforce its patent on the use of the MP3 algorithm and attempt to collect royalties for its use, or should it allow users and software/hardware manufacturers to make free use of the algorithm, allowing the momentum of the format to build? If it was to limit the use of the algorithm, it faced the risk of established rivals such as Microsoft and Sony developing competing formats, yet if it allowed free use of the algorithm, it would be difficult to profit on its invention.

Fraunhofer decided to pursue a partially open licensing approach, partnering with Thomson Multimedia as the exclusive licensing representative of MP3 patents in 1995.[b] Thomson, in turn, negotiated agreements with several companies including Apple, Adobe, Creative Labs, Microsoft, and many others. Such a broad base of MP3 licensees (100 by April 2001) provided consumers with easy access to encoders, decoders, and the format in general. Licensees generally opted to provide decoders free of charge, while charging a nominal fee to those who wished to encode MP3s.

Fraunhofer continued to innovate, introducing the mp3pro format and working on the Advanced Audio Coding (AAC) format with Dolby that Apple would later use. Many other companies also developed or adapted their own audio compression codecs including Sony (ATRAC codec, originally developed in 1991 for use with Mini Discs[c]) and Microsoft (WMA, launched in April 1999[d]). However, by 1996, MP3s could be found on computers worldwide, and it appeared that MP3 had won the battle for dominant design in compressed audio formats.

Napster Takes the Lead

In 1999, while a student at Northeastern University in Boston, Shawn Fanning released Napster—a software program that allowed users with Internet access to easily share MP3 files. Napster provided a user-friendly solution to music fans wishing to share and find music online. Napster provided a user interface with a search box that pointed individuals to other users with the files they wished to download. The Napster servers did not host any MP3 files; rather they hosted a database with information on which users had which files to share and whether they were online, and connected one computer to another for downloading. Napster was one of the first widely adopted "peer-to-peer" applications, and helped popularize the term.

Napster was free, and as the growing number of people with Internet access realized, so was the music that it allowed them to access. Users were increasingly trading copyrighted material—commercial records and songs. In fact, the great majority of music downloaded through Napster was copyrighted material. By March 2000, 5 million copies of Napster had already been downloaded.[e] At its peak, there were 70 million Napster users.[f]

While "music pirates" around the world embraced Napster, the Recording Industry Association of America (RIAA), the trade group that represents the leading music business entities in the United States, grew increasingly alarmed. The RIAA worried that the growing illegal trade of music would result in a loss of profits for its constituents—record labels that owned the rights to much of the popular commercial music that was being traded online. The RIAA initiated legal action against Napster and Napster users in an effort to take the service offline and curtail illegal file sharing. This move was controversial for several reasons. Some analysts believed that it would be difficult to fight a technological advance such as this by legal action alone, and that the RIAA would not be successful unless it offered a legitimate alternative for users who wished to purchase music online. Other analysts took an even stronger stance, arguing that the record labels were not only fighting to protect the rights of artists, but to protect a business model that had become outdated.[g] They argued that the popularity of Napster was partially due to the rigid and overpriced traditional music distribution model, where fans were forced to buy albums for prices that some felt were inflated, and did not have the choice to buy individual songs. This was not the first time the entertainment industry had resisted a change in business models and was reluctant to embrace a new technology. A 2001 article in *The Economist* pointed out that "Phonographs were going to kill sheet music, the rise of radio threatened to undermine sales of phonograph discs, video recorders were going to wipe out the film industry, and cassette recorders spelt doom for the music business. . . . In each case, their fears proved unfounded. The new technologies expanded the markets in unprecedented ways."[h] Some commentators believed that the new technology could be beneficial for the recording industry. If harnessed appropriately, it could enable an inexpensive distribution method, as well as direct intimate interaction with consumers that allowed for targeted marketing.

In 2001 Napster offered the RIAA a partnership that included a legitimate digital distribution model that would make online music available via a subscription service. The RIAA declined, and instead continued to pursue a legal judgment against Napster. In July 2001, the court ruled in the RIAA's favor, and the Napster service was taken offline. It was a blow to peer-to-peer fans worldwide.

Though the record labels had won the battle against Napster, they began to realize the war was far from over. Services similar to Napster began to sprout up online, offering "users in the know" the opportunity to continue pirating music. The record labels continued to pursue legal action against peer-to-peer services and users who engaged in illegal file trading, while coming to terms with the need to offer a legitimate alternative service. Subsequently, Warner Music teamed up with BMG, EMI, and RealNetworks to introduce MusicNet, and Sony Entertainment and Universal created Pressplay, both of which were subscription services that enabled individuals to download music legally from the Web. However, in an attempt to control their music catalogs, the labels used proprietary file formats and severely limiting digital rights management (DRM) schemes that confused users. Furthermore, neither service offered the breadth of selection offered by unauthorized peer-to-peer services such Kazaa or Gnutella. The popularity of peer-to-peer music swapping continued to grow. The RIAA needed a savior. Steve Jobs offered to be that guy.

iTunes Just in Time

On April 28, 2003, Apple opened its iTunes Music Store. After striking agreements with the five major record labels (Sony, Universal, BMG, Warner Music Group, and EMI), iTunes launched with an initial catalogs of 200,000 songs for purchase at 99 cents per song.[i] iTunes showed immediate signs of success, boasting 50 million downloads within the first year, and quickly became the leading distributor of music online.[j] Apple got the blessing of the recording industry after guaranteeing them that the files offered via the Music Store would allow for protection against illegal sharing thanks to the "FairPlay" DRM scheme. In essence, the iTunes Music Store offered audio in two file formats—Advanced Audio Coding (AAC) and modified MP3s. With Apple's Fairplay DRM, song files could be loaded on up to five computers only, and could not be played on non-iPod MP3 players. In addition, the files could not be e-mailed or distributed over the Web, and files were "hidden" on the iPod through a subdirectory structure that made it difficult to copy songs from a friend's iPod. All of these features helped to prevent users from mass-distributing songs to others, helping to ease the minds of record company executives.

The success of iTunes was fueled by a number of factors. The company had a "cool" image that was attractive to the recording industry and users alike. The company also used the familiar MP3 format, offered an attractive price tag for online music, and its licensing agreements with all five major labels enabled it to offer a one-stop source for customers. In addition, the FairPlay DRM was not as restrictive as other competing formats,[k] and this was important to many users. The success of iTunes was also accelerated by the success of Apple's iPods. iPods are hard-disk-based portable MP3 players that are well designed, well marketed, and user-friendly. Though there had been some criticisms concerning their dependability (chiefly related to battery life)[l] and sound quality issues,[m] casual music consumers took to these players in large numbers. To the appreciation of the RIAA, the iPods required synchronization with one's music collection via the iTunes application, thereby making it difficult to share music stored on the iPod, or purchased from iTunes.

The recording industry had found a new channel of distribution that earned significant revenues (about $.70 of every $.99 sale on iTunes is delivered directly to the record labels[n]), and Apple had licensing agreements with all the major labels, which afforded Apple access to a huge catalogs. Apple leveraged this catalogs to entice users to buy music through its iTunes Music Store, and this in turn helped drive sales of the Apple iPod, since files bought on iTunes could not be played on rival MP3 players. Apple was well positioned, but threats loomed on the horizon.

In March 2006, the French National Assembly approved a bill requiring Apple to open its FairPlay DRM technology to industry rivals in France.[o] This meant that Apple would have to allow songs downloaded from the French iTunes Music Store to be played on non-iPod MP3 players, and that iPods would need to play competing file formats, such as Sony's ATRAC3 files purchased through the Sony Connect online music store. Many users could appreciate this interoperability, yet it would challenge the "single operator license model" that had eased the minds of the recording industry and created a large and loyal customer base for Apple. Initially analysts speculated that Apple would withdraw from the French market, but instead Apple began working on negotiating fewer DRM restrictions from the record labels. By March of 2009 Apple had convinced all the major labels to permit their songs to be sold through iTunes without DRM. In return, Apple adopted the tiered pricing model that the major labels had long requested.

The rise of smartphones that could hold users' music digital libraries in addition to offering a host of other useful functions helped to fuel the growth of digital music sales, and in 2011, sales of digital music surpassed the sale of physical music for the first time ever, capturing 50.3 percent of the total market for music. However, analysts speculated that the near future of music might involve a transition away from sales of music completely. Rapidly growing services such as Pandora and Spotify offered streaming of music over the internet, enabling listeners to hear whatever music they wanted, whenever they wanted, on a wide range of devices without the user ever taking ownership of the music.

Discussion Questions

1. What industry conditions led to the revolution in audio distribution described above? Which stakeholders stand to benefit most (or least) from this revolution?
2. Why did the music stores created by the record labels fail to attract many subscribers? What, if anything, should the record labels have done differently?
3. What factors led iTunes to be successful?
4. What new models of music distribution have emerged, and what do you think will influence whether they endure?

[a] Adapted from a New York University teaching case by Shachar Gilad, Christopher Preston, and Melissa A. Schilling.

[b] "Thomson Multimedia Signs 100th mp3 Licensee," press release (PR Newswire), April 18, 2001.

[c] Junko Yoshida, "Sony Sounds Off about Mini Disc," *Electronic World News*, no. 41 (June 3, 1991), p.15.

[d] Jack Schofield, "Music Definitions," *The Guardian*, October 5, 2000, p. 3.

[e] Karl Taro Greenfeld, "The Free Juke Box: College Kids Are Using New, Simple Software Like Napster to Help Themselves to Pirated Music," *Time*, March 27, 2000, p. 82.

[f] Michael Gowan, "Easy as MP3," *PC World* 19, no. 11 (November 2001), p. 110.

[g] "The Same Old Song," *The Economist* 358, no. 8210 (January 24, 2002), pp. 19, 20.

[h] Ibid.

[i] Michael Amicone, "Apple Took a Big Bite Out of the Market," *Billboard* 116, no. 16 (April 17, 2004), p. 2.

[j] "iTunes Music Store Downloads Top 50 Million Songs," press release, March 15, 2004.

[k] Ibid.

[l] "Apple Faces Class Action Suits on iPod Battery," *Reuters*, February 10, 2004.

[m] Randall Stross, "From a High-Tech System, Low-Fi Music," *New York Times*, July 4, 2004, p. 3.

[n] Alex Veiga, "Recording Labels, Apple Split over Pricing," *Associated Press*, April 2, 2006.

[o] Rob Pegoraro, "France Takes a Shot at iTunes," *WashingtonPost.com*, March 26, 2006, p. F06.

OVERVIEW

A crucial element of formulating a firm's technological innovation strategy is determining whether and how to protect its technological innovation. Traditionally, economics and strategy have emphasized the importance of vigorously protecting an innovation in order to be the primary beneficiary of the innovation's rewards, but the decision about whether and to what degree to protect an innovation is actually complex. Sometimes *not* vigorously protecting a technology is to the firm's advantage—encouraging other producers (and complementary goods providers) to support the technology may increase its rate of diffusion and its likelihood of rising to the position of dominant design. In this chapter, we first will review the factors that shape the degree to which a firm is likely to appropriate the returns from its innovation, and the mechanisms available to the firm to protect its innovation. We then will consider the continuum between a wholly proprietary strategy and a wholly open strategy, examining the trade-offs inherent in decisions about whether (and to what degree) to protect or diffuse a technological innovation. The chapter concludes by listing factors the firm should consider in formulating its protection strategy.

APPROPRIABILITY

appropriability
The degree to which a firm is able to capture the rents from its innovation.

The degree to which a firm can capture the rents from its innovation is termed **appropriability**. In general, the appropriability of an innovation is determined by how easily or quickly competitors can imitate the innovation. The ease with which competitors can imitate the innovation is, in turn, a function of both the nature of the technology itself and the strength of the mechanisms used to protect the innovation.

Some technological innovations are inherently difficult for competitors to copy; the knowledge underlying the technology may be rare and difficult to replicate. A firm's unique prior experience or talent pool may give it a foundation of technical know-how that its competitors do not possess. If this knowledge base is **tacit** (i.e., it cannot be readily codified into documents or procedures) or **socially complex** (i.e., it arises through complex interactions between people), competitors will typically find it very difficult to duplicate.[1] For example, a firm that has a team of uniquely talented research scientists may have a rare and difficult-to-imitate knowledge base. While some of the skill of the research scientists may be due to imitable training procedures, *talent* typically implies that an individual (or group) has a natural endowment or ability that is very difficult, if not impossible, to replicate through training. Furthermore, if the unique capabilities of the research team arise in part from the nature of the interactions between the scientists, their performance will be socially complex. Interactions between individuals can significantly shape what each individual perceives, and thus what each individual—and the collective group—discovers or learns. The outcomes of these interactions are path dependent, and thus are idiosyncratic to the combination of individuals, the moment of the interaction, and the nature of the interaction. This means that knowledge can emerge from the interaction of a group that could not be replicated by any individual or any different group.

tacit knowledge
Knowledge that cannot be readily codified or transferred in written form.

socially complex knowledge
Knowledge that arises from the interaction of multiple individuals.

Many innovations, however, are relatively easy for competitors to imitate. Individuals and firms often employ legal mechanisms to attempt to protect their innovations. Most countries offer legal protection for intellectual property in the form of patent, trademark, copyright, and trade secret laws.

PATENTS, TRADEMARKS, AND COPYRIGHTS

patent
A property right protecting a process, machine, manufactured item (or design for manufactured item), or variety of plant.

trademark
An indicator used to distinguish the source of a good.

While patents, copyrights, and trademarks are all ways of protecting intellectual property, they are each designed to protect different things. A **patent** protects an invention, and a **trademark** protects words or symbols intended to distinguish the source of a good. A **copyright** protects an original artistic or literary work. Thus, a typical computer might have components whose designs are protected by patents, logos such as "IBM Thinkpad" that are protected by trademark law, and software that is protected by copyright (though as discussed later in the section on patents, many types of software are now also eligible for patent protection).

Most sources attribute the origin of formalized protection of intellectual property to fifteenth-century England, when the English monarchy began granting certain privileges to manufacturers and traders as signified by "letters patent," which were marked with the king's great seal. The first known of these was granted by Henry VI to John of

copyright
A property right protecting works of authorship.

Utynam in 1449. This patent gave John a 20-year monopoly on a method of producing stained glass that had not been previously known in England.[2] Copyright protection did not arrive until 1710, when an Act of Parliament gave protection to books and other written works. While the use of trademarks (or, more generally, marks of ownership) can be traced back as early as 3500 BC, trademark protection laws did not begin to emerge until the late 1700s. In 1791, Thomas Jefferson supported the requests of sailcloth makers by recommending the establishment of trademark protection based on the commerce clause of the Constitution. Trademark laws were later enacted in France (1857) and the United Kingdom (1862).[3] The first international trademark agreement was reached in 1883 at the Paris Convention for the Protection of Industrial Property.

Patents

In many countries, inventors can apply for patent protection for their inventions. In the United States, a patent is a property right granted by the federal government that excludes others from producing, using, or selling the invention in the United States, or from importing the invention into the United States, for a limited time in exchange for public disclosure of the nature of the invention at the time the patent is granted.[4]

Patents are often categorized into different types. In the United States, a *utility* patent may be granted to an inventor who creates or discovers a new and useful process, machine, manufactured item, or combination of materials. A *design* patent may be granted to the inventor of an original and ornamental design for a manufactured item. A *plant* patent may be granted to an inventor who invents or discovers and asexually reproduces any distinct and new variety of plant. Under U.S. patent law, an invention must pass three tests to be patentable:

1. It must be *useful* (i.e., it must produce a desirable result, solve a problem, improve on or propose a new use for an existing development or show potential of doing so).
2. It must be *novel* (i.e., it must not already be patented or described in public literature, or be in public use for more than a year).
3. It must *not be obvious* (i.e., a person with experience or skill in the particular art of the patent would not be expected to achieve the same invention with a normal amount of effort).

Discovery of scientific principles that pertain to natural laws (e.g., gravity) cannot be patented because they are considered to have always existed. Specifically, the following are not typically patentable:

- Substituting one material for another (e.g., plastic for metal).
- Merely changing the size of an already existing device.
- Making something more portable.
- Substituting an element for an equivalent element.
- Altering an item's shape.

Printed materials are not typically patentable, but it may be possible to protect them by copyright, as discussed in the next section.

Before 1998, most software algorithms were not eligible for patent protection—they were eligible only for copyright protection. However, when a Supreme Court case in 1998 upheld a patent on a computerized method of managing mutual funds that relied on software algorithms, it unleashed a flood of patent applications for software algorithms. From 1997 to 2000, patent filings for software-enabled methods of doing business increased more than 700 percent.[5] For example, Amazon patented its "1-click" system that streamlines the process by which customers place orders.[6]

Patenting an invention is a serious undertaking. To apply for a patent, the inventor must explain how to make and use the invention, and make claims about what it does that makes it a new invention. Drawings of the new invention are also often required. In the United States, this application is reviewed by a patent examiner who may modify the scope of the claims made by the patent. The patent is then published for a time in which other inventors can challenge the patent grant (if, for example, they believe that the patent infringes on previously granted patents). If the standards for patentability are met, the patent is then granted. The entire process from application to granting of the patent can take between two and five years, with an average time of 33 months in 2011. These delays in patent granting grew substantially over the last two decades, in large part due to rapid growth in both U.S. origin and non-U.S. origin patent applications that was not matched by growth in resources for patent examination. In industries in which product lifecycles are short, such delays significantly diminish the usefulness of patenting. This has led to a number of proposals for how the patenting system might be reformed to make it more efficient. (see Figure 9.1).

FIGURE 9.1
Growth in Patent Applications filed with the USPTO, 1980–2014

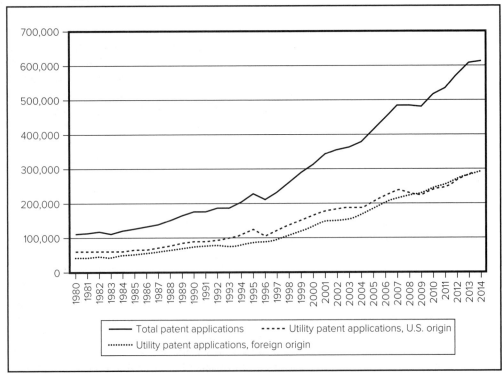

A number of costs are also involved in filing and maintaining a patent. The U.S. Patent and Trademark Office has two fee schedules—one for "small entities" (independent inventors and companies with less than 500 employees) and one for larger entities. The entire patenting process in the United States typically costs a small entity around $1,500 in filing fees and $5,000–$10,000 in attorney fees.

Utility patents are typically granted more protection than other types of patents. Before 1995, the United States granted patent owners a term of 17 years of protection; however, in 1995, that term was extended to 20 years. While patent law varies considerably by country (as discussed in more detail below), almost every country assigns a protection term of 20 years to utility patents. In a major study of historical success rates for U.S. patent applications, Michael Carley, Deepak Hegde, and Alan Marco followed the history of the 2.15 million new patent applications filed at the USPTO after 1996 and found that only 55.8 percent of the applications became granted. Patent applications in the "Drugs and Medical Instruments" sector had the lowest success on average (42.8%), and applications in the "Electrical and Electronics" had the highest (66.6%). They also found that success was generally lower for small firms and that overall, success rates for all types of applications had gone down over time.[7]

Patent Law around the World

Almost every country has its own laws governing patent protection. A patent granted in one country does not provide protection in other countries. People or firms seeking patent protection in multiple countries must apply in each of the countries in accordance with those countries' requirements.

Significant differences exist in national patent laws, and U.S. patent law is one of the more unusual. For example, in most other countries, publication of information about the invention before applying for a patent will bar the right to a patent, but the United States allows a one-year grace period (that is, an inventor can publish an invention up to a year before applying for the patent). Thus, if international patent protection will eventually be sought, inventors must uphold the stricter standard of applying for patent before publishing information about the patent, even if they plan to first patent the invention in the United States. Many countries also require that the invention be manufactured in the country in which a patent was granted within a certain time frame (often three years) from the time the patent is granted. This is called the "working requirement," and it effectively prevents inventors from patenting inventions in countries in which they have no intention of setting up production.

Several international treaties seek to harmonize the patent laws around the world. Two of the most significant are the Paris Convention for the Protection of Industrial Property and the Patent Cooperation Treaty.

The **Paris Convention for the Protection of Industrial Property** (also known as the Paris Convention Priority) is an international intellectual property treaty adhered to by 176 countries as of August 2015. Under the Paris Convention, a citizen of any member country may patent an invention in any of the member countries and enjoy the same benefits of patent protection as if the inventor were a citizen of those countries. That is, the Paris Convention eliminates (for its member countries) any differential patent rights afforded to citizens of the country versus foreign nationals.

Furthermore, the treaty also provides the right of "priority" for patents and trademarks. Once an inventor has applied for patent protection in one of the member countries, the inventor may (within a certain time period) apply for protection in all the other member countries. The time period is 12 months for utility patents and 6 months for design patents and trademarks. Most important, the applications to these later countries will be treated as if they were made on the same date as the first application. This enables the inventor to establish priority over any other patents applied for in those countries after the inventor made the first application. For example, if an inventor applied for a utility patent for an invention in Madagascar in January 2003, and another inventor applied for a patent for a very similar invention in France in June 2003, the Madagascar inventor could have applied for patent protection in France in December 2003 and claim priority over the French invention. The French inventor would have to prove that his or her invention was substantively different from the Madagascar invention, or the French inventor's patent would be denied.

As mentioned previously, in many countries, public disclosure of an invention makes it impossible to subsequently patent that invention. However, with the priority rights established under the Paris Convention, an inventor who patents an invention in one of the member countries can then publicly disclose information about that invention without losing the right to patent the invention in the other countries—each patent application will be treated as if it were applied for at the same time as the first application, and thus as if it were applied for before public disclosure. Without this treaty, it would be nearly impossible for an inventor to patent an invention first in the United States and then in other countries because U.S. patent applications are made available to the public.

Another very significant international patent treaty is the **Patent Cooperation Treaty**, or PCT. This treaty facilitates the application for a patent in multiple countries. An inventor can apply for a patent to a single PCT governmental receiving office, and that application reserves the inventor's right to file for patent protection in more than 100 countries for up to two-and-half years. Once the inventor has filed the application, a PCT governmental searching office will perform the patent search for the application (this search verifies that the invention is not already subject to a prior claim). Once the search is completed, the inventor can choose to enter Chapter II of the process wherein the PCT governmental office assesses the patentability of the invention subject to the standards of the Patent Cooperation Treaty. Eventually, the inventor must have the PCT application filed in each of the national patent offices in which the inventor is seeking protection.

Filing a single PCT application offers numerous advantages. First, applying for the PCT patent buys the inventor the option to apply to multiple nations later without committing the inventor to the expense of those multiple applications. With a PCT application, the inventor can establish a date of application in multiple countries (protecting the inventor's priority over later claims), while paying only the single PCT application fee rather than the numerous national application fees. Though the inventor will eventually have to pay for national applications in the countries in which protection is sought, the inventor can delay those costs. Thus, the inventor has time to assess the likelihood of the patent being granted and the potential profitability of the invention. If the PCT process suggests that the patent will not be granted or if it appears the invention has limited potential for earning returns, the inventor can forgo the expense of applying to the national offices.

Another advantage of the PCT process is that it helps make the results of patent applications more uniform. Though individual countries are not required to grant a patent to those inventions that are granted a patent by the PCT governing office, the granting of the patent by the PCT provides persuasive evidence in favor of granting the patent in the individual national offices. As of August 2015, there were 148 member states of the Patent Cooperation Treaty.

Patent Strategies

It is typical to assume that an inventor seeks a patent because they desire to make and sell the invention themselves. However, inventors and firms may monetize patents in a range of different ways, including licensing the technology to others or selling the patent rights to another firm that can better utilize the technology.[8] Furthermore, whereas the conventional wisdom is that most inventors prefer to keep the details of their invention secret before the patent is granted (to prevent rivals from having access to their proprietary knowledge), this turns out not to be the case. A study by Stuart Graham and Deepak Hegde found that the vast majority of patentees prefer to disclose their patent applications *before* they are granted. Both large and small inventors, across all major technology fields exhibited this preference for early disclosure, presumably because it allows them to publicize their invention's quality and scope to competitors, external investors, and potential licensees. Disclosure via patent application also establishes the date from which patentees can enjoy provisional patent rights.[9]

patent trolling
A pejorative term for when an individual or firm misuses patents against other individuals or firms in attempt to extract money from them.

Firms may also seek patents just to limit the options of competitors or to earn revenues through aggressive patent lawsuits. These actions are sometimes referred to as "**patent trolling**." A patent troll's primary purpose in owning patents is to extort money from other firms. For example, a patent troll might buy a patent from a bankrupt firm to sue another company that it claims is infringing on the purchased patent. Apple claims to be the #1 target for patent trolls, having faced nearly 100 lawsuits between 2011 and 2014.[10] According to RPX Corporation, a firm that helps companies resolve patent lawsuits through licensing, patent trolls filed more than 2,900 infringement suits in the United States in 2012.[11] This type of predatory patenting has sparked an effort by the U.S. Federal government to make patent granting stricter and to impose penalties against spurious patent lawsuits.[12]

patent thickets
A dense web of overlapping patents that can make it difficult for firms to compete or innovate.

In industries with complex technologies such as computers, software, and telecommunications, a dense web of overlapping patents known as "**patent thickets**" can make it very difficult for firms to compete without falling prey to patent suits by other firms in that technology domain. This can seriously stifle innovation and has resulted in the rather peculiar strategy of firms buying bundles of patents to create war chests that they hope will deter the patent attacks of others. For example, in 2011, the bankrupt Nortel auctioned off its massive patent portfolio. The auction was won by a consortium called Rockstar Bidco that included Microsoft, Apple, RIM, Sony, and Ericsson, who paid $4.5 billion for the war chest, beating out Google which bid $4.4 billion. Google subsequently bought 1,030 IBM patents that covered a range of technologies, from the fabrication of microprocessing chips, object-oriented programming, and other business processes. These patents were not necessary for Google's business directly; rather they provided a retaliation threat to others that might attack them through patent suits.[13] Google also bought Motorola Mobility for

$12.5 billion the same year, and it was widely believed that the purchase was almost solely for Motorola's patents, which would bolster Google's position in the lawsuit they expected would arise from the Nortel patents.[14] In October of 2013, confirming Google's fears, Rockstar Bidco filed suit against Google and seven companies that make phones for Google's Android operating system.[15] Google countersued based on its own patents, and in November 2014, it was reported that Google and Rockstar had reached a settlement.[16]

Trademarks and Service Marks

A trademark is a word, phrase, symbol, design, or other indicator that is used to distinguish the source of goods from one party from the goods of others. The "Intel Inside" logo on many computers is one example of a trademark, as is the familiar Nike "swoosh" symbol. A service mark is basically the same as a trademark, but distinguishes the provider of a service rather than a product. Often the term *trademark* is used to refer to both trademarks and service marks.

Trademarks and service marks can be embodied in any indicator that can be perceived through one of the five senses. Most marks are embodied in visual indicators, such as words, pictures, and slogans. However, marks are also registered that use other senses such as sound (e.g., tones that are associated with a particular company or brand) or smells (as in fragrance). Trademark rights may be used to prevent others from using a mark that is similar enough to be confusing, but they may not be used to prevent others from producing or selling the same goods or services under a clearly different mark.

The rights to a trademark or service mark are established in the legitimate use of the mark and do not require registration; however, registration provides several advantages. First, registering the mark provides public notice of the registrant's claim of ownership over the mark. Second, marks must be registered before a suit can be brought in federal court against an infringement of the mark. Third, registration can be used to establish international rights over the trademark, as when the U.S. registration is used to establish registration in other countries, and to protect the mark against infringement from imported products. As of April 2012, the U.S. Patent and Trademark Office charged a $375 application fee for trademark registration using paper filing, and $325 using electronic filing. It normally takes from 10 to 16 months to receive certification from the U.S. Patent and Trademark Office, but the protection offered by the registration of the trademark begins from the date of filing. Unlike patents and copyrights, trademark protection can last as long as the trademark is in use, but the registration requires periodic renewal.

Trademark Protection around the World

Nearly all countries offer some form of trademark registration and protection. National or regional offices maintain a Register of Trademarks that contains information on all trademark registrations and renewals. To eliminate the need to register separately in each country (or region), the World Intellectual Property Organization administers a System of International Registration of Marks governed by two treaties: the Madrid Agreement Concerning the International Registration of Marks and the Madrid Protocol. Countries that adhere to either (or both) the Madrid Agreement or Madrid Protocol are part of the Madrid Union. Any individual that lives in, is a citizen of, or maintains an establishment in a Madrid Union country can register with the trademark office of that country and obtain an international registration that provides protection in as many other Madrid Union countries as the applicant chooses. As of April 2014, there were 91 member countries of the Madrid Union.

Copyright

Copyright is a form of protection granted to works of authorship. In the United States, the authors of original literary, dramatic, musical, artistic, and certain other intellectual works can obtain copyright protection.[17] Like trademarks, the rights of copyright protection are established by legitimate use of the work. This protection is available whether or not the work is published and prevents others from producing or distributing that work. Under section 106 of the 1976 Copyright Act, the owner of the copyright has the exclusive right to do (or authorize others to do) the following:

- Reproduce the work in copies or phonorecords.
- Prepare derivative works based upon the work.
- Distribute copies or phonorecords of the work to the public by sale or other transfer of ownership, or by rental, lease, or lending.
- Perform the work publicly, in the case of literary, musical, dramatic, and choreographic works, pantomimes, and motion pictures and other audiovisual works.
- Display the copyrighted work publicly, in the case of literary, musical, dramatic, and choreographic works, pantomimes, and pictorial, graphic, or sculptural works, including the individual images of a motion picture or other audiovisual work.
- Perform the work publicly by means of a digital audio transmission (in the case of sound recordings).

There are, however, limitations to these rights. In particular, the doctrine of fair use stipulates that in most circumstances it is not a violation of copyright for others to use copyrighted material for purposes such as criticism, comment, news reporting, teaching, scholarship, or research. Furthermore, some types of work cannot be protected by copyright. For example, work that has not been fixed in a tangible form of expression (for example, a choreographed dance or improvisational speech that was not notated or recorded) is not eligible for copyright protection. Titles, names, short phrases, slogans, familiar symbols, and lists of ingredients also cannot be copyrighted.

Unlike patent protection, copyright protection is secured automatically when an eligible work is created and fixed in a copy or phonorecord for the first time. No publication or registration with the Copyright Office is necessary to establish this copyright, though registering the copyright is advantageous in that it establishes a public record of the copyright claim and is required before filing an infringement suit in court. As of August 2015 basic online registration of copyright with the U.S. Copyright Office cost $35, and it took about 3–10 months to receive a certificate of registration.

Before 1978, copyright protection lasted only 28 years from the time it was secured (though during the last year the author could opt to renew the protection for an additional term). Revisions to U.S. copyright law, however, give copyright protection to works created after 1978 that lasts for the author's life plus an additional 70 years.

Copyright Protection around the World

As with patents and trademarks, no international copyright law automatically protects an author's work throughout the world. Copyright protection varies from country to country. However, most countries do offer copyright protection to both domestic and foreign works, and there are international copyright treaties for simplifying the process of securing such protection. One of the most significant is the Berne Union for the Protection of Literary and Artistic Property (known as the Berne Convention). The Berne Convention specifies a minimum level of copyright protection for all member countries, and it requires member countries to offer the same protection to both its own citizens and foreign nationals. Other treaties include the Universal Copyright Convention (UCC); the Rome Convention for the Protection of Performers, Producers of Phonograms and Broadcasting Organizations; the Brussels Convention Relating to the Distribution of Program-Carrying Signals Transmitted by Satellite; and the World Intellectual Property Organization Copyright Treaty.

TRADE SECRETS

trade secret
Information that belongs to a business that is held private.

Rather than disclose detailed information about a proprietary product or process in exchange for the grant of a patent, inventors or firms often will choose to protect their intellectual property by holding it as a **trade secret**. A trade secret is information that belongs to a business that is generally unknown to others. Trade secrets need not meet many of the stringent requirements of patent law, enabling a broader class of assets and activities to be protectable. For example, while the formula for a beverage is not patentable, it can be considered a trade secret. Trade secret law traces its history back to Roman law punishing individuals who induced someone to reveal the details of their employer's commercial affairs.[18]

Information is typically considered to be a trade secret only if it (*a*) offers a distinctive advantage to the company in the form of economic rents, and (*b*) remains valuable only as long as the information remains private. Examples of trade secrets might include information about a firm's customers, its marketing strategies, or its manufacturing processes. Trade secret law protects such information from being wrongfully taken by another party. In the United States, trade secret law is implemented at the state level, but the Uniform Trade Secret Act attempts to make these laws consistent from state to state.

For information to qualify as a trade secret under the Uniform Trade Secret Act, the information must meet the following three criteria:

- The information must not be generally known or readily ascertainable through legitimate means.
- The information must have economic importance that is contingent upon its secrecy.
- The trade secret holder must exercise reasonable measures to protect the secrecy of the information.

If information meets these criteria, the Uniform Trade Secret Act stipulates that its owner can prevent others from benefiting from this information without the owner's permission. In particular, the act states that no individual or group can copy, use, or otherwise benefit from a trade secret without the owner's authorization if they meet *any* of the following conditions:

1. They are bound by a duty of confidentiality (e.g., employees, lawyers).
2. They have signed a nondisclosure agreement.
3. They acquire the secret through improper means such as theft or bribery.
4. They acquire the information from someone who did not have the right to disclose it.
5. They learn about the secret by mistake but have reason to know that the information was a protected trade secret.

   In most U.S. states, if owners of a trade secret believe that another party has stolen or improperly disclosed their trade secret, they can ask a court to issue an injunction against further use of the secrets, and they may also be able to collect damages for any economic harm suffered by the improper use of the trade secret. For example, in November 2002, Procter & Gamble sued Potlatch Corporation, claiming that Potlatch had stolen trade secret methods used to produce Bounty paper towels and Charmin bath tissue by hiring away two of Procter & Gamble's paper manufacturing experts. Potlatch is a large, private-label tissue manufacturer that produces toilet paper, facial tissues, napkins, and paper towels for grocery store chains such as Albertsons and Safeway. By March 2003, the two companies had reached an agreement to settle out of court, keeping the terms of the settlement confidential.[19]

THE EFFECTIVENESS AND USE OF PROTECTION MECHANISMS

The methods used to protect innovation—and their effectiveness—vary significantly both within and across industries.[20] In some industries, such as pharmaceuticals, legal protection mechanisms such as patents are very effective. In other industries, such as electronics, patents and copyright provide relatively little protection because other firms can often invent around the patent without infringing on it (as IBM discovered with its personal computer design as described in the accompanying Theory in Action). It is also notoriously difficult to enforce patents protecting industrial processes such as manufacturing techniques. If patents provide little protection, the firm may rely more heavily on trade secrets; however, the ability to protect trade secrets also varies with the nature of the technology and the industry context. To protect a trade secret, a firm must be able to expose its product to the public without revealing the underlying technology, but in many cases, revealing the product reveals all.

   For some competitive situations, protecting a technology may not be as desirable as liberally diffusing it. In industries characterized by increasing returns, firms sometimes choose to liberally diffuse their technologies to increase their likelihood of rising to the position of dominant design. As discussed in Chapter Four, learning-curve effects and network externalities can cause some industries to demonstrate increasing returns to adoption: The more a technology is adopted, the more valuable it becomes.[21] This dynamic can lead to winner-take-all markets that create natural monopolies. A firm that controls the standard can reap monopoly rents and can exert significant architectural control over both its own industry and related industries.[22]

This enviable position can be so lucrative that firms may be willing to lose money in the short term to improve their technology's chance of rising to the position of dominant design. Thus, firms may liberally diffuse their technologies (through, for example, **open source software** or liberal licensing arrangements) to accelerate the technology's proliferation and thereby jump-start the self-reinforcing feedback effect that can lead to the technology's dominance. However, the firm often faces a dilemma: If it liberally diffuses the technology to would-be competitors, it relinquishes the opportunity to capture monopoly rents when and if the technology emerges as a dominant design. Furthermore, once control of a technology is relinquished, it can be very hard to regain; thus, such diffusion may result in the firm losing all hope of controlling the technology. Finally, liberal diffusion of the technology can result in the fragmentation of the technology platform: As different producers add improvements to the technology that make it better fit their needs, the "standard" may be split into many nonstandardized versions (as with UNIX, as described in more detail later in the chapter). To resolve these trade-offs, firms often adopt a strategy of partial protection for their innovations, falling somewhere on the continuum between wholly proprietary systems and wholly open systems.

Wholly Proprietary Systems versus Wholly Open Systems

Wholly proprietary systems are those based on technology that is company-owned and protected through patents, copyrights, secrecy, or other mechanisms. Such technologies may be legally produced or augmented only by their developers. Wholly proprietary systems are often not compatible with the products offered by other manufacturers. Because their operation is based on protected technology, other manufacturers are often unable to develop components that may interact with the proprietary system. Proprietary systems typically provide their developers with the opportunity to appropriate rents from the technology. However, they might also be less likely to be adopted readily by customers as a result of their higher costs and the inability to mix and match components.

In **wholly open systems**, the technology used in a product or process is not protected by secrecy or patents; it may be based on available standards or it may be new technology that is openly diffused to other producers. Wholly open technologies may be freely accessed, augmented, and distributed by anyone. Such technologies are usually quickly commoditized and provide little appropriability of rents to their developers.

Many technologies are neither wholly proprietary nor wholly open—they are partially open, utilizing varying degrees of control mechanisms to protect their technologies. It is useful to think of a control continuum that stretches from wholly proprietary to wholly open (see Figure 9.2). For instance, most of the major video game console producers (Nintendo, Sony, and Microsoft) utilize a wholly proprietary strategy for their consoles, but a limited licensing policy for their games. The licensing policies are designed to encourage developers to produce games for the systems, while simultaneously enabling the console producers to retain a great deal of control over the games produced. All games developed for the consoles must be approved by the

open source software
Software whose code is made freely available to others for use, augmentation, and resale.

wholly proprietary systems
Goods based on technology that is owned and vigorously protected through patents, copyrights, secrecy, or other mechanisms. Wholly proprietary technologies may be legally produced and augmented only by their developers.

wholly open systems
Goods based on technology that is not protected and that is freely available for production or augmentation by other producers.

FIGURE 9.2
Examples on the Continuum from Wholly Proprietary to Wholly Open

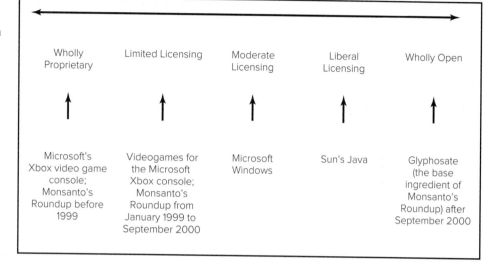

Wholly Proprietary	Limited Licensing	Moderate Licensing	Liberal Licensing	Wholly Open
Microsoft's Xbox video game console; Monsanto's Roundup before 1999	Videogames for the Microsoft Xbox console; Monsanto's Roundup from January 1999 to September 2000	Microsoft Windows	Sun's Java	Glyphosate (the base ingredient of Monsanto's Roundup) after September 2000

console producer before they can be made commercially available. For example, in the case of Microsoft, would-be Xbox games developers must first apply to the Xbox Registered Developer Program (for established games developers) or the Xbox Incubator Program (for smaller or newer games developers). If accepted into one of these two programs, the developer will receive access to development tools, but this does not guarantee the approval of any resulting game titles. The games are subjected to a separate, rigorous approval process.

By contrast, the licensing policies for Microsoft's Windows are more open. Windows is protected by copyright, and Microsoft defends its exclusive right to augment the software; however, it also permits complementary goods providers to access portions of the source code to facilitate development of complementary goods, licenses the rights to such providers to produce complementary applications, and licenses **original equipment manufacturers (OEMs)** to distribute the software by bundling it with hardware. Those who purchase a license for the software can execute and bundle the software with other goods but may not augment the software. For example, software applications developers may produce and distribute value-added applications for use with Windows as long as those applications do not affect the functionality of the Windows program itself.

As described in the Theory in Action section later in the chapter, Sun's "community source" (as opposed to "open source") policy for Java is even more open. This policy grants anyone immediate access to the complete source code for Java and allows users to develop commercial applications based on the code, or to augment the code for their own implementations. These developers pay no license fee to Sun. However, any augmentation to the core structure of Java must be approved by the Java Community Process, which is managed by Sun. Sun's "community source" principle is meant to encourage the broader software community to improve Java and develop complementary applications, but it allows Sun to retain some control over the core

original equipment manufacturers (OEMs)
Firms that assemble goods using components made by other manufacturers, also called value-added resellers (VARs).

In 1980, IBM was in a hurry to introduce a personal computer. When personal computers first began to emerge at the end of the 1970s, most of the major computer manufacturers considered it no more than a peculiar product for a hobbyist market. The idea that individuals would want personal computers on their desks seemed ludicrous. However, as total U.S. personal computer sales reached $1 billion, IBM began to worry that the personal computer market could actually turn out to be a significant computer market in which IBM had no share. To bring a personal computer to market quickly, IBM decided to use many off-the-shelf components from other vendors, including Intel's 8088 microprocessor and Microsoft's software. However, IBM was not worried about imitators because IBM's proprietary basic input/output system (BIOS), the computer code that linked the computer's hardware to its software, was protected by copyright. While other firms could copy the BIOS code, doing so would violate IBM's copyright and incur the legendary wrath of IBM's legal team.

However, getting around IBM's copyright turned out not to be difficult. Copyright protected the written lines of code, but not the functions those codes produced. Compaq was able to reverse-engineer the BIOS in a matter of months without violating IBM's copyright. First, a team of Compaq programmers documented every function the IBM computer would perform in response to a given command, without recording the code that performed the function. This list of functions was then given to another team of "virgin" programmers (programmers who were able to prove that they had never been exposed to IBM's BIOS code).[a] These programmers went through the list of functions and wrote code to create identical functions. The result was a new BIOS that acted just like an IBM BIOS but did not violate its copyright. Compaq sold a record-breaking 47,000 IBM-compatible computers in its first year, and other clones were quick to follow.

[a] R. Cringely, *Accidental Empires* (New York: HarperCollins, 1992).

platform to ensure that the platform does not become fragmented through unmanaged development by the software community.

Many technologies that were once wholly proprietary or partially open become wholly open once their patents or copyrights expire. For instance, Monsanto's highly profitable Roundup herbicide is based on a patented chemical ingredient called glyphosate. This extremely potent herbicide was adopted by farmers in more than 100 countries and accounted for a substantial portion of Monsanto's sales.[23] However, facing impending expiration of its patents, Monsanto began to license the rights to glyphosate production to a few other companies (including Dow Agrosciences, DuPont, and Novartis) in 1999. In September 2000, the U.S. patent on glyphosate expired, and any chemical company was free to produce and sell glyphosate-based herbicides in the United States, making glyphosate a wholly open technology.

ADVANTAGES OF PROTECTION

Because proprietary systems offer greater rent appropriability, their developers often have more money and incentive to invest in technological development, promotion, and distribution. If a single firm is the primary beneficiary of its technology's success, it has much greater incentive to invest in further developing the technology. The profits from the technology may be directly reinvested in further improvements in the technology. The sponsor of a proprietary technology might also adopt a penetration pricing strategy (that is, it may offer the technology at a low price or free) to rapidly build its installed base, it may spend aggressively on advertising to increase awareness of the technology, and it may even subsidize the production of complementary goods to increase the desirability of its technology to customers. A firm may be willing to lose money in the short term to secure the technology's position as the standard, because once the technology has emerged as a standard, the payoff can be substantial and enduring. By contrast, when multiple firms can produce a technology, losing money on the technology in the short term to promote it as a standard is highly risky because the long-term distribution of the payoffs is uncertain. While the technology's developer may have borne the bulk of the cost in developing the technology, multiple firms may vie for the profits to be made on the technology.

Protecting the technology also gives the developing firm architectural control over the technology. **Architectural control** refers to the firm's ability to determine the structure and operation of the technology, and its compatibility with other goods and services. It also refers to the firm's ability to direct the future development path of the technology. Architectural control can be very valuable, especially for technologies in which compatibility with other goods and services is important. By controlling the technology's architecture, the firm can ensure that the technology is compatible with its own complements, while also restricting its compatibility with the complements produced by others.[24] The firm can also control the rate at which the technology is upgraded or refined, the path it follows in its evolution, and its compatibility with previous generations. If the technology is chosen as a dominant design, the firm with architectural control over the technology can have great influence over the entire industry. Through selective compatibility, it can influence which other firms do well and which do not, and it can ensure that it has a number of different avenues from which to profit from the platform.

Microsoft's Windows is the quintessential embodiment of this strategy. Because Windows is the dominant operating system in the personal computing market and because it serves as the interface between a computer's hardware and software, Microsoft has considerable market power and architectural control over the evolution of the personal computer system. Among other things, Microsoft has been able to incorporate ever more utility programs into the core program, thereby expanding and taking over the roles of many other software components. Once a user purchased an operating system, uninstaller programs, disk-compression programs, and memory management programs separately, but Windows 95 and 98 integrated all these products and more into the operating system. This "feature creep" had a major impact on competition in the industry; many utility producers such as Qualitas, Stac Electronics, Microhelp, Quarterdeck, and others were forced to abandon their once-profitable products.

architectural control
The ability of a firm (or group of firms) to determine the structure, operation, compatibility, and development of a technology.

Advantages of Diffusion

The primary argument for diffusing a technology instead of protecting it is that open technologies may accrue more rapid adoptions. If multiple firms are producing, distributing, and promoting the technology, the technology's installed base may accumulate much more rapidly than if one firm alone is responsible for such activities.

Competition among producers may drive the price of the technology down, making it more attractive to customers. Both customers and complementary goods providers may also perceive the technology as better (or its future more certain) if there are multiple companies backing the technology. This perception can lead to much more rapid adoption of the technology by customers and complementary goods providers, which further stimulates more companies to back the technology. Thus, a liberal diffusion strategy can stimulate the growth of the installed base and availability of complementary goods.[25]

Open technologies can also benefit from the collective development efforts of parties external to the sponsoring firm. For instance, Netscape Navigator, UNIX, and Linux are all technologies that have benefited significantly from external development. By making the source code freely available to the vast world of developers who could benefit from the technology, the technologies reaped the advantages of having a much larger pool of talent and resources directed at improving the technologies than could have been rallied by the original developers.

External development, however, poses some costs and risks. First, external development efforts typically lack the coordination of internal development. External developers may have very diverse objectives for the technology; rather than work together toward some unified vision of what the technology could achieve in the future, they might work in different, possibly even conflicting, directions.[26] Much of their effort may be redundant, as different external developers work on solving the same problems without communicating with each other. Finally, whether and how these improvements get incorporated into the technology and disseminated to other users of the technology can prove very problematic. UNIX provides a stark example of this.

UNIX was an operating system first developed by AT&T's Bell Laboratories in 1969. Though a Department of Justice injunction forbade AT&T from selling software commercially, it made the source code for the product available through licensing arrangements. Early licensees (notably, University of California—Berkeley) began using and adapting the software for their purposes, causing many incompatible versions of the software to emerge. Though the software community made several attempts to standardize the UNIX operating language, their efforts failed. AT&T also challenged the commercialization of several UNIX variants, but to no avail. Ultimately, AT&T sold the division responsible for UNIX to Novell, and Novell handed over the rights to the UNIX trademark to the X/Open standards-setting body.[27]

Given the range of advantages (and risks) of protecting versus diffusing a technology, a firm must carefully consider the following factors in deciding whether, and to what degree, it should protect its innovation.

Production Capabilities, Marketing Capabilities, and Capital

If the firm is unable to produce the technology at sufficient volume or quality levels (or market the technology with sufficient intensity), then protecting the technology so that the firm is its sole provider may significantly hinder its adoption. For example, when JVC was promoting its VHS standard for video recorders, its management knew JVC was at a disadvantage in both manufacturing and marketing capabilities compared to Sony (which was promoting the Beta technology). JVC chose to vigorously pursue both licensing and OEM agreements, lining up Hitachi, Matsushita, Mitsubishi, and Sharp to boost the technology's production rate.

Similarly, if complementary goods influence the value of the technology to users, then the firm must (*a*) be able to produce the complements in sufficient range and quantity, (*b*) sponsor their production by other firms, or (*c*) encourage collective production of the complements through a more open technology strategy. The only firms that have been successful in the U.S. video game industry were those that were able to produce games in-house (ensuring that a wide range of games would be available at the console's launch) and that encouraged third-party development of games (to ensure that the number of game titles grew quickly). Both Nintendo and Sega had previous arcade experience, and thus possessed considerable game development expertise. Microsoft had long been a producer of PC-based video games, so it had some game developing experience, and it also acquired a few small game developers (e.g., Bungie) to expand its expertise in developing console-type games.[28] Sony had no prior game experience, but aggressively acquired in-house developers, licensed external developers, and set up a program with Metrowerks to provide developer tools that would make it easier for external developers to produce PlayStation games. If a firm lacks the production capability or expertise to produce a sufficient range of complementary goods, or the capital to acquire such capabilities quickly, it should encourage collective production of complements through a more open technology strategy and utilize forms of sponsorship.

Industry Opposition against Sole-Source Technology

Sometimes other industry members are able to exert strong pressure against the adoption of a technology that would give one (or a few) producer(s) undue control and power, causing a technology that is restricted to such production to be rejected or more hotly contested than a more open technology. This was the case with Sony and Philips' Super Audio CD (SACD) audio format. Sony and Philips had jointly created the original compact disc (CD) format and split the royalties on every CD player sold, totaling hundreds of millions of dollars. The rest of the world's leading consumer electronics producers (including Hitachi, JVC, Matsushita, Mitsubishi, and Toshiba) and record producers (including Time Warner and Seagram's Universal Music group) banded together to form the Digital Video Disk (DVD) Audio consortium. This consortium's purpose is to promote the DVD Audio standard that is intended to displace the CD and enable royalties to be split among the 10 companies that control the patents.[29] Industry observers note that a driving force underlying the formation of the consortium was to prevent Sony and Philips from controlling yet another generation of audio formats. The degree of industry opposition to a sole-source technology needs to be considered when the firm formulates its technology strategy. If the industry is able to pose significant opposition, the firm may need to consider a more open technology strategy to improve the technology's likelihood of being chosen as a dominant design.

Resources for Internal Development

If a firm does not have significant resources (capital, technological expertise) to invest in the technology's functionality, it may have difficulty producing a technology that has an initial performance level, and rate of improvement, that the market finds attractive. In such instances, it can be valuable to tap the external development efforts of other firms (or individuals) through utilizing a more open technology strategy. For example, when Netscape found itself in a race to match browser capabilities with Microsoft, it was at a tremendous disadvantage in both human resources and capital. Microsoft had legions of internal developers and a lot of money to invest in Explorer; there was no way that Netscape could match those resources internally. Instead, Netscape tapped the external development community by giving them access to its source code and incorporating their improvements into the Navigator product.

Control over Fragmentation

For technologies in which standardization and compatibility are important, maintaining the integrity of the core product is absolutely essential, and external development can put it at risk. As the UNIX example illustrates, if the developing firm relinquishes all control over the development of the technology, the technology will have no shepherd with the ability and authority to direct its trajectory and ensure that a single standard remains intact. This suggests that the developer of any technology that requires standardization and compatibility should retain some degree of control over the technology, or find/establish another governing body with the authority to do so.

Incentives for Architectural Control

Architectural control over the evolution of a technology is always valuable; however, it becomes particularly valuable if a firm is a significant producer of complements to the technology in question. A firm with architectural control can typically design the technology to be compatible with its own complements and incompatible with those of competitors. If the technology is chosen as the dominant design, this architectural control allows the firm to ensure that it reaps the lion's share of the rewards in complements production. Furthermore, by making the technology selectively compatible with some competitors and not others, the firm can exert great influence over the competitive field.

Architectural control can also enable the firm to direct the development efforts put into the technology so that it exploits the firm's core competencies. Technology trajectories are path dependent; minor events in their evolution can set them careening off into unexpected directions. A firm that has a significant stake in a particular evolution path (because, for example, it has technological competencies that are much more amenable to one path of evolution than other potential paths) may place a high value on architectural control, which can enable it to co-opt or destroy less favorable development paths by denying their progenitors access to the market.

Summary of Chapter

1. The degree to which a firm can capture the rents from its innovation efforts is largely determined by the degree to which competitors can quickly and easily imitate the innovation. Some innovations are inherently difficult to copy; others are difficult to copy because of the mechanisms the firm uses to protect its innovation.

2. The three primary legal mechanisms used to protect innovation in most countries are patents, trademarks, and copyrights. Each mechanism is designed to protect a different type of work or good.

3. International treaties have helped to harmonize patent, trademark, and copyright laws around the world. Most countries now have patent, trademark, and copyright laws of some form, and in some instances protection can be applied for in multiple countries simultaneously.

4. Trade secrets provide another mechanism of protecting innovation. Firms that protect their intellectual property as a trade secret often have legal recourse if another party wrongfully takes and uses such property.

5. Legal mechanisms for protecting innovation are more effective in some industries than others; in some industries, inventing around a patent or copyright is relatively easy. Similarly, in some industries it is nearly impossible to protect an innovation by using trade secrets because commercializing the innovation reveals its underlying technologies.

6. Sometimes the choice between protecting versus diffusing a technology is not obvious. Both strategies offer potential advantages. Many firms use neither a wholly open nor wholly proprietary strategy, but rather a partially open strategy.

7. Protecting an innovation helps ensure that the firm earns the lion's share of the returns from the innovation. These returns can then be reinvested in further developing the technology, promoting the technology, and producing complementary goods.

8. Protecting an innovation also preserves the firm's architectural control, enabling it to direct the technology's development, determine its compatibility with other goods, and prevent multiple incompatible versions of the technology from being produced by other firms.

9. Diffusing a technological innovation can encourage multiple firms to produce, distribute, and promote the technology, possibly accelerating its development and diffusion. Diffusion can be particularly useful in industries that accrue increasing returns to adoption. It is also useful when the firm has inadequate resources to be the sole developer, producer, distributor, and marketer of a good.

Discussion Questions

1. What are the differences between patents, copyrights, and trademarks?

2. What factors should a firm considering marketing its innovation in multiple countries use in formulating its protection strategy?

3. When are trade secrets more useful than patents, copyrights, or trademarks?

4. Identify a situation in which none of the legal protection mechanisms discussed (patents, copyrights, trademarks, trade secrets) will prove useful.

5. Describe a technological innovation not discussed in the chapter, and identify where you think it lies on the control continuum between wholly proprietary and wholly open.

6. What factors do you believe influenced the choice of protection strategy used for the innovation identified above? Do you think the strategy was a good choice?

Suggested Further Reading

Classics

Levin, R., A. Klevorick, R. Nelson, and S. Winter, "Appropriating the Returns from Industrial Research and Development," *Brookings Papers on Economic Activity, Microeconomics* 3 (1987), pp. 783–820.

Bound, J., C. Cummins, Z. Griliches, B. H. Hall, and A. Jaffe, "Who Does R&D and Who Patents? in *R&D, Patents, and Productivity*, ed. Z. Griliches (Chicago: University of Chicago Press for the National Bureau of Economic Research, 1984).

Teece, D. J., "Profiting from Technological Innovation—Implications for Integration, Collaboration, Licensing and Public-policy," *Research Policy* 15, no. 6 (1986), pp. 285–305.

Recent Work

Schilling, M.A., "Protecting or Diffusing a Technology Platform: Tradeoffs in Appropriability, Network Externalities, and Architectural Control," in Platforms, *Markets and Innovation*, ed. A. Gawer (Cheltenham, UK: Edward Elgar Publishing, 2009).

Graham, S., and D. Hegde, "Disclosing Patents' Secrets," *Science* 347 (2015), no. 6219, pp. 236–37.

Fisher, W.W., and F. Oberholzer-Gee, "Strategic Management of Intellectual Property," *California Management Review* 55, no. 4 (Summer 2013), pp. 157–83.

Somaya, D. "Patent Strategy and Management: An Integrative Review and Research Agenda," *Journal of Management,* 38 (2012), pp. 1084–114.

Astebro, T. B., and K. B. Dahlin, "Opportunity Knocks," *Research Policy* 34 (2005), pp. 1404–18.

de Laat, P. B., "Copyright or Copyleft? An Analysis of Property Regimes for Software Development," *Research Policy* 34 (2005), pp. 1511–32.

Jaffe, A. B., and J. Lerner, *Innovation and Its Discontents: How Our Broken Patent System Is Endangering Innovation and Progress, and What to Do about It* (Princeton, NJ: Princeton University Press, 2004).

Endnotes

1. J. B. Barney, "Firm Resources and Sustained Competitive Advantage," *Journal of Management* 17 (1991), p. 990.

2. U.K. Patent Office.

3. U.S. Trademark History Timeline at www.lib.utexas.edu/engin/trademark/timeline/tmindex .html.

4. Definition from the United States Patent and Trademark Office.

5. "Software Patent," *Bank Technology News* 14, no. 3 (2001), p. 25.

6. A. B. Silverman, "Software Patents for Methods of Doing Business—A Second Class Citizen No More," *Journal of Management* 52, no. 19 (2000), p. 64.

7. M. Carley, D. Hegde, and A. Marco, "What is the probability of receiving a US Patent?" *Yale Journal of Law & Technology*, 17 (2015), pp. 204–223.]

8. D. Alderucci and W. Baumol, "Patents and the dissemination of inventions," *Journal of Economic Perspectives*, 27 (2013), no. 4, pp. 223–26; D. Alderucci, "Monetization Strategies for Business Method Patents," *The Licensing Journal* (2000), November.

9. S. Graham and D. Hegde, "Disclosing Patents' Secrets," *Science* 347 (2015), no. 6219, pp. 236–37.

10. "Apple Complains of "Patent Trolls," *LA Times* (2014), February 8th.

11. A. Jones, "Tech Firms Back Obama Patent Move," *Wall Street Journal*, June 4th.

12. W. New, "White House Takes Major Action Against "Patent Trolls," *Intellectual Property Watch*, (2013), June 4th; "Hatch Introduces Measure to Stop Patent Trolls," *The Ripon Advance* (2013), November 4th; E. Wyatt, "FTC Settles First Case Targeting 'Patent Troll'," *New York Times* (2014), November 6th.

13. S. Decker and B. Womack, "Google Buys 1,023 IBM Patents to Bolster Defense of Android," *BloombergBusiness* (2014): September 14th.

14. Q. Hardy, "Google Buys Motorola for Patent Parts," *Forbes* (2011), August 15th.

15. J. Mullin, "Patent War Goes Nuclear: Microsoft, Apple-owned "Rockstar" Sues Google," *Arstechnica* (2013), October 31.

16. J. Roberts, "Apple-backed Rockstar Ends Patent War on Android, Deal Suggests," *GigaOM* (2014):November.

17. U.S. Copyright Office.

18. The Trade Secrets home page.

19. S. Decker, "Procter & Gamble, Potlatch Resolve Trade Secrets Suit," *Seattle Post Intelligencer,* March 14, 2003.

20. R. Levin, A. Klevorick, R. Nelson, and S. Winter, "Appropriating the Returns from Industrial Research and Development," *Brookings Papers on Economic Activity, Microeconomics* 3 (1987), pp. 783–820; and J. Bound, C. Cummins, Z. Griliches, B. H. Hall, and A. Jaffe, "Who Does R&D and Who Patents?" in *R&D, Patents, and Productivity,* ed. Z. Griliches (Chicago: University of Chicago Press for the National Bureau of Economic Research, 1984).

21. W. B. Arthur, *Increasing Returns and Path Dependency in the Economy* (Ann Arbor: The University of Michigan Press, 1994).

22. C. H. Ferguson and C. R. Morris, *Computer Wars* (New York: Random House, 1993); and R. Henderson and K. Clark, "Architectural Innovation: The Reconfiguration of Existing Product Technologies and the Failure of Established Firms," *Administrative Science Quarterly* 35 (1990), pp. 9–30.

23. S. Brooks, M. A. Schilling, and J. Scrofani, "Monsanto: Better Living through Genetic Engineering?" in *Strategic Management, Competitiveness and Globalization,* 5th ed., eds. M. Hitt, R. Hoskisson, and R. D. Ireland (Minneapolis/St. Paul: West Publishing, 2001).

24. M. A. Schilling, "Toward a General Modular Systems Theory and Its Application to Interfirm Product Modularity," *Academy of Management Review* 25 (2000), pp. 312–34.

25. C. W. L. Hill, "Establishing a Standard: Competitive Strategy and Technological Standards in Winner-Take-All Industries," *Academy of Management Executive* 11, no. 2 (1997), pp. 7–25; and M. A. Schilling, "Winning the Standards Race: Building Installed Base and the Availability of Complementary Goods," *European Management Journal* 17 (1999), pp. 265–74.

26. R. Garud, S. Jain, and A. Kumaraswamy, "Institutional Entrepreneurship in the Sponsorship of Common Technological Standards: The Case of Sun Microsystems and Java," *Academy of Management Journal* 45 (2002), pp. 196–214.

27. D. Essner, P. Liao, and M. A. Schilling, "Sun Microsystems: Establishing the Java Standard," Boston University teaching case no. 2001–02, 2001.

28. J. Kittner, M. A. Schilling, and S. Karl, "Microsoft's Xbox," New York University teaching case, 2002. 45.

29. J. Brinkley, "Disk versus Disk: The Fight for the Ears of America," *New York Times,* August 8, 1999.

Part Three

Implementing Technological Innovation Strategy

In this section, we will cover the key aspects of implementing a technological innovation strategy, including:

- Structuring the firm to improve its likelihood of innovating, its effectiveness at new product development, and its speed of new product development.
- Managing new product development processes to maximize fit with customer needs, while simultaneously minimizing development cycle time and controlling development costs.
- Composing, structuring, and managing new product development teams to maximize new product development effectiveness.
- Crafting a strategy for effectively deploying the innovation into the marketplace, including timing, licensing strategies, pricing strategies, distribution, and marketing.

Implementing Technological Innovation Strategy

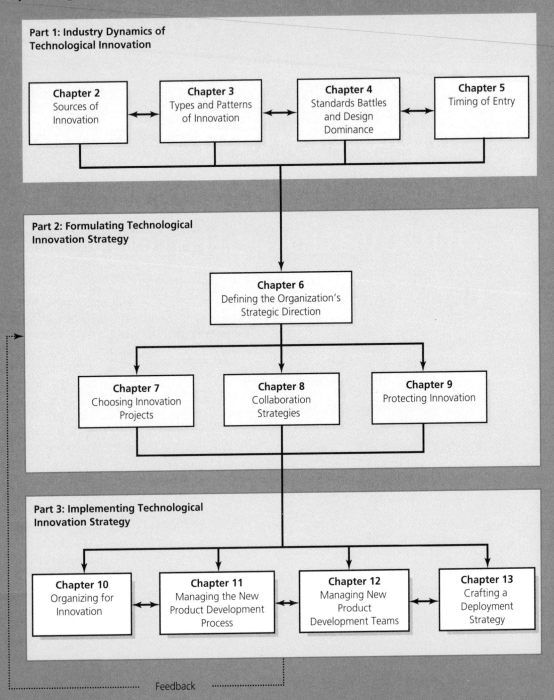

Part 1: Industry Dynamics of Technological Innovation

Chapter 2
Sources of Innovation

Chapter 3
Types and Patterns of Innovation

Chapter 4
Standards Battles and Design Dominance

Chapter 5
Timing of Entry

Part 2: Formulating Technological Innovation Strategy

Chapter 6
Defining the Organization's Strategic Direction

Chapter 7
Choosing Innovation Projects

Chapter 8
Collaboration Strategies

Chapter 9
Protecting Innovation

Part 3: Implementing Technological Innovation Strategy

Chapter 10
Organizing for Innovation

Chapter 11
Managing the New Product Development Process

Chapter 12
Managing New Product Development Teams

Chapter 13
Crafting a Deployment Strategy

Feedback

Chapter **Ten**

Organizing for Innovation

Organizing for Innovation at Google

Google was founded in 1998 by two Stanford Ph.D. students, Sergey Brin and Larry Page, who had developed a formula for rank ordering random search results by relevancy. Their formula gave rise to an incredibly powerful Internet search engine that rapidly attracted a loyal following. The search engine enabled users to quickly find information through a simple and intuitive user interface. It also enabled Google to sell highly targeted advertising space.

The company grew rapidly. In 2001, Brin and Page hired Eric Schmidt, former CTO of Sun Microsystems and former CEO of Novell, to be Google's CEO. In 2004, the company went public, raising $1.6 billion in one of the most highly anticipated IPOs ever. Under Schmidt, the company adhered to a broad yet disciplined mission: "To organize the world's information and make it universally accessible and useful." This led the company to leverage its core search and advertising capabilities into blogging, online payments, social networks, and other information-driven businesses.

By 2014, Google had sales of over $66 billion, and employed more than 57,000 people. Despite this size, however, the company eschewed hierarchy and bureaucracy and sought to maintain a small-company feel. As noted by Schmidt during an interview, "Innovation always has been driven by a person or a small team that has the luxury of thinking of a new idea and pursuing it. There are no counter examples. It was true 100 years ago and it'll be true for the next 100 years. Innovation is something that comes when you're not under the gun. So it's important that, even if you don't have balance in your life, you have some time for reflection. So that you could say, 'Well, maybe I'm not working on the right thing.' Or, 'maybe I should have this new idea.' The creative parts of one's mind are not on schedule."[a]

In accordance with this belief, Google's engineers were organized into small technology teams with considerable decision-making authority. Every aspect of the headquarters, from the shared offices with couches, to the recreation facilities and the large communal cafe known as "Charlie's Place," was designed to foster informal communication and collaboration.[b] Managers referred to Google as a flexible and flat "technocracy," where resources and control were allocated based on the quality of people's ideas rather than seniority or hierarchical status. Schmidt remarked, "One of the things that we've tried very hard to avoid at Google is the sort of divisional structure that prevents collaboration across units. It's difficult. So I understand why people want to build business units, and have their presidents. But by doing that you cut down the informal ties that, in an open culture, drive so much collaboration. If people in the organization understand the values of the company, they should be able to self-organize to work on the most interesting problems."[c]

A key ingredient in Google's organization is an incentive system that requires all technical personnel to spend 20 percent of their time on innovative projects of their own choosing. This budget for innovation is not merely a device for creating slack in the organization for creative employees—it is an aggressive mandate that employees develop new product ideas. As noted by one Google engineer, "This isn't a matter of doing something in your spare time, but more of actively making time for it. Heck, I don't have a good 20% project yet and I need one. If I don't come up with something I'm sure it could negatively impact my review."[d] Managers face similar incentives. Each manager is required to spend 70 percent of his or her time on the core business, 20 percent on related-but-different projects, and 10 percent on entirely new products. According to Marissa Mayer, Google's head of search products and user experience, a significant portion of Google's new products and features (including Gmail and AdSense) resulted from the 20 percent time investments of Google engineers.

In a Podcast interview at Stanford University, Andy Grove (former CEO of Intel) remarked that the company's organization appeared chaotic, even noting "From the outside it looks like Google's organizational structure is best described by . . . Brownian motion in an expanding model" and questioned whether Schmidt believed this model would continue to work forever. In his response, Schmidt responded, "There's an important secret to tell, which is there are parts of the company that are not run chaotically. Our legal department, our finances. Our sales force has normal sales quotas. Our normal strategic planning activities, our normal investment activities, our M&A activities are run in a very traditional way. So the part of Google that gets all the attention is the creative side, the part where new products are being built and designed, and that is different. And it looks to us like that model will scale for quite some time . . . it looks like small teams can run ahead and that we can replicate that model for that part of the company."[e]

Discussion Questions

1. What are the advantages and disadvantages of the creative side of Google being run as a flexible and flat "technocracy?"
2. How does Google's culture influence the kind of employees it can attract and retain?

3. What do you believe the challenges are in having very different structure and controls for Google's creative side versus the other parts of the company?

4. Some analysts have argued that Google's free-form structure and the 20 percent time to work on personal projects is only possible because Google's prior success has created financial slack in the company. Do you agree with this? Would Google be able to continue this management style if it had closer competitors?

[a] J. Manyika, "Google's View on the Future of Business: An Interview with CEO Eric Schmidt," *McKinsey Quarterly*, November 2008.

[b] From "The Google Culture," www.google.com.

[c] Manyika, "Google's View on the Future of Business."

[d] B. Iyer and T. H. Davenport, "Reverse Engineering Google's Innovation Machine," *Harvard Business Review*, April 2008.

[e] Podcast retrieved on April 13, 2009, at http://iinnovate.blogspot.com/2007/03/eric-schmidt-ceoof-google.html.

OVERVIEW

The structure of an organization and the degree to which it uses formalized and standardized procedures and controls can significantly influence its likelihood of innovating, the effectiveness of its innovation projects, and the speed of its new product development processes.[1] For example, it is often argued that small, flexible organizations with a minimum of rules and procedures will encourage creativity and experimentation, leading to more innovative ideas. At the same time, it is also frequently pointed out that well-developed procedures and standards can ensure that the organization makes better development investment decisions and is able to implement projects quickly and efficiently. How then do managers decide what structure and controls would make the most sense for their firm?

A vast majority of firms use some type of product team structure to organize their new product development process, and we will look closely at how teams are composed and structured in Chapter Twelve, Managing New Product Development Teams. This chapter focuses on the organization-wide structural dimensions that shape the firm's propensity and ability to innovate effectively and efficiently. We will review the research on how firm size and structural dimensions such as formalization, standardization, and centralization affect a firm's innovativeness. By focusing on these underlying structural dimensions, we will elucidate why some structures may be better for encouraging the creativity that leads to idea generation, while other structures may be better suited for efficient production of new products. We will also explore structural forms that attempt to achieve the best of both worlds—the free-flowing organic and entrepreneurial structures and controls that foster innovation, plus the formalized and standardized forms that maximize efficiency while ensuring coherence across all of the corporation's development activities. The chapter then turns to the challenge of managing innovation across borders. Multinational firms face particularly difficult questions about where to locate—and how to manage—their development activities. We will review some of the work emerging on how multinational firms can balance the trade-offs inherent in these choices.

SIZE AND STRUCTURAL DIMENSIONS OF THE FIRM

Size: Is Bigger Better?

In the 1940s, Joseph Schumpeter challenged supporters of antitrust law by proposing that large firms would be more effective innovators.[2] Schumpeter pointed out that (1) capital markets are imperfect, and large firms are better able to obtain financing for R&D projects, and (2) firms with larger sales volume over which to spread the fixed costs of R&D would experience higher returns than firms with lower sales volume. Large firms are also likely to have better-developed complementary activities such as marketing or financial planning that enable them to be more effective innovators, and they are also likely to have greater global reach to obtain information or other resources.

Another advantage of size may arise in scale and learning effects. If large firms spend more on R&D in an absolute sense, they might also reap economies of scale and learning curve advantages in R&D—that is, they may get better and more efficient at it over time.[3] Through investing in R&D, the firm develops competencies in the new product development process and thus may improve its development process. It may accumulate better research equipment and personnel. Furthermore, as a large firm gains experience in choosing and developing innovation projects, it may learn to make better selections of projects that fit the firm's capabilities and have a higher likelihood of success.

Large firms are also in a better position to take on large or risky innovation projects than smaller firms.[4] For example, only a large company such as Boeing could develop and manufacture a 747, and only large pharmaceutical companies can plow millions of dollars into drug development in hopes that one or two drugs are successful.[5] This suggests that in industries that have large development scale (i.e., the average development project is very big and costly), large firms will tend to outperform small firms at innovation. In theory a coalition of small firms ought to achieve the same scale advantages, but in practice, coordinating a coalition of firms tends to be very difficult. While a single large firm can exert hierarchical authority over all of the development activities to ensure cooperation and coordination, coalitions often do not have such a well-defined system of authority and control.

On the other hand, as a firm grows, its R&D efficiency might decrease because of a loss of managerial control.[6] That is, the bigger a firm gets the more difficult it can become to effectively monitor and motivate employees. Furthermore, as a firm grows, it becomes increasingly difficult for individual scientists or entrepreneurs to appropriate the returns of their efforts; therefore their incentives diminish.[7] Thus, as the firm grows, the effectiveness of its governance systems may decrease.

Large firms may also be less innovative because their size can make them less nimble and responsive to change. Large firms typically have more bureaucratic inertia due to many layers of authority and well-developed policies and procedures.[8] For example, in the early 1980s, Xerox discovered that the administrative layers it had added to prevent errors in new product development had the unintended effect of blocking a project's progress, making product development cycles unacceptably long and putting Xerox at a disadvantage to more nimble Japanese competitors.[9]

High numbers of employees, large fixed-asset bases, and a large base of existing customers or supplier contracts can also be sources of inertia, making it difficult for the firm to change course quickly. As the number of employees grows, communication and coordination may become more difficult and prone to decision-making delays. When large firms have large fixed-asset bases and/or significant fixed costs, they often prefer to stick with existing sources of cash flow rather than gambling on big changes. Strategic commitments to customers and suppliers can also tie the firm to its existing businesses and technologies, making it more difficult to respond to technological change. Strategic commitments can thus lead to an *Icarus Paradox*—a firm's prior success in the market can hinder its ability to respond to new technological generations (for more on the Icarus Paradox see the accompanying Theory in Action).

Small firms are often considered more flexible and entrepreneurial than large firms. They are unencumbered by multiple layers of administration, large fixed-asset bases, or strategic commitments to large numbers of employees, customers, and suppliers. Small firms may also find it much simpler to monitor employees and reward them for their effort or success at innovation.[10] Because resources are less abundant, small firms may also be more motivated to choose projects more carefully, leading to higher rates of new product success.

A number of empirical studies have attempted to test whether large size improves or hampers innovation productivity. Several studies of patent counts, new drug introductions, and technological innovations that improve product performance have indicated that small firms often outperform large firms in innovation.[11] For example, a few studies of patenting output have concluded that small firms appear to spend their R&D dollars more carefully and are more efficient, receiving a larger number of patents per R&D dollar.[12] One study of 116 firms developing new business-to-business products also found that small firms (those with annual sales less than $100 million) had significantly shorter development cycles than large firms (those with $100 million and more in sales), even when considering the relative magnitude of the innovation.[13] However, a few studies have indicated that large firms may still outperform small firms in innovation in some industries.[14]

While the firm's overall size is not an easy-to-manipulate attribute of the firm, many firms have found ways of making even large firms feel small. One primary method is to break the overall firm into several smaller subunits, and then encourage an entrepreneurial culture within these subunits. Multiple studies have observed that in industries characterized by high-speed technological change, many large and hierarchical firms have been **disaggregated** (or "unbundled") into networks of smaller, often more specialized, autonomous divisions or independent firms.[15] In such industries, many firms have undergone large-scale downsizing, with many functions and layers of management eliminated. The giant multidivisional firms of the twentieth century were replaced by leaner firms that were more focused and flexible, loosely coupled in a network of alliances, supplier relationships, and distribution agreements.[16] This phenomenon led to the rise of terms such as *virtual organization*,[17] *network organization*,[18] and *modular organization*.[19]

disaggregated
When something is separated into its constituent parts.

Since firms also use big company–small company hybrids to vary other structural dimensions of the firm (including formalization, standardization, and centralization), these ambidextrous approaches to organizing will be covered in more depth after the structural dimensions of the firm are reviewed.

STRUCTURAL DIMENSIONS OF THE FIRM

Firms vary on a number of structural dimensions that can influence the amount, type, and effectiveness of their Innovation. Key structural dimensions include centralization, formalization, and standardization.

Centralization

**centralization/
decentraliza-
tion**
Centralization
is the degree to
which decision-
making author-
ity is kept at
top levels of
management.
Decentralization
is the degree to
which decision-
making authority
is pushed down
to lower levels of
the firm.

Centralization is the degree to which decision-making authority is kept at top levels of the firm, while **decentralization** is the degree to which decision-making authority is pushed down to lower levels of the firm. Centralization can refer both to the geographical location of activities (that is, the degree to which activities are performed in a central location for the firm) and to where power and authority over activities are located. That is, activities might occur in locations far from the corporate headquarters, but the authority and decision making over those activities may be retained at headquarters—leading to greater centralization than their physical location would suggest.

For firms that have multiple R&D projects ongoing, whether to centralize or decentralize R&D activities is a complex issue. Decentralizing R&D activities to the divisions of the firm enables those divisions to develop new products or processes that closely meet their particular division's needs (see Figure 10.1). The solutions they develop are more likely to fit well within the operating structure of the division, and be closely matched to the requirements of the customers served by that division. The decentralization of development projects also enables the firm to take advantage of the diversity of knowledge and market contacts that may exist in different divisions. Consistent with this, studies by Felipe Csaszar show that when decision making about new projects is pushed down to the lowest levels of the firm, the firm ends up taking on both a greater quantity and variety of projects. Though there will be more failed projects, the firm

FIGURE 10.1
Centralized and Decentralized R&D Activities

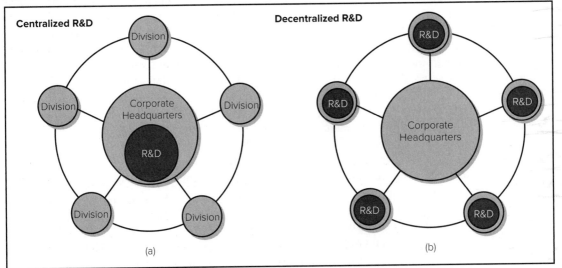

makes fewer "errors of omission."[20] However, there is much risk of reinventing the wheel when R&D activities are decentralized. Many redundant R&D activities may be performed in multiple divisions, and the full potential of the technology to create value in other parts of the firm may not be realized. Furthermore, having multiple R&D departments may cause each to forgo economies of scale and learning-curve effects.

By contrast, if the firm centralizes R&D in a single department, it may maximize economies of scale in R&D, enabling greater division of labor among the R&D specialists and maximizing the potential for learning-curve effects through the development of multiple projects. It also enables the central R&D department to manage the deployment of new technologies throughout the firm, improving the coherence of the firm's new product development efforts and avoiding the possibility that valuable new technologies are underutilized throughout the organization. For example, in the late 1980s, Intel realized that, as a result of the rising complexity and information processing demands in the semiconductor industry, its decentralized process development (which was scattered across diverse business groups) was resulting in serious delays and cost overruns. In the 1990s Intel thus centralized all process development, giving a single fabrication facility full responsibility for all new process generation. This development group would have maximum development resources (the highest in the industry). Once a new development process was completed and tested, it was replicated (in a process known in Intel as "copy exactly") in all of the company's other fabrication facilities.

The use of a centralized versus decentralized development process varies by type of firm and industry. For example, a study by Laura Cardinal and Tim Opler found that research-intensive firms that were highly diversified were more likely to establish separate research and development centers to facilitate communication and transfer of innovation across divisions.[21] A study by Peter Golder, on the other hand, found that consumer products companies tend to utilize more decentralized R&D, tailoring projects to local markets, while firms in electronics industries tend to centralize R&D in centers of excellence that are devoted to leveraging particular competencies.[22]

There is some disagreement about whether centralization enhances or impedes a firm's flexibility and responsiveness to technological change (or other environmental shifts). A highly centralized firm may be better able to make a bold change in its overall direction because its tight command-and-control structure enables it to impose such change on lower levels of the firm in a decisive manner. Decentralized firms may struggle to get the cooperation from all the divisions necessary to undergo a significant change. But decentralized firms may be better able to respond to some types of technological or environmental change because not all decisions need to be passed up the hierarchy to top management; employees at lower levels are empowered to make decisions and changes independently and thus may be able to act more quickly.

Formalization and Standardization

Formalization and standardization are closely related structural dimensions of organizations. The **formalization** of the firm is the degree to which the firm utilizes rules, procedures, and written documentation to structure the behavior of individuals or groups within the organization. **Standardization** is the degree to which activities in a firm are performed in a uniform manner. The rules and procedures employed in formalization can facilitate the standardization of firm activities and help to regulate employee

formalization
The degree to which the firm utilizes rules, procedures, and written documentation to structure the behavior of individuals or groups within the organization.

behavior by providing clear expectations of behavior and decision-making criteria. Formalization can substitute for some degree of managerial oversight, and thereby help large companies run smoothly with fewer managers. This is demonstrated in the accompanying Theory in Action about 3M, where both Lehr and Jacobson responded to the difficulty of managing the growing firm by imposing more discipline and rules. By creating formal processes for choosing and managing development projects, Lehr and Jacobsen hoped to improve the overall efficiency and coherence of the firm's many decentralized development activities. However, high degrees of formalization can also make a firm rigid.[23] If a firm codifies all of its activities with detailed procedures, it may stifle employee creativity. Employees may not feel empowered or motivated to implement new solutions. This is also noted in the 3M example, when employee resentment of the new planning methods led to morale and motivation problems.

standardiza-tion
The degree to which activities are performed in a uniform manner.

Similarly, while **standardization** can ensure that activities within the firm run smoothly and yield predictable outcomes, standardization can also stifle innovation. Standardization may be used to ensure quality levels are met and that customers and suppliers are responded to consistently and equitably. However, by minimizing variation, standardization can limit the creativity and experimentation that leads to innovative ideas.

Mechanistic versus Organic Structures

mechanistic
An organization structure characterized by a high degree of formalization and standardization, causing operations to be almost automatic or mechanical.

The combination of formalization and standardization results in what is often termed a **mechanistic** *structure*. Mechanistic structures are often associated with greater operational efficiency, particularly in large-volume production settings. The careful adherence to policies and procedures combined with standardization of most activities results in a well-oiled machine that operates with great consistency and reliability.[24] For example, Dell Computer achieves its operational excellence, delivering products cost-effectively and with minimal inconvenience, by being highly standardized, disciplined, and streamlined.[25] While mechanistic structures are often associated with high centralization, it is also possible to have a highly decentralized mechanistic structure by using formalization as a substitute for direct oversight. By establishing detailed rules, procedures, and standards, top management can push decision-making authority to lower levels of the firm while still ensuring that decisions are consistent with top management's objectives.

organic
An organization structure characterized by a low degree of formalization and standardization. Employees may not have well-defined job responsibilities and operations may be characterized by a high degree of variation.

Mechanistic structures, however, are often deemed unsuitable for fostering innovation. Mechanistic structures achieve efficiency by ensuring rigid adherence to standards and minimizing variation, potentially stifling creativity within the firm. **Organic** structures that are more free-flowing, and characterized by low levels of formalization and standardization, are often considered better for innovation and dynamic environments.[26] In the organic structure, employees are given far more latitude in their job responsibilities and operating procedures. Because much innovation arises from experimentation and improvisation, organic structures are often thought to be better for innovation despite their possible detriment to efficiency.[27]

Size versus Structure

Many of the advantages and disadvantages of firm size that were discussed at the beginning of the chapter are related to the structural dimensions of formalization,

In 1916, William McKnight, the then general manager of sales and production for 3M, authorized the creation of the company's first research laboratory to improve 3M's sandpaper. McKnight had a strong belief in the power of individual entrepreneurship and innovation. He encouraged innovation through a combination of setting ambitious goals for new product development and giving individuals considerable freedom in how they pursued those goals. For example, McKnight established a companywide objective that 25 percent of sales should come from products created in the last five years. He also endorsed a "bootlegging" program whereby researchers could spend up to 15 percent of their time on whatever projects they were interested in pursuing.

As the firm grew, McKnight continued to support a centralized R&D lab while also encouraging divisions to pursue their own development initiatives in response to market needs they encountered. However, as 3M's product portfolio grew, it became increasingly difficult for 3M to manage functions such as production and sales. In 1944, McKnight began to experiment with an even more decentralized organizational form wherein divisions would have not only their own R&D labs, but also their own production operations and sales force. McKnight believed that small independent businesses would grow faster than a large company, leading to his "grow and divide" philosophy: Each division would be independent, and as its development projects grew into successful departments, they too would be spun off into new divisions.

By 1980, when Lou Lehr took the helm, 3M had grown to have 85 basic technologies and competed in about 40 major product markets. Lehr feared that 3M's greatest strength had become its weakness—the proliferation of independent businesses had led to a fragmentation of effort. Lehr worried that divisions might be wasting too much time on redundant activities and not taking advantage of the opportunity to leverage technologies across multiple divisions where they might be valuable. He wanted to ensure that divisions with related technologies would cooperate on development projects, and that new technologies would be diffused across the company. So he consolidated the company's 42 divisions and 10 groups into four business sectors based on

their relatedness of technology. He also created a three-tiered R&D system: central research laboratories that concentrated on basic research with long-term potential, sector labs that would serve groups of related divisions and develop core technologies to drive medium-term (5 to 10 years) growth, and division labs that would continue to work on projects with immediate applications. Lehr also imposed much more formal planning on the development process—some of 3M's managers began to refer to it as "planning by the pound." He also eliminated many projects that had been struggling for years.

The arrival of "Jake" Jacobson in 1986 as the new CEO led 3M into an era of even greater discipline. Jacobson increased the target of sales from products developed within the past five years to 35 percent. He increased the R&D funding rate to about twice that of other U.S. companies, but also directed the company to become more focused in its project selection and to shorten development cycle times. He also implemented a companywide move toward using teams for development rather than encouraging individual entrepreneurs. Though Jacobson's initiatives improved efficiency, many researchers began to resent some of the changes. They believed that the move to manage all development projects with teams was destroying the individualistic culture of entrepreneurship at 3M and that the focus on discipline came at the expense of creativity and excitement. Motivation and morale problems began to emerge.

Thus, when "Desi" Desimone became the CEO in 1991, he eased the company back toward a slightly looser, more entrepreneurial focus. He believed his predecessors had established a good architecture for ensuring that innovation did not run away in an uncontrolled fashion, but he also believed the company needed more balance between freedom and control, as reflected in the following quote:

> Senior management's role is to create an internal environment in which people understand and value 3M's way of operating. It's a culture in which innovation and respect for the individual are still central. If you have senior management who have internalized the principles, you create a trust relationship in the company. The top knows it should

continued

Source: Adapted from C. Bartlett and A. Mohammed, "3M: Profile of an Innovating Company," Harvard Business School case no. 9-395-016, 1995.

trust the process of bottom-up innovation by leaving a crack open when someone is insistent that a blocked project has potential. And the lower levels have to trust the top when we intervene or control their activities.

standardization, and centralization. Large firms often make greater use of formalization and standardization because as the firm grows it becomes more difficult to exercise direct managerial oversight. Formalization and standardization ease coordination costs, at the expense of making the firm more mechanistic. Many large firms attempt to overcome some of this rigidity and inertia by decentralizing authority, enabling divisions of the firm to behave more like small companies. For example, firms such as General Electric, Hewlett-Packard, Johnson and Johnson, and General Motors have attempted to take advantage of both bigness and smallness by organizing their companies into groups of small companies that can access the large corporation's resources and reach while retaining a small company's simplicity and flexibility.[28] The next section examines several methods by which firms can achieve some of the advantages of large size, and the efficiency and speed of implementation afforded by mechanistic structures, while simultaneously harnessing the creativity and entrepreneurial spirit of small firms and organic structures.

The Ambidextrous Organization: The Best of Both Worlds?

Most firms must simultaneously manage their existing product lines with efficiency, consistency, and incremental innovation, while still encouraging the development of new product lines and responding to technological change through more radical innovation. Tushman and O'Reilly argue that the solution is to create an ambidextrous organization.[29] An **ambidextrous organization** is a firm with a complex organizational form that is composed of multiple internally inconsistent architectures that can collectively achieve both short-term efficiency and long-term innovation.[30] Such firms might utilize mechanistic structures in some portions of the firm and organic structures in others. This is one of the rationales for setting up an R&D division that is highly distinct (either geographically or structurally) from the rest of the organization; a firm can use high levels of formalization and standardization in its manufacturing and distribution divisions, while using almost no formalization or standardization in its R&D division. Incentives in each of the divisions can be designed around different objectives, encouraging very different sets of behavior from employees. A firm can also centralize and tightly coordinate activities in divisions that reap great economies of scale such as manufacturing, while decentralizing activities such as R&D into many small units so that they behave like small, independent ventures. Whereas traditionally research emphasized the importance of diffusing information across the firm and ensuring cross-fertilization of ideas across new product development efforts, recent research suggests that some amount of isolation of teams, at least in early development stages, can be valuable. When multiple teams interact closely, there is a risk that a solution that appears to have an advantage (at least at the outset) will be too rapidly adopted by other teams. This can cause all of the teams to converge on the same ideas, thwarting the development of

ambidextrous organization
The ability of an organization to behave almost as two different kinds of companies at once. Different divisions of the firm may have different structures and control systems, enabling them to have different cultures and patterns of operations.

Skunk Works®

Skunk Works® is a term that originated with a division of Lockheed Martin that was formed in June of 1943 to quickly develop a jet fighter for the United States Army. It has evolved as skunk works to refer more generally to new product development teams that operate nearly autonomously from the parent organization, with considerable decentralization of authority and little bureaucracy.

other creative approaches that might have advantages in the long run.[31] Consistent with this, a significant body of research on "**skunk works**" has indicated that there can be significant gains from isolating new product development teams from the mainstream organization.[32] Separating the teams from the rest of the organization permits them to explore new alternatives, unfettered by the demands of the rest of the organization.

Similarly, firms that have multiple product divisions might find that one or more divisions need a more organic structure to encourage creativity and fluid responses to environmental change, while other divisions benefit from a more structured and standardized approach. For example, when *USA Today* decided to establish an online version of the popular newspaper, management discovered it would need more flexible procedures to respond to both rapid technological change and the real-time information updating requirements of the online paper. The paper would also require different incentive schemes to attract and retain technologically savvy employees. The company established the online paper as a separate division with a different reporting structure, less formalization, a different pay structure, and even different cultural norms about appropriate work attire and working hours.

Apple provides another example. In 1980, Apple was churning out Apple II personal computers at a fast clip. However, Steve Jobs was not content with the product design; he wanted a product that would revolutionize the world by dramatically changing the way people interact with computers. He wanted to develop a computer so user-friendly and self-contained that it would appeal even to people who had no interest in the technological features of computers—it would become an extension of their everyday lives. Jobs began working with a team of engineers on a new project called Macintosh (originally developed by another Apple engineer, Jef Raskin). Jobs did not believe that the growing corporate environment at Apple was conducive to nurturing a revolution, so he created a separate division for the Macintosh that would have its own unique culture. He tried to instill a free-spirited entrepreneurial atmosphere reminiscent of the company's early beginnings in a garage, where individualistic and often eccentric software developers would flourish. The small group of team members was handpicked and sheltered from normal corporate commitments and distractions. He encouraged the Macintosh team members to consider themselves renegades, and even hung a pirate's skull-and-crossbones flag over their building. Jobs would also take the team on regular retreats to isolated resorts and reaffirm the renegade culture with quotes like "It's more fun to be a pirate than to join the Navy."[33]

If big firms can have internal structures with the incentives and behavior of small firms, then much of the logic of the impact of firm size on technological innovation rates becomes moot. A single organization may have multiple cultures, structures, and processes within it; large firms may have entrepreneurial divisions that can tap the greater resources of the larger corporation, yet have the incentive structures of small firms that foster the more careful choice of projects or enhance the motivation of R&D scientists. Such entrepreneurial units may be capable of developing discontinuous innovations within the large, efficiency-driven organizations that tend to foster incremental innovations.

Firms can also achieve some of the advantages of mechanistic and organic structures by alternating through different structures over time.[34] Schoonhoven and Jelinek studied Intel, Hewlett-Packard, Motorola, Texas Instruments, and National Semiconductor and found that these firms maintained a "dynamic tension" between formal reporting structures, quasiformal structures, and informal structures.[35] While the organizations had very explicit reporting structures and formalized development processes, the organizations were also reorganized frequently to modify reporting relationships and responsibilities in response to a changing environment. Thus, while the organizations used seemingly mechanistic structures to ensure systematic and efficient production, frequent reorganizing enabled the firms to be flexible.

These firms also used what Schoonhoven and Jelinek term *quasiformal structures* in the form of teams, task forces, and dotted-line relationships (that is, reporting relationships that were not formally indicated on the organizational chart). These quasiformal structures were more problem-focused and could change faster than the rest of the company. They also provided a forum for interaction across divisions and thus played an important boundary-spanning role. One advantage of quasiformal structures is that they fostered interactions based on interests rather than on hierarchy. This can foster more employee motivation and cross-fertilization of ideas. As noted by one employee: "Sometimes [innovation] happens in the men's room. One guy's talking to another guy, and another guy's standing, eavesdropping on the conversation, scribbling on a napkin."[36] Some of the downsides to such quasiformal structures were that they required time to manage, and they could be hard to kill. Since the quasi structures were not part of the formal reporting structure, it could sometimes be difficult to establish who had the authority to disband them.

MODULARITY AND "LOOSELY COUPLED" ORGANIZATIONS

Another method firms use to strike a balance between efficiency and flexibility is to adopt standardized manufacturing platforms or components that can then be mixed and matched in a modular production system. This enables them to achieve standardization advantages (such as efficiency and reliability) at the component level, while achieving variety and flexibility at the end product level.

Modular Products

Modularity refers to the degree to which a system's components may be separated and recombined.[37] Making products modular can exponentially increase the number of possible configurations achievable from a given set of inputs.[38] For example, many of IKEA's shelving systems are designed so that users can mix and match a number of components to meet their needs. The shelves and supports come in a range of standardized sizes, and they can all be easily attached with standardized connectors. Similarly, some stoves now offer customers the ability to expand the range of the stove's functionality by removing the burners and plugging in other cooking devices such as barbecue grills and pancake griddles. Publishers have even embraced modularity by offering digital content that enables instructors to assemble their own textbooks from book chapters, articles, cases, or their own materials.

Many other products are produced in a modular way, even though the customer does not perceive the modularity. By standardizing a number of common components and using flexible manufacturing technologies that can quickly shift from one assembly configuration to another, companies can produce a wide variety of product models just by changing which components are combined, while still achieving economies of scale and efficiency in the individual components. For example, Chrysler achieves one of the fastest new product development cycles in the automobile industry while also keeping new product development costs low through its practice of using a few standard platforms upon which all of its new car models are built. Tata Motors, the Indian company that introduced a $2,500 car in 2008, used modularity even more dramatically. The Nano is built in components that can be sold and shipped in kits to be assembled and serviced by local entrepreneurs. This both enables the distribution of the Nano to be fast and streamlined and enables better penetration of remote rural markets.[39]

Modularity is achieved in product design through the specification of standard interfaces. For example, by designing all of its shelving components to work with its standardized connectors, IKEA ensures that components can be freely mixed and matched. Individual components can be changed without requiring any design changes in the other components. Because modularity enables a wider range of end configurations to be achieved from a given set of inputs, it provides a relatively cost-effective way for firms to meet heterogeneous customer demands. Furthermore, since modularity can enable one component to be upgraded without changing other components, modularity can enable firms and customers to upgrade their products without replacing their entire system. The personal computer is an excellent example of a modular system that enables upgrading. For example, if users want their personal computer to have more memory or a better monitor, they do not need to replace their entire computer system—they can simply purchase and install additional memory or a new monitor.

Modular products become more valuable when customers have heterogeneous demands and there are diverse options for meeting them. For example, suppose a car may be assembled from a range of components. The wider the range of components that may be recombined into a car, the wider is the range of possible car configurations achievable through modularity, and the greater is the potential opportunity cost of being "locked in" to a single configuration. Furthermore, the more heterogeneous customers are in their demand for car features, the less likely they are to agree on a single configuration. By employing modularity, heterogeneous customers can choose a car configuration that more closely meets their preferences.[40] By contrast, if customers all want the same thing, then there is little to be gained through offering a modular system—it will be a simple matter to determine the best combination of components to meet customer demands and integrate them into a nonmodular system.

When products are made more modular, it enables the entire production system to be made more modular. The standard interfaces reduce the amount of coordination that must take place between the developers of different components, freeing them to pursue more flexible arrangements than the typical organizational hierarchy.[41] Such flexible arrangements are referred to as "loosely coupled organizational structures," as described in the next section.

Loosely Coupled Organizational Structures

Organizations can also be made modular through the adoption of structures that enable "loose coupling."[42] In a loosely coupled structure, development and production activities are not tightly integrated but rather achieve coordination through their adherence to shared objectives and common standards. If, for example, each development group agrees to a development plan and standardized interfaces that enable the components they develop to connect and interact effectively, there may be little need for close coordination between the groups. The standard interface provides "embedded coordination" among all the development and production participants.[43] This can enable components of a product to be produced by highly autonomous divisions of the firm, or even by multiple independent firms.

Advances in information technology have also enabled loosely coupled organizational structures to become more common.[44] Information technology can enable a firm to access and process more information at a lower cost, vastly increasing the firm's options for development configurations.[45] For example, information technology lowers a firm's search costs for locating suitable development partners, as well as the costs of monitoring the partner's performance. This was clearly demonstrated in a study by Nick Argyres of the development of the B-2 "Stealth" bomber, a highly advanced military aircraft, developed jointly by Northrop, Boeing, Vaught, and General Electric.[46] Argyres found that enhanced information technology limited the need for coordination of activities through hierarchical control. By using information technology and developing a standard interface—a shared "technical grammar" that facilitated communication across firms—the firms involved in the development of the bomber could work autonomously, yet cooperatively.

Less need for integration frees firms to pursue more flexible research and development and production configurations. For instance, firms can become more specialized by focusing on a few key aspects of technological innovation that relate closely to the firm's core competencies, while obtaining other activities through outsourcing or alliances. By focusing on those activities in which the firm has a competitive advantage, the firm can improve its chance of developing a product that has a price-to-value ratio that attracts customers while reducing the overhead and administrative complexity of maintaining a wide scope of activities. This can cause whole industries to be transformed as large vertically integrated firms are displaced by nimbler, more specialized producers.[47] For example, when computer workstations displaced their more integrated predecessors, minicomputers (which were traditionally built using a proprietary central processor, combined with a proprietary system bus, and run with a proprietary operating system), the entire computer industry began to become more modular as integrated producers like Prime, Wang, and Data General were displaced by a network of producers (including Sun Microsystems, Silicon Graphics, and Motorola), whose components could be combined in numerous end product configurations.

There are, however, disadvantages of loose coupling. Many activities reap significant synergies by being integrated.[48] In particular, activities that require the frequent exchange of complex or tacit knowledge are likely to need closer integration than a loosely coupled development configuration can offer. For example, suppose the design of a delivery mechanism for a drug will require intensive coordination with the design of the drug itself. It may be that the strength and dosage of the drug must be carefully calibrated and adjusted in accordance to the speed at which the delivery mechanism releases the drug. Alternative materials considered for the delivery mechanism may also have to be evaluated for their risk of potential interaction with chemicals used in the drug solution. If ongoing intensive coordination is required, the development activities might be better carried out through close integration of all parties.

When Boeing launched its sales program for the yet-to-be-built 787 Dreamliner in late 2003, it rapidly became the fastest-selling commercial jet liner in history. By 2011, Boeing had received more than 800 advance orders for the aircraft—more than any other plane in history.[b] The Dreamliner marked an important turning point for the company. Boeing had not built an all-new airliner since 1994, when the 777 took to the sky. Since that time, Airbus had led the way in aerospace innovation, while Boeing had been content to stretch and refine its existing families of airplanes such as the 737 and 747. Many had begun to believe that Boeing no longer had what it took to build an entirely new aircraft.[c] The Dreamliner's success or failure would thus send strong signals to the market about the company's prospects for the future.

The Dreamliner was a super-efficient long-range mid-sized airliner. It would be the first commercial jet manufactured primarily from carbon fiber composites, enabling it to be significantly lighter and thus more fuel efficient than traditional commercial jets. Because the composite material could be more easily sculpted than aluminum, the wings of the jet would have graceful curves like a bird's wings. Furthermore, since the composite material was exceptionally strong and resistant to corrosion, the cabin could be both more pressurized and more humidified, making air travel more comfortable.[d] Composites also allowed Boeing to easily assemble the forward, center, and rear sections of the fuselage, the wings, the horizontal stabilizers, and the vertical fins as large individual modules that could be quickly snapped together to form the airplane, instead of constructing the aircraft piece by piece using aluminum sheets as prior aircraft had been constructed.[e]

The innovations of the Boeing 787 program extended well past the actual composition of the aircraft. For the 787 project, Boeing also revolutionized the structure of the production processes involved in building a commercial aircraft. The production of the 787 would be significantly more loosely coupled than any commercial aircraft to date. Dozens of partners from around the world built and preassembled large pieces of the plane which were then delivered to the Boeing plant for final assembly.[f] For example, Mitsubishi, Kawasaki, and Fuji, all of Japan, were contracted to produce the wings, forward fuselage, and center wing box, respectively. Saab makes the cargo doors, and Alenia Aeronautica of Italy produces a horizontal stabilizer and central fuselage. Dozens of companies from other countries contribute other parts.[g] Roughly 70 percent of the Dreamliner would be built outside of the United States. The dramatic increase in outsourcing was expected to provide a range of benefits that included spreading the risk of developing the aircraft, containing costs, and improving the prospects for foreign sales since purchasers and their governments often like to see work done on the aircraft in their countries.[h]

Though Boeing had outsourced a portion of the work on its planes for decades, the 787 ushered in a new era of outsourcing, Boeing's role would shift from being the traditional designer and manufacturer to becoming "an essential elements company, reserving for itself optimum design and integration tasks and relying on a select group of outsiders for everything else."[i] The revolutionary new production process was not without its challenges, however. The sheer complexity of the project and the large number of suppliers involved made coordination much more complicated. Breakdowns in this coordination had led to several delays. Though the first Dreamliner had been slated to take flight in August of 2007, customers did not actually take delivery of the first Dreamliners until late 2011. The challenges of coordinating suppliers around the globe had led to numerous production delays and design adjustments. Boeing's managers indicated that the company would make little profit on the first several dozen planes because even after they rolled off the assembly line, they would require corrective work, including the repair of parts and design changes.[j] Boeing's management acknowledged that some mistakes had been made in the supply chain, and Engineering Vice President Mike Denton indicated that the company was considering bringing more of the work back

continued

concluded

in-house. He noted, "We will probably do more of the design and even some of the major production for the next new airplanes ourselves as opposed to having it all out with the partners."[k]

[a] Adapted from "The Loosely Coupled Production of Boeing's 787 Dreamliner" by Jaspal Singh and Melissa A. Schilling, New York University teaching case.

[b] C. Drew, "Boeing Posts 20% Profit Gain But Cuts Forecast For 2012 As Jet Completion Slows," *New York Times*, January 25, 2012.

[c] M. V. Copeland, "Boeing's Big Dream," *Fortune* 157, no. 9 (2008), pp. 180–91. The Dreamliner's success or failure would thus send strong signals to the market about the company's prospects for the future.

[d] S. Holmes, "Better Living at 30,000 Feet," *BusinessWeek*, August 2, 2007.

[e] R. Renstrom, "Boeing's Big Gamble: Half-Plastic Dreamliner," *Plastics News*, July 2, 2007.

[f] P. Hise, "How Many Small Businesses Does It Take to Build a Jet?" *Fortune Small Business* 17, no. 6 (2007), pp. 42–45.

[g] J. Weber, "Boeing to Rein in Dreamliner Outsourcing," *BusinessWeek Online*, January 19, 2009, p. 10.

[h] Ibid., and M. Mecham, "The Flat-Earth Airplane," *Aviation Week & Space Technology*, July 3, 2006, p. 43.

[i] Mecham, "The Flat-Earth Airplane."

[j] C. Drew, "Boeing Posts 20% Profit Gain But Cuts Forecast For 2012 As Jet Completion Slows." *New York Times*, January 25, 2012

[k] Weber, "Boeing to Rein in Dreamliner Outsourcing."

An integrated firm also has mechanisms for resolving conflict that may be more effective or less expensive than those available in the market.[49] For example, if a dispute should arise over the development of a new product among development groups that are within the same firm, top managers can decide what action to take and exercise their authority over the development groups. But if the development groups are in separate companies, developing a new product in a collaboration agreement, neither firm may possess the authority to resolve the dispute and enforce a particular outcome. If the firms are unable to resolve the dispute themselves, they may face going to court or arbitration to resolve the dispute, an expensive and time-consuming option.

MANAGING INNOVATION ACROSS BORDERS

The organization of innovation activities becomes particularly interesting for multinational firms. Many of the same issues that shape the centralization-versus-decentralization decision discussed earlier become highly amplified in the multinational firm. Foreign markets offer highly diverse sources of information and other resources. They may also have highly diverse product needs and different operating norms. This prompts many firms to consider decentralizing R&D to take advantage of local information and tailor innovation activities to the local market. However, innovations developed in this decentralized manner might never be diffused to the other divisions. The customization of products and processes to the local markets makes them particularly difficult to transfer to divisions serving different markets. Divisions that are accustomed to developing their own innovations may be reluctant to share them with others for fear of giving away their proprietary knowledge. They may also be reluctant to adopt other divisions' innovations because of the belief that innovations that are not developed locally will not suit their local market needs (a phenomenon known as *not-invented-here syndrome*). However, much of the value creation potential of a multinational is the opportunity to leverage technological innovation (and other core competencies) into multiple markets. Allowing innovation activities to become completely autonomous and disconnected risks forfeiting this opportunity. How does the multinational resolve this dilemma? A series of studies by Christopher Bartlett and Sumantra Ghoshal highlight some advantages and disadvantages of various approaches to the management of multinational innovation. They identify four primary strategies used by firms: center-for-global, local-for-local, locally leveraged, and globally linked.[50]

center-for-global strategy
When all innovation activities are conducted at a central hub and innovations are then diffused throughout the company.

The **center-for-global** strategy entails conducting all innovation activities at a centralized hub. These innovations are then deployed globally throughout the company. The centralization of innovation activities enables management to:

- Tightly coordinate all R&D activities (across both functions and projects).
- Achieve greater specialization and economies of scale in R&D activities while avoiding duplication of activities in multiple divisions.
- Develop and protect core competencies.
- Ensure that innovations are standardized and implemented throughout the company.

Managers are likely to choose a center-for-global approach to innovation when they have a strong desire to control the evolution of a technology, when they have strong concerns about the protection of proprietary technologies, when development activities require close coordination, or when there is a need to respond quickly to technological change and dispersed efforts are likely to create inefficiencies.[51] However, a center-for-global approach tends to not be very responsive to the diverse demands of different markets. Furthermore, the divisions that serve these markets might resist adopting or promoting centrally developed innovations. As a result, innovations developed centrally may not closely fit the needs of foreign markets and may also not be deployed quickly or effectively.

local-for-local strategy
When each division or subsidiary of the firm conducts its own R&D activities, tailored for the needs of the local market.

A **local-for-local strategy** is the opposite of the center-for-global strategy. Each national subsidiary uses its own resources to create innovations that respond to the needs of its local market. A local-for-local strategy takes advantage of access to diverse information and resources, and it customizes innovation for the needs and tastes of the local market. Managers are likely to choose a local-for-local strategy when divisions are very autonomous and when markets are highly differentiated.

locally leveraged strategy
When each division or subsidiary of the firm conducts its own R&D activities, but the firm attempts to leverage resulting innovations throughout the company.

There are several downsides to the local-for-local strategy, however. It can result in significant redundancy in activities as each division reinvents the wheel. Furthermore, each division may suffer from a lack of scale in R&D activities, and there is a risk that valuable innovations will not be diffused across the firm.

Over time, firms have developed variants of these strategies that attempt to reap advantages of both the center-for-global and local-for-local strategies. Bartlett and Ghoshal identify one such strategy as the **locally leveraged strategy**. A firm implementing a locally leveraged strategy attempts to take the most creative resources and innovative developments from the divisions and deploy them across the company. This strategy enables the firm to take advantage of the diverse ideas and resources created in local markets, while leveraging these innovations across the company. One way this strategy is employed in consumer markets is to assign an individual the role of international brand custodian. This person is responsible for ensuring that a successful brand is deployed into the firm's multiple markets while also maintaining consistency in the product's image and positioning.[52] Such a strategy can be very effective if different markets the company serves have similar needs.

globally linked strategy
Innovation activities are decentralized, but also centrally coordinated for the global needs of the corporation.

Another approach, the **globally linked strategy**, entails creating a system of decentralized R&D divisions that are connected to each other. Each geographically decentralized division might be charged with a different innovation task that serves the global company's needs. For example, a multinational auto manufacturer may empower one of its European divisions with the responsibility for developing new subcompact models that most closely fit the European markets but that may ultimately also be sold in the United States, Canada, and South America. In the meantime, its American division might bear the bulk of the responsibility for collaborating with other manufacturers to develop more efficient manufacturing processes that will ultimately be deployed corporatewide. Thus, while innovation is decentralized to take advantage of resources and talent pools offered in different geographic markets, it is also globally coordinated to meet companywide objectives. This approach also attempts to enable the learning accrued through innovation activities to be diffused throughout the firm. This strategy can be quite powerful in its ability to tap and integrate global resources, but it is also expensive in both time and money as it requires intensive coordination.

In both the locally leveraged and globally linked strategies, R&D divisions are decentralized and linked to each other. The difference lies in the missions of the R&D divisions. In the locally leveraged strategy, the decentralized R&D divisions are largely independent of each other and work on the full scope of development activities relevant to the regional business unit in which they operate. This means, for example, that if their regional business unit produces and sells health care items, beauty care products, and paper products, the R&D division is likely to work on development projects related to all of these products. However, to ensure that the best innovations are leveraged across the company, the company sets up integrating mechanisms (such as holding regular cross-regional meetings, or establishing a liaison such as an international brand custodian) to encourage the divisions to share their best developments with each other. By contrast, in the globally linked strategy, the R&D divisions are decentralized, but they each play a different role in the global R&D strategy. Instead of working on all development activities relevant to the region in which they operate, they specialize in a particular development activity. For example, an R&D division may be in a regional business unit that produces and sells health care, beauty care, and paper products, but its role may be to focus on developing paper innovations, while other R&D divisions in the firm work on health care items or beauty care products. Or it might focus on basic chemistry applications relevant to all of the products, while another division explores packaging innovations, and so on. The role of the division should exploit some local market resource advantage (such as abundant timber or a cluster of chemical technology firms). This strategy attempts to take advantage of the diversity of resources and knowledge in foreign markets, while still linking each division through well-defined roles in the company's overall R&D strategy.

Bartlett and Ghoshal argue that, overall, the multinational firm's objective is to make centralized innovation activities more effective (that is, better able to serve the various local markets) while making decentralized innovation activities more efficient (that is, eliminating redundancies and exploiting synergies across divisions). Bartlett and Ghoshal propose that firms should take a *transnational* approach wherein resources and capabilities that exist anywhere within the firm can be leveraged and deployed to exploit any opportunity that arises in any geographic market. They argue that this can be achieved by:

- Encouraging reciprocal interdependence among the divisions of the firm (that is, each division must recognize its dependency on the other divisions of the firm).
- Utilizing integration mechanisms across the divisions, such as division-spanning teams, rotating personnel across divisions, and so on.
- Balancing the organization's identity between its national brands and its global image.

Ericsson provides an excellent example of this approach. Instead of using a strictly centralized or decentralized structure for its innovation activities, Ericsson's structure ebbs and flows between centralization and decentralization. Sometimes Ericsson increases levels of centralization and global integration for particular projects, while other times it decentralizes much more authority over innovation activities to its geographically dispersed divisions. Similar to the dynamic tension approach described by Jelinek and Schoonhoven, Ericsson regularly modifies its structure to adjust the balance between integration and autonomy. To encourage interunit integration, Ericsson also sends teams of 50 to 100 engineers to a different subsidiary for a year or two. Such member rotation programs facilitate the diffusion of knowledge throughout the firm.[53] Furthermore, encouraging engineers to become integrated into multiple areas of the company helped the engineers identify with both the global company and particular divisions.

Summary of Chapter

1. The impact of firm size on innovation has been debated for more than 50 years. Size is thought to confer advantages such as economies of scale in R&D, greater access to complementary resources (like capital and market access), and learning benefits. However, size may also be associated with disadvantages such as inertia and governance problems.

2. Many firms attempt to make big companies feel small by breaking them into networks of more specialized divisions. These divisions can behave like smaller, more entrepreneurial firms.

3. Structural dimensions of the firm, including formalization, standardization, and centralization, also affect the firm's propensity to innovate and its effectiveness at innovation. Formalization and standardization tend to improve efficiency, but can stifle experimentation and creativity. Centralization has a more ambiguous effect

on innovation; in some cases, centralization can enable significant innovation to occur more rapidly, and in other situations, decentralization fosters more innovation by enabling managers to respond quickly to local needs.

4. Traditionally, scholars have divided organization structures into two major types: mechanistic structures, which are highly formalized and standardized, and are good for efficient production, and organic structures, which are loose and free flowing and are good for creativity and experimentation.

5. Ambidextrous organizations attempt to achieve both the efficiency advantages of large mechanistic firms and the creativity and entrepreneurial spirit of small organic firms. These firms may have divisions with different structures and control schemes, or they may alternate between different structures.

6. Recently, many firms have begun forming loosely coupled networks both within and between firms to conduct development activities. Part of this transition is attributed to the rise in information technology and the resultant decrease in coordination costs.

7. Multinational firms face significant challenges in determining where and how to conduct their R&D activities. One primary challenge is to balance the need to tap the knowledge and resources of local markets while also achieving coherence across the corporation and ensure that technological innovations are diffused and leveraged throughout the organization.

Discussion Questions

1. Are there particular types of innovation activities for which large firms are likely to outperform small firms? Are there types for which small firms are likely to outperform large firms?

2. What are some advantages and disadvantages of having formalized procedures for improving the effectiveness or efficiency of innovation?

3. What factors should a firm consider when deciding how centralized its R&D activities should be? Should firms employ both centralized and decentralized R&D activities?

4. Why is the tension between centralization and decentralization of R&D activities likely to be even greater for multinational firms than for firms that compete in one national market?

5. What are some of the advantages and disadvantages of the transnational approach advocated by Bartlett and Ghoshal?

Suggested Further Reading

Classics

Burns, T., and G. M. Stalker, *The Management of Innovation* (London: Tavistock Publications, 1961).

Chandler, A., *Strategy and Structure: Chapter in the History of the American Industrial Enterprise* (Cambridge, MA: Harvard University Press, 1962).

Ettlie, J. E., W. P. Bridges., and R. D. O'Keefe, "Organization Strategy and Structural Differences for Radical versus Incremental Innovation," *Management Science* 30 (1984), pp. 682–95.

Schilling, M. A., "Towards a General Modular Systems Theory and Its Application to Inter-firm Product Modularity," *Academy of Management Review*, 25 (2000): 312–34.

Schumpeter, J. A., *Capitalism, Socialism and Democracy* (New York: Harper & Brothers Publishers, 1942).

Thompson, J. D., *Organizations in Action* (New York: McGraw-Hill, 1967).

Recent Work

Argyres, N., and L. Bigelow, "Innovation, Modularity, and Vertical Deintegration: Evidence from the Early U.S. Auto Industry," *Organization Science* 21 (2010), pp. 842–53.

Fang, C., J. Lee., and M. A. Schilling, "Balancing Exploration and Exploitation through Structural Design: Advantage of the Semi-isolated Subgroup Structure in Organizational Learning," *Organization Science*, 21 (2010), pp. 625–42.

Arora, A, Belenzon, S. and Rios, LA. "The Organization of R&D in American Corporations: The Determinants and Consequences of Decentralization," NBER Working Paper No. 17013 (2011), May.

Lerner, J. and Wulf, J. "Innovation and Incentives: Evidence from Corporate R&D," *Review of Economics and Statistics*, 89 (2007): 634–44.

Tushman, M., W. K. Smith., R. C. Wood., G. Westerman., and C. O'Reilly, "Organizational Designs and Innovation Streams," *Industrial and Corporate Change* 19 (2010), pp. 1331–66.

Endnotes

1. D. Dougherty, "Reimagining the Differentiation and Integration of Work for Sustained Product Innovation," *Organization Science* 12 (2001), pp. 612–31; A. Griffin, "The Effect of Project and Process Characteristics on Product Development Cycle Time," *Journal of Marketing Research* 34 (1997), pp. 24–35; E. H. Kessler and A. K. Chakrabarti, "Innovation Speed: A Conceptual Model of Context, Antecedents, and Outcomes," *Academy of Management Review* 21 (1996), pp. 1143–91; and A. Menon, J. Chowdhury, and B. Lukas, "Antecedents and Outcomes of New Product Development Speed: An Interdisciplinary Conceptual Framework," *Industrial Marketing Management* 31 (2002), pp. 317–28.

2. J. A. Schumpeter, *Capitalism, Socialism and Democracy* (New York: Harper & Brothers Publishers, 1942).

3. W. M. Cohen and D. A. Levinthal, "Absorptive Capacity: A New Perspective on Learning and Innovation," *Administrative Science Quarterly* 35 (1990), pp. 128–52; and M. I. Kamien and N. L. Schwartz, "Market Structure and Innovation—A Survey," *Journal of Economic Literature* 13 (1975), pp. 1–37.

4. F. Damanpour, "Organizational Size and Innovation," *Organization Studies* 13 (1992) pp. 375–402.

5. R. L. Daft, *Organization Theory and Design* (Minneapolis: West Publishing Company, 1995).

6. W. Cohen and R. Levin, "Empirical Studies of Innovation and Market Structure," in *Handbook of Industrial Organization,* vol. II, eds. R. Schmalensee and R. D. Willig (Amsterdam: Elsevier Science Publishers B.V., 1989).

7. Ibid; and J. Rotemberg and G. Saloner, "Benefits of Narrow Business Strategies," *American Economic Review* 84, no. 5 (1994), pp. 1330–49.

8. G. Gilder, "The Revitalization of Everything: The Law of the Microcosm," *Harvard Business Review* 66, no. 2 (1988), pp. 49–61.

9. M. Kharbanda, "Xerox Corporation: A Case Study in Revitalizing Product Development," in *Time-Based Competition: The Next Battleground in American Manufacturing,* ed. J. D. Blackburn (Homewood, IL: Business One Irwin, 1991), pp. 177–90.

10. A. Cotterel, *The Encyclopedia of Mythology* (London: Smithmark, 1996).

11. J. Bound, C. Cummins, Z. Griliches, B. H. Hall, and A. Jaffe, "Who Does R&D and Who Patents?" in *R&D, Patents, and Productivity,* ed. Z. Griliches (Chicago: University of Chicago, 1984); A. K. Chakrabarti and M. R. Halperin, "Technical Performance and Firm Size: Analysis of Patents and Publications of U.S. Firms," in *Innovation and Technological Change: An International Comparison,* eds. A. J. Acs and D. B. Audretsch (Ann Arbor, MI: University of Michigan Press, 1991); S. B. Graves and N. S. Langowitz, "Innovative Productivity and Returns to Scale in the Pharmaceutical Industry," *Strategic Management Journal* 14 (1993), pp. 593–605; and G. N. Stock, N. P. Greis, and W. A. Fischer, "Firm Size and Dynamic Technological Innovation," *Technovation* 22 (2002), pp. 537–49.

12. Z. Griliches, "Patent Statistics as Economic Indicators: A Survey," *Journal of Economics Literature* 28 (1990), pp. 1661–1707; and F. M. Scherer, "The Propensity to Patent," *International Journal of Industrial Organization* 1 (1983), pp. 107–28.

13. A. Griffin, "Product Development Cycle Time for Business-to-Business Products," *Industrial Marketing Management* 31 (2002), pp. 291–304.

14. W. M. Cohen and S. Klepper, "A Reprise of Firm Size and R&D," *Economic Journal* 106 (1996), pp. 925–51; and R. Henderson and I. Cockburn, "Scale, Scope and Spillovers: The Determinants of Research Productivity in Drug Discovery," *Rand Journal of Economics* 27 (1996), pp. 32–59.

15. R. Ashkenas, D. Ulrich, T. Jick, and S. Kerr, *The Boundaryless Organization: Breaking the Chains of Organizational Structure* (San Francisco: Jossey-Bass Publishers, 1995); J. Hagel and M. Singer, "Unbundling the Corporation," *Harvard Business Review,* March–April 1999, pp. 133–41; M. A. Schilling and K. Steensma, "The Use of Modular Organizational Forms: An Industry Level Analysis," *Academy of Management Journal* 44 (2001), pp. 1149–69; C. Snow, R. Miles, and H. J. Coleman, "Managing 21st Century Network Organizations," *Organizational Dynamics* 20, no. 3 (1992), pp. 5–20; and T. R. Zenger and W. S. Hesterly, "The Disaggregation of Corporations: Selective Intervention, High-Powered Incentives, and Molecular Units," *Organization Science* 8 (1997), pp. 209–23.

16. R. S. Achrol, "Changes in the Theory of Interorganizational Relations in Marketing: Toward a Network Paradigm," *Academy of Marketing Science* 25 (1997), pp. 56–71.

17. H. Chesbrough and D. Teece, "When Is Virtual Virtuous? Organizing for Innovation," *Harvard Business Review,* January–February 1996, pp. 65–73; and D. Churbuck and J. S. Young, "The Virtual Workplace," *Forbes* 150, no. 12 (1992), pp. 184–90.

18. C. Jones, W. Hesterly, and S. Borgatti, "A General Theory of Network Governance: Exchange Conditions and Social Mechanisms," *Academy of Management Review* 22 (1997), pp. 911–45; R. E. Miles and C. C. Snow, "Organizations: New Concepts for New Forms," *California Management Review* 28, no. 3 (1986), pp. 62–73; and R. E. Miles and C. C. Snow, "Causes of Failures in Network Organizations," *California Management Review* 34, no. 4 (1992), pp. 53–72.

19. D. Lei, M. A. Hitt, and J. D. Goldhar, "Advanced Manufacturing Technology: Organizational Design and Strategic Flexibility," *Organization Studies* 17 (1996), pp. 501–24; R. Sanchez, "Strategic Flexibility in Product Competition," *Strategic Management Journal* 16 (1995), pp. 135–60; R. Sanchez and J. Mahoney, "Modularity, Flexibility, and Knowledge Management in Product and Organization Design," *Strategic Management Journal* 17 (1996), pp. 63–76; and Schilling and Steensma, "The Use of Modular Organizational Forms: An Industry Level Analysis."

20. Csaszar, FA. "Organizational Structure as a Determinant of Performance: Evidence from Mutual Funds," *Strategic Management Journal* 33 (2012):611–632; Csaszar, FA, "When Consensus Hurts the Company," *MIT Sloan Management Review*, (2015), Spring: 17–20.

21. L. Cardinal and T. Opler, "Corporate Diversification and Innovative Efficiency: An Empirical Study," *Journal of Accounting & Economics* 19 (1995), pp. 365–82.

22. P. N. Golder, "Insights from Senior Executives about Innovation in International Markets," *Journal of Product Innovation Management* 17 (2000), pp. 326–40.

23. Menon, Chowdhury, and Lukas, "Antecedents and Outcomes of New Product Development Speed."

24. P. S. Adler, "Building Better Bureaucracies," *Academy of Management Executive* 13, no. 4 (1999), pp. 36–50.

25. M. Treacy and F. Wiersema, "Customer Intimacy and Other Value Disciplines," *Harvard Business Review* 71, no. 1 (1993), pp. 84–94.

26. M. P. Miles, J. G. Covin, and M. B. Heeley, "The Relationship between Environmental Dynamism and Small Firm Structure, Strategy, and Performance," *Journal of Marketing Theory and Practice* 8, no. 2 (2000), pp. 63–75.

27. D. Leonard, *Well-Springs of Knowledge: Building and Sustaining the Sources of Innovation* (Boston: Harvard Business School Press, 1996); C. Moorman and A. Miner, "Organizational Improvisation and Organizational Memory," *Academy of Management Review* 23, no. 4 (1998), pp. 698–723; and D. Dougherty, "Reimagining the Differentiation and Integration of Work for Sustained Product Innovation," *Organization Science* 12 (2001), pp. 612–31.

28. Daft, *Organization Theory and Design;* and Menon, Chowdhury, and Lukas, "Antecedents and Outcomes of New Product Development Speed."

29. M. L. Tushman and C. A. O'Reilly, "Ambidextrous Organizations: Managing Evolutionary and Revolutionary Change," *California Management Review* 38, no. 4 (1996), pp. 8–31.

30. M. L. Tushman and C. A. O'Reilly, *Winning through Innovation: A Practical Guide to Leading Organizational Change and Renewal* (Boston: Harvard Business School, 1997); and M. L. Tushman and W. Smith, "Organizational Technology: Technological Change, Ambidextrous Organizations and Organizational Evolution," in *Companion to Organizations,* ed. J. A. Baum (New York: Blackwell Publishers, 2002), pp. 386–414.

31. C. Fang, J. Lee, and M. A. Schilling, "Balancing Exploration and Exploitation through Structural Design: Advantage of the Semi-isolated Subgroup Structure in Organizational Learning," *Organization Science* 21 (2010), pp. 625–42.

32. J. M. Benner and M. Tushman, "Exploitation, Exploitation, and Process Management: The Productivity Dilemma Revisited," *Academy of Management Review* 28 (2003), pp. 238–56; and J. L. Bower and C. M. Christensen, "Disruptive Technologies: Catching the Wave," *Harvard Business Review* 73, no. 1 (1995), pp. 43–53.

33. M. Rogers, "It's the Apple of His Eye," *Newsweek,* March 1, 2003.

34. N. Siggelkow and D. Levinthal, "Temporarily Divide to Conquer: Centralized, Decentralized, and Reintegrated Organizational Approaches to Exploration and Adaptation," *Organization Science* 14 (2003), pp. 650–69.

35. M. Jelinek and C. Schoonhoven, *The Innovation Marathon: Lessons from High Technology Firms* (Oxford, UK: Basil Blackwell, 1990); and C. B. Schoonhoven and M. Jelinek, "Dynamic Tension in Innovative, High Technology Firms: Managing Rapid Technological Change through Organizational Structure," in *Managing Strategic Innovation and Change,* eds. M. L. Tushman and P. Anderson (Oxford: Oxford University Press, 1996).

36. Schoonhoven and Jelinek, "Dynamic Tension in Innovative, High Technology Firms."

37. M. A. Schilling, "Toward a General Modular Systems Theory and Its Application to Interfirm Product Modularity," *Academy of Management Review* 25 (2000), pp. 312–34.

38. C. Y. Baldwin and K. B. Clark, *Design Rules, Volume 1: The Power of Modularity* (Cambridge, MA: MIT Press, 2000); R. Garud and A. Kumaraswamy, "Technological and Organizational Designs for Realizing Economies of Substitution," *Strategic Management Journal* 16 (1995), pp. 93–109; and Sanchez, "Strategic Flexibility in Product Competition."

39. J. Hagel and J. S. Brown, "Learning from Tata's Nano." *BusinessWeek,* February 27, 2008.

40. M. A. Schilling, "Towards a General Modular Systems Theory and its Application to Inter-firm Product Modularity," *Academy of Management Review* 25 (2000), pp. 312–34.

41. Hoetker, G. "Do Modular Products Lead to Modular Organizations?" *Strategic Management Journal* 27 (2006): 501–518; Cabigiosu, A and Camuffo, A. "Beyond the "mirroring" Hypothesis: Product Modularity and Interorganizational Relations in the Air Conditioning Industry," *Organization Science* 23 (2012): 686–703; Colfer, L. and Baldwin, CY. "The Mirroring Hypothesis: Theory, Evidence and Exceptions," Harvard Business School Finance Working Paper No. 10–058 (2010), June 4th.

42. Sanchez and Mahoney, "Modularity, Flexibility, and Knowledge Management in Product and Organization Design."

43. Schilling and Steensma, "The Use of Modular Organizational Forms"; and Sanchez and Mahoney, "Modularity, Flexibility, and Knowledge Management in Product and Organization Design."

44. E. Brynjolfsson, T. W. Malone, V. Gurbaxani, and A. Kambil, "Does Information Technology Lead to Smaller Firms?" *Management Science* 40 (1994), pp. 1628–45; and T. R. Zenger and W. S. Hesterly, "The Disaggregation of Corporations: Selective Intervention, High-Powered Incentives, and Molecular Units," *Organization Science* 8 (1997), pp. 209–23.

45. E. Brynjolfsson, "Information Assets, Technology, and Organization," *Management Science* 40 (1994), pp. 1645–63; and L. M. Hitt, "Information Technology and Firm Boundaries: Evidence from Panel Data," *Information Systems Research* 10, no. 2 (1999), pp. 134–50.

46. N. S. Argyres, "The Impact of Information Technology on Coordination: Evidence from the B-2 'Stealth' Bomber," *Organization Science* 10 (1999), pp. 162–81.

47. Schilling and Steensma, "The Use of Modular Organizational Forms."

48. Chesbrough and Teece, "When Is Virtual Virtuous?" and Schilling and Steensma, "The Use of Modular Organizational Forms."

49. Chesbrough and Teece, "When Is Virtual Virtuous?"

50. C. A. Bartlett and S. Ghoshal, "Managing Innovation in the Transnational Corporation," in *Managing the Global Firm,* eds. C. A. Bartlett, Y. Doz, and G. Hedlund (London and New York: Routledge, 1990).

51. Ibid; and A. M. Rugman, "Research and Development by Multinational and Domestic Firms in Canada," *Canadian Public Policy* 7 (1981), pp. 604–16.

52. Golder, "Insights from Senior Executives about Innovation in International Markets."

53. T. Madsen, E. Mosakowski, and S. Zaheer, "The Dynamics of Knowledge Flows: Human Capital Mobility, Knowledge Retention and Change," *Journal of Knowledge Management* 6, no. 2 (2002), pp. 164–77.

Managing the New Product Development Process

Skullcandy: Developing Extreme Headphones[a]

Founded in 2003 by Rick Alden, Skullcandy grew from a simple idea to a company with products distributed in approximately 80 countries and generating over $200 million in revenues annually. The company's core products, headphones with an extreme sport aesthetic, were sold in both specialty shops (e.g., skateboard, surf, and snowboard shops) and mass market channels such as Target, Best Buy, college bookstores, and more, and its iconic skull logo was recognizable by its core youth market worldwide. Rather than the simplistic and streamlined ear buds that dominated the headphone category throughout the 1990s, many of Skullcandy's designs had large ear cups with integrated amplifiers, akin to those worn by disc jockeys. As Alden notes, one of their first set of headphones, the Skullcrushers, provided sound that "rattles your head and bleeds through your eyes. It's a damage-your-hearing kind of bass."[b] The headphones also came in bold colors and patterns. Skullcandy had reinvented the headphone category from a commodity-like product to one that was highly differentiated and branded, with distinct designs that became as much about fashion and identity as functionality.

The Idea

In 2001, Rick Alden was riding up a ski lift and listening to music on an MP3 player when he heard his phone ringing, muffled in the pocket of his ski jacket. He fumbled around with his gloved hands, trying to get to the phone before it stopped ringing, and at that moment he thought "why not have headphones that connect to both a cell phone and an MP3 player?"[c] In January of 2002, he had his first prototype built by a Chinese manufacturer, and by January of 2003, he had taken out two mortgages on his home to launch his company, Skullcandy.[d]

Building an Action Sports Brand

Alden had an extensive background in the snowboarding industry, having previously founded National Snowboard Incorporated (one of the first companies to promote snowboarding) and having developed and marketed his own line of snowboard bindings. His father, Paul Alden, had played many roles in the industry, including serving as the president of the North American Snowboard Association, which helped open up ski resorts to snowboarders. His brother, David Alden, had been a professional snowboarder for Burton, and a sales representative for several snowboard lines. Thus, when Alden began creating an image and brand for the headphones, it only made sense to create a brand that would have the kind of dynamic edginess that would attract snowboarders and skateboarders. Alden could also use his deep connections in the snowboarding and skateboarding worlds to line up endorsements by pro riders and distribution by skate and snowboard shops. As Alden notes, "I'd walk into snowboarding and skateboarding shops that I'd sold bindings to or that I'd known for 15 years, and say, `Hey, man, I think you ought to sell headphones.'"[e] Soon he was developing headphones that were integrated into Giro ski and snowboard helmets, and MP3-equipped backpacks and watches. The graphic imagery of the brand—which draws from hip-hop culture and features a prominent skull—helped to turned a once placid and commoditized product category into an exciting and important fashion accessory for action sports enthusiasts.

The company grew quickly. By 2005, the company broke $1 million in sales, and in the following year sold almost $10 million worth of headphones and accessories. By 2007, Skullcandy's products were selling in Best Buy, Target, Circuit City, and most college bookstores in addition to the core market of action sport retailers, for total revenues of $35 million, greatly exceeding even the stretch targets the company was shooting for. By the end of 2011, Skullcandy sales had reached $232.5 million—a 44 percent increase from its 2010 sales. In the same year, the company went public in an initial public offering that raised $188.8 million.

The company was careful in its approach to selling to the mass market, carefully distinguishing between products that were sold to the core channel versus to big box retailers.[f] Alden's philosophy was that "Conservative guys buy core products, but core guys will never buy conservative. In other words, we've got to be edgy and keep our original consumer happy, because without him, we'll lose people like me—old guys who want to buy cool young products too."[g]

In 2009, the company began to target the hip-hop music aficionado market by partnering with key music industry veterans such as Calvin "Snoop Dogg" Broadus and Michael "Mix Master Mike" Schwartz of the Beastie Boys. The collaboration with Snoop Dogg resulted in the "Skullcrusher"—a headphone with extreme bass amplification perfect for listening to rap music. The collaboration with Mix Master Mike was intended to produce the "ultimate DJ headphone."

Developing the Ultimate DJ Headphone

To begin designing a set of headphones that would uniquely target disc jockeys/turntablists, Skullcandy assembled a team that included Mix Master Mike (who would lend insight into the key factors that would make the "ideal" DJ headphone, as well as lending his own personal design inspirations), Skullcandy's Director of Industrial Design, Pete Kelly (who would translate the desired features into engineering specifications), an external industrial design company that could quickly transform the team's ideas into photo-realistic renderings, Product Manager Josh Poulsen (who would manage the project milestones and communicate directly to the factory in China where the product would be manufactured), and team members with backgrounds in graphic arts or fine arts who would explore the potential color palettes, materials and form factors to use.

The small size and informal atmosphere at Skullcandy ensured close contact between the team members, and between the team and other Skullcandy personnel. For example, the director of industrial design and the art director shared an office, and all of the graphic designers worked in a common bullpen.[h] The team would schedule face-to-face meetings with Mix Master Mike and the external industrial design company, and Josh Poulsen would travel to China to have similar face-to-face meetings with the manufacturer.

In the first phase, the team met to analyze what functionality would be key to making a compelling product. For the DJ headphones, the team identified the following key factors that would help to significantly improve headphone design:

- Tough, replaceable and/or washable ear pads made of antimicrobial materials (ear pads were prone to getting soiled or torn)
- Headphones that could be worn by "righty" or "lefty" DJs (DJs typically have a preference for leaning on one side while they work, and this side determines the optimal cable location)
- Sound quality that was not too clear, not too bass, and not too muddy (DJs typically were not looking for the clear quality of studio sound)
- Coiled cord or straight cord options (many DJs preferred coiled cords, whereas mass market consumers typically preferred straight cords)

Above all, the team had the mandate given by Alden to create "headphones that don't look like headphones."

The product's aesthetic design would be heavily influenced by Mix Master Mike. As noted by Dan Levine, "When you attach yourself to someone iconic, you try to figure out what inspires their form sensibilities. For example, Mike likes transformers, Japanese robots, Lamborghinis, furniture by B&B Italia . . . we use these design elements to build inspiration boards."[i] The team initially met for three straight days in Mix Master Mike's studio. Then, after the team had created 6–12 initial sketches, they worked to narrow the list down to three of the best and then fine-tuned those until they had one best sketch. The external industrial design firm created photorealistic renderings that precisely portrayed what the end product was to look like. At this point, marketing people could be brought into the team to begin developing a marketing strategy around the product. The marketing team used "sneak peaks" of renderings and nonfunctioning prototypes to gain initial sales contracts.

The next phase was an iterative process of commercialization and design refinement. According to Levine, "That's when it feels like you're swimming in glue because it never happens fast enough. The design phase is exciting. Once you have that design you get impatient for it to come to market, but you can only work as fast as manufacturing capabilities dictate, and building technical products takes time."[j] First, CAD files would be brought to China where a manufacturer would use a stereolithography apparatus (SLA) to create prototypes of each part of the headphone in a wax resin. As described by Alden, "you can't see the lasers—the part just rises up out of this primordial ooze. Then you can sand it down, paint it, and screw it to your other parts. This part will end up costing $300 compared to the 30 cents the part will eventually cost when it's mass-produced using injection molding, but it's worth creating these SLA parts to make sure that they're accurate."[k] SLA versions of the products were also often taken to the trade shows to solicit customer feedback and generate orders. Every week or two, the Product Manager would need to talk to the Chinese factory about building or modifying SLA parts, until eventually a 100 percent complete SLA product was achieved. At that point, it was time to begin "tooling" (the process of building molds that would be used to mass produce the product). This phase took four to six weeks to complete and was expensive. Several samples would be produced while final modifications were made, and then once a perfect sample was obtained, the tools would be hardened and mass production would begin. As Alden described, "after you've got everything in place—after you've made the first one, then it's just like making doughnuts."[l]

All of the steps of the project were scheduled using a Gantt chart (a type of chart commonly used to depict project elements and their deadlines). Project deadlines were determined by working backward from a target market release date and the time required to manufacture the product in China. In general, the firm sought to release new products in September (before the big Christmas sales season), which required having the tooling complete in July.

Every major design decision was passed up to Dan Levine for approval, and when the design was ready for "tooling" (being handed off to manufacturing), it had to be approved by Rick Alden, as this phase entailed large irreversible investments. Most of the people at Skullcandy were involved with many projects simultaneously. As Levine emphasized, "This is a lean organization. At Nike you can work on a single or a few projects; when you have a brand that's small and growing fast, you work on a tremendous number of projects, and you also hire outside talent for some tasks."[m] According to Rick Alden, "We used to try to manage everything in-house, but we just don't have enough bodies. We've discovered that the fastest way to expand our development capacity is to use outside developers for portions of the work. We'll develop the initial idea, and then bring it to one of our trusted industrial design firms to do the renderings, for example."[n]

Team members did not receive financial rewards from individual projects. Instead, their performance was rewarded through recognition at monthly "Skullcouncil" meetings, and through quarterly "one touch" reviews. For the quarterly reviews, each employee would prepare a one-page "brag sheet" about what they had accomplished in the previous quarter, what they intended to accomplish in the next quarter, and what their strengths and weaknesses were. These reviews would be used to provide feedback to the employee and to determine the annual bonus; 75 percent of the annual bonus was based on the individual's performance, and 25 percent was based on overall company performance. According to Rick Alden, "In the early days, we did things very differently than we do now. Everyone received bonuses based on overall performance—there were so few of us that we all had a direct attachment to the bottom line. Now with a bigger staff, we have to rely more on individual metrics, and we have to provide quarterly feedback so that the amount of the annual bonus doesn't come as a surprise."[o] The company also relied on some less conventional incentives. Each year the board of directors would set an overarching stretch target for revenues, and if the company surpassed it, Alden took the whole company on a trip. In 2006, he took everyone heliboarding (an extreme sport where snowboarders are brought to the top of a snow-covered peak by helicopter). When the company achieved nearly triple its 2007 sales goal (earning $35 million instead of the targeted $13 million), Alden took the entire staff and their families to Costa Rica to go surfing.[p]

According to Alden, the biggest challenge associated with new product development has been managing three different development cycles simultaneously. "You have your new stuff that you're coming out with that you haven't shown anyone yet—that's the really exciting stuff that everyone focuses on. Then you have the products you have just shown at the last show but that aren't done yet—maybe the manufacturing process isn't approved or the packaging isn't finished. You're taking orders but you haven't yet finished the development. Finally, you have all of the products you've been selling already but that require little improvements (e.g., altering how something is soldered, improving a cord, and changing the packaging). We have so little bandwidth in product development that the big challenge has been managing all of these cycles. We just showed a product in January of this year [2009] that we still haven't delivered and it's now May. We were just too excited to show it. But that's risky. If you don't deliver on time to a retailer, they get really angry and they won't keep your product on the shelf."[q]

Soon a flurry of new headphone brands had followed in Skullcandy's footsteps—including the wildly successful Beats by Dre. The functionality and style trends in headphones were relatively easy to quickly imitate. The key source of advantage, then, was to create brand loyalty among consumers and distributors. Alden noted that though he had initially patented some of the individual headphone models or technologies, given the time lag between patent application and patent granting, and the expense involved in using patent attorneys, patenting didn't make much sense in his industry—he preferred to just beat his competitors to market with great products.[r]

Discussion Questions

1. How does Skullcandy's new product development activities affect its ability to (*a*) maximize the fit with customer needs, (*b*) minimize development cycle time, and (*c*) control development costs?

2. What are some of the ways that Skullcandy's size and growth rate influence its development process?

3. What are the advantages of using Computer Aided Design (CAD) and stereo-lithography to create prototypes of Skullcandy's headphones?

4. If you were advising the top management of Skullcandy about new product development processes, what recommendations would you make?

[a] Skullcandy 10-K reports; www.hoovers.com

[b] Alden, R. "How I did it." *Inc.* (2008), September: 108–112.

[c] A. Osmond, "Rick Alden: Founder & CEO Skullcandy," Launch, March/April 2007 (http://issuu.com/lumin/docs/launch200703)

[d] Rick Alden interviewed by Melissa Schilling, May 5, 2009.

[e] Rick Alden interviewed by Melissa Schilling, May 5, 2009.

[f] Anonymous. 2008. Caught on tape: Rick Alden, CEO of Skullcandy. *Transworld Business*, October 24th.

[g] Alden, R. "How I did it." *Inc.* (2008), September: 108–112.

[h] Dan Levine, interviewed by Melissa Schilling, May 2, 2009.

[i] Dan Levine, interviewed by Melissa Schilling, May 2, 2009.

[j] Dan Levine, interviewed by Melissa Schilling, May 2, 2009.

[k] Rick Alden, interviewed by Melissa Schilling, May 5, 2009.

[l] Rick Alden, interviewed by Melissa Schilling, May 5, 2009.

[m] Dan Levine, interviewed by Melissa Schilling, May 2, 2009.

[n] Rick Alden, interviewed by Melissa Schilling, May 5, 2009.

[o] Rick Alden, interviewed by Melissa Schilling, February 20, 2012.

[p] Rick Alden, interviewed by Melissa Schilling, May 5, 2009.

[q] Rick Alden, interviewed by Melissa Schilling, May 5, 2009.

[r] Interview with Rick Alden, February 2012.

OVERVIEW

In many industries, the ability to develop new products quickly, effectively, and efficiently is now the single most important factor driving firm success. In industries such as computer hardware and software, telecommunications, automobiles, and consumer electronics, firms often depend on products introduced within the past five years for more than 50 percent of their sales. Yet despite the avid attention paid to new product development, the failure rates for new product development projects are still agonizingly high. By many estimates, more than 95 percent of all new product development projects fail to result in an economic return.[1] Many projects are never completed, and of those that are, many flounder in the marketplace. Thus, a considerable amount of research has been focused on how to make the new product development process more effective and more efficient. This chapter discusses some strategic imperatives for new product development processes that have emerged from the study of best—and worst—practices in new product development.

We will begin by looking at the three key objectives of the new product development process: maximizing fit with customer requirements, minimizing cycle time, and controlling development costs. We then will turn to methods of achieving these objectives, including adopting parallel development processes, using project champions, and involving customers and suppliers in the development process. Next we will look at a number of tools firms can utilize to improve the effectiveness and efficiency of the development process, including creating go/kill decision points with stage-gate processes, defining design targets with quality function deployment, reducing costs and development time with design for manufacturing and CAD/CAM systems, and using metrics to assess the performance of the new product development process.

OBJECTIVES OF THE NEW PRODUCT DEVELOPMENT PROCESS

For new product development to be successful, it must simultaneously achieve three sometimes-conflicting goals: (1) maximizing the product's fit with customer requirements, (2) minimizing the development cycle time, and (3) controlling development costs.

Maximizing Fit with Customer Requirements

For a new product to be successful in the marketplace, it must offer more compelling features, greater quality, or more attractive pricing than competing products. Despite the obvious importance of this imperative, many new product development projects fail to achieve it. This may occur for a number of reasons. First, the firm may not have a clear sense of which features customers value the most, resulting in the firm's overinvesting in some features at the expense of features the customer values more. Firms may also overestimate the customer's willingness to pay for particular features, leading them to produce feature-packed products that are too expensive to gain significant market penetration. Firms may also have difficulty resolving heterogeneity in customer demands; if some customer groups desire different features from other groups, the firm may end up producing a product that makes compromises between these conflicting demands, and the resulting product may fail to be attractive to any of the customer groups.

Numerous new products have offered technologically advanced features compared to existing products but have failed to match customer requirements and were subsequently rejected by the market. For example, consider Apple's Newton MessagePad, a relatively early entrant into the personal digital assistant market. The Newton was exceptional on many dimensions. It had a highly advanced ARM610 RISC chip for superior processing performance. Its operating system was object oriented (a feature that software programmers had been clamoring for), and Apple openly licensed the architecture to encourage rapid and widespread adoption by other vendors. Also, its weight, size, and battery life were better than many of the other early competitors. However, the Newton MessagePad was still much too large to be kept in a pocket, limiting its usefulness as a handheld device. Many corporate users thought the screen was too small to make the product useful for their applications. Finally, early problems with the handwriting recognition software caused many people to believe the product was fatally flawed.

Another example is Philips' attempt to enter the video game industry. In 1989, Philips introduced its Compact Disc Interactive (CD-i). The CD-i was a 32-bit system (introduced well before Sega's 32-bit Saturn or Sony's 32-bit PlayStation), and in addition to being a game player, it offered a number of educational programs and played audio CDs. However, Philips had overestimated how much customers would value (and be willing to pay for) these features. The CD-i was priced at $799, more than double the cost of Nintendo or Sega video game systems. Furthermore, the product was very complex, requiring a half-hour demonstration by a skilled sales representative. Ultimately, the product failed to attract many customers and Philips abandoned the product.

Minimizing Development Cycle Time

Even products that achieve a very close fit with customer requirements can fail if they take too long to bring to market. As discussed in Chapter Five, bringing a product to market early can help a firm build brand loyalty, preemptively capture scarce assets, and build customer switching costs. A firm that brings a new product to market late may find that customers are already committed to other products. Also, a company that is able to bring its product to market early has more time to develop (or encourage others to develop) complementary goods that enhance the value and attractiveness of the product.[2] Other things being equal, products that are introduced to the market earlier are likely to have an installed base and availability of complementary goods advantage over later offerings.

development cycle time

The time elapsed from project initiation to product launch, usually measured in months or years.

Another important consideration regarding **development cycle time** relates to the cost of development and the decreasing length of product life cycles. First, many development costs are directly related to time. Both the expense of paying employees involved in development and the firm's cost of capital increase as the development cycle lengthens. Second, a company that is slow to market with a particular generation of technology is unlikely to be able to fully amortize the fixed costs of development before that generation becomes obsolete. This phenomenon is particularly vivid in dynamic industries such as electronics where life cycles can be as short as 12 months (e.g., personal computers, semiconductors). Companies that are slow to market may find that by the time they have introduced their products, market demand has already shifted to the products of a subsequent technological generation.

Finally, a company with a short development cycle can quickly revise or upgrade its offering as design flaws are revealed or technology advances. A firm with a short development cycle can take advantage of both first-mover *and* second-mover advantages.

Some researchers have pointed out the costs of shortening the development cycle and rushing new products to market. For example, Dhebar points out that rapid product introductions may cause adverse consumer reactions; consumers may regret past purchases and be wary of new purchases for fear they should rapidly become obsolete.[3] Other researchers have suggested that speed of new product development may come at the expense of quality or result in sloppy market introductions.[4] Compressing development cycle time can result in overburdening the development team, leading to problems being overlooked in the product design or manufacturing process. Adequate product testing may also be sacrificed to meet development schedules.[5] However, despite these risks, most studies have found a strong positive relationship between speed and the commercial success of new products.[6]

Controlling Development Costs

Sometimes a firm engages in an intense effort to develop a product that exceeds customer expectations and brings it to market early, only to find that its development costs have ballooned so much that it is impossible to recoup the development expenses even if the product is enthusiastically received by the market. This highlights the fact that development efforts must be not only *effective*, but also *efficient*. Later in the chapter, ways to monitor and control development costs are discussed.

SEQUENTIAL VERSUS PARTLY PARALLEL DEVELOPMENT PROCESSES

Before the mid-1990s, most U.S. companies proceeded from one development stage to another in a sequential fashion (see Figure 11.1a). The process included a number of gates at which managers would decide whether to proceed to the next stage, send the project back to a previous stage for revision, or kill the project. Typically, R&D and marketing provided the bulk of the input in the opportunity identification and concept development stages, R&D took the lead in product design, and manufacturing took the lead in process design. According to critics, one problem with such a system emerges at the product design stage when R&D engineers fail to communicate directly with manufacturing engineers. As a result, product design proceeds without manufacturing requirements in mind. A sequential process has no early warning system to indicate that planned features are not manufacturable. Consequently, cycle time can lengthen as the project iterates back and forth between the product design and process design stages.[7]

FIGURE 11.1
Sequential versus Partly Parallel Development Processes

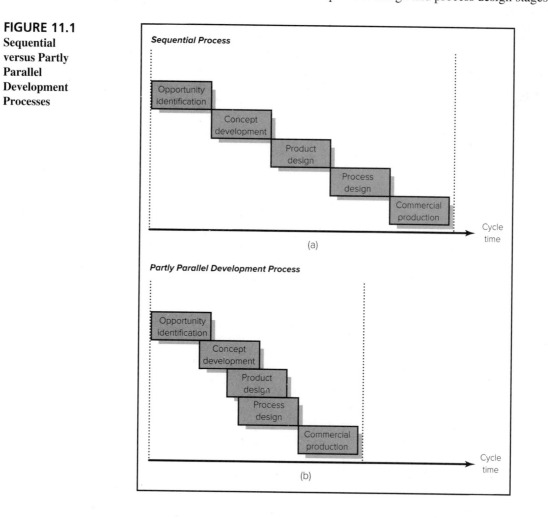

In the 1970s, Glaxo Holdings PLC of Great Britain was one of the larger health care conglomerates in the world, known principally for its baby food, but it needed a new hit product to stimulate sales. While contemplating research possibilities, the head of Glaxo's research laboratory, David Jack, attended a lecture by James Black, a Nobel Prize–winning scientist and researcher for U.S.-based SmithKline Beecham. During the lecture, Black described a new possibility for treating ulcers that involved compounds called H_2 blockers that would inhibit gastrointestinal cells from secreting acid. Jack was intrigued. Ulcers were a common problem, and thus represented a large market opportunity for an effective solution. Jack began experimenting with different compounds in pursuit of a formula that would be safe and effective. Unfortunately, researchers at SmithKline Beecham beat Glaxo to the finish line, introducing Tagamet in 1977. Tagamet revolutionized ulcer treatment, and sales grew phenomenally.[a]

Discouraged but not thwarted, Jack's team kept working. Other companies (including Merck and Eli Lilly) were also developing their own ulcer treatments, and Jack believed that beating them to market might still give the company a shot at a significant share. In that same year, the team came up with a compound based on ranitidine (Tagamet was based on a compound called cimetedine) that achieved the desired objectives. However, Jack realized that if Glaxo was going to beat Merck and Eli Lilly to market, it would need to radically shorten the typical 10-year testing period required to secure regulatory approval and bring the product to market. To achieve this, Jack proposed the first parallel development process used in the pharmaceutical industry. Instead of following the typical sequence of testing (e.g., from rats to monkeys, and from short-term toxicity to long-term toxicity), Jack proposed doing all of the tests concurrently.[b] This intensified development process could potentially cut the cycle time in half—to five years—however, it would also be expensive and risky. If the development efforts increased the research costs substantially, it would be much harder to recoup those expenses through sales of the drug.

Fortunately for Jack's team, Paul Girolami, Glaxo's director of finance, chose to champion the project. Girolami argued that the company should be willing to risk its range of decently profitable products for one potentially sensational drug, stating, "Having all your eggs in one basket concentrates the mind because you had better make sure it is a good basket."[c] Not only was he able to convince the company that it was worth investing in the shortened development process, but he also insisted that the product be modified so that it could be taken once a day (Tagamet required twice-a-day use) and so that the product would have fewer side effects than Tagamet. These features would help differentiate Zantac as a superior product, and it was hoped they would enable Glaxo to take share away from SmithKline Beecham. The development process was successful, and the product was ready for launch in 1982. To recoup its development costs, Girolami chose a premium pricing strategy for the product (one-third higher than Tagamet), arguing that its advantages would warrant its additional cost. He also insisted that the product be launched globally in all major markets, and he set up a distribution alliance with Hoffman-LaRoche to speed up the product's penetration of the U.S. market.

Girolami's strategies were successful, and by the end of the year, Zantac was stealing about 100,000 patients a month from Tagamet. By 1987, Zantac sales had exceeded Tagamet's, and by 1991 Zantac became the world's No. 1 selling prescription drug and the first drug ever to achieve $1 billion in U.S. sales.[d] Both David Jack and Paul Girolami were knighted, and Sir Paul Girolami was appointed chairman of Glaxo.[e]

[a] A. Corsig, T. Soloway, and R. Stanaro, "Glaxo Holdings PLC: Zantac," in *New Product Success Stories,* ed. R. Thomas (New York: John Wiley & Sons, Inc., 1995), pp. 242–52.
[b] Ibid.
[c] C. Kennedy, "Medicine Man to the World," *Director* 46, no. 4 (1992), pp. 106–10.
[d] "Anti-Ulcer Drugs: Too Much Acid," *The Economist* 318, no. 7700 (1991), pp. 82–84.
[e] Corsig, Soloway, and Stanaro, "Glaxo Holdings PLC: Zantac."

partly parallel development process
A development process in which some (or all) of the development activities at least partially overlap. That is, if activity A would precede activity B in a partly parallel development process, activity B might commence before activity A is completed.

To shorten the development process and avoid time-consuming and costly iterations between stages of the development cycle, many firms have adopted a **partly parallel development process**, as shown in Figure 11.1b.[8] Product design is initiated before concept development is complete, and process design is begun long before product design is finalized, enabling much closer coordination between the different stages and minimizing the chance that R&D will design products that are difficult or costly to manufacture. This should eliminate the need for time-consuming iterations between design stages and shorten overall cycle time. One type of parallel development process, **concurrent engineering**, involves not only conducting the typical product development stages simultaneously but also takes into account downstream stages of a product's lifecycle such as maintenance and disposal.

Parallel development processes are not universally endorsed, however. In some situations, using a parallel development process can substantially increase the risks or costs of the development process. If, for example, variations in product design require significant changes to the process design, beginning process design before product design is finalized can result in costly rework of the production process. Such risks are especially high in markets characterized by rapid change and uncertainty.[9] Furthermore, once process design has commenced, managers may be reluctant to alter the product design even if market testing reveals that the product design is suboptimal. It is precisely these risks that the stage-gate* process (discussed later in the chapter) attempts to minimize.

PROJECT CHAMPIONS

concurrent engineering
A design method in which stages of product development (e.g., concept development, product design, and process design) and planning for later stages of the product lifecycle (e.g., maintenance, disposal, and recycling) occur simultaneously.

A number of studies on new product development have suggested that firms should assign (or encourage) a senior member of the company to champion a new product development project.[10] Senior executives have the power and authority to support and fight for a project. They can facilitate the allocation of human and capital resources to the development effort, ensuring that cycle time is not extended by resource constraints, and help ensure that the project can sustain the necessary momentum to surmount the hurdles that inevitably will arise.[11] A senior project champion also can stimulate communication and cooperation between the different functional groups involved in the development process. Given that interfunctional communication and cooperation are necessary both to compress cycle time and to achieve a good fit between product attributes and customer requirements, the use of executive sponsors can improve the effectiveness of the development process. As of 2001, 68 percent of North American firms, 58 percent of European firms, and 48 percent of Japanese firms reported using senior managers to champion new product development projects.[12] An example of a successful use of project championing is described in the accompanying Theory in Action.

Risks of Championing

Vigorous project championing, however, also has its risks. A manager's role as champion may cloud judgment about the true value of the project. Optimism is the norm in product

*Note: Stage-Gate® is a registered trademark of Stage-Gate International Inc.

Research Brief   Five Myths about Product Champions

Stephen Markham and Lynda Aiman-Smith argue that a number of myths have become widely accepted about new product champions. While Markham and Aiman-Smith believe that product champions are critical to new product development, they also argue that for product champions to be effective, their role in the development process must be completely understood. Markham and Aiman-Smith conducted a systematic review of the theoretical and empirical literature on product champions and identified five popular myths:

Myth 1: *Projects with champions are more likely to be successful in the market.* Markham and Aiman-Smith's review of the empirical data on use of project champions found that projects with champions were just as likely to be market failures as market successes. Markham and Aiman-Smith point out that while champions may improve the likelihood of a project being completed, the factors determining its market success are often beyond the champion's control.[a]

Myth 2: *Champions get involved because they are excited about the project, rather than from self-interest.* Markham and Aiman-Smith report that empirical evidence suggests champions are more likely to support projects that will benefit the champion's own department.[b]

Myth 3: *Champions are more likely to be involved with radical innovation projects.* Empirical evidence from multiple large sample studies indicates that champions were equally likely to be involved with radical versus incremental innovation projects.

Myth 4: *Champions are more likely to be from high (or low) levels in the organization.* Markham and Aiman-Smith argue that there are myths about both high-level

and low-level managers being more likely to be product champions. Though stories abound featuring prominent senior managers supporting projects, as do stories featuring low-level champions fighting vigorously for a project's success, empirical evidence suggests that champions may arise from any level in the organization. (Note that this research does not indicate champions from all levels of the firm are equally effective.)

Myth 5: *Champions are more likely to be from marketing.* Markham and Aiman-Smith argue that while anecdotal evidence may more often emphasize champions who have marketing backgrounds, an empirical study of 190 champions found that champions arose from many functions of the firm. Specifically, the study found that 15 percent of champions were from R&D, 14 percent were from marketing, 7 percent were from production and operations, and 6 percent were general managers. Interestingly, 8 percent of champions were potential users of the innovations.[c]

[a] S. Markham, S. Green, and R. Basu, "Champions and Antagonists: Relationships with R&D Project Characteristics and Management," *Journal of Engineering and Technology Management* 8 (1991), pp. 217–42; S. Markham and A. Griffin, "The Breakfast of Champions: Associations between Champions and Product Development Environments, Practices, and Performance," The *Journal of Product Innovation Management* 15 (1998), pp. 436–54; and S. Markham, "Corporate Championing and Antagonism as Forms of Political Behavior: An R&D Perspective," *Organization Science* 11 (2000), pp. 429–47.

[b] Markham, "Corporate Championing and Antagonism as Forms of Political Behavior."

[c] D. Day, "Raising Radicals: Different Processes for Championing Innovative Corporate Ventures," *Organization Science* 5 (1994), pp. 148–72.

development—surveys indicate a systematic upward bias in estimates of future cash flows from a project.[13] In the role of champion, this optimism is often taken to extreme levels. Managers may fall victim to escalating commitment and be unable (or unwilling) to admit that a project should be killed even when it is clear to many others in the organization that the project has gone sour, or the factors driving the project's original value are no longer relevant. While it is common to read stories about projects that succeed against all odds because of the almost fanatical zeal and persistence of their champions, bankruptcy courts are full of companies that should have been less zealous in pursuing some projects. Managers who have invested their reputations and years of their lives in development projects may find it very difficult to cut their losses, in much the same way that individuals tend to hold losing stocks much longer than they should due to the temptation to try to recoup what they have lost. Though the champion's seniority is an asset in gaining access to resources and facilitating coordination, this same seniority may also make others in the firm unwilling to challenge the project champion even if it has become apparent that the project's expected value has turned negative.[14]

Firms may benefit from also developing "antichampions" who can play the role of devil's advocate. Firms should also encourage a corporate culture open to the expression of dissenting opinion, and champions should be encouraged to justify their projects on the basis of objective criteria, without resorting to force of personality.[15] The accompanying Research Brief describes five myths that have become widely accepted about project champions.

INVOLVING CUSTOMERS AND SUPPLIERS IN THE DEVELOPMENT PROCESS

As mentioned previously, many products fail to produce an economic return because they do not fulfill customer requirements for performance and price, or because they take too long to bring to market. Both of these problems can be reduced by involving customers and suppliers in the development process.

Involving Customers

Firms often make decisions about projects on the basis of financial considerations and level of production and technical synergy achieved by the new product proposal rather than on marketing criteria. This can lead to an overemphasis on incremental product updates that closely fit existing business activities.[16] The screening decision should focus instead on the new product's advantage and superiority to the consumer, and the growth of its target market.[17] The customer is often the one most able to identify the maximum performance capabilities and minimum service requirements of a new product. Including the customer in the actual development team or designing initial product versions and encouraging user extensions can help the firm focus its development efforts on projects that better fit customer needs.[18]

Many firms use *beta testing* to get customer input early in the development process. A "beta version" of a product is an early working prototype of a product released to users for testing and feedback. Beta versions also enable a firm to signal the market about its product features before the product reaches the commercial production stage.

Other firms involve customers in the new product development process in even more extensive ways, such as enabling customers to "cocreate" the end product (this is discussed more in the section below on crowdsourcing).

Some studies suggest that firms should focus on the input of lead users in their development efforts rather than a large sample of customers. **Lead users** are those who face the same needs of the general marketplace but face them months or years earlier than the bulk of the market, and expect to benefit significantly from a solution to those needs.[19] According to a survey by the Product Development & Management Association, on average, firms report using the lead user method to obtain input into 38 percent of the projects they undertake. Not surprisingly, when customers help co-create an innovation, the resulting innovations tend to better fit their needs or expectations.[20] More detail on how firms use lead users is provided in the accompanying Theory in Action section.

lead users
Customers who face the same general needs of the marketplace but are likely to experience them months or years earlier than the rest of the market and stand to benefit disproportionately from solutions to those needs.

Involving Suppliers

Much of the same logic behind involving customers in the new product development process also applies to involving suppliers. By tapping into the knowledge base of its suppliers, a firm expands its information resources. Suppliers may be actual members of the product team or consulted as an alliance partner. In either case, they can contribute ideas for product improvement or increased development efficiency. For instance, a supplier may be able to suggest an alternative input (or configuration of inputs) that would achieve the same functionality but at a lower cost. Additionally, by coordinating with suppliers, managers can help to ensure that inputs arrive on time and that necessary changes can be made quickly to minimize development time.[21] Consistent with this argument, research has shown that many firms produce new products in less time, at a lower cost, and with higher quality by incorporating suppliers in integrated product development efforts.[22] For example, consider Chrysler. Beginning in 1989, Chrysler reduced its supplier base from 2,500 to 1,140, offering the remaining suppliers long-term contracts and making them integrally involved in the process of designing new cars. Chrysler also introduced an initiative called SCORE (Supplier Cost Reduction Effort) that encouraged suppliers to make cost-saving suggestions in the development process. The net result was $2.5 billion in savings by 1998.

Boeing's development of the 777 involved both customers and suppliers on the new product development team; United employees (including engineers, pilots, and flight attendants) worked closely with Boeing's engineers to ensure that the airplane was designed for maximum functionality and comfort. Boeing also included General Electric and other parts suppliers on the project team, so that the engines and the body of the airplane could be simultaneously designed for maximum compatibility.

crowdsourcing
A distributed problem-solving model whereby a design problem or production task is presented to a group of people who voluntarily contribute their ideas and effort in exchange for compensation, intrinsic rewards, or a combination thereof.

Crowdsourcing

Firms can also open up an innovation task to the public through crowdsourcing. Many crowdsourcing platforms such as InnoCentive, Yet2.com, and TopCoder present an innovation problem identified by a firm on a public Web platform, and provide rewards to participants who are able to solve them. Some crowdsourcing initiatives target people with special skills (e.g., TopCoder matches companies that need technical expertise such as software design with experienced specialists), while others solicit participation from the general public (e.g., Quirky allows individuals to share their

Hilti AG, a European manufacturer of construction components and equipment, turned to the lead user method in its development of a pipe hanger (a steel support that fastens pipes to walls or ceilings of buildings). The firm first used telephone interviews to identify customers who had lead user characteristics (were ahead of market trends and stood to benefit disproportionately from the new solution). The lead users were invited to participate in a three-day product concept generation workshop to develop a pipe hanging system that would meet their needs. At the end of the workshop, a single pipe hanger design was selected as the one that best met all the lead users' objectives. The company then presented this design to 12 routine users (customers who were not lead users but who had a long, close relationship with Hilti). Ten of the 12 routine users preferred the new design to previously available solutions, and all but one of the 10 indicated they would be willing to pay a 20 percent higher price for the product. Not only was the project successful, but the lead user method was also faster and cheaper than the conventional market research methods the firm had used in the past to develop its product concepts. Hilti's typical process took 16 months and cost $100,000, but the lead user method took 9 months and cost $51,000.

Source: C. Herstatt and E. von Hippel, "Developing New Product Concepts via the Lead User Method: A Case Study in a Low-Tech Field," *Journal of Product Innovation Management* 9 (1992), pp. 213–21.

inventive ideas for others to review; companies or investors can then select the best ideas and help the inventor execute them). Many crowdsourcing programs offer some sort of prize to successful participants. For example, Ben & Jerry's asked its customers to invent their new varieties of ice cream flavors—the submitters of the best flavors were given a trip to the Dominican Republic to see a sustainable fair trade cocoa farm. However, individuals also often individuals participate for the sheer excitement and challenge of solving the problem,[23] or for social or reputational benefits.[24] For example, Fiat Brazil used crowdsourcing to develop a new concept car called the "Fiat Mio" ("My Fiat"). Fiat created a website inviting people to create the car of the future. More than 17,000 people from around the world submitted over 11,000 ideas—and not just in the design. Participants were invited to contribute solutions at every stage of the development process, including solving problems related to fuel efficiency and production. Participants received no rewards from their participation other than the pleasure they derived from interacting with Fiat and with each other, and the satisfaction they felt at having their ideas incorporated into the car. Hundreds of Fiat Mio's co-creators turned up at the unveiling of the car at a Sao Paulo motor show.

TOOLS FOR IMPROVING THE NEW PRODUCT DEVELOPMENT PROCESS

Some of the most prominent tools used to improve the development process include stage-gate processes, quality function deployment ("house of quality"), design for manufacturing, failure modes and effects analysis, and computer-aided design/computer-aided manufacturing. Using the available tools can greatly expedite the new product development process and maximize the product's fit with customer requirements.

Stage-Gate Processes

As discussed in a previous section, escalating commitment can lead managers to support projects long after their expected value has turned negative, and the cost of pushing bad projects forward can be very high. To help avoid this, many managers and researchers suggest implementing tough **go/kill decision points** in the product development process. The most widely known development model incorporating such go/kill points is the stage-gate process developed by Robert G. Cooper.[25] The stage-gate process provides a blueprint for moving projects through different stages of development. Figure 11.2 shows a typical stage-gate process.

At each stage, a cross-functional team of people (led by a project team leader) undertakes parallel activities designed to drive down the risk of a development project. At each stage of the process, the team is required to gather vital technical, market,

FIGURE 11.2
Typical Stage-Gate Process, from Idea to Launch

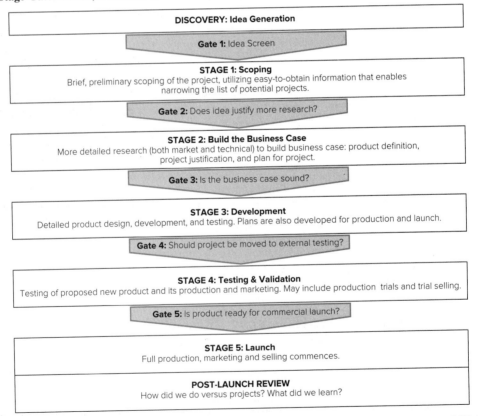

Source: R.G. Cooper, "Stage-Gate Idea to Launch System," *Wiley International Encyclopedia of Marketing: Product Innovation & Management* 5, B.L. Bayus (ed.), (West Sussex UK: Wiley, 2011).

and financial information to use in the decision to move the project forward (go), abandon the project (kill), hold, or recycle the project.

In Stage 1, the team does a quick investigation and conceptualization of the project. In Stage 2, the team builds a business case that includes a defined product, its business justification, and a detailed plan of action for the next stages. In Stage 3, the team begins the actual design and development of the product, including mapping out the manufacturing process, the market launch, and operating plans. In this stage, the team also defines the test plans utilized in the next stage. In Stage 4, the team conducts the verification and validation process for the proposed new product, and its marketing and production. At Stage 5, the product is ready for launch, and full commercial production and selling commence.[26]

Preceding each stage is a go/kill gate. These gates are designed to control the quality of the project and to ensure that the project is being executed in an effective and efficient manner. Gates act as the funnels that cull mediocre projects. Each gate has three components: *deliverables* (these are the results of the previous stage and are the inputs for the gate review), *criteria* (these are the questions or metrics used to make the go/kill decision), and *outputs* (these are the results of the gate review process and may include a decision such as go, kill, hold, or recycle; outputs should also include an action plan for the dates and deliverables of the next gate).

Because each stage of a development project typically costs more than the stage preceding it, breaking down the process into stages deconstructs the development investment into a series of incremental commitments. Expenditures increase only as uncertainty decreases. Figure 11.3 shows the escalation costs and cycle time for each stage of a typical development process in a manufacturing industry.

Many companies have adapted the stage-gate process to more specifically meet the needs of their firm or industry. For example, while managers at Exxon were strong advocates of using a stage-gate process to track and manage development projects, they also felt that the standard five-stage system did not adequately address the needs

FIGURE 11.3
Escalation of Development Time and Costs by Stage

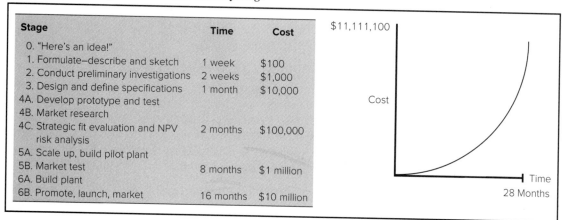

Stage	Time	Cost
0. "Here's an idea!"		
1. Formulate–describe and sketch	1 week	$100
2. Conduct preliminary investigations	2 weeks	$1,000
3. Design and define specifications	1 month	$10,000
4A. Develop prototype and test		
4B. Market research		
4C. Strategic fit evaluation and NPV risk analysis	2 months	$100,000
5A. Scale up, build pilot plant		
5B. Market test	8 months	$1 million
6A. Build plant		
6B. Promote, launch, market	16 months	$10 million

$11,111,100

Cost

Time
28 Months

Source: From Frederick D. Buggie, "Set the 'Fuzzy Front End' in Concrete," *Research Technology Management,* vol. 45, no. 4, July–August 2002. Reprinted with permission of Industrial Research Institute.

FIGURE 11.4
Exxon Research and Engineering's Stage-Gate System

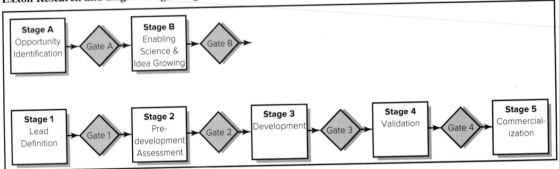

of a company in which basic research was a primary component in generating innovations. Exxon managers created their own extended stage-gate system to include directed basic research. The resulting stage-gate system included two basic research stages (Stages A and B in Figure 11.4) and five applied research and development stages. In Stage A, the company identifies the potential business incentives and competitive advantages of an envisioned technology. The company then develops a basic research plan that establishes specific scientific deliverables, the methods of achieving these deliverables, and the required resources. In Stage B, Exxon's research division begins to execute the plan developed in Stage A, using scientific methods to generate leads for addressing the business opportunity. Stage 1 then identifies the best leads, using "proof-of-principle" assessments to establish whether the leads are feasible.[27] Stages 2 through 5 proceed according to a typical stage-gate process.

According to studies by the Product Development and Management Association, nearly 60 percent of firms (including IBM, Procter & Gamble, 3M, General Motors, and Corning) use some type of stage-gate process to manage their new product development process. Corning has made the process mandatory for all information system development projects, and Corning managers believe that the process enables them to better estimate the potential payback of any project under consideration. They also report that the stage-gate process has reduced development time, allows them to identify projects that should be killed, and increases the ratio of internally developed products that result in commercial projects.[28]

Quality Function Deployment (QFD)—The House of Quality

QFD was developed in Japan as a comprehensive process for improving the communication and coordination among engineering, marketing, and manufacturing personnel.[29] It achieves this by taking managers through a problem-solving process in a very structured fashion. The organizing framework for QFD is the "house of quality" (see Figure 11.5). The house of quality is a matrix that maps customer requirements against product attributes. This matrix is completed in a series of steps.

1. The team must first identify customer requirements. In Figure 11.5, market research has identified five attributes that customers value most in a car door: it is easy to open and close, it stays open on a hill, it does not leak in the rain, it isolates the occupant from road noise, and it protects the passengers in the event of crashes.

FIGURE 11.5

Quality Function Deployment House of Quality for a Car Door

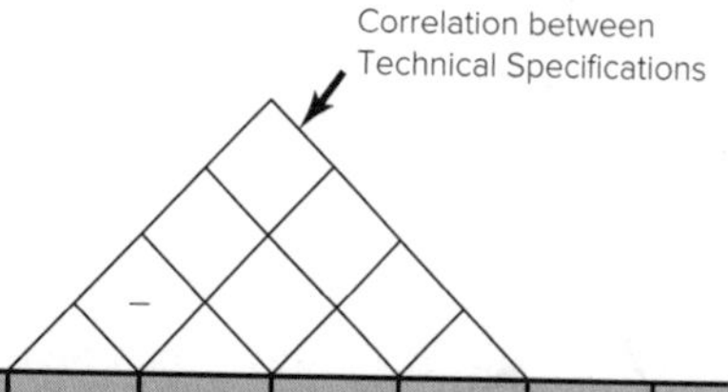

The House of Quality matrix:

Customer Requirements	Engineering Attributes	Importance	Weight of Door	Stiffness of Hinge	Tightness of Door and Seal	Tightness of Window Seal	Competitor A	Competitor B	Evaluation of New Design
Customer Requirements	Easy to Open	15	9	3			7	4	
	Stays Open on Hill	10	3	9			6	7	
	Does Not Leak	35			9	9	7	6	
	Isolates Occupant from Road Noise	20	1		9	9	4	7	
	Crash Protection	20	9				4	7	
Relative Importance of Each Engineering Attribute			365	135	495	495			
Design Targets									

2. The team weights the customer requirements in terms of their relative importance from a customer's perspective. This information might be obtained from focus group sessions or direct interaction with the customers. The weights are typically entered as percentages, so that the complete list totals 100 percent.

3. The team identifies the engineering attributes that drive the performance of the product—in this case the car door. In Figure 11.5, four attributes are highlighted: the weight of the door, the stiffness of the door hinge (a stiff hinge helps the door stay open on a hill), the tightness of the door seal, and the tightness of the window seal.

4. The team enters the correlations between the different engineering attributes to assess the degree to which one characteristic may positively or negatively affect another. The correlations are entered into the matrix that creates the peaked roof of the house. In this case, the negative sign between door weight and hinge stiffness indicates that a heavy door reduces the stiffness of the hinge.

5. The team fills in the body of the central matrix. Each cell in the matrix indicates the relationship between an engineering attribute and a customer requirement. A number (in this example, one, three, or nine) is placed in the cell located at the intersection of each row (customer requirements) with each column (engineering attributes), which represents the strength of relationship between them. A value of one indicates a weak relationship, a three indicates a moderate relationship and

a nine indicates a strong relationship. The cell is left blank if there is no relationship. The ease of opening the door, for example, is strongly related to the weight of the door and moderately related to the stiffness of the door hinge, but is not related to the tightness of the door seal or window seal.

6. The team multiplies the customer importance rating of a feature by its relationship to an engineering attribute (one, three, or nine). These numbers are then summed for each column, yielding a total for the relative importance of each engineering attribute. For example, the stiffness of the hinge influences how easy the door is to open, and whether the door stays open on a hill. Thus to calculate the relative importance of the stiffness of the hinge, the team multiplies the customer importance rating of how easy the door is to open by its relationship to the stiffness of the hinge ($15 \times 3 = 45$), then multiplies the customer importance rating of the door staying open on a hill by its relationship to the stiffness of the hinge ($10 \times 9 = 90$), and then adds these together for the total relative importance of the hinge stiffness ($45 + 90 = 135$). These scores indicate that the tightness of the door and window seals is the most important engineering attribute, followed by the weight of the door.

7. The team evaluates the competition. A scale of one to seven is used (one indicating a requirement is not addressed, and seven indicating a requirement is completely satisfied) to evaluate the competing products (in this case A and B) on each of the customer requirements. These scores go in the right-hand "room" of the house of quality.

8. Using the relative importance ratings established for each engineering attribute and the scores for competing products (from step 7), the team determines target values for each of the design requirements (for example, the door's optimal weight in pounds).

9. A product design is then created based on the design targets from step 8. The team then evaluates the new design that was created. The team assesses the degree to which each of the customer requirements has been met, entering a one to seven in the far right column of the house of quality, permitting it to compare the new design with the scores of the competing products.

The great strength of the house of quality is that it provides a common language and framework within which the members of a project team may interact. The house of quality makes the relationship between product attributes and customer requirements very clear, it focuses on design trade-offs, it highlights the competitive shortcomings of the company's existing products, and it helps identify what steps need to be taken to improve them. The house of quality is used in settings as diverse as manufacturing, construction, police service, and educational curriculum design.[30] Advocates of QFD maintain that one of its most valuable characteristics is its positive effect upon cross-functional communication and, through that, upon cycle time and the product/customer fit.[31]

Design for Manufacturing

Another method of facilitating integration between engineering and manufacturing, and of bringing issues of manufacturability into the design process as early as possible, is the use of design for manufacturing methods (DFM). Like QFD, DFM is simply a

FIGURE 11.6
Design Rules for Fabricated Assembly Products

Source: Adapted from M. A. Schilling and C. W. L. Hill, 1998, "Managing the New Product Development Process," *Academy of Management Executive,* vol. 12, no. 3, pp. 67–81.

Design Rule	Impact on Performance
Minimize the number of parts	Simplifies assembly; reduces direct labor; reduces material handling and inventory costs; boosts product quality
Minimize the number of part numbers (use common parts across product family)	Reduces material handling and inventory costs; improves economies of scale (increases volume through commonalty)
Eliminate adjustments	Reduces assembly errors (increases quality); allows for automation; increases capacity and throughput
Eliminate fasteners	Simplifies assembly (increases quality); reduces direct labor costs; reduces squeaks and rattles; improves durability; allows for automation
Eliminate jigs and fixtures	Reduces line changeover costs; lowers required investment

way of structuring the new product development process. Often this involves articulating a series of design rules. Figure 11.6 summarizes a set of commonly used design rules, along with their expected impact on performance.

As shown in Figure 11.6, the purpose of such design rules is typically to reduce costs and boost product quality by ensuring that product designs are easy to manufacture. The easier products are to manufacture, the fewer the assembly steps required, the higher labor productivity will be, resulting in lower unit costs. DEKA Research makes a point of bringing manufacturing into the design process early, because as founder Dean Kamen points out, "It doesn't make sense to invent things that ultimately are made of unobtanium or expensium."[32] In addition, designing products to be easy to manufacture decreases the likelihood of making mistakes in the assembly process, resulting in higher product quality.

The benefits of adopting DFM rules can be dramatic. Considering manufacturing at an early stage of the design process can shorten development cycle time. In addition, by lowering costs and increasing product quality, DFM can increase the product's fit with customer requirements. For example, when NCR used DFM techniques to redesign one of its electronic cash registers, it reduced assembly time by 75 percent, reduced the parts required by 85 percent, utilized 65 percent fewer suppliers, and reduced direct labor time by 75 percent.[33]

Failure Modes and Effects Analysis

Failure modes and effects analysis (FMEA) is a method by which firms identify potential failures in a system, classify them according to their severity, and put a plan into place to prevent the failures from happening.[34] First, potential failure modes are identified. For example, a firm developing a commercial aircraft might consider failure modes such as "landing gear does not descend," or "communication system experiences interference"; a firm developing a new line of luxury hotels might consider failure modes such as "a reservation cannot be found" or "guest experiences poor service by room service staff." Potential failure modes are then evaluated on three criteria of the risk they pose: severity, likelihood of occurrence, and inability of controls to detect it. Each criterion is given a score (e.g., one for lowest risk, five for highest risk), and then a composite risk priority number is created for each failure mode by multiplying its scores together (i.e., risk priority number = severity × likelihood of occurrence × inability of controls to detect). The firm can then prioritize its development efforts to target potential failure modes that pose the most composite risk. This means that rather than focus first on the failure modes that have the highest scores for severity of risk, the firm might find that it should focus first on failure modes that have less severe impacts, but occur more often and are less detectable.

FMEA was originally introduced in the 1940s by the U.S. Armed Forces and was initially adopted primarily for development projects in which the risks posed by failure were potentially very severe. For example, FMEA was widely used in the Apollo Space Program in its mission to put a man on the moon, and was adopted by Ford after its extremely costly experience with its Pinto model (the location of the gas tank in the Pinto made it exceptionally vulnerable to collisions, leading to fire-related deaths; Ford was forced to recall the Pintos to modify the fuel tanks, and was forced to pay out record-breaking sums in lawsuits that resulted from accidents).[35] Soon, however, FMEA was adopted by firms in a wide range of industries, including many types of manufacturing industries, service industries, and health care. A recent PDMA study found that firms report using FMEA in 40 percent of the projects they undertake.[36]

Computer-Aided Design Computer-Aided Engineering/Computer-Aided Manufacturing

Computer-aided design (CAD) and computer-aided engineering (CAE) is the use of computers to build and test product designs. Rapid advances in computer technology have enabled the development of low-priced and high-powered graphics-based workstations. With these workstations, it is now possible to achieve what could previously be done only on a supercomputer: construct a three-dimensional "working" image of a product or subassembly. CAD enables the creation of a three-dimensional model; CAE makes it possible to virtually test the characteristics (e.g., strength, fatigue, and reliability) of this model. The combination enables product prototypes to be developed and tested in virtual reality. Engineers can quickly adjust prototype attributes by manipulating the three-dimensional model, allowing them to compare the characteristics of different product designs. Eliminating the need to build physical prototypes can reduce cycle time and lower costs as illustrated in the accompanying Theory in Action. Visualization tools and 3-D software are even being used to allow nonengineering customers to see and make minor alterations to the design and materials.

three-dimensional printing
A method whereby a design developed in a computer aided design program is printed in three dimensions by laying down thin strips of material until the model is complete.

Computer-aided manufacturing (CAM) is the implementation of machine-controlled processes in manufacturing. CAM is faster and more flexible than traditional manufacturing.[37] Computers can automate the change between different product variations and allow for more variety and customization in the manufacturing process.

A recent incarnation of computer-aided manufacturing is **three-dimensional printing** (also known as additive manufacturing), whereby a design developed in a computer aided design program is literally printed by laying down thin horizontal cross sections of material until the model is complete. Unlike traditional methods of constructing a model, which typically involve machining a mold that can take several

Team New Zealand discovered the advantages of using sophisticated computer-aided-design techniques in designing the team's 1995 America's Cup yacht. The team had traditionally relied on developing smaller-scale prototypes of the yacht and testing the models in a water tank. However, such prototypes took months to fabricate and test and cost about $50,000 per prototype. This greatly limited the number of design options the team could consider. However, by using computer-aided-design technologies, the team could consider many more design specifications more quickly and inexpensively. Once the basic design is programmed, variations on that design can be run in a matter of hours, at little cost, enabling more insight into design trade-offs. Computer-aided design also avoided some of the problems inherent in scaling up prototypes (some features of the scaled-down proto-type boats would affect the flow of water differently from full-scale boats, resulting in inaccurate results in prototype testing). The team would still build proto-types, but only after considering a much wider range of design alternatives using computer-aided-design methods. As noted by design team member Dave Egan, "Instead of relying on a few big leaps, we had the ability to continually design, test, and refine our ideas. The team would often hold informal discussions on design issues, sketch some schematics on the back of a beer mat, and ask me to run the numbers. Using traditional design methods would have meant waiting months for results, and by that time, our thinking would have evolved so much that the rea-son for the experiment would long since have been forgotten."

Source: M. Iansiti and A. MacCormack, "Team New Zealand," Harvard Business School case no. 9-697-040, 1997.

days to complete, three-dimensional printing can generate a model in a few hours. By 2015, three-dimensional printing was being used to create products as diverse as food, clothing, jewelry, solid-state batteries, and even titanium landing gear brackets for supersonic jets.[38] Biotechnology firms were even using three-dimensional print-ing for use in creating organs by depositing layers of living cells onto a gel medium.[39] This method has recently begun rapidly replacing injection molding for products that are produced in relatively small quantities.

TOOLS FOR MEASURING NEW PRODUCT DEVELOPMENT PERFORMANCE

Many companies use a variety of metrics to measure the performance of their new product development process. In addition to providing feedback about a particular new product, such performance assessments help the company improve its innova-tion strategy and development processes. For example, evaluating the performance of its new product development process may provide insight into which core com-petencies the firm should focus on, how projects should be selected, whether or not it should seek collaboration partners, how it should manage its development teams, and so on.

At Microsoft, almost all projects receive either a post-mortem discussion or a written postmortem report to ensure that the company learns from each of its development experiences. These postmortems tend to be extremely candid and can be quite critical. As noted by one Microsoft manager, "The purpose of the document is to beat yourself up." Another Microsoft manager notes that part of the Microsoft culture is to be very self-critical and never be satisfied at getting things "halfway right." A team will spend three to six months putting together a postmortem document that may number anywhere from less than 10 pages to more than 100. These postmortem reports describe the development activities and team, provide data on the product size (e.g., lines of code) and quality (e.g., number of bugs), and evaluate what worked well, what did not work well, and what the group should do to improve on the next project. These reports are then distributed to the team members and to senior executives throughout the organization.

Source: M. A. Cusumano and R. W. Selby, *Microsoft Secrets* (New York: Free Press, 1995).

Both the metrics used by firms and the timing of their use vary substantially across firms. In a survey by Goldense and Gilmore, 45 percent of companies reported using periodic reviews at calendar periods (e.g., monthly or weekly) and at predetermined milestones (e.g., after product definition, after process design, post launch, etc.).[40] Microsoft, for example, uses postmortems to measure new product development performance, as described in the accompanying Theory in Action. Measures of the success of the new product development process can help management to:

- Identify which projects met their goals and why.
- Benchmark the organization's performance compared to that of competitors or to the organization's own prior performance.
- Improve resource allocation and employee compensation.
- Refine future innovation strategies.[41]

Multiple measures are important because any measure used singly may not give a fair representation of the effectiveness of the firm's development process or its overall innovation performance. Also, the firm's development strategy, industry, and other environmental circumstances must be considered when formulating measures and interpreting results. For example, a firm whose capabilities or objectives favor development of breakthrough projects may experience long intervals between product introductions and receive a low score on measures such as cycle time or percent of sales earned on projects launched within the past five years, despite its success at its strategy. Conversely, a firm that rapidly produces new generations of products may receive a high score on such measures even if it finds its resources are overtaxed and its projects are overbudget. Additionally, the success rate of new product development can vary significantly by industry and project type. Some authors argue that even firms with excellent new product development processes should not expect to have a greater than 65 percent success rate for all new products launched.[42]

New Product Development Process Metrics

Many firms use a number of methods to gauge the effectiveness and efficiency of the development process. These measures capture different dimensions of the firm's ability to successfully shepherd projects through the development process. To use such methods it is important to first define a finite period in which the measure is to be applied in order to get an accurate view of the company's current performance; this also makes it easier for the manager to calculate a response. The following questions can then be asked:

1. What was the average cycle time (time to market) for development projects? How did this cycle time vary for projects characterized as breakthrough, platform, or derivative?
2. What percentage of development projects undertaken within the past five years met all or most of the deadlines set for the project?
3. What percentage of development projects undertaken within the past five years stayed within budget?
4. What percentage of development projects undertaken within the past five years resulted in a completed product?

Overall Innovation Performance

Firms also use a variety of methods to assess their overall performance at innovation. These measures give an overall view of the bang for the buck the organization is achieving with its new product development processes. Such measures include:

1. What is the firm's return on innovation? (This measure assesses the ratio of the firm's total profits from new products to its total expenditures, including research and development costs, the costs of retooling and staffing production facilities, and initial commercialization and marketing costs.)
2. What percentage of projects achieve their sales goals?
3. What percentage of revenues are generated by products developed within the past five years?
4. What is the firm's ratio of successful projects to its total project portfolio?

Summary of Chapter

1. Successful new product development requires achieving three simultaneous objectives: maximizing fit with customer requirements, minimizing time to market, and controlling development costs.
2. Many firms have adopted parallel development processes to shorten the development cycle time and to increase coordination among functions such as R&D, marketing, and manufacturing.
3. Many firms have also begun using project champions to help ensure a project's momentum and improve its access to key resources. Use of champions also has its risks, however, including escalating commitment and unwillingness of others in the organization to challenge the project.
4. Involving customers in the development process can help a firm ensure that its new products match customer expectations. In particular, research indicates that involving lead users can help the firm understand what needs are most important

to customers, helping the firm to identify its development priorities. Involving lead users in the development process can also be faster and cheaper than involving a random sample of customers in the development process.

5. Many firms use beta testing to get customer feedback, exploit external development of the product, and signal the market about the firm's upcoming products.

6. Firms can also involve suppliers in the development process, helping to minimize the input cost of a new product design and improving the likelihood that inputs are of appropriate quality and arrive on time.

7. Stage-gate processes offer a blueprint for guiding firms through the new product development process, providing a series of go/kill gates where the firm must decide if the project should be continued and how its activities should be prioritized.

8. Quality function deployment can be used to improve the development team's understanding of the relationship between customer requirements and engineering attributes. It can also be a tool for improving communication between the various functions involved in the development process.

9. Failure Modes and Effects Analysis can be used to help firms prioritize their development efforts in order to reduce the likelihood of failures that will have the greatest impact on the quality, reliability, and safety of a product or process.

10. Design for manufacturing and CAD/CAM are additional tools development teams can use to reduce cycle time, improve product quality, and control development costs.

11. Firms should use a variety of measures of their new product development effectiveness and overall innovation performance to identify opportunities for improving the new product development process and improving the allocation of resources.

Discussion Questions

1. What are some of the advantages and disadvantages of a parallel development process? What obstacles might a firm face in attempting to adopt a parallel process?

2. Consider a group project you have worked on at work or school. Did your group use mostly sequential or parallel processes?

3. Name some industries in which a parallel process would not be possible or effective.

4. What kinds of people make good project champions? How can a firm ensure that it gets the benefits of championing while minimizing the risks?

5. Is the stage-gate process consistent with suggestions that firms adopt parallel processes? What impact do you think using stage-gate processes would have on development cycle time and development costs?

6. What are the benefits and costs of involving customers and suppliers in the development process?

Suggested Further Reading

Classics

Clark, K. B., and S. C. Wheelwright, *Managing New Product and Process Development* (New York: Free Press, 1993).

Cooper, R., and E. J. Kleinschmidt, "New Product Processes at Leading Industrial Firms," *Industrial-Marketing-Management* 20, no. 2 (1991), pp. 137–48.

Griffin, A., and J. R. Hauser, "Patterns of Communication among Marketing, Engineering and Manufacturing," *Management Science* 38 (1992), pp. 360–73; and Kahn, K. B. *The PDMA Handbook of New Product Development* (2005), Hoboken, NJ: John Wiley & Sons.

Recent Work

Carnevalli, J. A., and P. C. Miguel, "Review, Analysis and Classification of the Literature on QFD—Types of Research, Difficulties and Benefits," *International Journal of Production Economics* 114 (2008), pp. 737–54.

Gattiker, T. F., and C. R. Carter, "Understanding Project Champions' Ability to Gain Intra-organizational Commitment for Environmental Projects," *Journal of Operations Management* 28 (2010), pp. 72–85.

Lawson, B., D. Krause, and A. Potter, "Improving Supplier New Product Development Performance: The Role of Supplier Development." *Journal of Product Innovation Management* 32 (2015), pp. 777–92.

Chesbrough, H. W., and A. R. Garman, "How Open Innovation Can Help You in Lean Times." *Harvard Business Review* 87 (2009), issue 12, pp. 68–76.

Loch, C., and S. Kavadias, *Handbook of New Product Development Management.* (Oxford, UK: Elsevier Ltd., 2008).

Endnotes

1. E. Berggren and T. Nacher, "Introducing New Products Can Be Hazardous to Your Company: Use the Right New-Solutions Delivery Tools," *Academy of Management Executive* 15, no. 3 (2001), pp. 92–101.

2. M. A. Schilling, "Technological Lockout: An Integrative Model of the Economic and Strategic Factors Driving Success and Failure," *Academy of Management Review* 23 (1998), pp. 267–84; and W. B. Arthur, *Increasing Returns and Path Dependence in the Economy* (Ann Arbor: University of Michigan Press, 1994).

3. A. Dhebar, "Speeding High-Tech Producer, Meet Balking Consumer," *Sloan Management Review,* Winter 1996, pp. 37–49.

4. M. C. Crawford, "The Hidden Costs of Accelerated Product Development," *Journal of Product Innovation Management* 9, no. 3 (1992), pp. 188–200.

5. G. Pacheco-de-Almeida and P. Zemsky, "The Creation and Sustainability of Competitive Advantage: Resource Accumulation with Time Compression Diseconomies," mimeo, Stern School of Business, 2003.

6. E. J. Nijssen, A. R. Arbouw, and H. R. Commandeur, "Accelerating New Product Development: A Preliminary Empirical Test of a Hierarchy of Implementation," *Journal of Product Innovation Management* 12 (1995), pp. 99–104; R. W. Schmenner, "The Merits of Making Things Fast," *Sloan Management Review,* Fall 1988, pp. 11–17; A. Ali, R. Krapfel, and D. LaBahn, "Product Innovativeness and Entry Strategy: Impact on Cycle Time and Break-Even Time," *Journal of Product Innovation Management* 12 (1995), pp. 54–69; and R. Rothwell, "Successful Industrial Innovation: Critical Factors for the 1990s," *R&D Management* 22, no. 3 (1992), pp. 221–39.

7. A. Griffin, "Evaluating QFD's Use in US Firms as a Process for Developing Products," *Journal of Product Innovation Management* 9 (1992), pp. 171–87; and C. H. Kimzey, *Summary of the Task Force Workshop on Industrial-Based Initiatives* (Washington, DC: Office of the Assistant Secretary of Defense, Production and Logistics, 1987).

8. A. De Meyer and B. Van Hooland, "The Contribution of Manufacturing to Shortening Design Cycle Times," *R&D Management* 20, no. 3 (1990), pp. 229–39; R. Hayes, S. G. Wheelwright, and K. B. Clark, *Dynamic Manufacturing* (New York: Free Press, 1988); R. G. Cooper, "The New Product Process: A Decision Guide for Managers," *Journal of Marketing Management* 3 (1988), pp. 238–55; and H. Takeuchi and I. Nonaka, "The New Product Development Game," *Harvard Business Review,* January–February 1986, pp. 137–46.

9. K. Eisenhardt and B. N. Tabrizi, "Accelerating Adaptive Processes: Product Innovation in the Global Computer Industry," *Administrative Science Quarterly* 40 (1995), pp. 84–110; and C. Terwiesch and C. H. Loch, "Measuring the Effectiveness of Overlapping Development Activities," *Management Science* 45 (1999), pp. 455–65.

10. B. J. Zirger and M. A. Maidique, "A Model of New Product Development: An Empirical Test," *Management Science* 36 (1990), pp. 867–83; R. Rothwell, C. Freeman, A. Horley, P. Jervis, A. B. Robertson, and J. Townsend, "SAPPHO Updates—Project SAPPHO, PHASE II," *Research Policy* 3 (1974), pp. 258–91; A. H. Rubenstein, A. K. Chakrabarti, R. D. O'Keffe, W. E. Souder, and H. C. Young, "Factors Influencing Innovation Success at the Project Level," *Research Management,* May 1976, pp. 15–20; F. A. Johne and P. A. Snelson, "Product Development Approaches in Established Firms," *Industrial Marketing Management* 18 (1989), pp. 113–24; and Y. Wind and V. Mahajan, "New Product Development Process: A Perspective for Reexamination," *Journal of Product Innovation Management* 5 (1988), pp. 304–10.

11. T. F. Gattiker and C. R. Carter, "Understanding project champions' ability to gain intraorganizational commitment for environmental projects," *Journal of Operations Management* 28 (2010), pp. 72–85.

12. E. Roberts, "Benchmarking Global Strategic Management of Technology," *Research Technology Management,* March–April 2001, pp. 25–36.

13. E. Rudden, "The Misuse of a Sound Investment Tool," *Wall Street Journal,* November 1, 1982.

14. M. Devaney, "Risk, Commitment, and Project Abandonment," *Journal of Business Ethics* 10, no. 2 (1991), pp. 157–60.

15. Devaney, "Risk, Commitment, and Project Abandonment."

16. F. A. Johne and P. A. Snelson, "Success Factors in Product Innovation," *Journal of Product Innovation Management* 5 (1988), pp. 114–28; and F. W. Gluck and R. N. Foster, "Managing Technological Change: A Box of Cigars for Brad," *Harvard Business Review* 53 (1975), pp. 139–50.

17. R. G. Cooper, "Selecting Winning New Product Projects: Using the NewProd System," *Journal of Product Innovation Management* 2 (1985), pp. 34–44.

18. J. E. Butler, "Theories of Technological Innovation as Useful Tools for Corporate Strategy," *Strategic Management Journal* 9 (1988), pp. 15–29.

19. C. Herstatt and E. von Hippel, "Developing New Product Concepts via the Lead User Method: A Case Study in a Low-Tech Field," *Journal of Product Innovation Management* 9 (1992), pp. 213–21.

20. D. Mahr, A. Lievens, and V. Blazevic. "The value of customer cocreated knowledge during the innovation process." *Journal of Product Innovation Management* 31 (2014), 599–615.

21. Asmus and Griffin found that firms that integrate their suppliers with engineering, manufacturing, and purchasing gain cost reductions, shortened lead times, lowered development risks, and tightened development cycles. D. Asmus and J. Griffin, "Harnessing the Power of Your Suppliers," *McKinsey Quarterly,* no. 3 (1993), pp. 63–79. Additionally, Bonaccorsi and Lipparini found that strategic alliances with suppliers lead to shorter product development cycles and better products, particularly in rapidly changing markets. A. Bonaccorsi and A. Lipparini, "Strategic Partnership in New Product Development: An Italian Case Study," *Journal of Product Innovation Management* 11, no. 2 (1994), pp. 134–46.

22. L. Birou and S. Fawcett, "Supplier Involvement in New Product Development: A Comparison of US and European Practices," *Journal of Physical Distribution and Logistics Management* 24, no. 5 (1994), pp. 4–15; and A. Ansari and B. Modarress, "Quality Function Deployment: The Role of Suppliers," *International Journal of Purchasing and Materials Management* 30, no. 4 (1994), pp. 28–36.

23. N. Franke and M. Schreier. "Why customers value self-designed products: The importance of process effort and enjoyment." *Journal of Product Innovation Management* 27 (2010), pp. 1020–1031.

24. W. D. Hoyer, R. Chandy, M. Dorotic, M. Krafft, and S. S. Singh, "Consumer cocreation in new product development," in *Journal of Service Research* 13 (2010), issue 3, 283–296.

25. R. Cooper and E. J. Kleinschmidt, "New Product Processes at Leading Industrial Firms," *Industrial-Marketing-Management* 20, no. 2 (1991), pp. 137–48; and R. G. Cooper, "Doing It Right," *Ivey Business Journal* 64, no. 6 (2000), pp. 54–61; and R.G. Cooper, "Stage-Gate Idea to Launch System," *Wiley International Encyclopedia of Marketing: Product Innovation & Management* 5, B.L. Bayus (ed.), (West Sussex UK: Wiley, 2011).

26. R.G. Cooper, "Stage-Gate Idea to Launch System," *Wiley International Encyclopedia of Marketing: Product Innovation & Management* 5, B.L. Bayus (ed.), (West Sussex UK: Wiley, 2011).

27. L. Y. Coyeh, P. W. Kamienski, and R. L. Espino, "Gate System Focuses on Industrial Basic Research," *Research Technology Management* 41, no. 4 (1998), pp. 34–37.

28. A. LaPlante and A. E. Alter, "Corning, Inc: The Stage-Gate Innovation Process," *Computerworld* 28, no. 44 (1994), p. 81.

29. J. J. Cristiano, J. K. Liker, and C. C. White, "Key Factors in the Successful Application of Quality Function Deployment (QFD)," *IEEE Transactions on Engineering Management* 48, no. 1 (2001), p. 81.

30. I. Bier, "Using QFD to Construct a Higher Education Curriculum," *Quality Progress* 34, no. 4 (2001), pp. 64–69; N. Eldin, "A Promising Planning Tool: Quality Function Deployment," *Cost Engineering* 44, no. 3 (2002), pp. 28–38; and W. J. Selen and J. Schepers, "Design of Quality Service Systems in the Public Sector: Use of Quality Function Deployment in Police Services," *Total Quality Management* 12, no. 5 (2001), pp. 677–87; J. A. Carnevalli and P. C. Miguel, "Review, analysis and classification of the literature on QFD—types of research, difficulties and benefits," *International Journal of Production Economics* 114 (2008), pp. 737–54.

31. K. B. Clark and S. C. Wheelwright, *Managing New Product and Process Development* (New York: Free Press, 1993); J. R. Hauser and D. Clausing, "The House of Quality," *Harvard Business Review,* May–June 1988, pp. 63–73; A. Griffin, "Evaluating QFD's Use in US Firms as a Process for Developing Products," *Journal of Product Innovation Management* 9 (1992), pp. 171–87; and A. Griffin and J. R. Hauser, "Patterns of Communication among Marketing, Engineering and Manufacturing," *Management Science* 38 (1992), pp. 360–73.

32. E. I. Schwartz, "The Inventor's Play-Ground," *Technology Review* 105, no. 8 (2002), pp. 68–73.

33. Clark and Wheelwright, *Managing New Product and Process Development.*

34. S. Kumar, E. C. Aquino, and E. Anderson, "Application of a Process Methodology and a Strategic Decision Model for Business Process Outsourcing," *Information Knowledge Systems Management* 6 (2007), pp. 323–42; and J. W. Langford, *Logistics: Principles and Applications* (New York: McGraw-Hill, 1995).

35. L. P. Chao and K. Ishii, "Design Error Classification and Knowledge Management," *Journal of Knowledge Management Practice,* May 2004; and P. Valdes-Dapena, "Tagged: 10 Cars with Bad Reputations," CNNMoney.com (accessed April 23, 2009).

36. G. Barczak, A. Griffin, and K. B. Kahn, "Trends and Drivers of Success in NPD Practices: Results of the 2003 PDMA Best Practices Study," *Journal of Product Innovation Management* 26 (2009), pp. 3–23.

37. M. R. Millson, S. P. Raj, and D. Wilemon, "A Survey of Major Approaches for Accelerating New Product Development," *Journal of Product Innovation Management* 9 (1992), pp. 53–69.

38. "The printed World," *The Economist (2011),* February 10, 2011; K. Lee, "Foodini 3D printer cooks up meals like the Star Trek food replicator," www.inhabitat.com (2013): December 9th; Fitzgerald, M. "With 3-D printing the shoe really fits." *MIT Sloan Management Review* (2013), www.sloanreview.mit.edu:May 15th.

39. J. Silverstein, "Organ Printing Could Drastically Change Medicine," ABC News, February 10, 2006.

40. B. L. Goldense and J. Gilmore, "Measuring Product Design," *Machine Design* 73, no. 14 (2001), pp. 63–67.

41. T. D. Kuczmarski, "Measuring Your Return on Innovation," *Marketing Management* 9, no. 1 (2000), pp. 24–32.

42. Ibid.

Managing New Product Development Teams

Innovation Teams at the Walt Disney Company

The Walt Disney Company is probably the best known entertainment company in the world. Founded in 1923 as a producer of animated films, it grew to become an entertainment conglomerate that includes theme parks, live action film production, television, publishing, retail, and more. In 2014, it earned over $48 billion in revenues and had 180,000 employees.[a] Despite the range of its businesses, most of them (with some notable exceptions) leverage the same key competitive advantage: the magical and wholesome stories and characters of its animated films.

The Making of an Animated Film

In the very early stages of generating and refining an idea for a movie, the development department assembles a small incubation team that includes a director, a writer, some artists, and some storyboard people.[b] This team draws storyboards that are edited together with dialogue and temporary music, creating "story reels." These story reels show the sequence of the movie and help the team craft and refine the story into one that will have visual and emotional appeal. They also help to reveal problems that have to be solved, which tend to be numerous in the early stages of production.[c]

Once approved for development, a typical movie enters production using computer-aided design (CAD) systems. Artists would create a model in a CAD system, which could then apply mathematical models to simulate lifelike textures, movement, and lighting.[d] This computing intensive phase was also managed by small autonomous teams, each focused on a particular specialty such as Tech Support, Renderfarm, and Post Production. Disney's Director of Systems, Jonathan Geibel, had noticed that when teams had seven or more participants, individual contribution would drop significantly, lowering the quality of the discussion. Geibel thus determined that teams should only have between two and six people, including one who would be designated as a *Team Lead*. Team Leads were chosen because of their technical expertise and their vision for the project. Their seniority played little role—rather they were chosen based on how compelling their vision was, and how good management thought they would be in driving the progress of the team. The remaining employees were assigned as "primary" members to a particular team to which they would give most of their time and effort and might also serve as "secondary" members on other teams when those teams needed their help.[e]

Workspace and Collocation

Geibel was also concerned about how the physical structure of the workspace and proximity would influence team dynamics and productivity. After running several experiments involving the location of team members, he decided to reconfigure the entire division so that teams were collocated. He noted, "Collocating individuals allowed ideas to flow each day through ad hoc meetings. Individuals would often brainstorm, pause, and walk over to a whiteboard for further development rather than needing to arrange a specific time and space to meet. With high priority and chaotic work, physical proximity was key."[f] Geibel also believed that people tended to contribute less in formal conference rooms, so he created small casual meeting spaces that teams could meet in, that did not require advance scheduling.

In keeping with his belief that immediate and informal communication was key, Geibel himself gave up his office and moved to a desk without walls in the center of the Systems area. He would conduct frequent walkabouts, conferring with the teams so that if something was going on, he would know about it immediately.

Team Communication

To help foster communication and coordination between teams, teams were asked to create yearly roadmaps of their goals that were broadcast to everyone within the Systems group. A master calendar was also created on whiteboards in a main hallway that showed major milestones throughout the year. Teams put post-it notes on the calendar to show major events.[g]

The teams also used "dailies"—a practice from traditional film production that had been brought in when Disney acquired Pixar. In the "dailies," artists had to show their ongoing work to directors and peers. This informal audience could then provide direct feedback about both the creative and technical elements of the project. As Brad Bird, Oscar-winning director, described, "As individual animators, we all have different strengths and weaknesses, but if we can interconnect all our strengths, we are collectively the greatest animator on earth. . . We're going to look at your scenes in front of everybody. Everyone will get humiliated and encouraged together. If there is a solution, I want everyone to hear the solution, so everyone adds it to their tool kit."[h] Initially, people were afraid to speak up, but after two-months of seeing artists hear and benefit from the blunt suggestions of Bird and others, people began to feel safe enough to speak up.

Creating a Creative Culture

Teams were given considerable autonomy so long as their work got done. Teams could choose their own hours, attire, office arrangements, project management routines, meeting structure, and more. As described by Ed Catmull, president of both Pixar and Walt Disney Animation Studios, "We believe the creative vision propelling each movie comes from one or two people and not from either corporate executives or a development department. Our philosophy is: You get create creative people, you bet big on them, you give them enormous leeway and support, and you provide them with an environment in which they can get honest feedback from everyone."[i]

Initially, it was not always easy for the engineers to embrace this kind of autonomy—they tended to continue to ask permission about minor aspects of team organization. As Geibel noted, "We've built teams where technical leads don't have to ask for permission to change the way they are running their teams . . . We're still working on people thinking that way spontaneously. The culture is ingrained in everybody because the average tenure is 15–40 years. If you've worked in a top-down organization for that long, it's going to take a while to adapt to a new culture where everyone is expected to challenge the status quo and where there's an expectation that critical thinking is happening at all levels."

Discussion Questions:

1. Why does Disney keep its development teams small?
2. What are the pros and cons of the teams being so autonomous?
3. Is Disney's team approach mostly suited to creative projects, or would it work equally well in other kinds of industries?

[a] www.hoovers.com
[b] Catmull, E. "How Pixar fosters collective creativity," *Harvard Business Review* (2008), September: 65–72.
[c] Catmull, E. "How Pixar fosters collective creativity," *Harvard Business Review* (2008), September: 65–72.
[d] Edmondson, AC, Ager, DL, Harburg, E. and Bartlett, N. "Teaming at Disney Animation," *Harvard Business School* (2015), May 18th.
[e] Edmondson, AC, Ager, DL, Harburg, E. and Bartlett, N. "Teaming at Disney Animation," *Harvard Business School* (2015), May 18th.
[f] Edmondson, AC, Ager, DL, Harburg, E. and Bartlett, N. "Teaming at Disney Animation," *Harvard Business School* (2015), May 18th.
[g] Edmondson, AC, Ager, DL, Harburg, E. and Bartlett, N. "Teaming at Disney Animation," *Harvard Business School* (2015), May 18th.
[h] Rao, H, Sutton, R, and Webb, AP. "Innovation lessons from Pixar: An interview with Oscar-winning director Brad Bird," *McKinsey Quarterly*, April, 2008.
[i] Catmull, E. "How Pixar fosters collective creativity," *Harvard Business Review* (2008), September: 65–72.

OVERVIEW

New product development often requires activities that are the responsibility of different departments within the organization. To facilitate coordination and cooperation across division boundaries, many organizations create cross-functional new product development teams to lead and manage the development process for the project. There is considerable variation, however, in how teams are formed and managed. In this chapter, we will look at several factors that affect the new product development team's performance, including its size, composition, structure, administration, and leadership.

CONSTRUCTING NEW PRODUCT DEVELOPMENT TEAMS

In constructing new product development teams, the organization must consider how the team's size and composition will affect its mix of skills, its access to resources, and its effectiveness in providing communication and coordination across the divisions.

Team Size

New product development teams may range from a few members to hundreds of members. For example, the development team that created the IBM personal computer had 19 members, but the average team size for development projects at IBM is close to 200.[1] The Yahoo! Internet portal was developed by 13 software developers, split into several small teams of one to three members.[2] By combining the efforts and expertise of multiple individuals, groups can often outperform individuals on many problem-solving tasks, implying that the size of the development team might be related to its potential for success.[3]

Bigger, however, is not always better. Large teams can create more administrative costs and communication problems, leading to costly delays. Additionally, the larger the team, the harder it can be to foster a shared sense of identity among team members. Further, as the size of the team increases, the potential for **social loafing** also increases. Social loafing occurs when, as the size of the team increases, individuals perceive that they will not receive full credit (or blame) for their contribution to the group effort and so their effort and commitment decrease.[4] The average team size used by U.S. organizations is 11 members,[5] but there is considerable variance in the size of teams used by organizations, and each team may vary in size over the course of a new product development project.

social loafing
When an individual in a team does not exert the expected amount of effort and relies instead on the work of other team members.

Team Composition

A lack of communication among the marketing, R&D, and manufacturing functions of a company can be extremely detrimental to new product development. A lack of cross-functional communication can lead to a poor fit between product attributes and customer requirements. R&D cannot design products that fit customer requirements unless it receives *and* attends to input from marketing regarding those requirements. The manufacturing/R&D interface is also of critical importance because of manufacturing's role in determining two key attributes of a product—*quality* and *price*. By working closely with R&D, manufacturing can ensure that R&D designs products that are relatively easy to manufacture. Designing for ease of manufacturing can lower both unit costs and product defects, which translates into a lower final price and higher quality. Similarly, a lack of cross-functional communication between functions can lead to longer cycle times as a product iterates back and forth between different stages in the process.

One of the ways that firms address this problem is by building cross-functional product development teams.[6] **Cross-functional teams** include members drawn from more than one functional area, such as engineering, manufacturing, or marketing.[7] For instance, in Chrysler's "vehicle deployment platform teams," team members are drawn from design, engineering, purchasing, manufacturing, product planning, finance, and marketing. Firms around the world rely heavily on cross-functional teams for their new product development efforts. In 2000, 77 percent of U.S. firms, 67 percent of European firms, and 54 percent of Japanese firms reported using cross-functional teams.[8]

Teams that are composed of people from diverse backgrounds have several advantages over teams that are drawn from only one or a few functional areas.[9] A greater

cross-functional teams
Teams whose members are drawn from multiple functional areas in the firm such as R&D, marketing, manufacturing, distribution, and so on.

variety of specialists provides a broader knowledge base and increases the cross-fertilization of ideas.[10] Having specialists from different areas also allows the project to draw on a wider mix of information sources in the environment through scanning activities (for richer detail on this, see the accompanying Research Brief on boundary-spanning activities).[11] Functional experts often actively read journals and are involved in associations that directly affect their trade. These activities can lead to the creation and improvement of innovative ideas, as well as provide solutions to product development problems.[12] By combining members of different functional areas into one project team, a wide variety of information sources can be ensured.

A number of arguments also support other types of diversity. Individuals who enter the organization at different times (organizational tenure diversity) are likely to have different contacts outside of the team, enabling the team to draw from a wider mix of resources. Teams that incorporate cultural diversity should show better problem solving by incorporating multiple viewpoints, and teams composed of members who are diverse in terms of education, gender or age can help ensure a variety of viewpoints are considered and external resources are tapped.[13] Studies have demonstrated that demographic diversity in teams can increase innovative outcomes and overall performance.[14]

Diversity of team members, however, can also raise coordination and communication costs. Individuals tend to interact more frequently and more intensely with other individuals whom they perceive as being similar to them on one or more dimensions.[15] This phenomenon is known as **homophily**. Research on homophily suggests that individuals prefer to communicate with others they perceive as similar to them because it is easier and more comfortable to communicate with those who have similar dialects, mental models, and belief systems.[16] The perception of similarity can also be self-reinforcing—as individuals interact with frequency and intensity, they can develop a common dialect, greater trust, and greater familiarity with the knowledge each possesses. The common dialect, trust, and familiarity, in turn, make the individuals both more willing and more able to exchange information effectively in future interactions. When individuals perceive others as being very different from them, they may be less willing to interact frequently or intensely, and it may be more difficult for them to develop a shared understanding. Heterogeneous teams often have greater difficulty integrating objectives and views, leading to conflict and lower group cohesion.[17] Research has also indicated, however, that the communication and coordination differences between heterogeneous or homogeneous teams diminish if the groups maintain long-term contact. Presumably, through extensive interaction, heterogeneous teams learn to manage their group processes better.[18]

In sum, heterogeneous teams should possess more information, on average, than homogeneous groups. The heterogeneity of a team can also increase the creativity and variance in decision making, leading to more innovative outcomes and higher overall performance.[19] However, to realize this potential performance advantage, heterogeneous teams may require long-term contact and incentives to foster communication and cooperation.

The ability of team members to communicate and cooperate effectively is also a function of the personalities of the individuals on the team. A study by Susan

homophily
The tendency for individuals to like other people whom they perceive as being similar to themselves.

Research Brief   Boundary-Spanning Activities in New Product Development Teams

To be successful, new product development teams must be able to manage relationships with groups that are beyond the team's boundaries. Teams need to be able to collect information and resources both within and outside of their organizations, and they also need to represent the team to other groups in the organization to ensure that the team continues to receive support and that team members are not overloaded with non-team-related activities.[a] The most successful new product development teams have gatekeepers who provide important links to the environment.[b]

Deborah Ancona and David Caldwell conducted a study to explore the full range of boundary-spanning activities in which teams engage and to identify which of these activities enhanced team performance. They interviewed 38 experienced product development team managers and collected data from 45 product development teams in five high-technology companies in the computer, analytic instruments, and photographic equipment industries. Ancona and Caldwell found that teams engaged in three primary types of boundary-spanning activity:

Ambassador activities—These activities were directed at representing the team to others and protecting the team from interference. For example, an ambassador might convince other individuals in the organization that the team's activities are important.

Task coordination activities—These activities emphasized coordinating and negotiating the team's activities with other groups. For instance, task coordination activities might include negotiating delivery deadlines with other divisions of the firm or obtaining feedback about the team's performance.

Scouting activities—These activities were directed at scanning for ideas and information that might be useful to the team, enhancing its knowledge base. For example, scouting activities could include collecting data about what competitors were doing on similar projects or finding technical information that might be useful in the development project.

Ancona and Caldwell found that boundary-spanning activities affected the performance of the new product development team, and their impact depended on the timing of the activities. In particular, they found that scouting and ambassador activities were more beneficial if conducted early in the development project cycle, while task coordination activities were beneficial throughout the life of the team.[c]

[a] D. B. Ancona and D. F. Caldwell, "Making Teamwork Work: Boundary Management in Product Development Teams," in Managing Strategic Innovation and Change, eds. M. L. Tushman and P. Anderson (New York: Oxford University Press, 1997), pp. 433–42.
[b] M. L. Tushman, "Special Boundary Roles in the Innovation Process," *Administrative Science Quarterly* 22 (1977), pp. 587–605; and E. B. Roberts and A. R. Fusfeld, "Staffing the Innovative Technology-Base Organization," *Sloan Management Review* 22, no. 3 (1981), pp. 19–34.
[c] D. B. Ancona and D. F. Caldwell, "Bridging the Boundary: External Activity and Performance in Organizational Teams," *Administrative Science Quarterly* 37, (1992), pp. 634–65.

Kichuk and Willi Wiesner explored whether five personality factors (conscientiousness, extroversion, neuroticism, agreeableness, and openness to experience) influenced the likelihood of success in new product development teams. Kichuk and Wiesner found that the personality characteristics that enhanced the success of a new product development team were high extroversion, high agreeableness, and low neuroticism.[20]

THE STRUCTURE OF NEW PRODUCT DEVELOPMENT TEAMS

Teams can be structured in a number of ways. One well-known typology classifies teams into four types: functional, lightweight, heavyweight, and autonomous.[21] Figure 12.1 depicts each of these types graphically.

Functional Teams

In functional teams, members remain in their functional departments (e.g., R&D, marketing, manufacturing, etc.), and report to their regular functional manager (see Figure 12.1, panel a); however, they may meet periodically to discuss the project. Such teams are usually temporary, and individuals may spend less than 10 percent of their time working on team-related activities. Functional teams also typically do not have a project manager or dedicated liaison personnel. While this team structure is straightforward to implement because it requires little (if any) deviation from the firm's normal

FIGURE 12.1
Types of Development Teams

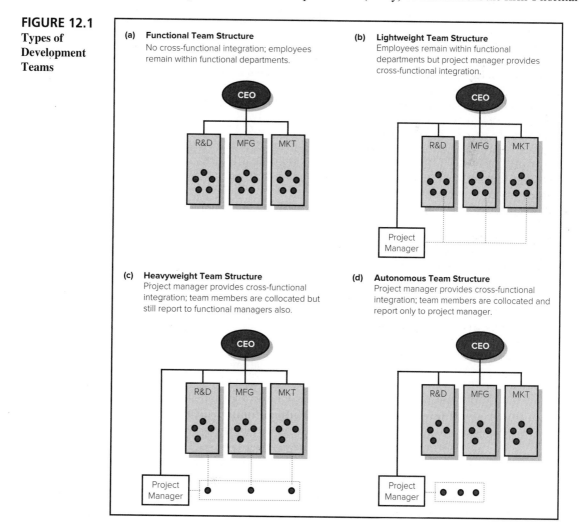

(a) **Functional Team Structure**
No cross-functional integration; employees remain within functional departments.

(b) **Lightweight Team Structure**
Employees remain within functional departments but project manager provides cross-functional integration.

(c) **Heavyweight Team Structure**
Project manager provides cross-functional integration; team members are collocated but still report to functional managers also.

(d) **Autonomous Team Structure**
Project manager provides cross-functional integration; team members are collocated and report only to project manager.

operations, this structure provides little opportunity for cross-functional coordination.[22] Further, since individuals are still evaluated and rewarded almost exclusively based on their functional performance, the team members may have little commitment to the development project. Functional teams are more likely to be appropriate for derivative projects that primarily affect only a single function of the firm.

Lightweight Teams

In lightweight teams, members still reside in their functional departments, and functional supervisors retain authority over evaluation and rewards (see Figure 12.1, panel b). Like functional teams, lightweight teams are typically temporary, and members spend the majority of their time on their normal functional responsibilities (up to 25 percent of their time might be spent on team-related activities). However, lightweight teams have a project manager and dedicated liaison personnel who facilitate communication and coordination among functions. Managers of lightweight teams are normally junior or middle management employees, who are not able to exert significant influence or authority over team members. As a result of these factors, lightweight teams offer a small improvement in team coordination and likelihood of success over functional teams. Such a team structure might be appropriate for derivative projects where high levels of coordination and communication are not required.

Heavyweight Teams

In heavyweight teams, members are removed from their functional departments so that they may be *collocated* with the project manager (see Figure 12.1, panel c). Project managers of heavyweight teams are typically senior managers who outrank functional managers, and have significant authority to command resources, and evaluate and reward team members.[23] The core group of team members in the heavyweight team is often dedicated full-time to the project. This combination of factors helps ensure that the team has strong cross-functional coordination and communication, and that team members are significantly committed to the development project. However, heavyweight teams are still often temporary; thus, the long-term career development of individual members continues to rest with their functional managers rather than the project manager. This type of team structure offers a significant improvement in communication and coordination over functional teams, and it is typically considered appropriate for platform projects.

Autonomous Teams

In autonomous teams, members are removed from their functional departments and dedicated full-time (and often permanently) to the development team (see Figure 12.1, panel d). Team members are collocated with the project manager, who is a very senior person in the organization. The project manager of an autonomous team is given full control over resources contributed from different functional departments, and the project manager has exclusive authority over the evaluation and reward of team members. Autonomous teams often do not conform to the operating procedures of the rest of the organization; instead they are permitted to create their own policies, procedures, and reward systems.[24] Autonomous teams are also held fully accountable for the success of the project; in many ways, autonomous teams act like independent divisions of the firm. Autonomous teams typically excel at rapid and efficient new product development, particularly when such development requires breaking away from the organization's existing technologies and routines. Thus, autonomous teams are typically considered to be appropriate for breakthrough projects and some major platform projects. They can be the birthplace of new business units.[25] However, the independence of the autonomous teams can cause them to underutilize the resources of the parent organization. Furthermore, autonomous teams are often hard to fold back into the organization if the project is completed or terminated. Many autonomous teams thus go on to become separate divisions of the firm, or may even be spun off of the firm as a subsidiary.

Figure 12.2 summarizes key dimensions across which the four teams vary, including a number of points that have not yet been dealt with in the text. The potential for conflict between the functions and the team, particularly the project manager, rises with the move from functional teams to autonomous teams. The independence of heavyweight and autonomous teams may prompt them to pursue goals that run counter to the interests of the functions. Senior managers should keep such conflict in check.

FIGURE 12.2
Summary of Characteristics of Team Types

Characteristics	Functional Team	Lightweight Team	Heavyweight Team	Autonomous Team
Project manager	None	Junior or middle manager	Senior manager	Senior manager
Power of project manager	NA	Low	High	Very high
Time spent on team activities	Up to 10%	Up to 25%	100%	100%
Location of team members	Functions	Functions	Collocated with project manager	Collocated with project manager
Length of commitment to team	Temporary	Temporary	Long-term but ultimately temporary	Permanent
Evaluation of team members	Functional heads	Functional heads	Project manager and functional heads	Project manager
Potential for conflict between team and functions	Low	Low	Moderate	High
Degree of cross-functional integration	Low	Moderate	High	High
Degree of fit with existing organizational practices	High	High	Moderate	Moderate-low
Appropriate for:	Some derivative projects	Derivative projects	Platform projects/ breakthrough projects	Platform projects/ breakthrough projects

THE MANAGEMENT OF NEW PRODUCT DEVELOPMENT TEAMS

For a new product development team to be effective, its leadership and administrative policies should be matched to the team's structure and needs.

Team Leadership

The team leader is responsible for directing the team's activities, maintaining the team's alignment with project goals, and serving as a communicator between the team and senior management. In heavyweight and autonomous teams, the team leader may also be the person who is primarily responsible for the evaluation, compensation, and promotion of individual team members. Effective team leaders are often much more directly related to the team's success than senior management or project champions. This may be because team leaders interact much more frequently with the team and more directly influence the team's behavior.[26]

As described in the team type and structure section above, different types of teams have different leadership needs. For instance, while lightweight teams might have a junior or middle-management leader who provides basic coordination between the functional groups, heavyweight and autonomous teams require senior managers with significant experience and organizational influence. In heavyweight and autonomous teams, the project manager must be someone who can lead and evaluate the team members, champion the development project both within the team and to the wider organization, and act as a translator between the various functions.[27] In particular, project managers in heavyweight and autonomous teams must have high status within the organization, act as a concept champion for the team within the organization, be good at conflict resolution, have multilingual skills (i.e., they must be able to talk the language of marketing, engineering, and manufacturing), and be able to exert influence upon the engineering, manufacturing, and marketing functions.[28] Other things being equal, teams whose project managers are deficient on one or more of these dimensions will have a lower probability of success.[29]

Team Administration

To ensure that members have a clear focus and commitment to the development project, many organizations now have heavyweight and autonomous teams develop a project charter and contract book. The *project charter* encapsulates the project's mission and articulates exact and measurable goals for the project. It might include a vision statement for the project (e.g., "Dell laptops will be the market standard for performance and value") and a background statement for why this project is important for the organization. The charter may describe who is on the team, the length of time members will spend on the team, and the percentage of their time that will be spent on team activities.[30] It may also stipulate the team's budget, its reporting timeline, and the key success criteria of the project (e.g., meeting a particular time-to-market goal, exceeding customer satisfaction criteria established for the project, capturing a target amount of market share within a defined period of time, etc.). Establishing an explicit set of goals for the project helps ensure that the team members have a common understanding of the project's overall purpose and priorities. Goals also help to structure the new product development process and can facilitate cooperation by keeping team members oriented toward a common outcome.[31]

Once the team charter is established, core team members and senior managers must negotiate a *contract book*. The contract book defines in detail the basic plan to achieve the goal laid out in the project charter. Typically, the contract book will estimate the resources required, the development time schedule, and the results that will be achieved. The contract book provides a tool for monitoring and evaluating the team's performance in meeting objectives by providing a set of performance benchmarks and deadlines to which the team's performance can be compared. More important, however, the contract book is an important mechanism for establishing team commitment to the project and a sense of ownership over the project. After negotiation and acceptance of this contract, all parties often sign the contract book as an indication of their intention to honor the plan and achieve the results. Team members who sign the contract book typically feel a greater sense of duty to work toward the project's goals. Furthermore, signing the contract book can give team members a sense of ownership over the project and empowerment to make decisions about the project. This ownership and empowerment can help team members identify with a project's outcome and can encourage them to exert extra effort to ensure its success.[32]

Managing Virtual Teams

virtual teams
Teams in which members may be a great distance from each other, but are still able to collaborate intensively via advanced information technologies such as videoconferencing, groupware, and e-mail or Internet chat programs.

Recent advances in information technology have enabled companies to make greater use of virtual teams. **Virtual teams** are teams in which members may be a great distance from each other, but are still able to collaborate intensively via advanced information technologies such as videoconferencing, groupware, and e-mail or Internet chat programs. Virtual teaming can enable individuals with unique skills to work on a project, regardless of their location. By meeting virtually, individuals who live at great distances can collaborate without incurring travel costs or disruption to their lives.[33] This is especially valuable for a company whose operations are highly global. For example, SAP Aktiengesellschaft is headquartered in Walldorf, Germany, but has large R&D centers in India, China, Israel, and the United States. Each location has deep expertise in particular areas but lacks functional breadth due to specialization. SAP's managers choose employees from different locations to assemble virtual teams that optimally integrate the expertise needed for a given project.[34] Similarly, when IBM began deploying more of its products globally, it increased its use of virtual teams. About one-third of IBM's employees will participate in virtual teams at some point in their career. When IBM needs to staff a project, it gives a list of the needed skills to the human resource division, which identifies an appropriate pool of people. If the skills and talent of the people are more important than their ability to meet face-to-face, a virtual team is formed.[35]

Virtual teams pose a distinct set of management challenges, however. As described earlier in the chapter, much of the work on the structure of new product development teams has emphasized the importance of collocation. Collocation facilitates communication and collaboration by giving team members opportunities for rich face-to-face communication and informal interaction.[36] Proximity and frequent interaction help teams to develop shared norms and a dialect for communicating about the project. Virtual teams, by contrast, must often rely on communication channels that

Research Brief   Virtual International R&D Teams

Gassman and von Zedtwitz build on the transnational corporation model discussed in Chapter Ten by examining how such firms coordinate their international innovation efforts via virtual teams. As in some of the arguments made in Chapter Ten about loosely coupled R&D activities, virtual international R&D teams may jointly work on a single development project, utilizing information technologies (rather than geographical proximity) to achieve coordination. However, while information technology decreases the need to collocate R&D activities, it does not readily solve problems related to building trust and transferring tacit knowledge. The type of innovation project being undertaken and the type of knowledge that must be shared should influence the degree to which firms rely on decentralized, virtual coordination processes.

Gassman and von Zedtwitz studied 37 technology-intensive multinationals and identified four patterns of teams: (1) decentralized self-coordination, (2) system integrator as coordinator, (3) core team as system architect, and (4) centralized venture team. In the *decentralized self-coordinating* teams, there was no single source of power or authority over the teams. Teams communicated primarily through telephone, the Internet, shared databases, and groupware. Coordination was relatively weak and relied largely on a strong corporate culture. Decentralized self-coordination was more likely to arise if there were well-developed standard interfaces between components being developed in dif-ferent locales; thus, it tended to be suited to modular innovation as opposed to architectural innovation (see Chapter Three).

In teams with a *system integrator as R&D coordinator,* a single individual or office takes responsibility for helping different divisions coordinate. The system integrator helps to build a common understanding of the project among each of the divisions, translates knowledge from one division to another, and tracks progress and contributions.

While the overall project is decentralized, the system integrator enables some centralized coordination.

In the *core team as system architect* model, a core team of key decision makers from all of the decentralized R&D groups meets regularly to coordinate the otherwise decentralized groups. The core team often includes a strong project manager, leaders from each of the decentralized groups, and occasionally external customers or consultants. The core team constructs the overall architecture of the development project and maintains its coherence throughout its development. Because the core team has more direct authority over the individual divisions than the system integrator described above, the core team is better able to resolve conflict and enforce standards across the divisions. Because core teams can provide a significant level of integration across the divisions, core teams are often able to conduct architectural innovation. In the *centralized venture team,* R&D personnel and resources are relocated to one central location to enable maximum integration and coordination. The team is likely to have a very powerful senior project manager with significant authority to allocate resources and define the responsibilities of individual team members. Gassman and von Zedtwitz describe two examples of centralized venture teams—Asea Brown's "High Impact Projects" and Sharp's "Golden Badge" projects. Because of their high expense, such teams are likely to be used only for strategic innovations of the utmost importance.

Gassman and von Zedtwitz's model is summarized in Figure 12.3. Overall, Gassman and von Zedtwitz argue that innovations that are radical, are architectural, or require the intensive transfer of complex or tacit knowledge will require greater centralization. Innovations that are incremental, are modular, and do not require the frequent transfer of complex or tacit knowledge can be more decentralized.

continued

concluded

FIGURE 12.3
Gassman and
von Zedtwitz's
Typology of
International
Virtual Teams

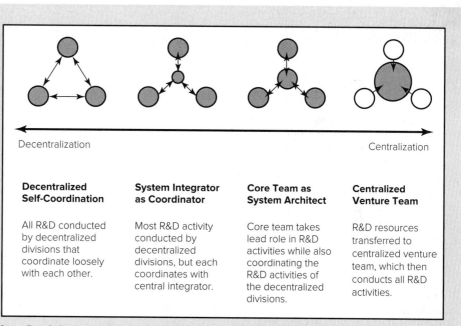

Decentralization   Centralization

Decentralized Self-Coordination	**System Integrator as Coordinator**	**Core Team as System Architect**	**Centralized Venture Team**
All R&D conducted by decentralized divisions that coordinate loosely with each other.	Most R&D activity conducted by decentralized divisions, but each coordinates with central integrator.	Core team takes lead role in R&D activities while also coordinating the R&D activities of the decentralized divisions.	R&D resources transferred to centralized venture team, which then conducts all R&D activities.

Source: From O. Gassman and M. von Zedtwitz, 2003, "Trends and Determinants of Managing Virtual R&D Teams," *R&D Management*, vol. 33, no. 3, pp. 243–62. Reprinted with permission of Blackwell Publishing.

are much less rich than face-to-face contact and face significant hurdles in establishing norms and dialects and may suffer from greater conflict. They may also have trouble negotiating multiple time zones, which can lead to frustration.[37]

In the forming of virtual teams, it is important to select personnel who are both comfortable with the technologies being used to facilitate collaboration and who have strong interpersonal skills.[38] Team members must be able to work independently and have a strong work ethic. Since distance makes it easy for team members to deflect opportunities for interaction, it is important to choose individuals who tend to seek interaction rather than avoid it. It is important that members of the team establish standards for how quickly they will respond to messages, and how often they will be available for synchronous communications (communications where the involved parties must participate at the same time, such as telephone calls, videoconferencing, and instant messaging).[39] Furthermore, because many of the opportunities for informal interaction may be lost in a virtual environment, more types of interaction may have to be incorporated into the ground rules of the team.[40] For example, the team leader might schedule daily or weekly unstructured "chat" times where team members are required to participate in a group conference call or online conference to share ideas that may not be uncovered in the team's more formal interactions.

Virtual teams also face challenges in developing trust, resolving conflict, and exchanging tacit knowledge, as discussed in the accompanying Research Brief about virtual international R&D teams.

**Summary
of
Chapter**

1. Bringing multiple people together into a team enables multiple bases of expertise to be collectively directed toward problem solving; thus, teams are powerful mechanisms for problem solving. However, if teams become too big, administrative costs and communication problems can become significant.

2. Diversity of team members ensures that the team can draw on different perspectives and bases of expertise. In particular, functional diversity is often sought in new product development teams. Cross-functional teams enable design, manufacturing, and marketing objectives to be integrated in the new product development process.

3. Diversity of team members ensures that the individuals in the team not only possess different knowledge or viewpoints, but also have different sources of extra-team resources upon which to draw through boundary-spanning activities.

4. Diversity can also make it more difficult for teams to develop a common understanding of the new product development project and can result in lower group cohesion. Teams may need long-term contact and incentives for cooperation to overcome these challenges.

5. The way in which a team is structured (collocation, permanence, supervisory relationships, etc.) significantly influences how team members interact and the likely outcomes of a development project. Different types of teams are appropriate for different types of development projects.

6. Attributes of the team leader (seniority, authority, multilingual skills) must match the team type for teams to be most effective.

7. Many firms have teams develop and sign a project charter and contract book to ensure that all team members have a common understanding of the project's goals and possess a sense of ownership and commitment to the project's success.

8. When a company wishes to form a team with individuals who have unique skills but live great distances from each other, it might opt to form a virtual team. Virtual teams use information technologies to achieve communication and coordination. Virtual teams face a distinct set of challenges in promoting participation, cooperation, and trust. As a result, they require special consideration of the selection of team members and the team administration processes.

**Discussion
Questions**

1. What are the trade-offs in choosing a team's size and level of diversity?

2. How can managers ensure that a team reaps the advantages of diversity while not being thwarted by some of the challenges team diversity raises?

3. Identify an example of a development project, and what type of team you believe they used. Do you think this was the appropriate type of team given the nature of the project?

4. What are some advantages and disadvantages of collocation? For what types of projects are virtual teams inappropriate?

Suggested Further Reading

Classics

Allen, T. J., *Managing the Flow of Technology: Technology Transfer and the Dissemination of Technological Information within the R&D Organization* (Cambridge, MA: MIT Press, 1977).

Ancona, D. G., and D. F. Caldwell, "Bridging the Boundary: External Activity and Performance in Organizational Teams," *Administrative Science Quarterly* 37 (1992), pp. 634–65.

Edmondson, A., "Psychological Safety and Learning Behavior in Work Teams." *Administrative Science Quarterly* 44 (1999), pp. 350–83.

Hansen, M. T., "The Search-transfer Problem: The Role of Weak Ties in Sharing Knowledge across Organization Subunits," *Administrative Science Quarterly* 44 (1999), pp. 82–111.

Williams, K., and C. A. O'Reilly, "Demography and Diversity in Organizations: A Review of 40 years of Research," *Research in Organizational Behavior* 20 (1998), pp. 77–140.

Recent Work

Edmondson, A. C., and I. M. Nembhard, "Product Development and Learning in Project Teams: The Challenges Are the Benefits," *Journal of Product Innovation Management* 26 (2009), pp. 123–28.

Hulsheger, U. R., N. Anderson, and J. F. Salgado, "Team-level Predictors of Innovation at Work: A Comprehensive Meta-analysis Spanning Three Decades of Research." *Journal of Applied Psychology* 40 (2009), pp. 1128–45.

Malhotra, A., A. Majchrzak, and B. Rosen, "Leading Virtual Teams," *Academy of Management Perspectives* 21 (2007), pp. 60–69.

Ostergaard, C. R., B. Timmermans, and K. Kristinsson, "Does a Different View Create Something New? The Effect of Employee Diversity on Innovation." *Research Policy* 40 (2011), pp. 500–9.

Reagans, R., and E. Zuckerman, "Networks, Diversity, and Productivity: The Social Capital of Corporate R&D Teams," *Organization Science* 12 (2001), pp. 502–17.

Endnotes

1. M. A. Cohen, J. Eliashberg, and T. Ho, "New Product Development: The Performance and Time-to-Market Trade-Off," *Management Science* 42 (1996), pp. 173–86.
2. M. Iansiti and A. MacCormack, "Living on Internet Time: Product Development at Netscape, Yahoo!, NetDynamics, and Microsoft," *Harvard Business School case* no. 9-697-052, 1996.
3. B. E. Collins and H. Guetzkow, *A Social Psychology of Group Processes for Decision Making* (New York: Wiley, 1964); V. B. Hinsz, "Cognitive and Consensus Processes in Group Recognition Memory Performance," *Journal of Personality and Social Psychology* 59 (1990), pp. 705–18; and M. E. Shaw, "Comparison of Individuals and Small Groups in the Rational Solution of Complex Problems," *American Journal of Psychology* 41 (1932), pp. 491–504.
4. S. J. Karau and K. D. Williams, "Social Loafing: A Meta-Analytic Review and Theoretical Integration," *Journal of Personality and Social Psychology* 65 (1993), pp. 681–706.

5. D. J. Devine, L. D. Clayton, J. L. Philips, B. B. Dunford, and S. B. Melner, "Teams in Organizations: Prevalence, Characteristics, and Effectiveness," *Small Group Research* 30 (1999), pp. 678–711.

6. S. Brown and K. Eisenhardt, "Product Development: Past Research, Present Findings, and Future Directions," *Academy of Management Review* 20, no. 2 (1995), pp. 343–78.

7. Ibid.

8. E. Roberts, "Benchmarking Global Strategic Management of Technology," *Research Technology Management*, March–April 2001, pp. 25–36.

9. L. Rochford and W. Rudelius, "How Involving More Functional Areas within a Firm Affects the New Product Process," *Journal of Product Innovation Management* 9 (1992), pp. 287–99.

10. J. R. Kimberly and M. Evanisko, "Organizational Innovation: The Influence of Individual, Organizational, and Contextual Factors on Hospital Adoption of Technological and Administrative Innovations," *Academy of Management Journal* 24 (1981), pp. 689–713; F. Damanpour, "Organization Innovation: A Meta-Analysis of Effects of Determinants and Moderators," *Academy of Management Journal* 34, no. 3 (1991), pp. 555–90; and M. Aiken and J. Hage, "The Organic Organization and Innovation," *Sociology* 5 (1971), pp. 63–82.

11. T. J. Allen, *Managing the Flow of Technology: Technology Transfer and the Dissemination of Technological Information within the R&D Organization* (Cambridge, MA: MIT Press, 1977); D. G. Ancona and D. F. Caldwell, "Demography and Design: Predictors of New Product Team Performance," *Organization Science* 3 (1992), pp. 321–41; and D. G. Ancona, and D. F. Caldwell, "Bridging the Boundary: External Activity and Performance in Organizational Teams," *Administrative Science Quarterly* 37 (1992), pp. 634–65.

12. P. Jervis, "Innovation and Technology Transfer—The Roles and Characteristics of Individuals," *IEEE Transaction on Engineering Management* 22 (1975), pp. 19–27; and D. Miller and P. H. Friesen, "Innovation in Conservative and Entrepreneurial Firms: Two Models of Strategic Momentum," *Strategic Management Journal* 3 (1982), pp. 1–25.

13. I. L. Janis, *Victims of Groupthink* (Boston: Houghton Mifflin, 1972); Ostergaard, C. R., B. Timmermans, and K. Kristinsson, "Does a different view create something new? The effect of employee diversity on innovation." *Research Policy* 40 (2011), 500–9.

14. S. E. Jackson, K. E. May, and K. Whitney, "Understanding the Diversity of Dynamics in Decision Making Teams," in *Team Effectiveness and Decision Making in Organizations,* eds. R. A. Guzzo, E. Salas, and Associates (San Francisco: Jossey-Bass, 1995), pp. 204–61; and R. L. Priem, D. A. Harrison, and N. K. Muir, "Structured Conflict and Consensus Outcomes in Group Decision Making," *Journal of Management* 21 (1995), pp. 691–710; Reagans, R. and McEvily, B. "Network structure and knowledge transfer: The effects of cohesion and range." *Administrative Science Quarterly* 48 (2003), pp. 240–267.

15. P. F. Lazarsfeld and R. K. Merton, "Friendship as a Social Process: A Substantive and Methodological Analysis," in *Freedom and Control in Modern Society,* ed. M. Berger (New York: Van Nostrand, 1954), pp. 8–66.

16. B. Uzzi, "Social Structure and Competition in Interfirm Networks: The Paradox of Embeddedness," *Administrative Science Quarterly* 42 (1997), pp. 35–67.

17. K. L. Bettenhausen, "Five Years of Groups Research: What We Have Learned and What Needs to Be Addressed," *Journal of Management* 17 (1991), pp. 345–81; and K. Williams and C. A. O'Reilly, "Demography and Diversity in Organizations: A Review of 40 Years of Research," *Research in Organizational Behavior* 20 (1998), pp. 77–140.

18. W. Watson, K. Kumar, and L. K. Michaelsen, "Cultural Diversity's Impact on Interaction Process and Performance: Comparing Homogeneous and Diverse Task Groups," *Academy of Management Journal* 36 (1993), pp. 590–602; R. Reagans and B. McEvily, "Network Structure and Knowledge Transfer: The Effects of Cohesion an Range," *Administrative Science Quarterly* 48 (2003), pp. 240–67.

19. Jackson, May, and Whitney, "Understanding the Diversity of Dynamics in Decision Making Teams."

20. S. L. Kichuk and W. H. Wiesner, "The Big Five Personality Factors and Team Performance: Implications for Selecting Successful Product Design Teams," *Journal of Engineering and Technology Management* 14, nos. 3–4 (1997), pp. 195–222.

21. S. C. Wheelwright and K. B. Clark, *Revolutionizing Product Development: Quantum Leaps in Speed, Efficiency and Quality* (New York: Free Press, 1992).

22. K. B. Clark and S. C. Wheelwright, "Organizing and Leading 'Heavyweight' Development Teams," *California Management Review* 34, no. 3 (1992), pp. 9–29.

23. Ibid.

24. Damanpour, "Organization Innovation."

25. Clark and Wheelwright, "Organizing and Leading 'Heavyweight' Development Teams."

26. E. F. McDonough, "Investigation of Factors Contributing to the Success of Cross-Functional Teams," *Journal of Product Innovation Management* 17 (2000), pp. 221–35.

27. K. B. Clark and S. C. Wheelwright, *Managing New Product and Process Development* (New York: Free Press, 1993); E. F. McDonough and G. Barczak, "Speeding Up New Product Development: The Effects of Leadership Style and Source of Technology," *Journal of Product Innovation Management* 8 (1991), pp. 203–11; and G. Barczak and D. Wilemon, "Leadership Differences in New Product Development Teams," *Journal of Production and Innovation Management* 6 (1989), pp. 259–67.

28. Brown and Eisenhardt, "Product Development."

29. M. A. Schilling and C. W. L. Hill, "Managing the New Product Development Process: Strategic Imperatives," *Academy of Management Executive* 12, no. 3 (1998), pp. 67–81.

30. C. W. Miller, "Hunting for Hunting Grounds: Forecasting the Fuzzy Front End," in *The PDMA Toolbook for New Product Development*, eds. P. Belliveau, A. Griffin, and S. Somermeyer (New York: John Wiley & Sons, 2002).

31. McDonough, "Investigation of Factors Contributing to the Success of Cross-Functional Teams."

32. Ibid.

33. C. Joinson, "Managing Virtual Teams: Keeping Members on the Same Page without Being in the Same Place Poses Challenges for Managers," *Human Resource Magazine,* June 2002.

34. Siebdrat, F, Hoegl, M and Ernst H. "How to manage virtual teams." *MIT Sloan Management Review* (2009) Summer: July 1.

35. Ibid.

36. Siebdrat, F, Hoegl, M and Ernst H. "How to manage virtual teams." *MIT Sloan Management Review* (2009) Summer: July 1.

37. Siebdrat, F, Hoegl, M and Ernst H. "How to manage virtual teams." *MIT Sloan Management Review* (2009) Summer: July 1.

38. B. L. Kirkman, B. Rosen, C. B. Gibson, P. E. Tesluk, and S. O. McPherson, "Five Challenges to Virtual Team Success: Lessons from Sabre, Inc.," *Academy of Management Executive* 16, no. 3 (2002), p. 67.

39. M. M. Montoya, A. P. Massey, Y. C. Hung, and C. B. Crisp, "Can You Hear Me Now? Communication in Virtual Product Development Teams," *Journal of Product Innovation Management,* 26 (2009), pp. 139–55.

40. A. Malhotra, A. Majchrzak, and B. Rosen, "Leading Virtual Teams," *Academy of Management Perspectives* 21 (2007), pp. 60–69.

Crafting a Deployment Strategy

Deployment Tactics in the Global Video Game Industry

In the global video game industry, the introduction of each generation of console has ushered in a new battle for market dominance. New entrants have made startling entrances and toppled seemingly invincible incumbents. Game developers, distributors, and customers have had to watch the battle closely in order to place their bets about which console would emerge as the generation's victor. Each generation has also revealed which deployment strategies have paid off—or proven fatal—for the contenders.[a]

Pong: The Beginning of an Era

In the fall of 1972, Nolan Bushnell founded a company called Atari and introduced Pong, a Ping-Pong-like game that was played on a user's television set with the aid of the Atari console. Though considered to be the "second generation" of home video game consoles (a console called the Odyssey, released by Magnavox early 1972 is considered the first generation), Pong was the first home console to become known around the world. In its first year, Pong earned more than $1 million in revenues. Pong and over 60 similar knockoffs soon flooded the market. In these early years of the video game industry, swift advances in integrated circuits enabled a rapid proliferation of new consoles and games. By 1984, video game console and games sales had reached $3 billion in the United States alone. However, console makers in this era did not utilize strict security measures to ensure that only authorized games could be played on their consoles, leading to explosive growth in the production of unauthorized games (games produced for a console without authorization of that console's producer). As a result, the market was soon saturated with games of dubious quality, and many unhappy retailers were stuck with video game inventories they were unable to move. Profits began to spiral downward, and by 1985, many industry observers were declaring the video game industry dead.

The Emergence of 8-Bit Systems

Much to everyone's surprise, however, two new companies from Japan entered the U.S. video game market, initiating the home video game console's third generation: Nintendo, with its 8-bit Nintendo Entertainment System (NES), introduced in 1985, and Sega, which launched its 8-bit Master System in the United States in 1986. Unlike Atari, which had spent only a few hundred thousand dollars on advertising, Sega and Nintendo spent $15 million promoting their systems. Both systems offered technological advantages over the previous generation of video game consoles. Sega's Master System appeared to be slightly superior to Nintendo's, but Nintendo spent much more on the development of quality games and characters and had more game titles available than Sega. The NES sold over 1 million units in the first year, sold 19 million units by 1990, and could be found in more than a third of the households in America and Japan.[b]

From 1985 to 1989, Nintendo held a near monopoly of the U.S. video game industry. The company sold its consoles for a price very close to production costs, while earning the bulk of its profits from games. Nintendo both made games for its system in-house and licensed third-party developers to produce games through very strict licensing policies that (a) limited the number of titles a developer could produce each year, (b) required the developer to preorder a minimum number of cartridges from Nintendo (which had its own contract manufacturers produce the games), and (c) restricted the developers from making similar games for other consoles. Nintendo also restricted the volume and pricing of consoles sold through distributors, ensuring that no single distributor acquired significant bargaining power.[c] Nintendo's restrictive policies were very profitable; however, they also incurred sanctions by the Federal Trade Commission, and they alienated distributors and developers, potentially leaving the company more vulnerable to a competitor.

The 16-Bit Video Game Systems

In September 1989, Sega launched the fourth generation of video game console competition when it introduced its 16-bit Genesis to the U.S. video game market. The Genesis offered dramatic performance enhancement over 8-bit systems. Further, Sega leveraged its popular arcade games to the Genesis and made it backward compatible with its 8-bit Master System games. There were 20 Genesis game titles available by December 1989. NEC also introduced a 16-bit system, the TurboGrafx-16, in the fall of 1989 and had 12 game titles by December 1989. Though Nintendo had its own 16-bit system in the works, it delayed introducing it to the United States for fear of cannibalizing its 8-bit system sales.

By the end of 1989, Sega had already sold 600,000 consoles in the United States, and NEC had sold 200,000. In 1990 and 1991, both Sega and NEC added game titles to their lists, bringing their totals to 130 and 80, respectively. By the end of 1991, Sega had sold 2 million consoles in the United States, and NEC had sold 1 million. Unlike Sega, which produced a major portion of its games in-house, NEC relied completely on external games developers, who found the system to have only a small technological advantage over 8-bit systems.[d] Developers began to abandon the NEC platform, and NEC exited the market in 1991.

Nintendo finally introduced its own 16-bit Super Nintendo Entertainment System (SNES) in 1991, but it was too late to quell Sega's momentum. In 1992 Nintendo controlled 80 percent of the video game market (based on combined 8-bit and 16-bit sales), but by 1994, Sega was the market leader.

Like Nintendo, Sega made little profit on the consoles and focused instead on increasing unit sales to drive game sales and software developer royalties. Sega, however, used less restrictive licensing arrangements than Nintendo and rapidly lured a large number of developers to make Sega game titles. Further, though Nintendo could have made its 16-bit system backward compatible, thus linking the value consumers possessed in their 8-bit game libraries to the new system, Nintendo chose to make the system incompatible with the 8-bit games. By the end of 1991, the SNES had 25 game titles compared to the 130 available for Genesis. Nintendo had given Sega two years of installed base lead on a system that offered a significant technological advantage and then entered the market at a ground-zero position with respect to the availability of complementary goods. The consequence of Nintendo's late move is aptly captured in a review of video game players published in *Fortune*: "To tell the truth, Nintendo just isn't cool anymore. This one is 16 bits, so it's better than the original Nintendo. But the company only made it to compete with Sega, and most kids already have that. So they don't need Super Nintendo, unless they're jerks and have to have everything. That's just idiotic."[e] Over time, sales of the Nintendo SNES accelerated, and it would ultimately prove to be one of the more successful game systems ever introduced, but Nintendo's near-monopoly position had been broken; Sega had successfully leapfrogged Nintendo.

32/64-Bit Systems

The late 1980s and early 1990s, new competitors were attracted to the video game market, with fifth generation machines that had either 32 or 64-bit systems. In 1989, Philips announced its 32-bit Compact Disc Interactive (CD-i), an interactive multimedia compact disc system that would serve as a game player, teaching tool, and music system. However, the CD-i was very complex, requiring a 30-minute demonstration. Furthermore, it was expensive—introduced at $799 and later reduced to a below-cost $500 (more than twice the cost of Nintendo or Sega systems).[f] While the product was actually much more than a video game console, customers compared it to the popular Nintendo and Sega systems and were dismayed by its price and complexity. Making matters worse, Philips was reluctant to disclose the technical specifications, greatly limiting the software development for the system. The Philips CD-i never attained more than a 2 percent market share.[g] Other companies also introduced 32-bit systems, including Turbo Technologies' Duo and 3DO's Interactive Multiplayer, but the cost of the systems ($600 to $700) was prohibitive. Turbo Tech's Duo was very short-lived and received little attention. But 3DO's system received considerable attention. The company was founded in October 1993 by Trip Hawkins, formerly of video games developer Electronic Arts. However, 3DO's unique strategy of licensing out all game and hardware production made it impossible to achieve the low console prices of Sega and Nintendo by subsidizing console production with game royalties. The hardware producers (Matsushita and Panasonic) for 3DO did not sell games and were unwilling to sell the consoles without a margin. Sales of the machine never took off, and 3DO exited the market. Atari also made a surprising return to the video game market in 1993 with the technologically advanced Jaguar. However, Atari's long struggle had not inspired great confidence in either developers or distributors, and several of the large retail chains chose not to carry the product.[h]

In 1995, two 32-bit systems arrived on the scene that would survive: Sega's Saturn and Sony's PlayStation. Both systems were introduced with great fanfare and considerable developer support. Although only Sega had experience and brand image in the video game market, Sony entered with tremendous brand image in consumer electronics and access to (and leverage in) extensive distribution channels in electronics and media. To rapidly gain insight into the toy industry, Sony hired experienced toy industry veteran Bruce Stein to head the video game unit. Sony's size and previous success in several electronics markets (including the development and control of the compact disc format) also enabled it to persuade several games developers (including Electronic Arts, the largest game developer in the United States at that time) to produce only PlayStation titles for the first six months after its introduction. There were 50 PlayStation titles by the end of 1995, and this number had grown to 800 by the end of 2000.

Though Sega's Saturn had beaten Sony's PlayStation to market by several months, it was shipped to only four retailers due to limited supply: Toys "R" Us, Babbage's, Software Etc., and Electronics Boutique. This aggravated retailers such as Best Buy and WalMart, which had long supported Sega.[i] Developers also felt that it was easier to program for the PlayStation than the Saturn, causing it to lose crucial developer support.[j] By the end of 1996, the installed base of Sony PlayStation in the United States (2.9 million units) was more than double that of the Sega Saturn (1.2 million units).

In 1996, after more than two years of announcements, Nintendo finally introduced its 64-bit game system called Nintendo 64. Though only two software titles were available at the console's release (one being Super Mario), the game units were sold out within weeks of their release. Though Nintendo's 64-bit system gained rapid consumer acceptance, neither Nintendo nor Sega was able to reclaim dominance over the video game industry. Though several new entrants (and one returning entrant, Atari) had tried to break into the video game industry through technological leapfrogging, only Sony had the successful combination of a product with a technological advantage, strategies, and resources that enabled it to rapidly build installed base and availability of complementary goods, and a reputation that signaled the market that this was a fight it could win.

128-Bit Systems

In September 1999, Sega launched the first sixth-generation console, its 128-bit Dreamcast, a $199 gaming system that enabled access to the Internet. Before the Dreamcast release, Sega was suffering from its lowest market share in years at 12 percent. The Dreamcast was the first 128-bit system to market, and 514,000 units were sold in the first two weeks. An installed base of 5 million was achieved by October 2000. Sega's success turned out to be short-lived, however. In March 2000, Sony launched its 128-bit PlayStation2 (PS2) in Japan and introduced the system to the United States in October. Despite price cuts on the Dreamcast and a promotion rebate that would make the console essentially free (in exchange for a two-year contract for Sega's SegaNet Internet service), the Dreamcast was crushed in the holiday sales season. In early 2001, Sega announced it would cease making consoles and transform itself into a third-party developer of games for other consoles.

Sony's PS2 was an unprecedented success. Not only did it offer a significant technological advantage over the 32-bit systems, but it was also backward compatible, enabling gamers to play their PlayStation games on the console until they amassed new game libraries.[k] During the opening sales weekend of March 4, 2000, PS2 sales reached about 1 million units, a figure that eclipsed by 10 times the amount of original PlayStation units sold during the three-day release period in 1994. Demand for the new unit was so high that on the opening day of pre-orders on Sony's Web site, more than 100,000 hits in one minute were received, and Sony was forced to briefly shut down the Web site.

At the time of the PS2 release, Nintendo had just postponed the launch of its new 128-bit system, the GameCube, to a release date in the first half of 2001. Unlike the PS2, the GameCube did not offer backward compatibility with Nintendo 64 games. The GameCube was also targeted toward a younger market (8- to 18-year-olds) than Sony's 16- to 24-year-old demographic. The real threat to Sony's PS2 came in the form of a new entrant to the video console industry: Microsoft's Xbox. The Xbox, launched in November 2001, was targeted at the 18- to 34-year-old male, positioning it directly against the PS2.

Microsoft had previously produced PC-based computer games (such as Flight Simulator and the Age of Empires series) and operated an online gaming service (Microsoft Gaming Zone) and thus had some familiarity with the industry. However, it did not have either the arcade experience of Sega or Nintendo or the consumer electronics experience of Sony. By the time the Xbox hit the market, PS2 already had a significant lead in installed base and availability of games (more than 300 PS2 game titles were available at the end of 2001), but Microsoft was counting on the technological advantages offered by the Xbox to tip consumer preferences. The Xbox offered a faster processor and more memory than the PS2. Furthermore, customers did not have to trade-off technological advantages against price: The Xbox launched at a retail price of $299, significantly less than its production costs (it is estimated that Microsoft lost between $100 and $125 per unit).[l]

To rapidly deploy the console and build installed base, Microsoft leveraged its existing relationships with distributors that carried its software, though it was now forced to seek much greater penetration into distributors such as Toys "R" Us, Babbages, and Circuit City. Microsoft also faced the challenge of cultivating a radically different brand image in the game console market than the one that it had achieved in the software market, and to make much greater use of marketing channels such as television advertising and gaming magazines. To that end, Microsoft budgeted $500 million to be spent over 18 months to market the Xbox—more than any other marketing campaign in the company's history.[m] Microsoft planned to produce 30 to 40 percent of its games in-house and gave away $10,000 game development kits to attract third-party games developers.

Both the Xbox and Nintendo's GameCube were launched just in time for the extremely important 2001 Christmas season and sold briskly. By the year's end, it was estimated that 1.3 million GameCube units had been sold, and 1.5 million Xbox units had been sold.[n] However, both of the new consoles were outrun by PS2, which sold 2 million units in the month of December alone. This market share pattern remained remarkably consistent over the next few years. By the end of fiscal year 2005, Microsoft reported it had shipped a total of 22 million Xbox consoles, which was slightly more than Nintendo's 20.6 million GameCube shipments, and far behind the Sony PS2's 100 million consoles shipped.[o]

The Seventh Generation: A Second Round of Competition in 128-bit Systems

In late 2005, Microsoft was first to introduce a seventh-generation console: Xbox 360. Though severe manufacturing shortages resulted in only 600,000 units being sold in the 2005 Christmas season, Microsoft was hoping its head start over Sony and Nintendo (both of which would not debut their next generation consoles until late 2006) would enable it to attain a dominant position.

The console was designed around a custom IBM processor that had three Power PC processors on a single chip, and a custom graphics processor from ATI. The result was a powerful console that generated high-definition video with stunning graphics. The Xbox 360 was also backward compatible with a portion of the Xbox game library (though not with all Xbox games). At launch, buyers could get a basic model for $299 or a premium model for $399.[p] More important (from Microsoft's perspective at least), the console was supposed to be for more than just games—it was Microsoft's next attempt to secure control over the digital living room. Users could download music, movies, TV shows, and purchase premium content. With an optional high-definition DVD drive users could also watch high-definition movies (or at least they could have if Microsoft's bet on Toshiba's HD-DVD standard had not gone awry—in early 2008, Toshiba conceded defeat to Sony in the high-definition DVD format war, and announced that it would stop making the drives). By early 2006, Microsoft had sold 3.2 million Xbox 360s. The number would have been higher but the company could not keep up with demand.[q]

Sony launched its Playstation3 (PS3) in November of 2006. The console had a powerful IBM cell processor; it included Sony's Blu-ray disc player (for playing high-definition DVDs) and launched with a hefty price tag of $599 for a 60-gigabyte model, or $499 for a 20-gigabyte model. Estimates put the cost of the components used to produce the consoles at $840 and $805, respectively, meaning that Sony lost more than $200 on every unit.[r] Sony claimed that the PS3 was backward compatible with all games written for the Playstation and PS2, but it turned out that not all of the older games would play on the new system. Though the console sold out within minutes of its launch, by early 2007, Sony had sold only 3.5 million PS3s worldwide—significantly less than it had forecasted.

Instead of joining Sony and Microsoft in a technological arms race, Nintendo changed the rules of the game with its Wii console in time for the Christmas season of 2006. Instead of a controller with buttons or a joystick that players had to vigorously manipulate, it offered an innovative wireless motion-sensing remote that enabled users to simulate real play, such as swinging a tennis racket in a tennis match or punching an opponent in a boxing match. The console was also launched at a price of $250—significantly cheaper than the Xbox 360 or PS3. It was fully compatible with Game Cube games, and because it was much cheaper to develop a Wii game (as little as $5 million compared to the $20 million for a PS3 game, for example), it attracted third-party developers in droves. The net result was dramatic—the console attracted casual gamers in unprecedented numbers, and from a remarkably wide range of demographics. Wiis were being used in nursing homes, for Wii bowling leagues, and on cruise ships.[5] Instead of simply being purchased by soccer moms for their children, they were being played by the soccer moms themselves. By mid-2007, the Wii was selling twice as fast as the Xbox 360 and four times as fast as the PS3. While Microsoft and Sony lost money on every console in hopes of profiting on future game sales, Nintendo was estimated to make $50 on every unit of the Wii sold.

In fall of 2008, Microsoft slashed the price of the Xbox 360 to $199, making it the cheapest console of the generation. However, even Don Mattrick, senior vice president of Microsoft's Interactive Entertainment Business admitted that the Xbox 360 was unlikely to overtake the Wii, noting: "I'm not at a point where I can say we're going to beat Nintendo . . . we will sell more consoles this generation than Sony."[t] Sony followed suit by lowering the price of its starter model to $399. The years 2009 and 2010 were worse for all of the console companies—the recession lead to a significant drop in sales and profits for all three companies and they responded by dropping the price of their consoles. However, the pattern of sales remained the same. By December of 2010, over 75 million, Wii's had been sold worldwide, compared to 45 million Xbox 360's, and 42 million PS3s.

In 2010, both Sony and Microsoft launched their own motion-based controllers. The Playstation Move was a handheld motion sensor wand, similar to the Wii Remote. Microsoft's Kinect, on the other hand, did not require holding anything—it was a webcam-style peripheral that detected user motion within a range of play in front of the device. Both devices were sold as add-on units to the companies' consoles and were priced at over $150 (nearly as much as the entire Wii console). However, despite the high price, by March 2011, Microsoft reported that it had sold more than ten million Kinect sensors worldwide, making it the fastest selling consumer device ever, according to the Guinness World Records Committee.

The Eighth Generation: Increasing Competition from Mobile Devices

The eighth generation saw the video game console makers focusing on further integration with other media and connectivity. In late 2012, Nintendo launched its Wii U, a tablet/controller hybrid with an embedded touch screen that would enable users to get a different perspective than the one on the main display. The Wii U was backward compatible with most Wii games, but the initial lineup of games written specifically for the device was weak at the consoles launch. Furthermore, because Nintendo had beaten Sony and Microsoft to market by a year, many customers decided to wait until they could compare all three consoles, leading to sluggish sales for the Wii U.

Sony launched its Playstation4 (PS4) in November of 2013, a device which would emphasize connectivity with other devices (such as the PlayStation Vita or Apple iOS or Android powered mobile devices), social game play, and cloud-based subscription gaming. The device launched at a price of $399, signaling that Sony had learned a painful-but-important lesson with PS3. Microsoft released its Xbox One the same month, billing the device as an "all-in-one entertainment system." Like the PS4, the device enabled game streaming from the cloud and included a Blu-Ray player. However, it also gave users the ability to connect to their television set-top box and overlay live television with gaming in a split-screen and to record and share highlights of game play. The console was launched at a price of $499.

The eight generation also brought increasing competition from new players. Mobile device platforms such as Android and Apple's iOS were beginning to account for significantly more gaming. Though the devices were small and the games lacked the high fidelity and motion-based play offered by the home consoles, they made up for it—at least in part—by a rapid proliferation of free or low-cost games (Angry Birds had over 3 billion downloads worldwide by mid-2015), and the fact that their owners tended to have them available at all times. Despite the increasing pressure, sales of the home video game consoles were reasonably strong. By early 2015, Sony had sold 22.3 million PS4s, Microsoft had sold 10 million Xbox Ones, and Nintendo had sold 9.54 million Wii Us.[u]

Discussion Questions

1. What factors do you think enabled Sega to break Nintendo's near monopoly of the U.S. video game console market in the late 1980s?

2. Why did Nintendo choose not to make its early video game consoles backward compatible? What were the advantages and disadvantages of this strategy?

3. What strengths and weaknesses did Sony have when it entered the video game market in 1995? What strengths and weaknesses did Microsoft have when it entered the video game market in 2001?

4. In what ways did Nintendo's Wii break with the norms of competition in the video game industry? How defensible was its position?

5. Comparing the deployment strategies used by the firms in each of the generations, can you identify any timing, licensing, pricing, marketing, or distribution strategies that appear to have influenced firms' success and failure in the video game industry?

[a] Adapted from M. A. Schilling, "Technological leapfrogging: Lessons from the U.S. videogame industry," *California Management Review* 45, no. 3 (2003), pp. 6–32.

[b] D. Sheff, *Game Over: How Nintendo Zapped an American Industry, Captured Your Dollars and Enslaved Your Children* (New York: Random House, 1993).

[c] A. Brandenberger, "Power Play (A): Nintendo in 8-Bit Video Games," Harvard Business School case no. 9-795-167, 1995.

[d] A. Brandenberger, "Power Play (B): Sega in 16-Bit Video Games," Harvard Business School case no. 9-795-103, 1995.

[e] J. Hadju, "Rating the hot boxes," *Fortune* 128, no. 16 (1993), pp. 112–13.

f N. Turner, "For Giants of Video Games It's an All-New Competition," *Investor's Business Daily*, January 24, 1996, p. A6.

g J. Trachtenberg, "Short Circuit: How Philips Flubbed Its U.S. Introduction of Electronic Product," *Wall Street Journal*, June 28, 1996, p. A1.

h Y. D. Sinakin, "Players Take Bold Step to Keep Up with New Rules," *Electronic Buyers' News*, February 19, 1996, p. 50.

i P. Hisey, "Saturn lands first at toys 'R' Us," *Discount Store News* 34, no. 11 (1995), pp. 6–8.

j T. Lefton, "Looking for a sonic boom," *Brandweek* 39, no. 9 (1998), pp. 26–30.

k M. A. Schilling, R. Chiu, and C. Chou, "Sony PlayStation2: Just Another Competitor?" in *Strategic Management: Competitiveness and Globalization*, 5th ed., eds. M. Hitt, D. Ireland, and B. Hoskisson (St. Paul, MN: West Publishing, 2003).

l D. Becker and J. Wilcox, "Will Xbox Drain Microsoft?" *CNET News.com*, March 6, 2001; L. P. Norton, "Toy Soldiers," *Barrons* 81, no. 20 (2001), pp. 25–30; and S. H. Wildstrom, "It's All about the Games," *BusinessWeek* 37, no. 63 (2001), p. 22.

m T. Elkin, "Gearing up for Xbox launch," *Advertising Age* 71, no. 48 (2000), p. 16.

n D. Frankel, "Video game business Boffo on big launches," *Video Business*, December 31, 2001, p. 38.

o Microsoft 2005 Annual Report; Nintendo 2005 Annual Report; Sony Corporation press release, November 30, 2005.

p S. H. Wildstrom, "Xbox: A Winner Only at Games" *BusinessWeek Online*, December 1, 2005.

q K. Terrell, "Gamers Push Pause," *U.S. News & World Report* 140, no. 18 (2006), pp. 42–43.

r A. Hesseldahl, "Teardown of Sony's Playstation 3," *BusinessWeek Online*, December 24, 2008, p. 10.

s J. M. O'Brien, "Wii will rock you," *Fortune* 155, no. 11 (2007), pp. 82–92.

t J. Greene, "Microsoft will cut Xbox prices in the U.S.," *BusinessWeek Online*, September 4, 2008, p. 2.

u Sony. "Consolidated Financial Results for the Fiscal Year Ended March 31, 2015" www.Sony.com, Retrieved April 30, 2015.

OVERVIEW

The value of any technological innovation is only partly determined by what the technology can *do*. A large part of the value of an innovation is determined by the degree to which people can understand it, access it, and integrate it within their lives. Deployment is not just a way for the firm to earn revenues from its innovations; deployment is a core part of the innovation process itself.

Deployment strategies can influence the receptivity of customers, distributors, and complementary goods providers. Effective deployment strategies can reduce uncertainty about the product, lower resistance to switching from competing or substitute goods, and accelerate adoption. Ineffective deployment strategies can cause even brilliant technological innovations to fail. As shown in the opening vignette, 3DO's Interactive Multiplayer and Philips' Compact Disk Interactive were two of the first 32-bit video game systems introduced to the market and offered significant technological advantages over previous generations of consoles. However, both were priced so high and introduced with so few games that neither was able to attract a significant share of the market. When Sega introduced its 32-bit system to the market—beating Sony's PlayStation by several months—the price was low and some popular games were available, but weak distribution ultimately hobbled the console's deployment. On the other hand, despite being a newcomer to the video game industry, Sony's exceptionally executed deployment strategies for the PlayStation made the console a nearly overnight success. Sony used a combination of intense marketing, low prices, strong games availability, and aggressive distribution to ensure that the product launched with unmistakable impact.

We will cover five key elements of the deployment process in this chapter: launch timing, licensing and compatibility, pricing, distribution, and marketing. Several of these topics warrant entire courses and textbooks in their own right; only an introduction to the issues most central to the deployment of a new technological innovation will be covered here.

LAUNCH TIMING

As illustrated by the video game industry, the timing of the product launch can be a significant part of a company's deployment strategy. For example, even though Nintendo had a 16-bit video game system in development when Sega's 16-bit Genesis was introduced, Nintendo delayed introducing a 16-bit system for fear of cannibalizing its 8-bit system sales. The advantages and disadvantages of being a first, early-but-not-first, or late mover were discussed in Chapter Five; the focus here is on how a firm can use timing as a deployment strategy.

Strategic Launch Timing

Generally, firms try to decrease their development cycles in order to decrease their costs and to increase their timing of entry options, but this does not imply that firms should always be racing to launch their products as early as possible. A firm can strategically use launch timing to take advantage of business cycle or seasonal effects, to position its product with respect to previous generations of related technologies, and to ensure that production capacity and complementary goods or services are in place. The role of each of these tactics is illustrated in the video game industry.

Nintendo, Sony, and Microsoft all took advantage of seasonal effects by introducing their consoles shortly before Christmas so that the hype of the consoles' launch would coincide with the Christmas buying season. The majority of video game consoles are sold in December. By launching their consoles close to December, firms could target their advertising for this time and leverage the free publicity that surrounded a console's launch such as press releases announcing the introduction and external product reviews.

Because the video game industry is characterized by distinct generations of technology, the timing of a console's launch also plays a key role in its positioning within a technological generation and with respect to competing consoles. If a console is introduced too early, it may receive a tepid welcome because customers want to wait to compare the consoles with others that will compete in the generation. Furthermore, by launching well ahead of competitors, a console maker may forfeit the opportunity to incorporate more advanced technology or may create customer confusion about which generation the product belongs to. For example, though the Xbox offered a processor that was double the speed of the PS2, its introductory timing positioned it as being in the same generation as the PS2. Many customers saw it as a competitor to a product they already had, rather than as a next generation technology. For example, though the Xbox offered a processor that was double the speed of the PS2, its introductory timing positioned it as being in the same generation as the PS2. Many customers saw it as a competitor to a product they already had, rather than as a next generation technology. If the console is introduced too late, the company can lose its image as a technological leader and may have already conceded a considerable installed base lead to earlier entrants. This is aptly illustrated in the quote about Nintendo's late introduction of the SNES in the opening vignette: "To tell the truth, Nintendo just isn't cool anymore. This one is 16 bits, so it's better than the original Nintendo. But the company only made it to compete with Sega, and most kids already have that. So they don't need Super Nintendo . . . ."

Finally, timing the introduction of a console to coincide with production capacity and games availability has proven very important in the video game console industry. For example, in Sega's rush to ensure that the Saturn beat Sony's PlayStation to market, it introduced the product before it had built adequate production capacity. Sega was subsequently unable to stock many important distributors, and it alienated companies that had supported Sega in previous generations. Similarly, the importance of having games available at the time of launch is also clearly demonstrated: Every video game console producer that has been successful in at least one generation (e.g., Atari, Nintendo, Sega, Sony, Microsoft) has ensured that games would be available at the console's launch, even if that meant buying games development companies to force them to produce compatible games! Games availability was also encouraged through licensing strategies, as discussed later in the chapter.

Optimizing Cash Flow versus Embracing Cannibalization

cannibalization
When a firm's sales of one product (or at one location) diminish its sales of another of its products (or at another of its locations).

A second key point about timing of entry is also illustrated in the video game industry. For firms introducing a next generation technology into a market in which they already compete, entry timing can become a decision about whether and to what degree to embrace **cannibalization**. Traditionally, research on product life cycles has emphasized the importance of timing new product introduction so as to optimize cash flows or profits from each generation and minimize cannibalization. If a firm's current product is very profitable, the firm will often delay introduction of a next generation product until profits have begun to significantly decrease for the current product. This strategy is intended to maximize the firm's return on investment in developing each generation of the product. However, in industries driven by technological innovation, delaying the introduction of a next generation product can enable competitors to achieve a significant technological gap. If competitors introduce products that have a large technological advantage over the firm's current products, customers might begin abandoning the firm's technology.

Instead, if the firm invests in continuous innovation and willingly cannibalizes its existing products with more advanced products, the firm can make it very difficult for other firms to achieve a technological lead large enough to prove persuasive to customers. By providing incentives for existing customers to upgrade to its newest models, the firm can further remove any incentive customers have to switch to another company's products when they purchase next generation technology. Many would argue that this is where Nintendo made a key mistake. In the late 1980s, Nintendo was deriving significant profits from its 8-bit system and thus was reluctant to cannibalize those sales with a 16-bit system. However, by not embracing cannibalization, Nintendo enabled Sega to steal customers away by offering a product with a significant technological advantage.

LICENSING AND COMPATIBILITY

Chapter Nine revealed how making a technology more open (i.e., not protecting it vigorously or partially opening the technology through licensing) could speed its adoption by enabling more producers to improve and promote the technology and allowing complementary goods developers to more easily support the technology. However, the chapter also pointed out that making a technology completely open poses several risks. First, if a firm completely opens its technology, other producers may drive the price of the technology down to a point at which the firm is unable to recoup its development expense. If competition drives the price down so no producer earns significant margins on the technology, no producer will have much incentive to further develop the technology. Finally, opening a technology completely may cause its underlying platform to become fragmented as different producers alter it to their needs, resulting in loss of compatibility across producers and the possible erosion of product quality.

Each of these effects was demonstrated in the opening vignette. By not protecting their technologies enough, video game console producers in the first generation relinquished their ability to control game production quantity and quality. The resulting market glut of poor-quality games decimated the video game industry. But Nintendo's highly restrictive licensing policies for its 8-bit system made games developers eager to give their support to the first rival that appeared viable. In the 16-bit, 32/64-bit, and 128-bit generations, the console makers sought to achieve a delicate balance of making licensing open enough to attract developer support while making licensing strict enough to control game quantities and quality.

In deploying a technological innovation, often a firm must decide how compatible (or incompatible) to make its technology with that provided by others or with previous generations of its own technology. If there is an existing technology with a large installed base or availability of complementary goods, the firm can sometimes leverage the value of that installed base and complementary goods by making its technology compatible with current products. For instance, producers of IBM-compatible computers (as detailed in Chapter Nine) were able to tap IBM's installed base and complementary goods advantages by offering computers that operated identically to those made by IBM. Users of IBM compatibles reaped the same installed base advantages and had access to all the same software as they would have with an IBM computer.

backward compatible
When products of a technological generation can work with products of a previous generation. For example, a computer is backward compatible if it can run the same software as a previous generation of the computer.

If the firm wishes to avoid giving away its own installed base or complementary goods advantages to others, it may protect them by ensuring its products are incompatible with those of future entrants. Most competitors in the U.S. video game industry (with the exception of Atari) have been fairly successful at this strategy. Nintendo, for example, uses a security chip to ensure that only licensed Nintendo games may be played in its consoles, and only Nintendo consoles may be used to play Nintendo games.

Firms must also decide whether or not to make their products **backward compatible** with their own previous generations of technology. Nintendo repeatedly opted not to make its consoles backward compatible, believing it would be more profitable to require customers to purchase new games. This is understandable given that the consoles were sold at cost and profits were made through game sales; however, it also meant that Nintendo forfeited a significant potential source of advantage over Sega. In contrast, Sega made its 16-bit Genesis compatible with its 8-bit Master System games—though this may not have proven terribly persuasive to customers given the limited success of the Master System. More significantly, Sony made its PS2 console backward compatible with PlayStation games, thereby not only ensuring a tremendous existing library of compatible games at its launch but also providing a significant incentive to PlayStation owners who were considering upgrading to a 128-bit system to choose the PS2 as opposed to Sega's Dreamcast, or waiting for the Xbox or GameCube.

Some firms use a particularly powerful strategy that combines continuous innovation with backward compatibility. A firm that both innovates to prevent a competitor from creating a technological gap and utilizes backward compatibility so that its new platform or models are compatible with previous generations of complementary goods can leverage the existing value yielded by a large range of complementary goods to its new platforms. While such a strategy may cause the firm to forfeit some sales of complementary goods for the new platform (at least initially), it can also effectively link the generations through time and can successfully transition customers through product generations while preventing competitors from having a window to enter the market. Microsoft has utilized this strategy deftly with Windows—though the operating system is regularly updated, each successive generation provides backward compatibility with most of the major software applications developed for previous generations. Thus, customers can upgrade without having to replace their entire libraries of software applications.

PRICING

Pricing is a crucial element in the firm's deployment strategy. Price simultaneously influences the product's positioning in the marketplace, its rate of adoption, and the firm's cash flow. Before a firm can determine its pricing strategy, it must determine the objectives it has for its pricing model. For example, if a firm is in an industry plagued with overcapacity or intense price competition, the firm's objective may be simply *survival*. A survival price strategy prices goods to cover variable costs and some fixed costs. It is a short-run strategy, however; in the long run, the firm will want to find a way to create additional value. One common pricing objective is to *maximize current profits*. Under this pricing strategy, the firm first estimates costs and demand and then sets the price to maximize cash flow or rate of return on investment. This strategy emphasizes current performance, but may sacrifice long-term performance.

For new technological innovations, firms often emphasize either a *maximum market skimming* objective or a *maximum market share* objective. To skim the market, firms will initially set prices high on new products. The high price may signal the market that the new product is a significant innovation that offers a substantial performance improvement over previously available products. The high price can also help the firm recoup initial development expenses, assuming there is also high initial demand. However, high initial prices may also attract competitors to the market and can slow adoption of the product. If costs are expected to decline rapidly with the volume of units produced, a skimming strategy can actually prove less profitable than a pricing strategy that stimulates more rapid customer adoption.

When achieving high volume is important, firms will often emphasize a maximum market share objective. To maximize market share, firms often use **penetration pricing**.

penetration pricing
When the price of a good is set very low (or free) to maximize the good's market share.

The firm will set the lowest price possible hoping to rapidly attract customers, driving volume up and production costs down. Effective utilization of penetration pricing often requires that the firm builds large production capacity in advance of demand. In the short run, the firm may bear significant risk from this capital investment, and it may lose money on each unit if the price is less than its initial variable costs. However, if its volume increases and drives its production costs down, the firm can achieve a very powerful position: It can have a low-cost position that enables it to earn profits despite a low price, and it can have a substantial share of the market.

Firms in industries characterized by increasing returns (strong learning-curve effects and/or network externalities) will often use the objective of maximizing market share and a penetration pricing strategy. In such industries, there is strong pressure for the industry to adopt a single dominant design (as discussed in Chapter Four). It is in the firm's best interest to accelerate adoption of its technology, building its installed base, attracting developers of complementary goods, and riding down the learning curve for its production costs.

For example, Honda's first hybrid electric vehicle, the Insight, was introduced at a price ($20,000) that actually caused Honda to lose money on each Insight it sold. However, Honda believed the hybrid technology would become profitable in the long term, and that the experience it would gain by working with hybrid technology and the continuance of its "green" car company image were strong enough motivations to sell the Insight at a loss for the first few years.[1]

Sometimes firms price below cost because the losses are expected to be recouped through profits on complementary goods or services. In the video game industry, this has proven to be a very important strategy. Nintendo, Sega, Sony, and Microsoft have each sold their video game consoles at a price very close to (or below) production costs while profiting from subsequent game sales and licensing royalties. Similarly, when Microsoft launched its Internet Explorer Web browser, it gave the product away so it could quickly catch up to Netscape's Web browser, which had been introduced to the market almost a year earlier. Though consumers paid nothing for the Internet Explorer browser, Microsoft earned profits selling other compatible software products to businesses.

Firms can also influence cash flow and the customers' perception of costs through manipulating the timing of when the price of a good is paid. For instance, while the most typical pricing model requires the customer to pay the full price before taking ownership, other pricing models enable the customer to delay paying the purchase price by offering a free trial for a fixed time. This permits the customer to become familiar with the benefits of the product before paying the price, and it can be very useful when customers face great uncertainty about a new product or service. Another pricing model enables customers to pay as they go, such as through leasing programs, or a pricing model whereby the initial product is free (or available at a low price) but the customer pays for service. For example, when cable television subscribers order cable service, they typically pay little or no fee for the equipment and instead pay a significant amount (often between $20 and $90 depending on the package) for monthly service that may include some portion for the equipment expense. Another example is the **"freemium"** model, where the base product is free, but additional features or capacity have a price. For example, when Drew Houston and Arash Ferdowsi founded Dropbox, a popular cloud storage and file synchronization service, they quickly realized they

freemium
A pricing model where a base product or service is offered for free, but a premium is charged for additional features or service.

could not afford to use advertising programs such as Google's AdWords to promote the service—it was simply too expensive. They thus combined a freemium model with a very successful referral program. First, users could get an initial storage allotment for free (two gigabytes in 2012), but would have to pay to get additional storage. Since users' reliance upon the service and storage needs both tend to increase over time, ultimately they often end up paying for additional capacity. By mid-2015, Dropbox had over 400 million registered users, the vast majority of which were using free accounts.[2]

When it is unclear how customers will respond to a particular price point, firms often use introductory pricing that indicates the pricing is for a stipulated time. This allows the company to test the market's response to a product without committing to a long-term pricing structure.

DISTRIBUTION

Selling Direct versus Using Intermediaries

manufacturers' representatives
Independent agents that promote and sell the product lines of one or a few manufacturers. They are often used when direct selling is appropriate but the manufacturer does not have a sufficiently large direct sales force to reach all appropriate market segments.

wholesalers
Companies that buy manufacturer's products in bulk, and then resell them (often in smaller or more diverse bundles) to other supply channel members such as retailers.

retailers
Companies that sell goods to the public.

Firms can sell their products directly to users through their direct sales force or an online ordering system or mail-order catalog. Alternatively, firms can use intermediaries such as **manufacturers' representatives**, **wholesalers**, and **retailers**. Selling direct gives the firm more control over the selling process, pricing, and service. For example, when Tesla Motors launched its Model S electric vehicle, its managers suspected that the dealer networks used by other automakers were not the best distribution method: electric vehicles require more explanation to consumers about estimating fuel savings, how often and where they will charge their automobiles, battery life and resale value, etc. Salespeople at dealerships would require extensive training, and additional incentives to motivate them to invest that amount of time in customer education. Management at Tesla Motors thus decided to utilize a direct-to-customer model whereby it operates its own boutique stores in high-traffic urban locations. In many situations, however, selling direct can be impractical or overly expensive. Intermediaries provide a number of important services that can make distribution more efficient. First, wholesalers and retailers *break bulk*. In general, manufacturers prefer to sell large quantities of a limited number of items, while customers prefer to buy limited quantities of a large number of items. Wholesalers and retailers can pool large orders from a large number of manufacturers and sell a wider range of goods in small quantities to customers.

For example, a typical book publisher produces a limited range of book titles, but desires to sell them in high volume. The average final consumer may wish to purchase only one copy of a particular book title, but often wants a wide range of book titles to choose from. Both wholesalers and retailers provide valuable bulk-breaking services in this channel. A wholesaler such as Ingram will purchase pallets of books from many different publishers such as McGraw-Hill, Simon & Schuster, and Prentice Hall. It then breaks apart the pallets and reassembles bundles of books that include titles from multiple publishers but have fewer copies of any particular book title. These bundles are then sold to retailers such as Barnes & Noble, which offers a wide range of titles sold on an individual basis. Though publishers could sell directly to final consumers using the Internet or a mail-order catalog, customers would have to examine the offerings of many different publishers to be able to consider the same range of books offered by a retailer.

Intermediaries also provide a number of other services such as transporting goods, carrying inventory, providing selling services, and handling transactions with customers. Many intermediaries also offer greater convenience for customers by offering geographically dispersed retail sites. Location convenience can be particularly important if customers are geographically dispersed and they are likely to want to examine or try different product options or to need on-site service. By contrast, if the product is primarily sold to a few industrial customers or if the product can be routinely ordered without close examination, trial, or service, geographic dispersion may be less important.

original equipment manufacturer (or value-added reseller)
A company that buys products (or components of products) from other manufacturers and assembles them or customizes them into a product that is then sold under the OEM's own name.

Original equipment manufacturers (OEMs) (also called **value-added resellers**, or VARs) provide an even more crucial role in the distribution process. An OEM buys products (or components of products) from other manufacturers and assembles them into a product that is customized to meet user needs. The OEM then sells this customized product under its own name and often provides marketing and service support for the product. OEMs are very common in the computer and electronics industries where manufacturers are often specialized in the production of individual components but users prefer to purchase whole, assembled products. Dell Computer, for example, is a very successful OEM in the computer industry. OEMs can provide a very valuable coordinating function in an industry by aggregating components and providing a single contact point for the customer.

disintermediation
When the number of intermediaries in a supply channel is reduced; for example, when manufacturers bypass wholesalers and/or retailers to sell directly to end users.

In some industries, advances in information technology (such as the Internet) have enabled **disintermediation** or a reconfiguration in the types of intermediaries used. For example, online investing services such as E-trade or Ameritrade caused some disintermediation in the investment market by enabling customers to bypass brokers and place their own stock or bond orders online. In industries where the product is information that can be conveyed digitally, such as newspapers, software, and music, the Internet can deliver the product from the manufacturer straight to the consumer. In most industries, however, information technology has simply shifted the roles of intermediaries or expanded the services they provide. For example, online stores such as Dell.com or Amazon.com enable customers to bypass traditional retail outlets such as computer stores or bookstores. However, in most cases this has not shortened the supply chain by which goods are delivered to customers—it has just rerouted it. In other instances, moving commerce online has required creating additional intermediaries (such as companies specialized in delivering the goods of others) or enhanced the services that intermediaries provide. For example, while grocers traditionally required customers to provide their own distribution for "the last mile" (the distance between the store and the customer's home), online grocery shopping shifts the responsibility of moving goods "the last mile" to the stores, requiring them either to develop their own delivery services or to purchase delivery services from other providers. Barnes & Noble uses online sales to complement its bricks-and-mortar retail outlets: Customers can come into the stores to see and physically handle books (an option many book shoppers express a strong preference for), but they can also order books online—from home or from within a Barnes & Noble store—if they are looking for a book that is not stocked at a convenient location.

To determine whether to use intermediaries and what type of intermediaries would be appropriate, the firm should answer the following questions:

1. *How does the new product fit with the distribution requirements of the firm's existing product lines?* Whether the firm already has an existing sales channel that would suit the product will be a primary consideration in how the product should be distributed. For example, if the firm already has a large direct sales force and the new product would fit well with this direct sales system, there may be no need to consider other distribution options. On the other hand, if the firm does not have an existing direct sales force, it will have to determine whether the new product warrants the cost and time of building a direct sales force.

2. *How numerous and dispersed are customers, and how much product education or service will customers require? Is prepurchase trial necessary or desirable? Is installation or customization required?* If customers are dispersed but require little product education or service, mail order or online ordering may suffice. On the other hand, if customers are dispersed and require moderate amounts of education, service, or prepurchase trial, using intermediaries is often a good option because they can provide some on-site education and service and/or trial. If customers are not dispersed, or will require *extensive* education and service, it may be necessary for the firm to provide the education and service directly. Furthermore, if the product will require installation or customization, the firm will often need to employ either a direct sales force or an intermediary capable of providing extensive service.

3. *How are competing products or substitutes sold?* The firm must consider how competing or substitute products are sold, because this both determines the nature of the existing distribution channel options and shapes customer expectations about how products will be purchased. For example, if customers are used to purchasing the product in a retail environment where the product can be viewed and handled and where customers can receive personal sales assistance, they may be reluctant to switch to a sales channel with less contact, such as online purchasing or mail order. How the product is sold may also affect the product's positioning from the perspective of the customer. For example, if competing products are primarily sold in a high-contact mode such as specialty stores or via a direct sales force, selling the new product in a lower-contact channel such as mass discounters or through mail order might cause the customer to perceive the product as being of lower quality or more economical. Market research can assess how the sales channel influences the customer's perception of the product.

Strategies for Accelerating Distribution

When the industry is likely to select a single technology as the dominant design, it can be very important to deploy the technology rapidly. Rapid deployment enables the technology to build a large installed base and encourages the developers of complementary goods to support the technology platform. As the technology is adopted, producer and user experience can be used to improve the technology, and producer costs should also decrease due to learning effects and economies of scale. The firm can use a variety of strategies to accelerate distribution, such as forging alliances with distributors, creating bundling relationships, sponsoring or contracting with large customer groups, and providing sales guarantees.[3]

Alliances with Distributors

Firms introducing a technological innovation can use strategic alliances or exclusivity contracts to encourage distributors to carry and promote their goods. By providing a distributor a stake in the success of the new technology, the firm may be able to persuade the distributor to carry and promote the new technology aggressively. Firms that already have relationships with distributors for other goods are at an advantage in pursuing this strategy; firms without such relationships may need to cultivate them, or even consider forward vertical integration to ensure that their product is widely available.

Lack of distribution may have contributed significantly to the failure of the Sega Saturn to gain installed base. Sega had very limited distribution for its Saturn launch, which may have slowed the building of its installed base both directly (because customers had limited access to the product) and indirectly (because distributors that were initially denied product may have been reluctant to promote the product after the limitations were lifted). Nintendo, by contrast, had unlimited distribution for its Nintendo 64 launch, and Sony not only had unlimited distribution, but also had extensive experience negotiating with retailing giants such as WalMart for its consumer electronics products. Consequently, Sony PlayStation had better distribution on its first day of business than the Sega Saturn, despite Sega's decade of experience in the market.[4]

Bundling Relationships

Firms can also accelerate distribution of a new technology by bundling it with another product that is already in wide use.[5] Bundling enables the new technology to piggyback on the success of another product that already has a large installed base. Once customers acquire the new product in tandem with something else that they already use, switching costs may prevent customers from changing to a different product, even if the different product might have initially been preferred. As customers become familiar with the product, their ties to the technology (for instance, through the cost of training) increase and their likelihood of choosing this technology in future purchase decisions may also increase. Bundling arrangements have proven to be a very successful way for firms to build their installed base and ensure provision of complementary goods. Consider, for example, Conner Peripherals (whose disk drives were bundled with Compaq's personal computers), Microsoft's MS-DOS (whose initial bundling with IBM led to bundling arrangements with almost all PC clone makers and also facilitated the later bundling of Windows with PCs), and Microsoft's Internet Explorer (which gained a larger installed base through a bundling arrangement with America Online, one of the largest Internet providers in the United States).

Contracts and Sponsorship

Firms can also set up contractual arrangements with distributors, complementary goods providers, and even large end users (such as universities or government agencies) to ensure that the technology is used in exchange for price discounts, special service contracts, advertising assistance, or other inducements. For example, when medical equipment manufacturers introduce significantly new medical devices such as new ultrasound equipment or magnetic resonance imaging machines, they will often donate or lend a number of these machines to large teaching hospitals. As the new equipment's benefits become clear to the doctors and hospital administration, their likelihood of purchasing additional machines increases. Because large teaching hospitals train medical staff that may ultimately work for other hospitals and are often influential leaders in the medical community, providing these hospitals with free equipment can be an effective way of encouraging the rest of the medical community to adopt the product.

Guarantees and Consignment

If there is considerable market uncertainty about the new product or service, the firm can encourage distributors to carry the product by offering them guarantees (such as promising to take back unsold stock) or agreeing to sell the product on consignment. For example, when Nintendo introduced the Nintendo Entertainment System to the U.S. market, distributors were reluctant to carry the console or games because many had been stuck with worthless inventory after the crash of the video game market in the mid-1980s. Nintendo agreed to sell the Nintendo Entertainment System to distributors on consignment: Nintendo would be paid only for consoles that were sold, rather than requiring distributors to buy consoles up front. Retailers bore little risk in distributing the good because unsold units could be returned to Nintendo, and the video game industry was reborn.

A similar argument can be made for offering guarantees to complementary goods producers. If complementary goods producers are reluctant to support the technology, the firm can guarantee particular quantities of complementary goods will be purchased, or it can provide the capital for production, thus bearing the bulk of the risk of producing complementary goods for the technology. The complementary goods producer may still have forfeited time or effort in producing goods that may not have a long-term market, but its direct costs will be less at risk.

MARKETING

The marketing strategy for a technological innovation must consider both the nature of the target market and the nature of the innovation. For example, is the target market composed primarily of large industrial users or individual consumers? Is the innovation likely to appeal only to technophiles or to the mass market? Are the benefits of the technology readily apparent, or will they require considerable customer education? Will customers respond more to detailed technical content or eye-catching brand images? Can the marketer alleviate customer uncertainty about the innovation? Major marketing methods are briefly reviewed next, along with how marketing can be tailored to particular adopter categories. Also explored is how marketing can shape perceptions and expectations about the innovation's installed base and availability of complementary goods.

Major Marketing Methods

The three most commonly used marketing methods include advertising, promotions, and publicity/public relations.

Advertising

Many firms use advertising to build public awareness of their technological innovation. Doing so requires that the firm craft an effective advertising message and choose advertising media that can convey this message to the appropriate target market.

In crafting an advertising message, firms often attempt to strike a balance between achieving an entertaining and memorable message versus providing a significant quantity of informative content. Too much focus on one or the other can result in advertisements that are memorable but convey little about the product, or advertisements that are informative but quickly lose the audience's attention. Many firms hire an advertising agency to develop and test an advertising message.

The media used are generally chosen based on their match to the target audience, the richness of information or sensory detail they can convey, their reach (the number of people exposed), and their cost per exposure. Some of the advantages and disadvantages of various advertising media are provided in Figure 13.1.

Promotions

Firms can also use promotions at the distributor or customer level to stimulate purchase or trial. Promotions are usually temporary selling tactics that might include:

- Offering samples or free trial.
- Offering cash rebates after purchase.
- Including an additional product (a "premium") with purchase.
- Offering incentives for repeat purchase.
- Offering sales bonuses to distributor or retailer sales representatives.
- Using cross-promotions between two or more noncompeting products to increase pulling power.
- Using point-of-purchase displays to demonstrate the product's features.

Publicity and Public Relations

Many firms use free publicity (such as articles that appear in a newspaper or magazine about the company or its product) to effectively generate word of mouth. For example, Pfizer's drug Viagra got an enormous amount of free exposure from unofficial celebrity endorsements and humorous coverage on TV shows such as *The Tonight Show* and *Late Show with David Letterman*. Other firms rely on internally generated publications (e.g., annual reports, press releases, articles written by employees for trade magazines or other media) to reach and influence target markets. **Viral marketing** is an attempt to capitalize on the social networks of individuals to stimulate word-of-mouth advertising. Information is sent directly to a set of targeted consumers (a process called "seeding") that are well-positioned in their social networks in some way (e.g., they may be "hubs" in that they have many more friends than others, or may have high potential for opinion leadership). The objective is to spark rapid spreading of the information through social networks, akin to a viral epidemic. Such strategies leverage the fact that people may be more receptive to, or have greater faith in, information that comes through personal contacts.[6] Firms may also sponsor special events (e.g., sporting events, competitions, conferences), contribute to good causes (e.g., charities), exhibit at trade associations, or encourage online consumer reviews to generate public awareness and goodwill.[7] Farmos even involved potential customers in the testing process of its drug Domosedan to generate awareness, as described in the accompanying Theory in Action.

viral marketing
Sending information directly to targeted individuals in effort to stimulate word-of-mouth advertising. Individuals are typically chosen on the basis of their position or role in particular social networks.

FIGURE 13.1
Advantages and Disadvantages of Major Advertising Media

Media	Advantages	Disadvantages
Online Advertising: Pay-per-click (search engines)	Can be highly targeted to a particular audience; pay only for results (clicks); fast to deploy—can gain immediate visibility, and can be adjusted or deleted just as quickly; enables rapid and efficient tracking of responses for analyzing effectiveness of the ad	Vulnerable to click-through fraud (e.g., clicks by a competitor or an unhappy customer or employee), which could result in wasted advertising spend
Online Advertising: Social Media	Can connect with customers in a rich way; potential for broad reach and viral marketing; can be highly targeted to a particular audience; relatively inexpensive; can be quickly deployed and adjusted; can track visitors in real-time	Conversion of visitors to customers is often low; can be difficult to build awareness and traffic to social media site
Television	High sensory richness that combines sight, sound, and motion; high geographic and demographic reach; independent stations offer new opportunities to more directly target-specific audiences	Increasingly fragmented audience due to proliferation of stations; increasing use of DVR's enables viewers to skip the advertising; high absolute cost; fleeting exposure
Radio	High geographic and demographic selectivity; medium reach; relatively low cost	Audio presentation only; advertisers may need to buy ads with multiple stations to achieve desired audience reach; fleeting exposure
Newspaper	Timeliness; good local market coverage; broad acceptance; high believability; audience can keep or revisit the advertisement; wide price ranges available	Newspaper audiences are decreasing; easy for audience to skip over ad; relatively poor production quality; high advertising clutter; may be difficult to selectively target a particular audience
Magazine	High geographic and demographic selectivity; high quality visual production; long life; can enable significant technical content; good pass-along readership	Slow deployment (long ad purchase lead times); some waste circulation; may require advertising in multiple magazines to achieve desired reach
Direct Mail	High audience selectivity; no ad competition within the same medium; personalization; enables communication of significant technical content; may be passed along to others; responses can usually be efficiently tracked	Relatively high cost; "junk mail" image; requires access to good mailing lists; requires relatively long lead times for printing and mailing
Outdoor (e.g., billboards, banners)	High repeat exposure; low cost; low competition	Limited audience selectivity; very limited technical content
Telephone	High audience selectivity; can give personalized message	Relatively high cost; can be perceived as an annoyance

Tailoring the Marketing Plan to Intended Adopters

As described in Chapter Three, innovations tend to diffuse through the population in an s-shape pattern whereby adoption is initially slow because the technology is unfamiliar; it then accelerates as the technology becomes better understood and utilized by the mass market, and eventually the market is saturated so the rate of new

When the Finnish company Farmos Group Limited introduced its veterinary drug Domosedan, executives knew that building awareness of the drug among known opinion leaders would be crucial. Domosedan represented a disruptive innovation in painkillers for horses and cattle; it would significantly alter the way veterinarians performed their examinations and treatments. Unlike previous sedatives and painkillers used in the treatment of large animals, Domosedan enabled veterinarians to conduct clinical and surgical examinations without tying up or anesthetizing their patients. Animals could be treated while standing, and in most instances they would not have to be transported to the veterinarian's clinic.

Farmos knew that university professors and advanced practitioners were important opinion leaders in veterinary medicine. To educate this group and encourage them to support the product, Farmos asked them to help with the testing process required for the drug's approval and sales permit. University professors were involved in the preclinical testing, and visionary practitioners were utilized for clinical testing. By proactively involving these influential potential adopters, the testing simultaneously acted as a premarketing tool while establishing the drug's efficacy and safety. This enabled opinion leaders to acquire advanced knowledge of and experience with the product before it was released. By the time the drug was launched, many of these influential users were already enthusiastic supporters of the product.

Because the drug represented a scientific breakthrough, it was featured in presentations at scientific conferences and was investigated in numerous dissertations, generating further awareness and excitement about the drug. When it was launched in Finland, the company hosted a large dinner party for all practicing veterinarians to attend, creating a celebratory atmosphere for the drug's introduction. Farmos' tactics were successful—Domosedan was adopted rapidly, spreading quickly around the world, and became a significant commercial success.

Source: Adapted from Birgitta Sandberg, "Creating the Market for Disruptive Innovation: Market Proactiveness at the Launch Stage," *Journal of Targeting, Measurement and Analysis for Marketing* 11, no. 2 (2002), pp. 184–96.

adoptions declines. These stages of adoption have been related to the adopter categories of *innovators* (in the very early stages); followed by *early adopters*, which cause adoption to accelerate; then the *early majority* and *late majority* as the innovation penetrates the mass market; and finally the *laggards* as the innovation approaches saturation.[8] The characteristics of these groups make them responsive to different marketing strategies.

Innovators and early adopters are typically looking for very advanced technologies that offer a significant advantage over previous generations. They are willing to take risks and to pay high prices, and they will accept some incompleteness in the product, but they may also demand considerable customization and technical support.[9] They are more likely to respond to marketing that offers a significant amount of technical content and that emphasizes the leading-edge nature of the innovation. Marketing channels that enable high content and selective reach are appropriate for this market. To market to the early majority, on the other hand, requires that the company communicate the product's completeness, its ease of use, its consistency with the customer's way of life, and its legitimacy. For this market segment, detailed technical information is not as important as using market channels with high reach and high credibility.

Firms often find it is difficult to make the transition between successfully selling to early adopters versus the early majority. While early adopters may be enthusiastic about the innovation's technological features, the early majority may find the product too complex, expensive, or uncertain. This can result in a chasm in the product's diffusion curve: Sales drop off because the early adopter market is saturated and the early majority market is not yet ready to buy (see Figure 13.2).[10] The company must simultaneously weather a period of diminished sales while scaling up its production capacity and improving efficiency to target the mass market.

To target the late majority and laggards, firms will often use similar channels as those used to target the early majority, although emphasizing reducing the cost per exposure. The marketing message at this stage must stress reliability, simplicity, and cost-effectiveness. The marketing channel need not enable high content, but it must have high credibility and not be so expensive as to drive product costs up significantly.

Recently, marketers have begun to tap the contagion-like spread of information by targeting individuals most likely to rapidly spread information. This is described in detail in the accompanying Research Brief.

Using Marketing to Shape Perceptions and Expectations

As described in Chapter Four, when distributors and customers are assessing the value of a technological innovation, they are swayed not only by evidence of the innovation's actual value, but also by their perception of the innovation's value and their expectations for its value in the future. Advertising, promotions, and publicity can play a key role in influencing the market's perceptions and expectations about the size of the installed base and the availability of complementary goods. Preannouncements can generate excitement about a product before its release, while press releases extolling forecasted sales can convince customers and distributors that the product's installed base will increase rapidly. The firm can also shape expectations about the future of the technology by signaling the market (including distributors, end users, manufacturers of complementary goods, and perhaps even other potential contenders for the new standard) that this is a battle it intends to win and is capable of winning. The firm's reputation may create a signal about its likelihood of success. Firms may also use credible commitments such as major fixed capital investments and guarantees to convince stakeholders that the firm has what it takes to challenge the incumbents.

FIGURE 13.2
The Chasm between Early Adopters and Early Majority Customers

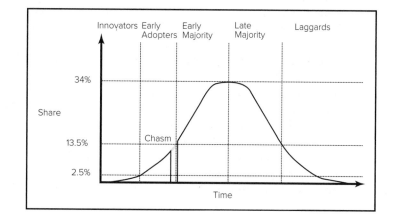

Preannouncements and Press Releases

A firm that aggressively promotes its products can increase both its actual installed base and its perceived installed base. Even products that have relatively small installed bases can obtain relatively large mindshares through heavy advertising. Since perceived installed base may drive subsequent adoptions, a large perceived installed base can lead to a large actual installed base. Such a tactic underlies the use of "vaporware"—preadvertised products that are not actually on the market yet and may not even exist—by many software vendors. By building the impression among customers that a product is ubiquitous, firms can prompt rapid adoption of the product when it actually is available. Vaporware may also buy a firm valuable time in bringing its product to market. If other vendors beat the firm to market and the firm fears that customers may select a dominant design before its offering is introduced, it can use vaporware to attempt to persuade customers to delay purchase until the firm's product is available.

The Nintendo 64 provides an excellent example. In an effort to forestall consumer purchases of 32-bit systems, Nintendo began aggressively promoting its development of a 64-bit system (originally named Project Reality) in 1994, though the product would not actually reach the market until September 1996. The project underwent so many delays that some industry observers dubbed it "Project Unreality." Another interesting vaporware example was Nintendo's rewritable 64M disk drive. Though the product was much hyped, it was never introduced.

Major video game producers also go to great lengths to manage impressions of their installed base and market share, often to the point of exaggeration or deception. For example, at the end of 1991, Nintendo claimed it had sold 2 million units of the SNES to the U.S. market, while Sega disagreed, arguing that Nintendo had sold 1 million units at most. Nintendo also forecast that it would sell an additional 6 million units by the end of 1992 (actual installed base of Super Nintendo systems in the United States reached just over 4 million units in 1992). By May 1992, Nintendo was claiming a 60 percent share of the 16-bit market, and Sega was claiming a 63 percent share. Similar tactics were deployed in the battle for the 32/64-bit market. For example, in October 1995, Sony announced to the press that it had presold 100,000 consoles in the United States, to which Mike Ribero, Sega's executive vice president for marketing and sales, countered that Sony's figures were deceptive, arguing that many preorders would never materialize into actual purchases.[11]

Reputation

When a firm is poised to introduce a new technological innovation, its reputation for both technological and commercial competence will critically influence the market's expectation about its likelihood of success.[12] Customers, distributors, and complementary goods producers will use the firm's track record for technological innovation as an indicator of the new product's functionality and value. The firm's prior commercial success acts as an indicator of the firm's ability to build and manage the necessary support network around the new technology (distribution, advertising, alliances) to create the necessary momentum in the installed base–complementary goods cycle.

When Sega entered the video game market, it had the benefit of having several highly successful arcade games to its credit (both Atari and Nintendo had also been arcade game producers before developing home video games). The company had a reputation for

Research Brief   Creating an Information Epidemic

Some individuals, by virtue of their natural proclivities and talents, can initiate a cascade of information that travels with startling momentum through a population. Such individuals can have a remarkable effect on marketplace behavior. Gladwell identifies three distinct types of individuals who have such a disproportionate amount of influence: connectors, mavens, and salespersons.[a]

Connectors are individuals who tend to form an exceptionally large circle of acquaintances. Sociologists have found that if a random sample of people is asked to identify the individuals they know on a first-name basis, connectors will identify many times the number of people an average person identifies.[b] These people may have an exceptionally high social drive; they also tend to have a knack for remembering people's names and keeping track of social details such as birthdays. However, it is not just the quantity of acquaintances that distinguishes connectors. Connectors also tend to have a diverse array of affiliations. They may belong to a number of different kinds of clubs, associations, or other social institutions. They belong to multiple social worlds. Thus, connectors can bring together people who would otherwise be unlikely to meet.

Mavens are individuals who are driven to obtain and disseminate knowledge about one or more of their interests. Economists have widely studied "market mavens," otherwise known as "price vigilantes." These individuals will closely track the prices charged by various retailers (or other market outlets) and will vociferously complain if they find something inappropriate, such as a promotion that is misleading.[c] Other mavens may take great pride in always knowing the best restaurants or hotels, or they may be avid readers of *Consumer Reports*. Mavens not only

collect information, but they are also keenly interested in educating others. They will frequently volunteer information and derive great pleasure out of helping other consumers.

Finally, *salespersons* are those individuals who are naturally talented persuaders. Such individuals are gifted at providing verbal responses that their listener is likely to find compelling. They may also have an acute ability to send and respond to nonverbal cues, enabling them to influence other people's emotional response to something. These individuals can infect others with their mood![d]

Any of these individuals is capable of sparking an information epidemic. While a connector with a valuable piece of information is likely to expose a great number and diversity of people, the maven is likely to convey the information to fewer people but in more detail, making it more convincing. The salesperson may not expose as many people as the connector and may not be driven to acquire and disseminate the volumes of information that the maven transmits, but the people the salesperson does transmit information to are likely to find it irresistible. Some individuals possess more than one of these traits simultaneously, making them a veritable typhoon of influence in the marketplace.

[a] Adapted from M. Gladwell, *The Tipping Point* (Boston: Little, Brown and Company, 2000).
[b] A. L. Barabasi, *Linked: The New Science of Networks* (Cambridge, MA: Perseus Books, 2002).
[c] L. F. Feick and L. L. Price, "The Market Maven: A Diffuser of Marketplace Information," *Journal of Marketing* 51 (1987), pp. 83–97.
[d] E. Hatfield, J. T. Cacioppo, and R. L. Rapson, *Emotional Contagion* (Cambridge: Cambridge University Press, 1994); and H. Friedman et al., "Understanding and Assessing Nonverbal Expressiveness: The Affective Communication Test," *Journal of Personality and Social Psychology* 39, no. 2 (1980), pp. 333–51.

developing exciting games, and this reputation may have facilitated customer acceptance of its 16-bit challenge to Nintendo's 8-bit dominance. By contrast, when Sony entered the video game market, it did not have the arcade background that underscored the other primary competitors. However, it did have a wealth of technological expertise as a consumer electronics manufacturer and exceptional brand equity in electronic products. Furthermore, Sony had demonstrated its ability to win a format war through its successful introduction of the CD format (with Philips) that supplanted vinyl records and analog cassettes.

Similarly, reputation was probably Microsoft's greatest strength in the battle for dominance over 128-bit video game systems. Microsoft's near monopoly in the personal computer operating system market was achieved through its unrivaled skill in using network externalities to its advantage. Microsoft had skillfully leveraged its controlling share in PC operating systems into domination over many categories of the software market, obliterating many would-be competitors. Microsoft's reputation sent a strong signal to distributors, developers, and customers that would shape their expectations for its future installed base and availability of complementary goods. Microsoft's success was not assured, but it was a powerful force to be reckoned with.

Credible Commitments

A firm can also signal its commitment to an industry by making substantial investments that would be difficult to reverse. For example, it was well publicized that Sony spent more than $500 million developing the PlayStation, in addition to manufacturing the system and establishing an in-house games development unit. By contrast, 3DO's cumulative research and development costs at the launch of its multiplayer were less than $37 million, and the company utilized a strategy whereby all console and game production was performed by third parties. Thus, 3DO may not have signaled the market that it had enough confidence in the platform to bear the brunt of the capital risk.

Summary of Chapter

1. A firm can use its launch timing strategy to take advantage of business cycle or seasonal effects, to influence its positioning vis-à-vis competitors, and to ensure that production capacity and complementary goods are sufficiently available at time of launch.

2. The launch timing decision must also consider the need to harvest cash flows from existing product generations versus the advantages of willingly cannibalizing existing products to preempt competitors.

3. Successful deployment requires striking a careful balance between making a system open enough to attract complementary goods providers (and/or other producers if that is desirable) and protected enough to ensure that product quality, margins, and compatibility can be sustained.

4. Common pricing strategies for technological innovations include market skimming and penetration pricing. While the first attempts to maximize margins earned on early sales of the product, the second attempts to maximize market share. Pricing strategies should consider the firm's ability to earn profits from sales of complementary goods or services—if profits from complements are expected to be high, lower prices on the platform technology may be warranted.

5. Firms can manipulate the customer's perception of the product's price (and the timing of cash flows) through the timing of when the price is paid.

6. Intermediaries provide a number of valuable roles in the supply chain, including breaking bulk, transporting, carrying inventory, providing selling services, and managing customer transactions.

7. Sometimes a firm can accelerate distribution of its innovation by forging relationships with distributors, bundling the good with others that have a wider installed

base, sponsoring large customer groups, or providing sales guarantees to distributors or complements producers.

8. Marketing methods vary in attributes such as cost, reach, information content, duration of exposure, flexibility of message, and ability to target particular segments of the market. When designing the marketing plan, the firm must take into account both the nature of the innovation (e.g., Is it complex? Are benefits easy to observe?) and the nature of the customer (e.g., Does the customer require in-depth technical detail? Is the customer likely to be influenced by brand images and/or reputation? How much uncertainty is the customer likely to tolerate?).

9. Marketing strategies can influence the market's perception of how widely used the product is or will be, and thus can influence the behavior of customers, distributors, and complementary goods producers. Preannouncements, the firm's reputation, and credible commitments can all influence the market's assessment of the product's likelihood of success.

Discussion Questions

1. Identify one or more circumstances when a company might wish to delay introducing its product.
2. What factors will (or should) influence a firm's pricing strategy?
3. Pick a product you know well. What intermediaries do you think are used in bringing this product to market? What valuable services do you think these intermediaries provide?
4. What marketing strategies are used by the producers of the product you identified for Question 3? What are the advantages and disadvantages of these marketing strategies?

Suggested Further Reading

Classics

Corey, E. R., F. V. Cespedes, and V. K. Rangan, *Going to Market: Distribution Systems for Industrial Products* (Boston: Harvard Business School Press, 1989).

Gladwell, M., *The Tipping Point* (Boston: Little, Brown and Company, 2000).

Mohr, J. J., S. Sengupta, and S. F., Slater, *Marketing of High-Technology Products and Innovations*, 3rd ed. (Upper Saddle River, NJ: Prentice Hall, 2009).

Moore, G., *Crossing the Chasm: Marketing and Selling Technology Products to Mainstream Customers* (New York: HarperCollins, 1991).

Rogers, E. M., *Diffusion of Innovations,* 5th ed. (New York: Free Press, 2003).

Schilling, M. A., "Technological Leapfrogging: Lessons from the U.S. Videogame Industry," *California Management Review* 45, no. 3 (2003), pp. 6–32.

Recent Work

Aral, S. and D. Walker, "Creating Social Contagion through Viral Product Design: A Randomized Trial of Peer Influence in Networks," *Management Science* 57 (2011), pp. 1623–1639.

Chen, Y., and J. Xie, "Online Consumer Review: Word-of-mouth as a New Element of Marketing Communication Mix," *Management Science* 54 (2008), pp. 477–91.

Hinz, O, B. Skiera, C. Barrot, and J. U. Becker, "Seeding Strategies for Viral Marketing: An Empirical Comparison," *Journal of Marketing* 75, no. 6 (2011), pp. 55–71.

Liu, H., "Dynamics of Pricing in the Video Game Console Market: Skimming or Penetration Pricing?" *Journal of Marketing Research* 47 (2010), pp. 428–443.

Reinders, M. J., R. T. Frambach, and J. P. L., Schoormans, "Using Product Bundling to Facilitate the Adoption Process of Radical Innovations," *Journal of Product Innovation Management* 27 (2010), pp. 1127–1140.

Endnotes

1. J. Johng, Y. Kang, M. A. Schilling, J. Sul, and M. Takanashi, "Honda Insight: Personal Hybrid," New York University teaching case, 2003.
2. Lynley, M. "Dropbox now has more than 400 million registered users," www.techcrunch.com (2015), June 24th.
3. Schilling, "Technological Leapfrogging"; and M. A. Schilling, "Winning the Standards Race: Building Installed Base and the Availability of Complementary Goods," *European Management Journal* 17 (1999), pp. 265–74.
4. D. Machan, "Great Job—You're Fired," *Forbes* 158, no. 7 (1996), pp. 145–46.
5. Reinders, MJ, Frambach, RT, and Schoormans, JPL. "Using Product Bundling to Facilitate the Adoption Process of Radical Innovations," *Journal of Product Innovation Management* 27 (2010):1127–1140.
6. O. Hinz, B. Skiera, C. Barrot, and J. U. Becker, "Seeding Strategies For Viral Marketing: An Empirical Comparison," *Journal of Marketing* 75 (2011) (November), pp. 55–71; see also M. Bampo, M. T. Ewing, D. R. Mather, D. Stewart and M. Wallace, "The Effects Of Social Structure Of Digital Networks On Viral Marketing Performance," *Information Systems Research* 19 (2008) (3), pp. 273–90.
7. P. Kotler, *Marketing Management* (Upper Saddle River, NJ: Prentice Hall, 2003). See also Y. Chen and J. Xie, "Online Consumer Review: Word-Of-Mouth As A New Element Of Marketing Communication Mix," *Management Science* 54 (2008), pp. 477–91.
8. E. M. Rogers, *Diffusion of Innovations,* 3rd ed. (New York: Free Press, 1983).
9. J. Mohr, *Marketing of High-Technology Products and Innovations* (Upper Saddle River, NJ: Prentice Hall, 2001).
10. G. Moore, *Inside the Tornado* (New York: Harper Business, 1995).
11. M. E. McGann, "Crossing Swords," *Dealerscope Consumer Electronics Marketplace* 37, no. 10 (1995), pp. 63–65; and Schilling, "Technological Leapfrogging."
12. R. K. Chandy and G. Tellis, "The Incumbent's Curse? Incumbency, Size, and Radical Product Innovation," *Journal of Marketing* 64, no. 3 (2000), pp. 1–18.

Index